STARKWEATHER

STARKWEATHER

THE UNTOLD STORY OF
THE KILLING SPREE
THAT CHANGED AMERICA

HARRY N. MACLEAN

COUNTERPOINT
BERKELEY, CALIFORNIA

STARKWEATHER

Copyright © 2023 by Harry N. MacLean

All rights reserved under domestic and international copyright. Outside of fair use (such as quoting within a book review), no part of this publication may be reproduced, stored in a retrieval system, or transmitted in any form or by any means, electronic, mechanical, photocopying, recording, or otherwise, without the written permission of the publisher. For permissions, please contact the publisher.

First Counterpoint edition: 2023

Library of Congress Cataloging-in-Publication Data
Names: MacLean, Harry N., author.
Title: Starkweather : the untold story of the killing spree that changed America / Harry N. MacLean.
Description: First Counterpoint edition. | Berkeley, California : Counterpoint, 2023.
Identifiers: LCCN 2023019009 | ISBN 9781640095410 (hardcover) | ISBN 9781640095427 (ebook)
Subjects: LCSH: Spree murderers—United States. | Murder—United States. | Starkweather, Charles Raymond, 1938-1959. | Fugate, Caril Ann.
Classification: LCC HV6529 .M33 2023 | DDC 364.152/30973—dc23/eng/20230531
LC record available at https://lccn.loc.gov/2023019009

Jacket design by Robin Bilardello
Jacket photograph © John Finney Photography / Getty
Book design by tracy danes and Laura Berry

COUNTERPOINT
2560 Ninth Street, Suite 318
Berkeley, CA 94710
www.counterpointpress.com

Printed in the United States of America

1 3 5 7 9 10 8 6 4 2

For
Hulya
My Partner in Crime

ALL POINTS BULLETIN

LINCOLN POLICE DEPARTMENT

JANUARY 27, 1958
5:43 PM

Be on the lookout for a 1949 black Ford. Nebraska license number 2-15628. Radiator grill missing. No hubcaps. Believed to be driven by Charles Starkweather, a white male, nineteen years old, 5 feet 5 inches tall. 140 pounds, dark red hair, green eyes. Believed to be wearing blue jeans and black leather jacket. Wanted by Lincoln police for questioning in homicide. Officers are warned to approach with caution. Starkweather is believed to be armed and dangerous.

Starkweather is believed to be accompanied by Caril Fugate, fourteen years old, female, white, 5 feet 1 inch tall, 105 pounds, dark brown hair, blue eyes, sometimes wears glasses. Usually wears hair in ponytail, appears to be about eighteen years old. Believed wearing blue jeans and blouse or sweater. May be wearing medium-blue parka and a gold ring set with a glass ruby.

CONTENTS

INTRODUCTION

IN 1958, AMERICA WAS AT THE PEAK OF THE POST-WWII boom. The country had emerged from the war as the strongest economic and military power in the world. Prosperity abounded. Returning soldiers went to college on the G.I. Bill, which also offered longer-term loans to allow the purchase of larger homes in areas that would come to be called suburbs. The middle class was expanding. Wages were increasing. Production was up. Ninety percent of adults had cars. Consumerism was flourishing almost without limit; the acquisition of material goods soared: Frigidaires with freezer compartments to hold four TV dinners, dishwashers, second cars, vegetable slicers, Electrolux vacuum cleaners—anything to increase the comfort of modern living. By the mid-1950s, two-thirds of U.S. households had at least one telephone. The baby boom had hit: 70.2 million people were born between 1946 and 1964, the largest generation in American history. Families were now wealthy enough to have more children and buy bigger houses to hold them. They could afford to travel, and many did so on propeller planes like the DC-3 and DC-4. Passengers could walk right through the airport door onto the tarmac and up the steps to sit wherever they chose. Smoking was allowed after takeoff. (You could also smoke in the waiting room of your doctor's office. Some doctors even recommended smoking to decrease stress.)

In 1950, 9 percent of households in the United States had televisions. By 1959, the number had risen to 86 percent. The average viewer watched almost three hours of TV a day. TV stations went off the air at midnight to the music of "The Star-Spangled Banner." Most people still got their news from the newspapers, but by 1958, coaxial cables allowed for the transmission of images from the local stations to the networks in New York and the evening news. With the introduction of video, a local story could be shared all over the country on the evening news. The era of mass media had arrived.

In 1950 there were forty million cars on the road in America. By the end of the decade, that number had doubled. Cars signaled the new, space age America; they grew bigger and flashier with long tail fins, shiny strips of chrome, wraparound windshields, and burnished hood ornaments. They ran hard and fast with powerful V-6 and V-8 engines.

There were gross inequities in the postwar boom. The prosperity mainly benefited the white middle class. Women were expected to stay home and raise kids, and most of them did. Black people in many southern states still lived in poverty and were subject to repressive Jim Crow laws. In 1955, Rosa Parks refused to give up her seat on a city bus in Montgomery, Alabama, and set off a boycott. That same year, Emmett Till was murdered in Mississippi. In *Brown vs. Board of Education*, the Supreme Court found "separate but equal" school systems to violate the equal-protection clause of the Constitution. The South resisted school integration with violence. In 1959, President Eisenhower, who had been opposed to the integration of the army while he was a general, sent the 101st Airborne Division to Little Rock to force the integration of public schools. The great migration of Black people to the northern industrial cities, which had begun in the 1920s and '30s, grew in force after WWII and maintained into the 1950s.

There were literary and musical stirrings against the conformity of the time. The Beats surfaced in New York and made their way to San Francisco, where Lawrence Ferlinghetti opened City Lights Bookstore. He published "Howl" by Allen Ginsberg, which was seen as an original and powerful protest against the middle-class values and numbing sameness of American culture. Pete Seeger wrote and sang a song entitled "Little Boxes," which made fun of the cookie-cutter homes of the growing suburbs. Jackson Pollock threw canvases on the floor and splashed paint on them. Dr. Salk developed a vaccine for polio.

There were things to fear: Joe McCarthy launched a fanatical investigation into supposed Communists in the State Department and Hollywood. He was brought down in part by Edward R. Murrow, a newsman who broadcast the war from London and became the first celebrity television journalist. Ike had put the Korean War to bed, but the Cold War was raging. The hydrogen bomb was exploded in the atolls of the Pacific with one thousand times the force of the atom bomb dropped on Hiroshima. School kids crouched under their desks when the sirens sounded. Rock and roll surfaced in the form of musicians like Elvis Presley and Jerry Lee Lewis whitewashing Black gospel and rhythm and blues. Elvis, with his gyrating hips and suggestive lyrics, was seen by many parents as a serious threat to family values. But Elvis was more than music; he was the force behind a lot of the cultural changes forming on the horizon. As John Lennon would say, "Before Elvis, there was nothing." In high school, there were good girls and bad girls, football players and bookworms. Every boy had a bike, but few were locked up on the school bike rack. Change was on the way, but it wasn't here yet. If people had heard of Vietnam, it was probably as a French colony in Indochina.

The homicide rate (murder and nonnegligent manslaughter) in the country had dropped from 4.6 per 100,000 in 1950 to 4.0 in 1957. (By 1973, the rate had more than doubled to 9.4 per 100,000.) Drugs, even marijuana, were unheard of in middle-class America. Ozzie and Harriet and their two sons, David and Ricky, were the beloved American family. DNA was discovered, drive-in theaters now offered in-car heaters, Golden Arches sprung up like weeds, and the second volume of the Kinsey Report—*Sexual Behavior in the Human Female*—was published.

That was about it. The major vibrations of the time were peace and prosperity (although, later on, the more astute claimed to have picked up the ominous rumbles down the road). There was a stability and predictability to life that hadn't been seen in the country since before the Great Depression. Life was good, and the future looked even better.

If the 1950s in the United States was a time of innocence, Lincoln, Nebraska, was the beating heart of it. The population had grown to 128,000 by 1958. It was the home office of thirty-three national insurance companies and had packing plants and wholesale warehouses. Ten thousand students attended the University of Nebraska, on the edge of downtown. The football team was on the verge of national fame. The rains on the prairies had been good the previous few years and crop prices were high, which brought farmers into town to shop retail and invest in new equipment. Lincoln was a hub of railroad activity, with five lines running through town. Although there were still some two-party phone lines, Lincoln had gotten direct dial, and the phone book contained detailed instructions on how to operate the black clicking wheel. Above all, the city was a safe place to raise a family. From 1947 to 1957, seven murders were reported in the city. All seven were eventually solved. In the same time period, six manslaughter incidents were reported, and five of them were solved.

So the stage was set as 1957 came to a close. The country was filled with self-confidence and a bustling optimism. There was no real fear of an evil out there, no real fear of an evil inside. As cruel as war was, it was never random. You knew the face of your enemy. Someone won and someone lost. Play by the rules, be decent and respectful of another, take care of your family and go to church, and *life will be good.* Yes, terrible things happen, like a car-versus-train accident that kills a family of four, but seldom at the intentional hand of another, seldom at the arbitrary hand of another here, in Nebraska.

The American lexicon did not include the word *mass murderer.* Or *spree killer.* Or *serial killer.* Not that some hadn't existed in the past, but they were never mythologized or given a categorical title. They hadn't been brought into your living room through the eye of television or given front-page coverage day after day for weeks.

Enter Charlie Starkweather and Caril Ann Fugate.

I WAS FIFTEEN in January 1958. Caril was thirteen; Charlie was nineteen. We all lived in Lincoln. My middle-class home was a little over a mile from the house where, at the end of that month, a wealthy couple and their maid would die. I knew their son. My older brother, Mike, was in shop class with Charlie. The only thing I knew of Belmont, where Caril lived, was that it was on the wrong side of the tracks. Both Mike and I were away at prep school when the killings happened, as was the son of the wealthy couple. I went on to college and became a lawyer and writer in Denver. I drove to Lincoln two or three times a year to visit my parents—mother and stepfather—and siblings, never staying more than a day or two. As the years passed, I thought about writing the Starkweather murder story on several occasions, but I always veered off. I sensed something, I guess.

It's amazing how sometimes life-changing decisions can turn on the smallest point. The sail catches a slight gust of wind, swings one way a little, and there's your future.

I wrote only about crimes with some hook that I could use to explore larger themes, like vigilante justice or repressed memories or the indelible imprint of past crimes on the present. In 2021, my wife, Julya (Hulya), and I were in Florida for the winter. In the mornings she walked the beach and collected shells. I wrote. I had started a novel; there were two threads, one about a badly busted-up marriage and the other about a young couple somewhat like Charlie and Caril, who were traveling a blood-splattered road of escape through the Sandhills. One day, when I was trying to get a feel for my fictional Caril, I decided to look at the real one. I found her on YouTube, in a 1988 episode of a show called *A Current Affair*. It was startling to see the fourteen-year-old girl as a middle-aged woman. She was dramatic and very convincing in her claim of innocence. Then I took a slap in the chops: Well, was she guilty? Everything I'd ever seen or read about her almost assumed ab initio that she was. She had been tried and convicted, but that was in the justice system of the 1950s. Maybe the issue needed to be reexamined after all these years. I knew how to look objectively at the evidence of a conflict or dispute and construct a story of *what happened*. I had done it for years as a magistrate in juvenile court and an arbitrator.

I flicked the TV off and flopped in a chair. I closed my eyes, waited for the curtain to drop. I was seventy-nine years old. If I went in, I would be eighty-one when I came out. If I was going to write this story, about the crime but also about the place where I grew up, I should have done so thirty-five years ago. Now, I wasn't sure I had the heart for it. It would be a rough couple of years. And there was Lincoln. The 1950s had not been a good time in my life. My gut was against it.

My approach to writing a book was complete immersion. I turned over every rock, knocked on every door, drew endless lists of names and questions and went after the answers one by one. For days, weeks, months, years if necessary. I tried to research and absorb everything. This story would be different. I'd be walking through my past. Before, I'd been on the outside looking in. Now, I would be on the inside looking in.

Bruce Springsteen wrote a song about Nebraska. Caril had heard it. She grew disturbed on the TV show as she described the line in the song when Charlie says he and Caril had had "some fun" on the murder rampage. Fun? She cried.

That was the small point, the shift of the sail in a mild gust of wind. If I had picked one of the other videos, or looked away the moment she lowered her head in despair, I might have shrugged off the impulse and gone on with my novel. So in the end, I ignored my gut and went with my head: Was Caril Ann Fugate a murderer? Sort that out, and answer the question, and there's the story.

Not that that lessened the lingering sense of dread. I wanted out the minute before I agreed to write this book and the minute after. But I was in. I usually wrote from 6:00 a.m. to 1:00 or 2:00 p.m. One afternoon about six months or so into the writing, I exited my office and met Julya in the hallway. She stared at me for a moment, then suggested I go into the bathroom and take a look at myself in the mirror. "Pass," I said, and made my way outside. Thank God for the Florida sun, I thought. January in Nebraska could freeze your blood.

So, one day in May 2021, I packed up my car and headed out northeast on I-76 and then east on I-80 to Lincoln. By the time I hit the Colorado desert, I was filled with a mixed sense of foreboding and determination. There was another thread: I knew how people looked at Nebraska. Flat. Boring. Endless. I was going to show them beauty. I wanted to take them through the Sandhills; float them down the wide and deep Niobrara River flowing east from Valentine and past Bassett, the little ranch town where I lived for a few years after the war, when my father and sister were still alive; and walk them up the mile-and-a-half-long trail to the top of magnificent Scotts Bluff, where they could look down on the countryside and imagine the endless line of immigrant wagons and animals and people trudging their way alongside the North Platte to Oregon.

IN AN EFFORT like this one, the author seeks to come up with a coherent narrative of events. One doesn't—because one can't—attempt to establish the actual truth of what happened; rather the author sets forth a (hopefully) convincing presentation of the way he sees it and why he sees it that way. One obstacle in this effort was the massive number of documents involved, because of the two trials and many confessions; another was the fact that most of the main participants have passed on. Another stems from the fact that the critical part of the story is the series of ten murders in eight days. There are only two people who know the truth of what happened from January 21, 1958, to January 29, 1958. One of them, Charlie Starkweather, gave at least ten different versions of the murders. Almost every time he spoke or wrote something about the spree, his story changed on key facts. The other, Caril Fugate, gave pretty much the same story in and out of court; some of it jibed with Charlie's, but many of the critical parts of it—who was where and who did what to whom during the spree—are diametrically opposed. This is why Part II, entitled "The Killings," sets forth two versions of each killing: one from Charlie's point of view, the other from Caril's. The reader will read the versions that came from their mouths, as best as I can stitch them together.

Part I, "The Setup," introduces Charlie and Caril and their relationship. Part III, "The Trials," takes the reader in some detail through the trials of both Charlie and Caril. In IV, "Guilt or Innocence," I lay out my analysis and conclusions as to who killed whom, murder by murder, for the reader to either accept or question, in whole or in part. Part V, "The Consequences," describes the effect of the killing spree on various characters in the book. In Part VI, "Impact," I discuss the impact of the murder spree on the culture of America.

Finally, before I began this book, I knew that me growing up in Lincoln during the 1950s might color my perception of the facts, and that delving deeply into the details of the murders and the lives of the people involved might have a personal effect on me. I decided early on to keep this theme out of the telling of the story and to save it, as I have, for the epilogue.

I

THE SETUP

1

CHARLES RAYMOND STARKWEATHER WAS NEITHER AS ordinary nor as complex a person as commonly portrayed. He was born on November 24, 1938, the third of seven children. WWII was just getting underway, and he lived with his family in a small apartment in a poor section of Lincoln. His father, Guy, a swarthy, good-looking fellow, was from a small town in northeastern Nebraska. He was born in 1910 and completed eighth grade. Initially he worked as a baker, later a handyman, but by the time Charlie came along he was usually unemployed because of arthritis. Charlie's mother, Helen, born in 1915, grew up in a different small town in northeastern Nebraska. She worked as a waitress in a local café.

The average size for a male in 1958 was five foot eight. Charlie eventually reached five foot five, although he claimed only five foot four on his driver's license. He had light freckles, slightly bowed legs, and his mother's red hair, described by one observer as the color of Lucille Ball's and another as that of Bozo the Clown's. He spoke with a lisp and had terrible eyesight and according to some reports was slightly pigeon-toed. Despite the consistent effort of the press and even his own lawyers to portray him as stupid or "weak-minded," his IQ at the time of his trial tested out at 110, which puts him in the high normal or average range. He was never a behavior problem in school and he had considerable artistic talent, as shown in his drawings—a few of them quite remarkable—but did little to develop it. He was held over in sixth grade in order to give him a "chance to mature," although the school psychologist felt that he had a "special insight" into himself and his surroundings. One teacher even wrote that "he is much more reachable than others in my room," and a sixth-grade teacher noted on his report card that Charlie "was very eager to work and to please."

He was happy to work the projector, sweep the auditorium, and assist in gym class.

While slightly intimidated by his father, in his writings Charlie makes constant reference to his affection for the man and his gratitude for teaching him to hunt and how to avoid dangerous snakes and taking him to the zoo. Guy Starkweather was a serious drunk—neighbor kids scattered across the lawns when they saw his car careening up the street—and was known to have smacked Charlie at least twice, but he did not, to all known facts, abuse his wife or other children. It was a chaotic home, perhaps, with seven children, but not necessarily a violent one. Charlie worried that his mother would get so exhausted from working and running the house and having children that one day she would up and leave. By all accounts, he loved her and got along with his siblings, particularly his sister Laveta, who regularly cleaned his room. While it was commonly reported that he had no police record, in fact he received one ticket for allowing Caril to drive his car when she was fourteen and a second one for possessing beer underage.

Charlie saw his childhood as the best time of his life, truly an "enchanted forest": "I would set down against a large tree, and enjoy the scenery . . . The fallen trees lay in a frightful tangle, and over and above them grew the undergrowth, the tropical trees stood stern."

In Charlie's mind, he exited the enchanted forest on the first day of kindergarten at Saratoga Elementary School, and life went bad after that. In his teen years, he longed more than anything to return to the forest. He would write:

> I was two going on three when we moved into the house which was in the South part of town, and still in Lincoln, Nebraska. I was raised in this house through most of my childhood, this place to me looked an enchanted forest, with its large trees surrounding the house, and at time in the evening when the sun was setting in its tender glory, with its beautiful colors in the western sky, and the birds singing in their melodys tha came softly from the trees—every-thing was nice and pretty, so peaceful and

tranquil—it was though time itself was standing still. I fell in love with this adventurous land in my earlier days, and the flames still burns deep down inside of me for the love of the enchanted forest.

The road from a child in the enchanted forest to feared tough guy was a tortuous one. On his first day of school, when it came time for him to stand and introduce himself, he stuttered and stammered so badly that the teacher told him to sit down, much to the amusement of the other students. He was humiliated. From that moment on, his days in school were marked by constant teasing. A "bow-legged red-headed woodpecker" they called him, and they suggested over and over that his legs were bent out that way because he was born riding a barrel. A welfare worker wrote in a report that his speech defect was so bad she could not understand him. He said "Wodney" when he meant *Rodney* or "wouse" for *house*. His severe astigmatism was not diagnosed until the sixth grade when a teacher discovered he could not read the words on the blackboard. Although he was a good athlete, he was picked last, if he was picked at all, for team sports. The boys mocked him for thinking he could kick a soccer ball with such bent legs. They would imitate his speech defect and bow their legs out. The girls were the worst; Charlie would come to hate them for their giggling and sly looks. He would feel a rage building within him, and his legs began to shake and tears came to his eyes. "Look!" a girl called. "He's beginning to cry!"

Charlie and siblings Rodney and Laveta attended catechism class at Trinity Lutheran Church on Sunday mornings. A neighbor often picked them up while they were waiting at the bus stop. Charlie sat in the back of the room and seldom spoke. After class, when the kids gathered outside on the lawn, the teasing would begin again. One of the girls whinnied like a horse, mocking his bow legs. Another would call out, "Who shot your horse?" The teasing never let up.

Charlie's father noticed his son's rumpled clothes and tearstained cheeks and Charlie told him of the teasing at school. His father called the school. He set up an appointment the next morning to meet with the principal, but nothing came of it. The school said there was nothing they could do.

One morning a few weeks later, his teacher, seeing Charlie's drawing talent, gave him a little tin of watercolors and some paper and suggested he paint a picture for his mother. He did so and was quite proud of his work. It was a "farm picture, with a house, barns, a fence, sky and a couple trees and chickens and cows." He rolled it up and walked home with it grasped in his hand. Charlie would later write:

> Walking home I didn't notice anyone walking behind me until I heard giggles and laughter. I kept walking as I glance back over my shoulder and there they were, a half dozen girls and boys making wise cracks about my bow legs and hair and speech. I could hear them imitating my speech as I kept walking. I walked two or three blocks before I thought if I turn, go home a different way that maybe they would keep walking without following up behind me. At the next corner I turned to head a different way home, but the wise cracks, the imitating giggles and laughter was still following behind me.
>
> . . . I began to quicken my steps a little fast but my . . . footsteps were coming rapitly up behind me, then a boys voice broked out an I new the voice was that of the boy that seem to be the leader, "look at those legs would you," the giggles and laughter started in I noticed of the girls giggles were higher pich that the rest and it seemed to crack and as she giggled, "hey what you got in your hand," the leader boy demanded. and at the same time I jerked the paper that was round up and had in my hands and was the painting I had made for mom. I stopped a few steps ahead of them and gared at the boy who had jerked my painting from me and now was unwrowing it. They all gathered around the boy that had my painting and right away they started making wise cracks about it . . . The boy with my picture, looking at me with a big smile said "this is piece of junk, besides being a red head, bow-legged, wood pecker—you can't even draw," and at that, tore it in

half and as the laughter and giggling began he glanced around at the finished ripping it into little pieces. I stood watching my painted picture being tore into little pisces an had to gripped my jaw tooth against toot to keep from crying at least I thought it would keep me from crying and it did at least from crying out loud but it didn't keep the tears from creeping from my eyes the tears came rowing down my cheeks as I looked at my painted picture what was left of it all scattered in little bits on the ground then of the girls yelled sarcastically he is going to cry he is a cry baby then they started in the red headed bowlegged wood pecker is cry baby . . . at that I turned ran as fast as my bowlegs would carry me.

His father was at the table "eating in his graceful manner and in silence" when Charlie came in the door. His mother noticed his face and asked if the kids were teasing him again. He nodded. Charlie told his father the whole story, from the teasing at school to the ripping up of his painting. His dad got on the phone to the school for a second time and after a loud and angry exchange was essentially told that the kids were just having fun. He hung up the phone. He turned to Charlie and told him that from then on if anybody started picking on him to "knock the devil out of them. You won't get a licking from us and if that school tries to because of your fighting for your rights well you just tell your mother." His father finished his coffee and kissed his wife and left to return to work.

Charlie hit the threshold. The hate germinating inside began consuming him; his black moods would immobilize him for long periods of time and his guts tightened. But now he had permission to deal with the world in a way he could grasp. Don't ignore the kids. Don't try to please them. Smack them. Hard. Charlie took this advice to heart.

WHAT ROLE THE taunting and teasing played in Charlie's evolution into a killer is subject to considerable debate. William Reinhardt, a respected criminologist at the University of Nebraska at the time, spent over forty hours interviewing Charlie and wrote a book entitled *The Murderous Trail of Charles Starkweather*. The short book is an odd, disjointed version of what he makes of Charlie, a mixture of psychological constructs, moral judgments, novelistic flights of fancy, and cloudy conclusions. He is clearly personally revolted by what he sees as Charlie's lack of humanity; he downplays if not dismisses outright the notion that Charlie's experiences at the hands of his classmates in grade school—if in fact they happened at all—were behind Charlie's ability to kill without feeling as an adult. Reinhardt sees Charlie's reliance on these childhood events in his memoir as a carefully constructed facade, as a way for Charlie to explain and even excuse his murderous behavior. Reinhardt wrote that Charlie had a "weak ego" that was obsessed with gaining power. Killing innocents was his way of achieving that power.

Other writers have the same take on the minimal impact of Charlie's early school days. A March 1959 piece in *Parade* magazine by the *Evening Journal* reporter Marjorie Marlett, which reprinted parts of his memoir, and for which Charlie received one thousand dollars, seemed to mock the very idea that children teasing and taunting a boy over his physical handicaps could have an effect on the boy's psychological evolution. Indeed, the six psychiatrists who examined Charlie for his trial made only passing mention of his childhood.

Psychology in 1958 wasn't about trauma. It was at the tail end of the Freudian years, where the focus on childhood trauma was pretty much limited to the impact of sexual abuse of girls. The first *Diagnostic and Statistical Manual* (*DSM*), which attempted to classify personality disorders, was published in 1952 and was based mainly on the Veterans Administration's system of psychiatric diagnoses. Concepts such as dissociation, multiple personalities, and repressed memories resulting from early life traumas weren't part of the psychological landscape in the 1950s. The notion that personalities could "split" into different people, or that a person could repress a memory too painful to remember—and then recover it in original form years later—or that a traumatized person could in effect repeat a childhood trauma in modified form over and over in his adult life, did not come into vogue until the 1980s, with books such as *Sybil*. Today, the *DSM-5* recognizes dissociative amnesia (the new name for repressed memories), differentiated personalities (the new name for multiple personalities), and depersonalization/derealization disorder. By the 1990s, it was not uncommon to see one or more of these diagnoses raised as a defense in criminal trials.

All of which is not to suggest that the relentless taunting and mocking of Charlie for his physical attributes should be seen as the direct and simple cause for his conscience-free murder spree. Direct causal relationships are difficult to prove in human behavior. But of one thing there can be no doubt: Charlie loved his mother. He wrote of it, his siblings spoke of it, and a psychiatrist described the depth of it in his testimony. Charlie wrote a one-line poem to her from his prison cell: "The stranger asks no greater glory till life is through than to spend one last minute in wilderness."

The incident in which the painting he had made for his mother was ripped from his hands and torn to pieces in front of him and in the midst of the relentless mocking and name-calling of his classmates could easily have had a serious impact on his psychological development. Charlie would write that in reaction to all this, he turned inward and became immersed in a bitter and deep hatred of others. He never used the word *freak*, but it is not hard to believe that he saw himself as one through the eyes of his fellow students: you can't talk right, you can't see, you're so bowlegged you roll from side to side when you walk, you're slightly pigeon-toed, you're short, and you have thick, flaming red hair. (In his mid-teens Charlie tried bleaching his hair blond. It didn't go well.) And he was constantly reminded of all this through the taunts and shunning of his classmates.

CHARLIE FINALLY MADE it out of elementary school and was assigned to Irving Junior High. His reputation as a fighter preceded his arrival. One student, a year ahead of Charlie, was so scared of him that if he passed him in the hallway or on the playground, he would look down to avoid eye contact. If their eyes had ever met, he would "have set a new world's record in the marathon" to get away. In one incident, he witnessed Charlie chasing a boy across the playground with a base-ball bat, but he fell behind because his bowlegs couldn't carry him fast enough. The observer was amused and scared at the same time.

By junior high, those that made fun of him did it behind his back. He was generally considered to be pretty dumb, and the silly grin he often wore did not help the image. He was short but stocky and squared off. One day, a student was drawn to a commotion on the playground and walked closer to see Charlie punch a guy in the face. The boy fell to the ground and Charlie kicked him several times before casually walk-ing away. The onlookers were stunned: Fights in those days usually con-sisted of two boys wrestling around, one getting the other in a headlock, both falling to the ground and tussling until one boy got on top of the other and held him down until he called, "Give." Boys didn't kick each other. The onlooker kept a safe distance from the fight, lest Charlie turn his way. Charlie was also known to chase girls and threaten to cut off their braids with a knife.

Not everybody stayed out of Charlie's way. Three tall basketball players took to harassing him. On one side of the three-story varie-gated brick school with white-trimmed windows was a series of steps leading down to a basement room. Near the entrance was a bike rack. One morning, when Charlie was at the rack, the three basketball players jerked Charlie's bicycle from his hands and tossed it down the stairwell. Another time, when Charlie was riding home, the same three boys spit on him one by one as they rode by on their bikes. One witness testified at Charlie's trial that when the two were in junior high, Charlie approached him and told him he wanted his bike and to get off it. When the boy re-fused, Charlie bloodied his nose and knocked him to the ground. He walked off grumbling. A few days later, the two had another encounter, and Charlie whipped him again. Don Wendling and Charlie's younger brother, Bobby, had built a fort in the Starkweather garage, and one day, as the two approached the garage, Charlie suddenly appeared and yelled at them not to come any farther and shot Wendling with a BB gun.

It was the downright meanness of the red-haired boy that made an impression on the other students. He didn't just smack an opponent in the face until he fell to the ground; he got on top of him and ground his face into the gravel. Other times, he punched him out in a focused burst of violence and walked away. Not that he always walked away unmarked. More than once he showed up at home with a bloody nose or split lip and black eye.

Charlie claimed, and it was frequently written, that he got kicked out or dropped out of Irving after eighth grade. The records show that in fact he was transferred to Everett Junior High for ninth grade by agreement that the school would be a better fit for him. By this time, Charlie had a citywide reputation. But Everett already had a resident tough guy: Robert Von Busch. Taller, bulkier than Charlie, he wore his hair in a flattop with wings pomaded back on the sides into a ducktail. Bob had also earned a reputation as a fighter, and for a few weeks the two roosters circled each other waiting and watching. Finally, the tension flared into a brawl in the classroom—Bob claimed Charlie started it—which soon spilled out into the hall. Both gave and took blows. In Von Busch's recollection, the fight ended in a draw. It also ended in the beginning of a fast friendship, one that lasted five years. When these two tough guys were running together, others pretty much stayed out of their way. Their buddies were usually boys they had already fought. Von Busch claims that Charlie started most of the fights; he would decide he didn't like the look on the face of some guy and he would set out to change it with his fists. He would get nervous and begin shaking before he threw a punch. Charlie never backed down.

Von Busch would also say that Charlie was James Dean before James Dean was James Dean, and in some ways Charlie bore a striking resemblance to the actor: his thick hair combed straight back (among other styles), his intense but brooding eyes, the sullenness, his way of standing with the faint hint of a sneer, the fact that Dean was always smoking, holding a cigarette loosely and a little off-center in his lips. A popular photo of Charlie after his arrest shows him in cuffs, without glasses, a cigarette between slightly open lips, wearing a quizzical smile. This dangling-cigarette look was mastered by Dean in the scene in *Rebel Without a Cause* where two guys are driving cars car full tilt toward the edge of a cliff in a game of "Chickie Run." The first one to swerve lost. In Lincoln's version of the game, simply called "chicken," two cars ran straight at each other until one of them swerved. Charlie never swerved. When a new James Dean movie came to town, Charlie and Bob went to see it again and again at a theater in downtown Lincoln. Charlie wore black jeans, cowboy boots, and a leather jacket with the collar turned up.

Von Busch also described the different sides of Charlie. "He'd be the kindest person you've ever saw. He'd do anything for you if he liked you. He was a helluva lot of fun to be around, too. Everything was just one big joke to him. But he had this mean side. He could be mean as hell, cruel. If he saw some guy on the street who was bigger than he was, better looking, or better dressed, he'd try to bring the poor bastard down to his size."

2

CARIL ANN FUGATE LIVED THE FIRST EIGHT YEARS OF her life in a cloud of alcoholic violence. Her father, William Fugate, a convicted pedophile, drank up what meager funds he managed to earn and regularly returned home from a bar to wreak violence on his wife and kids. When her mother, Velda, or Betty, as she was sometimes called, heard him banging at the door, she would hide Caril and her older sister, Barbara, in the closet, where they stayed, crying and hugging each other until their father stumbled off to bed. Eviction was a regular event in their lives. Time after time, Caril returned home from grade school to find the room piled high with packing boxes. The records show she attended six schools (one of them twice) from kindergarten through sixth grade and moved five times in two years. Not surprising, she did average at best in school and was held back two semesters for falling behind. But there were no behavior problems. Although some observers would later point to a streak of rebelliousness in her, she was on time for school, did her work, and did not draw attention to herself. When her father's conviction for molesting a ten-year-old girl in the State Theater (for which he served a hard six months in jail for the second offense) hit the newspapers, she and Barbara were humiliated at school.

This grim phase of Caril's life came to an abrupt end one night in her seventh year. She and her sister were hiding in the closet of a tenement on Tenth Street when the screaming in the kitchen turned into blows and then a loud thud. The sisters ran from the closet to find their father with his hands around their mother's throat, her head flat on the kitchen table. Barbara grabbed a butcher knife as Caril grabbed a hammer, and the two threatened and screamed at their father to let her go, until finally their grandmother, Pansy Street, who lived in the same building, burst into the room. William Fugate fled the apartment. He returned a week later to grab a suitcase full of clothes and left the apartment and his family.

Velda filed for divorce on October 16, 1950, and it was granted on February 20, 1951. The judge gave her custody of the two children and ordered William to pay fifty dollars a month for child support. Velda herself had been raised in terrible poverty, and now the family went on welfare in the fall of 1950. The caseworker noted that both girls were "attractive, well-mannered, normal and had a good relationship with their mother."

Velda and her two daughters remained in the tenement on Tenth Street. There was a brief reconciliation with William, but eventually Velda met and fell in love with Marion Bartlett, a skinny fifty-six-year-old WWII vet. Velda and Marion were married on March 26, 1954, when Caril was ten years old. The family eventually moved to 924 Belmont Avenue. Caril's life stabilized; while Marion was strict—no candy, no pop—and didn't make much money, he was regularly employed and he wasn't a drunk. On February 11, 1955, Velda gave birth to Betty Jean. From that day on, Caril's home life centered around her little sister. When she came home from Whittier Junior High in the eighth grade, the tiny two-year-old with the curly blond hair called her name and came running into her arms.

Besides being small, Caril was considered to be quiet—so quiet that when she became world-famous, several of her classmates could barely remember who she was. That may be, but she had a streak of the rebel in her; she often wore jeans and a man's shirt with the cuffs rolled up rather than the skirts and blouses of her classmates. According to some, she could swear up a storm and blew up quickly when challenged. Bad mouth and a rough temper aside, there was not, to credible perception, the sign of a seed of destruction germinating inside the usually well-behaved little girl.

In January 1958, Caril and her family were living in an area of north Lincoln called Belmont, a poor neighborhood, sometimes referred to as a slum in the newspapers. A dirt road ran in front of her house, and the family had been using an outhouse in the backyard until a few months earlier, when her stepfather managed to roughly plumb the house and install an indoor toilet. The house was basically a shack, with an uneven linoleum floor laid by her stepfather. Sheets were hung to divide the rooms, and clotheslines were strung across the ceiling of the living room. Clothes and bedding were washed by hand. The outside walls were plastered with tarpaper made to look like bricks. The backyard was so littered with junk that planks had been laid so the family could get safely from the dirt drive to the back door. The house had neither an air conditioner nor a phone.

Maria Diaz, who as a child lived with her family next door to the Fugates, was told by her mother to stay away from the father because he was a "window peeper." In 1958, William Fugate was working as a janitor at Park Elementary School. He died in jail in 1964 while serving time for contributing to the delinquency of a six-year-old girl in the Varsity Theater.

3

BOB VON BUSCH AND CHARLIE STARKWEATHER WERE still running together when Bob began dating Caril's older sister, Barbara, in 1956. Barbara and Caril had become quite close during the violent tumult of their childhood and had stayed close in their teenage years. They slept in the same bed and loved to spend time together caring for little sister Betty Jean. When Bob and Barb went to movies or the Runza Drive-In, little sister Caril was always along. It was fine with Bob. He liked Caril. (A runza, a fiercely popular sandwich in Nebraska, is fresh bread baked with a filling of beef, cabbage or sauerkraut, onions, and seasoning. It was brought to Nebraska as a bierock in the 1870s by German Russian immigrants).

So it worked out when Bob showed up at the Bartlett house with Charlie one night and suggested the four of them go to a movie together. For Charlie, it was all over from the very beginning. Caril was cute and wore a dark brown ponytail. She acted older than her age and had lots of opinions about things. She swore readily. All of which appealed to Charlie. More than that, *she liked him*, his funny stories about being a sheriff from Texas, running a gang of outlaws; she liked that he was short like her, she liked his bowlegs because they made him unusual, and she loved his thick red hair. As Caril would put it, "I wanted to be number one for someone, to get all of their attention, and he was a James Dean sort of character."

The four of them went out a few more times, but soon it was just Caril Ann and Charlie, or Chuck, as she called him. One boy made the mistake of asking Caril for a date, and Charlie heard about it and had a brief "conversation" with the boy, who never came around again.

Only a few weeks after their double date, Charlie and Caril were spending their evenings and weekends together. Caril seemed drawn to the older "bad boy," a known tough guy who bought her things, raced hot rods at Capitol Beach, and let her drive his Ford.

Caril was Charlie's first real girlfriend. The few others had been passing fancies, at best. Charlie began stopping by the Bartlett house in his 1941 Ford, hanging around until Caril asked her mother for permission to leave on a date. Soon, they were going steady. Caril would spend evenings in Charlie's room reading comics and watching Charlie throw a hunting knife at the wall. Charlie had left home after a fight with his father and lived in the same tenement on Tenth Street where Bob and Barb, now married, and Caril's maternal grandmother, Pansy Street, lived.

Marion Bartlett, Caril's stepfather, fiercely disapproved of the match. He not only took an instant dislike to Charlie but also thought the seventeen-year-old boy was way too old for Caril. He accused Charlie of getting her pregnant. Caril's mother also had little use for Charlie, but she defended her daughter's right to go out with whomever she chose.

The Starkweathers didn't so much dislike Caril as they did the impact she was having on their son. To Helen, Charlie's mother, her son was a different boy after he and Caril got together; it seemed like Caril had some sort of hold over him. He began arguing with his brothers, which he had never done before, and he had no time for family or even her. His whole life centered around Caril. In his father's eyes, his son became stubborn and impossible to reason with.

Charlie quit school after ninth grade. He got a job as a stock boy at Western Newspaper Union, where he baled newspapers and loaded and unloaded trucks. He earned forty-five dollars a week and gave fifteen dollars of it to his mother. Charlie taught thirteen-year-old Caril to drive his car, and some days he would allow her to drive it home from school. In September 1957, Charlie traded in his 1941 Ford for a light blue 1949 Ford. His father put up $150 for the purchase, and the title was in his name. One day, Caril pulled out of a parking spot without looking and a car banged into her, sending her into a third car. Charlie's father was outraged and insisted that Charlie promise not to let Caril drive the car anymore. Charlie refused. A tussle ensued in the living room of the house, and it ended with Charlie crashing through the front window. His father always insisted that he had only pushed Charlie. He told his son to get out and not come back.

Charlie left the house for good, although he would soon apparently reconcile with his father. He moved into the tenement on North Tenth Street, where Bob and Barbara, now married, and Pansy Street lived. Charlie was living there when the trouble began a few months later.

SOMETIMES CARIL'S FAST-RUNNING bad mouth shocked even Charlie, who told one psychiatrist that Caril used language in front of her mother that he would never use in front of his. Classmates heard Caril use swear words they'd never heard before. Another friend who used to walk home from school with Caril said she would go on a rant about how she hated her teachers and once threatened to kill one of them for keeping her late. And yet one of Caril's eighth-grade teachers would say that Caril, whom she described as cute in an elfish way, made a fine adjustment to junior high school; she had perfect attendance, made friends, and was anxious to do her schoolwork to the best of her ability.

There was a certain duality to Caril's personality. An electrician who came to the house on Belmont for a repair listened in shock as Caril cussed her stepfather a blue streak for refusing to give her money so she and Charlie could go to the state fair. He tried to reason with her—she and Charlie had gone to the fair the previous night—but she didn't buy it and cursed him even louder than before.

And yet Caril was wonderful with children. At age thirteen she babysat the five children of Virginia and Sonny Von Busch after school five nights a week from 4:00 to 9:30, when the parents came home from work. She cooked and cleaned and bathed them and put them to bed. The children loved her, and still loved her, Virginia would testify at Caril's trial.

Some evenings Charlie and Caril hung out in Charlie's room watching TV and reading comics—he trained her to toss the bone-handled hunting knife and stick it in the wall—and sometimes they cruised the streets of Lincoln, dragging Charlie's Ford one way on Sixteenth Street and back the other way on Seventeenth. They'd go to movies, usually a double feature on Sunday, or out to Pioneers Park on the southwest edge of town, where there were buffalo and horses, and they'd stop at the Runza Drive-In on the way back. Charlie saw that Caril admired his love of guns and his ability to fix beat-up cars. She was keen to watch him race his hot rod on the dirt track at Capitol Beach. One Sunday evening, he was the last car running in the demolition derby and won a twenty-five-dollar prize. He took Caril out to a fancy steak restaurant to show off and celebrate.

Charlie was never happier than those days, and yet being with Caril made him realize why he hated the rest of the world so much. He'd heard it worked otherwise, but loving her didn't come to mean he could love others or hate the world any less. There were times when the two of them lay in each other's arms "not talking much, just kind of tightening up and listening to the wind blow or looking at the same star and moving our hands over each other's faces ... We knowed that the world had given us to each other. We was going to make it leave us alone ... if we'da been let alone we wouldn't a hurt nobody."

4

HATRED. REVENGE. RAGE. BITTERNESS. SELF-LOATHING. None of these things leached out of Charlie's soul by his slow turn from the taunted, left-out, harassed crybaby kid into the scary rock-fisted teenager. Likely a sense of satisfaction, of relief, perhaps even triumph, would momentarily overcome him when he pounded some kid insensate. It may have tempered the intensity of the boiling hatred inside him, but it did not cool it off. With a reputation as a mean fighter, he was somebody other than a bow-legged runt (a phrase the AP would later use to describe him). But he would stand in front of the window of the restaurant of the Cornhusker Hotel and watch the finely dressed people sitting at their tables with silverware and wineglasses and realize he would never get there, like he would never get to New York or Los Angeles or anywhere else in the world. He was a garbage man, and he would never amount to much else. Looking in the widow, he would hear the taunts of his classmates in the schoolyards and he would mumble a vow of silent revenge. His hatred wasn't limited to those who once made fun of him; he hated everybody, a world that had no use for him, no place for him. He may have dreamed of a return to the enchanted forest, but even he knew the pathway into the innocence of that place was lost to him forever. He treasured guns. The smell of them, the feel of them. His brother Rodney would say that even when Charlie had shot and killed a rabbit, he kept on shooting it until he'd emptied the .22.

Charlie had bought a 1932 Model A Ford coupe and rented space in a garage on Woodsdale Boulevard from an elderly couple named the Southworths. He worked on it day and night. He knew how to tear down a car and put it back together blindfolded, but if he had to choose between guns and cars, he would easily choose guns. "The gun," he would say, "gave me a feeling of power that nothing else could match." As a pretend Texas sheriff, he stood in front of the mirror in his small room and practiced drawing on himself. He told stories of his gang's activities to his friends. He read comics and watched cowboy shows on TV until he could see his world as made up of fictional people. His dreams could soften the conflicted reality of his life, and they would often seep into the daylight hours.

Sometimes he would wake up from a terrifying dream and be quieted by a silver shaft of moonlight lying across his bed. The moonlight seemed alive. "Sometimes," he said, "it took me away from the things I hated . . . it made me forget." In the moonlight the cheap pieces of furniture seemed suddenly clothed in the silken raiment of a king in full possession of his kingdom. "I knowed better," he explained, "but that I imagined, I guess, it was what I wanted to imagine."

Standing in front of the mirror, he would pull a pistol and kill thousands of people. It was something that had to be done. Even then it was not an unpleasant thought. He had dreams of something closing in around him: "smiling faces, dreams of wishing death would come soon." He had dreams of walking freely in a forest as a boy. After spending hours in a neighborhood bar, he would walk home and it would seem like the trees and the shadows were singing to him. In bed, he would lie for hours while images and sounds of childhood taunts and insults played around in the room. Often the dreams wove their way into his waking hours and he was unable to differentiate the realities. He eventually came to an understanding of his place in the world that would link the images together to show the path that lay ahead of him. He was seventeen when Death made her initial appearance. She showed in the window of his room just before dawn:

"I don't know how it was, but I would always wake up and see her standing there in the window . . . and all I could see would be the part from the waist up . . . It was kind of a half human and half bear . . . only it didn't have no neck. It just tapered off from a big chest to a small pointed head. It didn't have no arms and no ears." He seemed to read her mind. "Don't be in no hurry. I won't let you forget." Sometimes she would appear when he was awake. She could come in the sound of a whistle. "It was close and loud at first, but it got further and further away and the sound became mournful and sad until I couldn't hear it no more." The whistle left him paralyzed. "For about a minute or two, I couldn't move my arms or legs."

"One time, Death comed to me with a coffin and tolded me to get in . . . then the coffin sailed away with me in it till it came to a big fire . . . the coffin sort of melted, I guess, I was down there on a street with great flames of fire on each side of me. But it wasn't hot like I'd always thought hell would be . . . it was more like beautiful flames of gold . . . then I woke up."

Charlie's fury coalesced around that dream. He now had an understanding, a purpose, a path, and whatever fear he might have had of dying had flown away along with the image in his window. He was now a free man. He understood he wouldn't last long and that was fine with him. He wouldn't have to listen to the taunts anymore; he would walk the streets without his hands out in front of him. Death had marked him. Death was coming for him.

Caril was in his death dreams, white and beautiful. She would ride with him, and they would go out in a blaze of glory. She would see him kill for her. She would die with him. The coffin dream told him it was better on the other side, that the fires were cold, and he wanted her with him when he got there. But he needed to start making things happen. To move from the riverbank into the river, from the fantasy outlaw into the real outlaw.

Charlie's head was by then a stream of fantasies. Even in the presence of Death laying out the path before him, the hatred still churning within seemed to almost immobilize him. Caril understood. She was more than a refuge from the hate. She was willing to go with him, and knowing that made Charlie feel renewed. Sometimes, he felt like with her he was an infant again; other times he wanted to be "forever lost in her arms." She stirred up strong, sometimes fearful forces inside him. Another time in a dream he felt his car swerve, heard the singing of bullets and "the frightened laughter of Caril as she clung to his arms." They went out in a blaze of glory while the hushed and frightened voices of everyone who'd ever made fun of him spoke in awe. Still, self-doubt never washed out. One night he lay in bed and sensed Caril was thinking about him. She was wondering if there was anything worth saving in him, anything worth standing by. Would he fight for her if the chips were down? What would he do if her parents threatened to kill him if he didn't let her alone? Then it cleared up: "I'd let her see that I'll kill for her."

5

I N THE POPULAR VERSION OF THE STATE, NEBRASKA IS simply a wide, flat land with fields of corn and beans stretching from border to border. For many Americans, their only experience of Nebraska, if they have one, is driving across it on the interstate from one border to another. They bemoan the lack of anything to see on the endless plains. Corn in the east. Cattle in the west. The Platte River? Wide, shallow, and shifting. (*Platte* is the French word for *flat*.) What did Mark Twain call it? "A miserable, yellow melancholy stream." "If it were my river," he said, "I wouldn't let it out at night." Most people driving across the state on I-80 today or on Highway 26 in the 1950s don't realize that they are following in the footsteps of the pioneers heading west from St. Louis or Independence in covered wagons along the Oregon and Mormon Trails. The Platte River provides the best path across the state because it *is* so flat. It was a great natural highway for Native Americans long before European settlers arrived. General William Tecumseh Sherman loved traveling the Platte Trail because, he said, it was dry, it was flat, and it went in the right direction. One hundred and twenty-five years later, deep ruts still cut the earth where the wagon wheels rolled. The North Platte, which flows from the Wyoming Rockies, and the South Platte, which flows from the Colorado Rockies, conjoin in the town of North Platte, just about in the middle of the state. Turn north from here, and in a mile or two you enter a strange land of gorgeous frozen waves of sand blanketed in a tall prairie grass. Hills rise up from nowhere and disappear just as suddenly. Even in daylight, you can drive for miles without seeing a human or animal. The occasional pond, or stream, the cowboy boots stuck upside down on top of fence posts, the dancer-like bending of the delicate prairie grasses in the wind—it all gives the land an even deeper sense of stark beauty and loneliness. On a moonlit night, the hills form wavering ghostly shapes.

The Sandhills consist of 19,500 square miles and run for 265 miles, from one end of the state to the other. They are the largest sand dune formation in the Western Hemisphere. Every ten years or so, a serious publication like *National Geographic* discovers the Sandhills and sends a photographer to fly over the freaky, rolling hills in a small plane in an attempt to capture their ethereal beauty.

West from the Sandhills lies the Panhandle. The northwest corner is the Pine Ridge region, which has rocky buttes and forests that are reminiscent of northern New Mexico. Below the South Dakota border is the historic site of Fort Robinson, an army fort that played a major part in the Sioux Wars from 1876 to 1890. Crazy Horse surrendered his band of Oglala Sioux here in 1877, and here he was killed over a year later by a soldier. The biography of the great Oglala warrior-chief is beautifully told by Mari Sandoz, one of Nebraska's most notable writers, in *Crazy Horse: The Strange Man of the Oglalas*. The fort served as the training center in the country for eight thousand war dogs during WWII. The fort was also the site of a WWII German prisoner-of-war camp.

The Wildcat Hills lie to the south. A rugged country bounded by the North Platte, it is populated with ponderosa pine, has small mountains and deep canyons cut by the river, and has striking rock formations, such Chimney Rock, Scotts Bluff, and Courthouse Rock. Mountain lions, wolves, elk, bighorn sheep, coyotes, and wild turkeys roam the countryside.

Over three hundred miles to the east lies the Ashfall Fossil Beds, a site containing complete fossils in the ground of rhinos, horses, and sixteen other species of animals perfectly preserved in volcanic ash that fell on the poor beasts twelve million years ago.

"River Country" is a phrase often used to describe the southeastern part of the state. It is bounded on the east by the Missouri River, on the west by the Little Blue River, and on the north by the Platte River. It includes Lincoln and Nebraska City and was initially populated by both

proslavery and antislavery homesteaders. The land is fertile and productive, in part due to the bottom soil of the three rivers. It is the country of
apple orchards and dairies, as well as alfalfa, corn, and soybeans.

Nebraska has rough weather. The warm air from the Gulf collides
with the cold air from the north and sets off tornadoes, flooding, and
blizzards. The blizzard of 1949 killed seventy-six people, even with the
U.S. Army and the National Guard providing relief. The drought of the
Great Depression devastated the people and the land.

A traveler will not see perhaps the most stunning and critical geo-
graphical feature of the state: the Ogallala Aquifer. Covering 174,000
square miles, the aquifer is essentially an underground lake stretching
from North Dakota south to Texas and from Kansas west to Colorado.
The deepest part lies under the Sandhills. It provides the water for most
of the farming and residential use in the Great Plains, which stretches
from the Rocky Mountains to the Missouri River and from the Rio
Grande to Canada. For years, the aquifer has been losing volume.

For most of Nebraska's history, water to irrigate crops was either di-
verted from streams and rivers or pumped from groundwater. Pumping
required windmills or, later, gas engines, which were expensive; divert-
ing and building irrigation ditches was not only time-consuming and
expensive but also depended on the flow of the rivers. The Sandhills
were far too expansive to irrigate. And yet right below the Sandhills and
the rest of the state lay the aquifer. In 1948, a farmer from Columbus
by the name of Frank Zybach invented the center-pivot sprinkler system, which he patented in 1952. The pump is fixed on top of the well,
and irrigation pipes are set on top of large towers on wheels. The force
of the water pumping swings the towers in a large circle. The pipes are
fitted with nozzles that spray water out onto the crops at set intervals.
(Electric motors are now used to turn the wheels.) A center-pivot irrigation system in the Sandhills can cover 130 acres, leaving green crop circles in otherwise arid land. The invention transformed the Great Plains
(and marginal land in many other countries) into a huge breadbasket.
Crops could now be grown in the flatter areas of the Sandhills. Bushels

of corn per acre increased from 75 to 250. Feed lots and meat-packing plants sprang up around the state. Many old ranching families objected to turning the fragile prairie grass and sandy soil. But good-paying jobs at equipment dealers and grain silos and seed dealerships were created in many small farming communities.

Nebraska was a latecomer to the Union. The land was acquired in 1803 as part of the Louisiana Purchase, in which the United States acquired France's claim to 828,000 square miles of land from Napoleon for $15 million. In 1854 the Territory of Nebraska was created by the Kansas-Nebraska Act, and it included portions of what today is Wyoming, Montana, Colorado, and North and South Dakota. In 1867 the territory was reduced to the current boundaries of Nebraska and admitted to the Union as the thirty-seventh state of the Union. It changed the name of its capital city from Lancaster to Lincoln. Lancaster became the county.

In the great settlement of the west, Nebraska was mainly a stretch of land crossed by pioneers and settlers on the way to Oregon and California. The prairie was so treeless and devoid of water that it was christened by an early explorer as "The Great American Desert." Paleontologists believe that Native Americans inhabited the land at least 11,500 years ago, in the time of mastodons and mammoths and saber-toothed cats. The Pawnees were early inhabitants. Other tribes were the Poncas, Omahas, Otoe-Missourias, Ioways, and Lakotas. Lewis and Clark traveled from St. Louis up the Missouri, which formed Nebraska's eastern border.

The Oregon Trail opened in 1841, not long after a pass through the Rockies was discovered in Wyoming. In the next twenty-five years, over half a million people traveled across Nebraska on their way west in covered wagons or on foot, pushing carts (Mormons), many seeking gold in California or good farmland in western Oregon. At the time, the government thought so little of Nebraska for farming and settlements that it declared it permanent "Indian country." But by 1850, the transcontinental railroad was on the horizon, and the railroad needed grain- and cattle-producing towns along the route. The territory was opened for settlement, and towns sprang up along the Missouri River, such as Nebraska City and Council Bluffs. These towns received cargo by steamboat and sent it out over the prairies on wagons.

By the time of the Civil War, Nebraska had only twenty-nine thousand people, excluding Native Americans. Slavery was legal in Nebraska from the territory's inception in 1854 to its abolishment in 1861.

In 1862, the federal government passed the Pacific Railway Act, which provided for the building of the transcontinental railroad by the Union Pacific Railroad heading west from the Missouri and the Central Pacific Railroad heading east from California. Almost simultaneously, the government passed the Homestead Act, which provided 160 acres of land to anyone, including freed slaves, women, and immigrants, who would pay a small fee and occupy and farm the land for five years. Soon, immigrants from Sweden, Germany, England, Ireland, Poland, and Czechoslovakia began coming to claim land. In the 1870s, the Union Pacific and Burlington Railroads began passing out brochures and tacking up posters in towns across central Europe advertising for immigrants. They promised free passage and land. Willa Cather, from Red Cloud, perhaps Nebraska's most well-known author, captured the immigrant pioneer experience in a remarkable novel, *O Pioneers!*, published in 1913.

Soon, the settler wagons rattling across the prairie of central and eastern Nebraska began stopping for the inhabitants to claim land. In the absence of trees, the houses had to be built from sod. It turned out that 160 acres was insufficient for a ranch in the Sandhills, so in 1904 the government passed the Kincaid Act, which allowed claims of 640 acres in the thirty-seven western counties of Nebraska.

At the time of statehood in 1867, the Indian Wars were still raging in western Nebraska. Either peacefully or otherwise—mainly otherwise—Native Americans were eventually pushed off the land and onto reservations. In 1879, in a lawsuit brought by Chief Standing Bear, a Ponca man whose tribe was forced by the U.S. Department of the Interior, in violation of their treaty rights, to leave Nebraska for the unfamiliar climate, landscape, and diseases of the Indian Territory (Oklahoma), a federal district court in Omaha ruled that a Native American was legally a person and therefore able to sue. When Nebraska was granted statehood, it was on the condition that it amend its charter to exclude the provision limiting the right to vote to white males.

Something had to be done about the treeless prairie of the new state. J. Sterling Morton, owner of the *Nebraska City News* and later the first secretary of agriculture, began a determined campaign to plant trees, and in a year more than one million trees had been planted in the state. Arbor Day became a state holiday, and it is now celebrated in all the states except Delaware. Nebraska City also became a stop on the underground railroad, providing safe houses and tunnels for escaped slaves on their way north.

Nebraska sent its seriously mentally ill patients over the border to Iowa for treatment or housing. When Lincoln became the state capitol in 1867, a commission was appointed to find a site in Nebraska for a state "lunatic asylum." The Nebraska State Hospital for the Insane was built near Lincoln, and the first patient was admitted in 1870. The hospital burned to the ground in a few months but was soon rebuilt. In 1921, the name of the institution was changed to the Lincoln State Hospital, which name it still bore when fourteen-year-old Caril Ann Fugate was admitted there on the evening of January 31, 1958, pursuant to the directive of the county attorney, who two days earlier had charged her with first-degree murder.

6

REFERRED TO OCCASIONALLY AS THE HOLY CITY BE-
cause of the number of Methodist churches, Lincoln was a
straight-up-and-down place. On top of the 400-foot-high tower
of the state capitol was a nineteen-foot-high bronze statue of a man scattering grain (*The Sower*), which could be seen from twenty miles around
in any direction. The numbered streets ran north to south, and the
lettered streets ran east to west. The church pews were full on Sunday.
Thursday was shopping night downtown. In 1922, Charles Lindbergh
learned to fly at the Nebraska Aircraft Corporation in Lincoln, and locals tell the stories of their parents or grandparents seeing him fly over
the country club golf course in his biplane.

Any crime in Lincoln was mainly small-time; there had been only
seven murders in the last ten years, and all of them had been solved. If
there were gangs anywhere, they were sixty miles east in Omaha, which
sits on the edge of the Missouri River and is a hub of the Union Pacific
Railroad. Omaha had been the territorial capital, and it fought bitterly
to remain the state capital upon statehood in 1867. The university in Lincoln drew students from small farm towns across the state; on a football
Saturday, the stadium was the third largest city in the state, after Lincoln
and Omaha. Nebraskans went bananas for Big Red.

Lincoln was the heart of the heartland. It was safe. Front doors were
often left unlocked; cars were parked in the drive or garage with keys in
the ignition. Elementary school kids walked blocks to school by themselves. Men wore hats to work. Women wore hats to church. Every boy
had a bike and a baseball glove. Girls wore skirts and blouses to school
and played jacks or hopscotch at recess. Most mothers stayed home to
raise their children. Men retired at sixty-five. Lincoln was a large rural
town of peace, predictability, and relative prosperity.

As in most towns, there were class divisions. O Street (the longest straight main street in the world, it was claimed back then) split the town down the middle; north of town were the blue-collar and poor neighborhoods like Belmont; south of O were the middle-class and wealthy neighborhoods, the brick boulevards and parkways and mansions, the beautifully manicured Lincoln Country Club golf course. The few thousand Black Lincolnites mostly lived north of O street in an area known as T-town.

In the fall of 1957, Charlie lived north of O Street, in a two-story gray stone building at 455 North Tenth Street. Every time Charlie went to see Caril, which was almost every day in the autumn of 1957, he drove or walked by an area known as the North Russian Bottoms, which had been settled by ethnic Germans whose families had moved to Russia in the 1770s under Catherine the Great and left under the oppressive edicts of Alexander II in the 1870s. He also crossed over a stream called Salt Creek, a small saline river that winds its way unobtrusively through Lincoln from south to north and eventually links up with the Platte River. In the 1850s, a large area of salt flats existed northwest of what is now Lincoln and was a primary reason for the town being settled where it was. For the frontiersman, as well as Native Americans, salt was necessary for the diet and was used for preserving meat; salt hunters traveled hundreds of miles to the flats to harvest it for use and sale. J. Sterling Morton and other entrepreneurs laid claim to a substantial portion of the flats, but they eventually proved commercially unviable because of the lack of wood on the empty plains necessary to boil away the water from the brine.

December 1, 1957, was a bitter-cold night with a cutting wind. In the early morning, a traveler found a body on a deserted section of Superior Street, not too far north of Salt Creek. A young man in white coveralls lay in the middle of the road with his head blown open. The night attendant at the Crest Service Station on close-by Cornhusker Highway had taken two shotgun blasts to the head.

The gas station was a futuristic glass structure with a slanted roof and a large apron in front. The CREST sign sat on top of a tall pole in front outlined in bright bulbs and small plastic flags. On the drive stood a sign advertising a gallon of permanent antifreeze for $1.71. A nude calendar hung on the wall inside, behind the cash register.

The murder was a big deal in peaceful Lincoln. The *Star* ran the story in a bold headline the next day: LINCOLNITE SLAIN: THEFT MOTIVE SEEN. Next to the headline was a photo of Robert George Colvert, looking as young and innocent as a Boy Scout. Twenty-one, a few months out of the navy, newly married, and an expectant father, he had been employed at the station less than a month, earning fifty-five dollars a week working the shift from 11:00 p.m. to 7:00 a.m.

The *Nebraska State Journal* noted that it was the third killing in Lincoln that year. (A man charged with murdering his three-year-old child had died by suicide in his prison cell, and a woman beat her husband to death with an iron sash in their bedroom.) But still, it was the north side of O Street, even the other side of Cornhusker Highway, which slices diagonally through north Lincoln, and it was simply a robbery gone bad. Probably a transient. Papers from the hundreds of small towns around Nebraska carried the story.

Days passed. Snows came and went. The earth was frozen. The icy wind blew without letup. Nothing came of the murder. There was concern, yes. But fear, a personal fear, not yet.

7

THE AFTERNOON OF NOVEMBER 30, CHARLIE DROVE to Sonny Von Busch's house and took a 12-gauge shotgun from his garage. Dressed in cowboy boots, black jeans, a black shirt, he pulled into the Crest station at approximately 3:30 a.m. in his light blue 1949 Ford and saw a new guy there dressed in a white mechanic's suit. He went inside, bought a pack of Winstons and a pack of gum, and left. He got a little way down the highway and turned back. At the station, he bought another pack of gum but left the place when another car drove in. He returned in a few minutes and parked off to the side. He pulled a red scarf up to just below his eyes, put on a red hunting hat, slipped his hands into brown leather gloves, lifted the shotgun from underneath the seat, got out of the car, and walked into the station. He thrust a canvas money sack he'd found on his garbage route at Robert George Colvert and told him to fill it. Colvert dug money from his pocket and put it and money from the register in the sack. He handed Charlie a silver change holder and stacks of wrapped coins. (Charlie says the total was $108; the law says $160.) Colvert told Charlie he couldn't open the safe. Charlie hustled him out to his car and told him to drive to Superior Street, a lonely stretch of road on the outskirts of town. In the middle of nowhere, Charlie told him to stop and ordered him out of the car.

As Charlie was getting out behind him, Calvert grabbed the end of the shotgun and tried to jerk it away. Charlie cocked the gun and fired, hitting Colvert on the right side of the head, dropping him to the ground. When Colvert started to get up, Charlie pumped another shell in the chamber and shot him again in the head. This time he stopped moving. Charlie picked up his hat, threw the gun in the car, and took off. Just before the bridge over Salt Creek, he recalled the spent shell and returned to retrieve it. The body still lay in the middle of the road, face-down. Farther down the road a ways, Charlie threw the two shells out the window. He returned to his apartment, passing by the Crest station, and noted a car at the pumps. He slept until 8:00 a.m., and around 11:00 a.m. he drove to Caril's house with the shotgun still under the front seat of the Ford.

That night he stopped at a bridge over Salt Creek and threw the gun and the change holder in the water. A few days later, he painted the blue Ford black in his dad's garage, ripped out the grill, and painted the inside red. He also changed all four wheels on the car. Three days later, he retrieved the shotgun from the creek, cleaned the sand out of it, and returned it to Sonny's garage. He couldn't find the change holder.

Charlie might have told the law and perhaps even himself that his only intention in going out to the gas station that night was to rob the place. He knew better. From the moment he slid in the driver's seat of the 1949 Ford and drove to Sonny's house to get the shotgun, he knew he was going to kill. By his own words, there was no sign that Colvert recognized him. He could have tied him up or locked him in the bathroom, grabbed the cash, and walked right out of the station. But to set the right story in motion, to bind Caril to him forever, he needed to get out of his imagination and into the reality of a true outlaw; he needed to point a gun at a man and pull the trigger and watch him die. The way out of his darkness lay before him like a bright path into the long-lost magical forest of his childhood. He would write the ending to his own story. Caril would go along down the road with him "to the next world."

This is what he thought the night before his first murder: "I am not scared of anybody that ever live[d], I've got a gun . . . I know how to shoot . . . I've got a girl. She likes my way of doing things and I am not afraid of dyin', if I have to. I am not going to die like a rabbit. I am going to have something worth dyin' about . . . and I'm not going to be the first person to die either."

After the shooting, Charlie was no longer depressed, and headaches he'd had for several years were gone. Whatever capacity for remorse he might once have had was now extinguished. It was as if the murder had balanced things out. He regained that lost feeling of peace and happiness from his childhood. Reinhardt, the criminologist from the University of Nebraska, would later write that the killing of Colvert resulted in the death of the old Charles and the birth of a new one. It was now him and Caril against the world.

In the next seven weeks, the law failed to arrest anybody for the murder of Robert Colvert. The law operated on the mistaken assumption that the killer was a transient and long gone. The law failed to come across a young man who would in hindsight seem like an obvious suspect. A short, red-haired young fellow who hung around the station and bummed change for cokes and candy bars and, when locked out of his room for nonpayment of rent, often slept outside in his car, a 1949 Ford. Who suddenly had lots of bills and pockets full of silver to pay his back rent and buy better clothes than usual at the thrift store. Who bought his girlfriend presents, including a small dog for five dollars. A physical description was given to the cops, but the man had never stood for a mug shot. No one put two and two together.

The murder had major consequences for Charlie. As he would say later, the crime seemed to almost make him whole; it seemed to move him from a life of fiction and fantasy into action, from drawing pistols in front of a mirror and pretending he was Roy Rogers or a Texas sheriff or the leader of a gang of bad guys into the reality of violent crime. The killing made him feel good; that was the short of it.

The confused bitterness, the rage, had given way to clarity; the path in front of him, of them, wound out like a shining stream, free and open and short. The two lovers would not last long with their guns and damning sense of purpose. Even the iron rock of hate in his soul was cooling off. Caril used to run her fingers through his red hair and say she loved every strand. She cheered loudly when he won the demolition derby at the Capitol Beach racetrack in Lincoln. She brought a magic into his life, and he swore they would be together for eternity. The December murder of the gas station attendant showed the way. The end would be going out in a blaze of glory. They "would leave a trail that couldn't rub out, like tracks cut in a rock." Charlie would later say, "Caril put a spark and thrill into the killing."

As one psychiatrist would testify, the crust was broken. Charlie's primitive mind had kicked in. He got his first taste of blood that night, and things were never going to be the same.

II

THE KILLINGS

8

THE CITY WAS PITCH-BLACK ON THE MORNING OF JAN-
uary 21, 1958, when Charlie Starkweather got out of bed in his
small apartment on the north side of Lincoln. It was Tuesday,
which meant he had to help his older brother Rodney on his garbage
route. It was hard, dirty work, and he hated it. Rodney drove the truck
and Charlie hung on the back, jumping off to pick up cans, tossing the
refuse into the back of the truck, then dropping the cans on the street.
He stank by the end of the route. He had been working on Rodney's
route the previous summer and fall but was fired in November because
he was obnoxious to customers and drivers. He'd been rehired during
the holiday season and stayed on, making forty-five dollars a week,
which he spent mainly on his girlfriend. He'd bought most of the stuff
in her room. Jewelry. Stuffed animals. A radio. It was never enough. He
needed more money, and he would never make it hauling garbage. The
best part of the job was that he was done at 1:00 or 1:30, which meant
he could pick up Caril after school and hang around with her the rest
of the day.

The memory of what had happened at the Bartlett house two days
earlier, Sunday, was burning inside him. He had stopped by to see Caril,
as usual, thinking they might go to the races at Capitol Beach. He found
Caril washing clothes in the tub on the back porch. Out of nowhere,
she told him not to come around anymore. She didn't want to see him
again. "Don't pick me up after school. Don't come over." She walked to
the kitchen and repeated what she told Charlie to her mother. She told
Charlie to leave. He left, and he hadn't seen his girlfriend on Monday.
Today was going to be different. His days as a garbage man were over.
His days of fighting with his fists were over. He needed a gun.

He stood outside in the bitter cold waiting for Rodney to pick him up. He told his brother he was going to go hunting with Caril's stepdad and needed to borrow his .22. Rodney thought that was odd—Charlie hated Mr. Bartlett, and the feeling was surely mutual—but he told him to stop by after work and pick up the rifle.

Charlie got home around 1:00 p.m. He felt good; things had cleared up for him. Caril's rejection had flipped the switch. Caril's sister, Barbara, greeted Charlie in the hallway. Charlie cleaned up, put on a fresh pair of jeans, his favorite blue-and-white cowboy boots with butterflies on the tips, a gray shirt, and his black leather jacket. He went outside and fired up the 1949 Ford. He drove to Rodney's, where he picked up his .22. From there, he headed to Caril's house in Belmont.

January 21 was a relatively pleasant day in midwinter Lincoln. At 2:00 a.m., the temperature was 3 degrees Fahrenheit. By noon the sun was out, and by 4:00 p.m. the temperature had risen to 39.9 degrees, melting a light snow that had fallen in the night.

THE KILLINGS OF MARION, VELDA, AND BETTY JEAN BARTLETT
January 21, 1958

Charlie

Charlie drives north on Tenth Street past the football stadium. He crosses Cornhusker Highway, not far from the Crest Service Station, and angles left onto Belmont Avenue. Around 1:30, he parks the Ford on the street in front of the house. Wearing the black leather motorcycle jacket with the collar up, and carrying the single-shot .22 in one hand and a couple of carpet scraps he brought as a favor for Velda in the other, Charlie walks around back to the kitchen door. Velda opens the door before Charlie can knock. In the kitchen beside Velda are Marion and the blond curly-haired two-year-old Betty Jean. Charlie asks Velda if she still wants the carpet scraps, and she says she does. Charlie walks past them into the living room where the television and stove sit and drops the scraps on the floor. He lays the rifle down, crouches, unties the scraps, and spreads them out. Velda looks at the scraps and retreats to the kitchen. Charlie sits on the couch with the rifle on his lap. He dusts the gun, takes out the bolt lever action, cleans it with a cloth, and reinserts it. After several minutes, Marion walks in, gives Charlie a dirty look, and crosses the floor to the far bedroom. Then Velda and Betty Jean go to Caril and Betty Jean's bedroom, the closer of the two. Charlie isn't surprised by Marion's behavior; Marion has always hated him. More than once he accused Charlie of getting Caril pregnant. Charlie also knows Marion works at night and usually sleeps in the afternoon.

Charlie gets up with the .22 and follows Velda and Betty Jean into the bedroom. Velda is lying on the king-size bed; Betty Jean is fooling with the radio on a stand against the wall. The room is lit by southern exposure. He leans the rifle against the wall. He asks Velda if Marion is going hunting with him, and when Velda tells him she doesn't think so, he sits down on an orange crate stood on end and asks why. Out of nowhere, Velda tells him he'll have to leave and never come back. Charlie again asks why, but she says he's not to see Caril anymore. She won't give him a reason, so he tells her to go to hell, and she comes up off the bed and slaps the shit out of him. Charlie is pissed, but he says nothing. He walks from the room, leaving the gun standing against the wall; goes out the front door to cool off; and gets in his car, thinking about what he's going to do next. He drives around the block, only to return and park in exactly the same spot. He walks around back and knocks on the kitchen door, and Velda lets him in. Marion jumps him with a long line of shit about him and Caril. Charlie gets pissed because he can't even get a word in, and he finally decides to get out of the house. He heads to the front door, and he no sooner has it open than Marion comes up from behind and kicks him in the ass so hard he flies out the door. Hard enough to hurt him for the next three days.

That's it, then and there, for Charlie. He has done what he could to make peace. The old man will die.

He picks himself up, thinks a little ahead. Marion usually goes to work around 5:30 or 6:00. There's no phone in the house, so when he doesn't show up, someone will come to the house looking for him. He needs to stop that from happening. He gets in his car and drives to Hutson's, a local market a block and a half away. Inside are rows of grocery items, boxes of gum and candy and cartons of cigarettes and a counter with a business phone. He looks up the number of Watson Brothers Trucking Line in a phone book, but rather than using the phone on the counter he drops a dime in a pay phone a few feet away. A lady answers, and without saying who he is he tells her Marion Bartlett is sick and won't be coming to work for a couple days. He drives back to Bartlett's and, for the third time that day, around 2:30, parks out front.

He knocks on the kitchen door. No one answers this time. He walks to the front and knocks on the door, and again no one answers. They are lying low inside. Around three o'clock, he figures he might as well go and pick up Caril from school. He gets in his car and drives off in the direction of Whittier but gets only a few blocks before the car begins making weird sounds. He pulls into the drive of some neighbors, the Griggses, and arranges to leave his car there until he can get it fixed. He walks back to the Bartlett house and sits on the back porch awaiting Caril's return. After a while, he hears a dog barking and figures Caril is home. Then he hears Caril and her mother arguing, and he hesitates but gets up and lets himself in the kitchen door. Caril and her mother are in Caril's bedroom yelling at each other. "Yes, he did." "No, he didn't." He can't quite make it out. Betty Jean is lying on the king-size bed. Caril whips by him and heads to the bathroom. Velda now turns on him, yelling a bunch of crazy things, one being that he got Caril pregnant. He says something back to her, and she rises from the bed and slaps the shit out of him again, once on each side of the face. He whacks her back this time, an open hand to the head, and she falls, letting out a loud cry as she stumbles, and Marion comes flying into the room. He grabs Charlie by the neck and starts hauling him to the front door. Charlie gives him a good kick, fists fly, and Marion drops him to the living room floor. They wrestle around until Marion finally gets up and takes off for a small room where he keeps his tools. Charlie goes into the bedroom and grabs his gun. Velda is watching from the doorway as Charlie takes a hollow-nose .22 shell from the pocket of his leather jacket and slips it in the chamber. He turns to look, and Marion is coming at him with a hammer in his right hand. Charlie cocks the gun and pulls the trigger. The bullet hits Marion in the head, and he falls to the floor. Caril enters the living room and looks at her bleeding stepfather on the floor but says nothing. Velda runs toward the kitchen, and the situation holds momentarily, until a minute or so later when she returns with a black-handled butcher knife, its long blade curved at the tip. When Caril angrily asks her what she's going to do with the knife, she tells her she's going to chop Charlie's head off. Charlie ejects the spent shell, slips a live round in the chamber, and slams the bolt closed. Caril jerks the gun away from Charlie and tells her mother she's going to blow her to hell. Velda gives Caril a shove, knocking her to the floor, and Charlie grabs the gun from Caril and whirls around and shoots Velda in the mouth. Betty Jean is watching from the doorway. Velda reels but does not go down. She gets herself past Charlie and heads toward the baby but then turns around and looks Charlie in the eye, the knife still in her hand. Charlie raises the rifle butt in the air and brings it smashing down on her head. She falls down, but not all the way—she's sitting on the floor—so he smashes the butt into her head again. She topples over and lies on her right side.

Betty Jean is now screaming her head off. So after Charlie hits Velda the second time, he brings the butt of the gun up and smashes the little girl in the head. She wobbles against the table but keeps screaming. Caril yells at her little sister to shut up. She tells Charlie that her stepfather is still moving around.

Charlie picks up the butcher knife and starts for him, but the little girl is still screaming, so he flips the butcher knife and it sticks in her throat. She goes only partway down. He grabs a hunting knife from his boot and proceeds to finish off Marion on the floor. He thrusts the knife into his side, but it won't go in. He jams it in the old man's throat, but it goes in only about an inch. He hits the handle with his fist, and it finally sinks all the way in. Charlie sits on the bed and watches for five minutes to make sure he's dead. He's still moving. He stabs him in the back and in the neck. Charlie goes into the kitchen and gets a drink of water. Caril comes in and asks, "What are we going to do now?" Charlie doesn't answer.

"What are we going to do with the bodies?" she asks.

"What do you think we should do?" Charlie says.

Caril goes into the living room and sits on the couch. Charlie follows, asks her what the matter is.

"Nothing," she says.

"We've got ourselves in a helluva mess."

"It's what we've always wanted," Caril adds. "We'd better clean them up."

Charlie tells her not to worry, he'll do it himself. They sit on the couch for a while, until Charlie, thinking the house is too quiet, turns on the television. Then he sets to work; first, he loads another shell into the .22 in case someone shows up, and then he pulls the knife out of Betty Jean's throat and washes it off in the sink. She's still bleeding pretty bad, so he picks her up and places her in the sink. He cuts the clotheslines overhead in the living room and ties Velda up around the neck and knees. Then he wraps her in a blanket from one of the bedrooms, scrounges a rug from the tool room and wraps her up again, then ties the bundle up tight.

He turns back to Betty Jean in the sink, goes to the girls' bedroom and gets a blanket, wraps her up in it, and lays her in a grocery box half full of garbage. He carries Velda and Betty Jean onto the back porch and then carries Betty Jean to the outhouse, where he lays the box down. Then he carries the "old lady" out to the toilet and lays her down on the seat, sticks her head down one of the holes. He returns to deal with Marion. In the bedroom, he spots the old man's false teeth on the floor, picks them up, and then drags the body into the kitchen. He wraps him in a sheet and some building paper he found in the tool room and ties the bundle up tight. He can't fit the body through the kitchen door, so he pries off the screen door with a screwdriver and pulls the body through the frame and across the yard and lays him out on the floor of the chicken shack. He lays the screen door on top of him. When he returns to the house, Caril is sitting in a rocking chair outside her room. He sees from the bloody rags in the rag box that she has cleaned up some. He drops the false teeth in the box and finishes cleaning up the blood himself. All in all, it takes him well over three hours.

He leaves the house and walks to Hutson's and buys three bottles of Pepsi and a bag of potato chips. He and Caril snack, watch television, and play gin rummy. He eventually falls asleep in the rocker and Caril falls asleep on the couch. He wakes up when the television is static, turns it off, and falls asleep beside Caril on the couch. Around 6:30 a.m., when a little gray is showing in the sky, the dog barks. Someone's at the house.

Caril

Caril's life has been looking up. She adores her little sister, and while her stepfather is a little strict—he doesn't like pop or candy because it rots your teeth and gives you worms—at least he puts food on the table and doesn't come home drunk and mean. And she hasn't moved houses in two years; eighth grade at Whittier is her second year at the same school, which is a first. She was held back twice in grade school, but she is starting to like school and most of the teachers. She dreams of becoming a nurse.

Caril has made up her mind to break up with Charlie. He was getting obsessive and accusing her of going out with other boys behind his back and saying nasty things about her. On Sunday afternoon, when she is washing clothes, he shows up. She tells him not to come around anymore; she doesn't ever want to see him again. She goes into the kitchen and tells her mother, who comes onto the porch and repeats her daughter's directive: don't come around anymore. Charlie looks at Caril like he can't believe it: "You don't want to see me anymore?" he demands. "That's right," she says. Charlie turns red; hangs around for a few minutes, slapping his fist into his hand; then leaves, slamming the door behind him.

Caril is not feeling well on Monday morning—her appendix is bothering her—and she doesn't go to school. Charlie doesn't come by on Monday, the first day in many that she hasn't seen him. On Tuesday morning, Bonnie Gardner, her friend who lives two houses down and

across the street, stops by to pick her up for school, as usual. She kisses
her mother, father, and little sister goodbye, and the two of them head
out the front door. They catch the bus on a corner close to Hutson's and
Highway 6. From there it's a ten- or fifteen-minute ride to Whittier.

THE DAY PROCEEDS like an ordinary school day. Classes start at 8:00.
An hour for lunch, which is long enough for her to go up the street to a
drugstore for a soda and a snack. In the last class of the day, the students
practice square dancing in the gym, one of her favorite things to do. The
bell rings at 3:15, and she and Bonnie walk to the bus stop. By the time
they reach Caril's house, it's almost 4:00 p.m. The wintry sky is dark-
ening. Her dad's car is in the drive, which means he's probably inside
sleeping before going to work. The two friends say goodbye, agreeing to
see each other the next morning. Caril notices a green sheet in the living
room window. She crosses the lawn to the front porch, where her collie
puppy, King, is waiting for her. The two enter through the screen door.
Standing inside is Charlie Starkweather, and he's got a gun in his hand
pointed at her face. She recognizes it as his brother Rodney's .22. He
orders her to sit down, and she tells him to put the gun down and stop
acting silly. He pushes her down in the rocking chair. His face is red and
he's jumpy, nervous, in a way she's never seen him before. She gets up,
he pushes her back down, she gets up again, and he slaps her across the
face. Now she's getting scared. Her family is nowhere to be seen. Betty
Jean always runs into her arms the second she steps through the door.
Through tears, she demands to know where her family is, and Charlie
says they're at the Southworths' house on Woodsdale Boulevard, where
he has rented garage space to work on a Model A. "Why?" she asks, and
he says, "Because they know too much." His gang is going to pull off a
robbery somewhere, and if she does what he says, her family will return
unharmed. It goes on like this for a while. He never makes any sense.
She asks if she can talk with her family, and he says maybe later. She
cries, telling him over and over that she doesn't believe him—it's just too
fantastic. He throws the rifle at her and says if she doesn't believe him,
she should go ahead and shoot him. She throws the rifle on the floor and

says she won't do it, she's never shot anyone. He keeps on going, and the more he keeps talking, the more scared she becomes. He rubs the gun with a cloth while he talks.

Caril asks him if she can get up and he says no; she asks to make some coffee, thinking it might calm him down, and he allows it. He follows her to the kitchen. She makes the coffee and has a cup. She's still in her skirt and blouse, and he tells her to change into jeans and a shirt. She says she won't. "Well, I'll do it for you then," he says, so she gets up and goes into her bedroom. He sits outside the door in the rocker while she changes into her black jeans and a shirt. He throws her mother's butcher knife into the wall off and on and sticks it every time. They spend the rest of the night inside the house. They watch television until it goes off, and then she lies down on the davenport and goes to sleep. He's in the rocker, and at some point he comes over and joins her. She tells him to leave, but he doesn't.

Hours later, their other dog, Nig, hooked to a clothesline in the yard, starts barking. Charlie looks out the window, sees Bonnie coming up to the door, and tells Caril to get rid of her. Caril goes to the door and tells her friend she doesn't feel well and won't be going to school. Bonnie seems to hesitate—her friend was fine yesterday—but then turns and leaves. Charlie keeps an eye on Caril every minute; she has to ask permission to go to the bathroom; then he sits on the bed listening to her. He makes her sit on the bed when he goes to the bathroom so he can hear if she leaves. He ties her up when he leaves the house that night.

9

AFTER KILLING THE BARTLETTS AND WITH CARIL AT his side, Charlie's violence cools; there is a six-day pause before it kicks in again. During this time, it almost seems as if he and Caril are two young lovers who have run off to escape their evil parents. (In fact, Charlie claims Caril did suggest more than once that they run off to Missouri to get married; Charlie didn't think much of the idea.)

The bloodless interlude for Charlie is like "paradise." He and Caril do whatever they want: watch TV, play cards, eat ice cream and potato chips, and drink Pepsi after Pepsi. They have sex at night, in the morning, and twice on Sunday. Charlie leaves the house only twice to go to the store, and he ties Caril up only the first time. Other than that, she is always free to leave.

Charlie needs another weapon. Caril tells him her stepfather has a gun, and that first night they find a .410 shotgun in a case at the back of her closet. The next day, Charlie saws nine inches off the barrel with a hacksaw. He lays the piece on top of the piano. He and Caril scour the house for shells and find two boxes for the .410 underneath her bed. Charlie now has a .410, Rodney's .22, Velda's .32 caliber pistol, for which he has no shells, and the butcher knife. He notices the metal plate on the butt of the .22 is broken off and figures it must be from smashing it on the heads of Velda and the little girl.

He tracks who comes to the house. On Wednesday night, Rodney stops by looking for Charlie. Caril tells him she hasn't seen him, and Rodney comes back again on Friday and tells her he wants his .22 back. Rodney is married to Barbara, a daughter of the Griggs family, where Charlie left his car, so on Saturday Charlie takes the .22 and puts it inside his car and asks Mrs. Griggs to tell Rodney it's in there.

There is a steady stream of people coming to the front door of 924

Belmont in the next few days. Caril always goes to the door and, on Charlie's instructions, tells them that the family has the flu. The bread man and the milk man come on Wednesday, and Caril tells them she will pay them next time. They return on Saturday, and Charlie gives Caril cash to pay them. On Thursday, Marion's boss and another man come to the house to see if Marion will be coming to work the next day. He's still sick, Caril tells them. Marion has a little side business where he buys a big carton of eggs from the market and marks them up for sale to neighbors. Mrs. Yordy Kane comes by for eggs on Tuesday, only to be told by Caril they haven't been to the store. The landlord comes on Friday. Charlie's sister Laveta shows up twice, and each time Caril sends her away. Barbara and Bob Von Busch show up in a cab on Saturday morning, and Caril tells them to stay away because they are all sick inside. Later that day, Bob Von Busch and Rodney return, and Caril again tells them Charlie's not there.

Saturday evening, the dog barks, and Caril peers out the window and sees two cops coming to the front door. Charlie is asleep on the couch. She wakes him, tells him the law is here. He watches from a window as Caril talks to the two cops and they leave. Sunday night, Caril writes "Stay Away. Everybody is sick with the flu." on the back of a yellow building permit and attaches it to the front screen door with bobby pins.

Paradise can't last, and Charlie knows it. Three bodies lay frozen in outbuildings, the Bartlett car is in the drive, and they're running low on money. One of these days someone is bound to force their way through the door. He's told Caril that he'll shoot anyone who makes it inside, even Rodney and Robert Von Busch, and he means it. He would have no choice. He's prepared to die, but the violent road they are walking can't end at the place it started.

Monday morning, Bonnie comes to the front door to pick up Caril for school. She notices the note on the screen door as Caril, in a blue housecoat, comes to the door and says she's still sick. It's the end of the semester, so she asks Bonnie to turn in her schoolbooks and bring her notebooks back to her.

Caril's grandmother Pansy Street shows up at the door around 9:00 a.m. She's been turned away before. Today, Caril, looking pale, tells her, "Go home, Grandma. Oh, Granny, go away! Mama's life is in danger if you don't." Pansy responds by yelling past Caril into the house, "Betty! You say something so I'll know you're all right!" With no response, she then yells loud enough for all the neighbors to hear: "Caril, you open this door this second. I'm going to get in this house and see what's wrong with Betty. If you don't open this door, I'm going to go to town and get a search warrant. You got Chuck in there with you, and don't tell me you don't!" She leaves.

Charlie is agitated; he doesn't doubt Pansy will come back with the cops. They need to get out of there. Caril packs a little red swim bag with a few clothes and family photos. Charlie puts on his blue cowboy shirt with snap buttons that Caril had been wearing before the killings, cowboy boots, and black leather jacket. Caril slips on her white majorette boots, black jeans, blue-and-white shirt, blue coat, and a red scarf, which she ties around her head. Charlie puts a handful of shotgun shells in his jacket and wraps the .410 in a blue blanket. The pair leaves through the kitchen door and heads up an alley toward the Griggses' house to get Charlie's car. Charlie is carrying the shotgun.

Caril's version of the six days tells a different story of the bloodless interim. Specifically, she says she was a hostage. The first night Charlie tore a dish towel into strips and tied her up before he left. She got the knots undone just as he was coming through the door. Charlie then cut up the clotheslines running across the living room ceiling and used those to tie her up. One time he stuffed a rag in her mouth. She could barely breathe. He told her what to say to those who came and was always watching and listening. She could have escaped when getting the mail or feeding the dogs, she could have told the cops that came to the door that Charlie was inside with a gun, she could have gotten in the cab with her sister and brother-in-law, she could have left when Charlie was sleeping, and so on, but the fact was that *she believed* Charlie would have killed her family if she tried to escape and that it would have been her fault. She went along with him because she felt she had no choice. She

had signed the note posted on the screen door "Miss Bartlett," thinking that anyone who read it would be tipped off because "Miss Bartlett"
could only refer to little Betty Jean. When the cab pulled up the drive,
she went out and told her sister and brother-in-law that they had to leave
or her mother could get hurt. She whispered to Laveta that her older
brother was hiding behind the door with a gun, but Laveta didn't hear
her. Caril was scared to death of Charlie. Whatever she did was only to
keep her parents and little sister alive.

10

THE CITY OF LINCOLN PASSED THE SIX DAYS FROM January 21 to January 27 in peaceful unknowingness. The countryside was frozen, the days were short and gray, and a light snow often blew sideways across the landscape. The fields were cold and lonely places. Cattle huddled in the protection of haystacks or fences. Months earlier, the prehistoric sandhill cranes had fled the cold by migrating to the Southwest and Mexico. In six or seven weeks, 650,000 of the great birds with wingspans exceeding eight feet would begin descending onto the Platte River, honking like bassoons, to stage their journey north to Alaska and Canada. Now the bare limbs of the ghostly cottonwoods and tall elms were free of birds and stretched like black veins into the wintry sky. A pale moon seemed frozen in its path.

On the morning of January 27, around 10:30, Pansy Street returned to 924 Belmont with two detectives. The doors were locked, and their knocks went unanswered. The detectives consented to break in only with Pansy's specific permission, and eventually one of them found an unlocked window at the back of the house. The three of them walked through the house room by room looking for something amiss. Although there were plenty of signs, such as clusters of knife holes in the walls, bullets on top of the dresser, the sawed-off gun barrel on top of the piano, a hacksaw in the kitchen, and shell casings on the carpet, both detectives and Pansy found nothing suspicious. They left without checking the outbuildings or even investigating the family car in the drive. The detectives drove Pansy home and on the way suggested that maybe she should butt out of the lives of her daughter and her family. But Pansy knew something was terribly wrong. At the café where she worked as a fry cook, she convinced her employer to allow her to listen to the radio for the bad news she knew was on the way.

Charlie's plan, after leaving 924 Belmont and getting his car, was to drive out of Lincoln and head southeast sixteen miles to the small town of Bennet, where his friend August Meyer lived on a farm.

The Griggses' house is only two blocks away. Charlie grabs the .410 and the two set out. Charlie sees that the 1949 Ford—their escape vehicle—has a flat tire. After putting the .410 in the passenger's side of the car, Charlie and Caril go to the house and retrieve the keys from Betty Griggs. A few minutes later, Charlie sends Caril back to the house to borrow a screwdriver to open the trunk and get the spare. Caril says nothing to Mrs. Griggs.

Charlie changes the tire, and they drive to the Crest station, where Charlie gets a few bucks' worth of gas. The spare tire he's put on has a bent rim, and it causes a bad shimmy over forty miles an hour, so he stops at "the old lady's house"—the Southworths'—where he stores his hot rod and a bunch of wheels. None of them fit the Ford. He throws a few in the back seat and drives off, heading south to Highway 77 on the way to Homer Tate's Conoco, only to hear a loud growling in the transmission. He pulls into Dale's Champion Service at Seventeenth and Burnham, only a few blocks from the Safety Patrol headquarters, and stops in front of one of the bays. Charlie tells the attendant, a fellow he knew in school, that he needs the transmission packed. He tells Caril to stay in the car and drives it forward over the X hoist. He gets her a Pepsi. While sitting high up in the car, Caril finds a piece of paper and a pen in the dash and writes on the paper, "Help Police—Don't Ignore." She sticks the note in her blue coat.

About 1:00 p.m., Charlie pulls into Homer Tate's on Highway 77, about six miles south of Lincoln and on the road to Bennet. Charlie stops at a pump close by Brickey's Café, adjacent to the station, and buys forty-five cents' worth of gas. As owner Homer Tate moves toward the pump, he glances in the car and sees the butt of a gun sticking out from a blue blanket on the front seat between the driver and his passenger. He figures maybe the couple was on their way to do some bird hunting.

Charlie gives Caril ten bucks to get something to eat, and she goes inside the café. He drives his car behind the garage out of sight to get the tire fixed. In the café, Caril orders four hamburgers. The waitress, Juanita Bell, notices the girl in a blue jacket, pink kerchief, and white boots and thinks she seems a little nervous. Inside the station, Charles flashes the .32 pistol to the attendant and asks if they have any shells for it. They don't. He buys three boxes of .22 longs and a box of shells for a .410 and picks up maps of Nebraska, Kansas, and Missouri. In the ten minutes Caril waits for her order, she sits quietly at the counter. Charlie walks in just as the burgers come up. He stands aside while Caril pays, then takes the change. She kind of pushes Charlie to get him out the door. As Caril walks away, she stares plaintively at the waitress through the window, just as she had when sitting at the counter.

The Ford heads down Highway 77 to Highway 2. Caril complains the burgers taste like dog food and swears they should take them back. Charlie, probably figuring that by now someone has found the three bodies in the backyard of 924 Belmont, refuses and continues on.

It is now 1:30 p.m., roughly three hours after Pansy Street and the cops searched the house and found nothing. The pair is just leaving the Lincoln area. An APB released around 11:00 a.m. might have caught them, particularly since they have about ten miles to go on the highway. Instead, a few miles down the road the Ford swings right on Highway 43 toward Bennet. The temperature has risen from 22 to 31 degrees.

Caril by now knows where they are headed. She and Charlie, along with her sister Barb and brother-in-law Bob Von Busch, had been out to a farm in Bennet hunting just a few months earlier. Charlie had taught Caril how to shoot the .22, and she plinked at tin cans. She'd seen Charlie's friend, the farmer, but hadn't talked to him. On the way to the farm today, Charlie tells her members of his gang might meet them there.

Bennet is a small farming town of around four hundred people. It has a gas station, a store, a farmer's co-op, a blacksmith shop, a school for grades K to 12, and the newly dedicated Bennet Community Church. Highway 43 is the main street and the only paved road in town. In 1958, the junior class has eight students, all of whom are in school this January afternoon. Heading into town, Charlie and Caril pass the town cemetery on the right. Just before the church, Charlie turns left on a gravel road and heads east to the farm of his friend August Meyer. Charlie has known August since boyhood. His father used to take him there hunting squirrels as a boy, and he has eaten at his table. He usually gives August half of the rabbits he's shot.

August Meyer, seventy-one years old, is of solid German Lutheran stock. One of seven kids, he'd lived with his mother on the 207-acre farm after his father died. A stoic, soft-spoken man, he retired from the rigors of farming a few years earlier, shortly after his mother died. Even after the advent of tractors and combines, he continued using horses to plow, plant, and harvest crops. Now, he keeps a few cattle and cuts firewood and hauls it to customers in Bennet by horse. He is known for keeping his farm in good repair and the farmhouse neat as a pin. He attends Lutheran church in a nearby town every Sunday. Mr. Meyer keeps mainly to himself—some would describe him as reclusive—but he is happy to let decent people like the Starkweathers hunt on his land.

In a few miles, Charlie turns north through the rolling, wooded countryside and in a quarter mile comes to what is referred to as "the lane" but which is actually a driveway leading to the back of Meyer's house about a mile east. The lane is marked by a mailbox shot full of holes by marauding teenagers. The lane itself is narrow, with shallow ditches on either side. A creek runs through the property. Charlie turns right up the lane. He doesn't get far. The day is clear and cold, but it has warmed up just enough to melt a few inches of snow that had fallen the night before. The tires break through the crust and churn the dirt to a muddy slush. Twenty feet up the road, the front end of the car slides over the edge of the ditch. Charlie curses Meyer for not clearing the road; Caril swears she'd like to kill him for it. Charlie and Caril get out of the car and try pushing it out of the ditch, without success. Charlie jacks up the front of the car and pushes it back several times. Nothing works.

A little more than a hundred yards up from the county road are the remains of an old rural schoolhouse torn down years earlier: a water pump, a concrete floor, a coal bin, partial brick walls, and a scattering of boards. Fifteen yards north of the lane is a storm cellar, sometimes called a bomb shelter or the "cave" by the local kids. A deep hole in the ground with twelve steep cement steps leading down a dark, narrow passage to a small room, it is heaped with school desks and piles of litter. A heavy wooden door off its hinges lies over the opening.

It's freezing, the wind is blowing hard, and the two of them are getting cold. Charlie gets the .410, the butcher knife, the .32-caliber pistol, and a battery-operated lantern from the car and the two descend into the cellar to warm up. Charlie turns on the four-sided lantern and hangs it from the ceiling. Caril watches as he takes shells from his jacket and loads her stepfather's shotgun. Charlie tells her they are going to walk up to the Meyer farmhouse to get his horses to pull the car out. They leave the cave, not any warmer than when they went in, and begin walking the hilly road to the two-story white farmhouse. Charlie is carrying the .410. They finally make it to the barn, where a dog starts barking. The dog draws Mr. Meyer to the back porch.

THE KILLING OF AUGUST MEYER
January 27, 1958

Caril

Charlie tells her to shut up and not say anything as Mr. Meyer walks toward them. The farmer agrees to use his horses to pull Charlie's car out but says he has to go into the house to get a coat. Charlie follows Mr. Meyer, and Caril follows behind Charlie. Suddenly, just as Meyer is opening the kitchen door, Charlie runs up behind him and lifts the gun and shoots him in the back of the head.

Mr. Meyer falls, although Caril can't see where he lands. She wants to get away but can't move. She's frozen. She sees herself screaming, but she can't hear a sound. Charlie is red-faced and highly agitated, and she figures he plans to kill her next. She is scared to death. Charlie drags the body off the porch and into a small building a few feet away. At his direction, she picks up Meyer's hat and throws it in after him.

The dog begins growling at Charlie. He holds the .410 by the barrel and swings the butt hard into the dog, who runs off yelping. Now the gun is jammed up. Charlie tries to shoot the animal, but the shotgun won't fire.

Charlie drags a rug over the blood on the porch. Inside the house, he begins searching for guns and money. He tells Caril there should be an envelope with about five hundred dollars in it, and Caril follows him from room to room upstairs as he tears each one apart. Charlie next tears the downstairs rooms apart and eventually finds three guns—two big ones and a small one—and throws them down on a mattress. He finds a brown money pouch, and he takes out a bunch of bills and sticks them in his billfold. He gives Caril the change for her purse. In a kitchen cupboard, he finds some cookies and Jell-O and sets them on the table. He puts his finger in the Jell-O, tells Caril it's good, but she doesn't want any. She is scared and keeps saying she wants to go. Mr. Meyer is dead, and she's afraid of his ghost. She looks nervously out the window to see if anyone is coming while Charlie takes a short nap. Well over half an hour passes by the time they finally leave the house and head back to the car. Charlie makes her carry the .410, and he carries Meyer's .22. After all this, Caril is weak, cold, and tired. He holds her up by the arm as they walk. She falls and hits her head on a fence.

Charlie
Charlie and Caril are walking to the house when Meyer comes out the back door. Charlie tells him he wants to use his horses to get his car out of the ditch, and Meyer agrees but says he needs to get a coat. He suggests they warm up in the small house to the side. On the porch, Meyer and Charlie get into a fierce argument about why the car is so far away. Mr. Meyer goes in the house, comes back with a .22, points the gun at Charlie, and takes a shot. The bullet whizzes by Charlie's head. Meyer tries another shot, but the gun jams. As he is starting back in the house, Charlie charges up the steps and shoots him in the back of the head, almost at point-blank range. The farmer drops to the floor. Caril is around the corner. The dog is barking a few feet away, and Charlie shoots him with the .410. The dog yelps and takes off. Charlie places some rags over

the pool of blood on the porch and throws a blanket over the body, and he and Caril go in the house. After the search yields the guns and the money, and after Charlie puts on a pair of Mr. Meyer's new socks and sets out a meal of Jell-O and cookies, which Caril refuses to eat, the two leave. On the way out, Charlie grabs a sweatshirt, a pair of gloves, and a straw cowboy hat, which he sticks on his head. He goes looking for the dog and finds it lying down by the river. He grabs a shovel from the barn, and he and Caril walk back to the car to dig it out. He is carrying the .22, Caril the .410. They pause for a few minutes in the cellar to get out of the biting wind. The lantern hangs right where Charlie left it.

At the car, Charlie digs under the wheels and, with Caril steering, jacks up the front end and pushes it over. After an hour, the wheels finally grab enough to spin the car up onto the lane.

It is now well below freezing, and winter's dim light is fading; the sharp Nebraska wind is flesh-burning. But Charlie is feeling better: his car is running, his girl is at his side, and perhaps most important he now has a pump .22 and a few bucks in his pocket. The decision to kill Meyer and take his new rifle had coagulated in his mind several days earlier. The pump .22 means he doesn't have to stick a new bullet in after every shot. Meyer had money; he'd heard him talking about getting five hundred dollars cash to have the road to the house scraped. And Meyer lived way out in the middle of nowhere at the end of a long, empty road. After the state maps he's picked up at Tate's, the cops will be expecting him to be long gone by now. The fact that the most recent blood spilled was that of a friend doesn't bother him. The world of make-believe that feeds the murderous spring inside him is blossoming into reality. The straw cowboy hat on his head makes it all perfect.

11

WITH THE CAR BACK ON THE LANE, CHARLIE AND Caril push the vehicle slowly toward the road, wary of the ditches on either side. Yet the car slides again headfirst into the ditch. They are out of ideas. Just then, two headlights come around the curve. A 1936 Ford pulls to a stop a few feet away. Charlie tells Caril to keep her mouth shut. A man in coveralls gets out and asks if they need any help. Charlie explains his transmission is shot. The man offers to pull him out if he has a rope. Charlie uses the black-handled butcher knife to open the trunk of his car and pulls out a length of quarter-inch steel cable. He hooks one end to his back bumper and the other to the back bumper of the other car. He pushes while Caril guides and the man drives his car, and the 1949 Ford pops out of the ditch. Caril fears that now Charlie is going to shoot the man, just as he had shot Mr. Meyer. Instead, Charlie asks the man what he owes him. "Forget it," the farmer says, "you don't owe me a thing." "Sure I do," Charlie says, and he digs two dollars out of his wallet and hands it to him. The farmer gets in his car and drives off.

Charlie is now without a plan. It's dark, and they have no place to go. Except back to the farmhouse. This time, he circles around and turns in on an access road heading west to the front of the farmhouse. There are two gates, and Caril gets out and opens them. They park about one hundred yards from the buildings. Charlie sneaks up on the small building where the body is, looks in the window, and sees that the blanket he put over the body is gone. "Shit," he says. "We've got to get out of here." They run back to the car, and on the way he tells Caril about the missing blanket. In the car, he decides to take a shortcut back to the highway but ends up at a dead end. He tries to turn around, but his front wheel gets stuck in a rut, so he simply guns it and tears straight through a farmer's field, cornstalks flying, and finally springs out onto a gravel road. They wander the back roads to Tate's Conoco. They get there around 5:30 p.m.

At Tate's, attendant Martin Krueger senses something is off when the 1949 Ford pulls into the station. The girl sitting in the passenger's seat has both a rifle and a shotgun lying in plain view across her lap, with the barrels pointing out the window. In the back seat are several car wheels. Martin wonders if the pair had been out stealing. He jots down the license plate and calls it in. Nothing comes of it.

Charlie goes inside and buys two boxes of .22 hollow points and picks up a couple more maps. Now where? Lincoln? Washington, where one of his brothers lives? To the house on Belmont? None of those. He heads south on 77, back to Bennet, back to the Meyer farm. Despite everything, it's a safe, warm place to spend the night. Maybe the wind blew in through a window or under the door and rustled the blanket off the body. Turning up the front lane, Caril has a premonition that Meyer's soul is there to haunt them and tells Charlie to stop. She says she's afraid Meyer's ghost might be waiting for them in the small house. Charlie freaks out himself and decides they need to get out of there. He tries turning the car around and the car gets stuck again, for the fourth time. It's no use trying to free it now in the pitch-black and icy cold, the shape they're in. It is about 7:30 when they finally abandon the Ford and begin walking back on the lane, Caril with the .410 in her hand and Charlie swinging Meyer's .22. Caril spots the lights of several farmhouses and suggests they stop at one to get warm. Charlie refuses. They walk on and eventually turn onto the county road and keep walking in the direction of Bennet. Caril sees car lights coming around a curve. Charlie tells her he'll do the talking and sticks out his thumb.

12

RODNEY HAD NOTICED THE DAMAGE TO HIS .22 WHEN Charlie returned it—not only was the stock plate missing; a decal was gone and the wood was badly scratched—and he told his father. On Sunday the twenty-sixth, Guy Starkweather locked the windows and doors and called the cops and told them to pick up his son because he was scared he was coming to shoot him. He seemed drunk to the cops. Charlie's father kept his door locked and called the cops again Monday morning to insist they pick up his son. Robert Von Busch was also concerned for his safety. Charlie was holding a grudge against him because he'd heard Robert and his wife, Barbara, were trying to break up him and Caril so they could set her up with another boy, a relative of Bob's.

On Monday, after Pansy and the detectives had left, Rodney and Robert decided to make another visit to 924 Belmont. They arrived around 4:00 p.m. and looked in the windows. The house was dark and empty. They decided to check the outbuildings. Bob went to the chicken coop and cracked open the door. He was hit by the sweet smell of cologne. A screen door was lying on top of something wrapped in green paper. The paper was torn, and he saw a white shirt. He kicked the door off, tore the green paper open, reached in, and came out with an arm. He replaced the door on the body and closed the door to the chicken shack behind him. He yelled for Rodney that they needed to get out of there. Rodney told him to come to the toilet. Inside were the wrapped-up body of Velda laid across the two holes and Betty Jean's body stuffed in the grocery box. The two men took off for the police station.

The cops arrived at the house at 4:34 p.m. Detectives, state patrolmen, sheriff deputies, local uniforms, and the district attorney gathered in the backyard. They questioned Rodney, who suggested his brother

Charles might be involved. Initially, the cops thought that Charlie might have killed Caril as well. Nonetheless, at 5:43, nearly six days after the murders, an APB went out over the radio for Charles Starkweather and Caril Ann Fugate, traveling in a black 1949 Ford. Armed. Dangerous.

One rookie cop spent a long night at the crime scene. Patrolman Dean Leitner later told reporter Bill Kelly of station WOWT-TV, in Omaha, that he spent the night inside the chicken coop on the off chance the killer might return to the scene of the crime. Dean later became chief of police in Lincoln.

13

Two blocks off Main Street stands the home of the Jensen family. Robert Jensen Sr. owns a general store and has a son, Bobby, president of his high school junior class. Bobby works at the store with his dad after school running errands and delivering groceries. A big, friendly kid who played high school football before childhood polio caught up with him, he has been going steady with Carol King, a pretty, slender brunette who lives on a farm south of town. Carol is a high school junior and cheerleader and sings in the church choir and is active in Future Homemakers of America. Her father died unexpectedly only a few weeks earlier. She and her mother have moved temporarily into Carol's brother and his wife's home, just down the road from the Jensens'. She and Bobby haven't seen each other since her father's funeral.

The high school semester is over. After school, King gives her mother a report card showing perfect grades. She eats dinner with her mother, her brother, Warren, and his wife. She helps her mother clean up after the meal. Carol isn't feeling well and plans to stay in and study. But Bobby calls around seven and says he has something he wants to talk to her about and suggests they go for a ride. She readily agrees. Bobby runs another errand for his dad in his 1950 Ford, which runs on a Flathead V-8 and has dual exhausts, twin antennas on the rear fenders, and white walls. In the back seat is his letter jacket. He stops by the gas station to fill up and then swings by to pick up Carol. He wears jeans, a sweatshirt, and a black jacket. In his wallet is a picture of Carol; on the back are the words "A very happy birthday, I wish I had a better picture for you but this will have to do. With all my love, Carol."

Carol has on jeans, a white sweatshirt, a red scarf, and a light winter coat. She tells her mother she will be home by ten.

THE KILLINGS OF ROBERT JENSEN AND CAROL KING
January 27, 1958

Charlie

The 1950 Ford slows on the two-lane gravel road. Charlie drops his thumb. The car angles over, comes to a stop. The driver, a big guy with glasses, rolls down his window and asks Charlie if he's lost. No, Charlie tells him; his car has gone in a ditch about a mile back. "Is it a black Ford?" Jensen asks. "It is," Charlie says, figuring that Jensen must have recognized him from the Capitol Beach racetrack, which isn't good. Charlie asks him for a ride into Bennet. Jensen opens the back door. As Charlie climbs in, Jensen grabs the barrel of the .22 and says, "I'll take that." Charlie tells him the gun's not loaded. Caril, getting in behind him with the .410, chimes in, "We don't walk around with loaded guns." Jensen lets go of the barrel. Caril settles in, with the .410 on her lap, behind the girl, and Charlie hunches behind the driver with the .22. He asks Jensen to take him into Bennet. As they approach the town, Charlie tells Jensen he needs to make a phone call. Jensen tells him that the station with the pay phone in town is closed and they'll have to find another phone. Charlie doesn't like the idea and tells Jensen to keep on driving. When Jensen resists, Charlie tells him, "Look, do as we tell you before somebody gets hurt."

"I don't think you'll shoot me," Jensen responds. Caril, pointing the shotgun to the front, blurts, "You do as we tell you or you'll find out, and I'll shoot the girl to show you." Heading north, Jensen asks if Charlie wants to go to Lincoln. "You heard him," Caril says, but Charlie is no longer sure. Where would he go in Lincoln? Three or four miles outside of town, he tells Jensen to turn back around and asks him if he knows where the cave is, and when Jensen says he does, Charlie tells him to drive there. On the way, Jensen and King talk to each other about school stuff, and at one point King turns in her seat and thanks Charlie for not being mean to them. Caril gets pissed and tells King to turn around and shut up. Caril asks Charlie if he'd asked for Jensen's billfold yet. He hasn't, but he does now, and Jensen passes it to Charlie, who hands it to

Caril. Caril takes out some cash, hands the wallet to King, then stuffs the cash in Charlie's billfold and gives it back to him. They continue on without incident until they reach Bennet. Jensen swings left before the community church on the gravel road leading to the cave and Meyer's farm. He asks Charlie if he is going to take his car. Charlie says he is, and Jensen reminds him to keep the oil filled so as to not burn up the engine. If there are people in the back seat, be careful going over bumps because the driveshaft is so low it might bounce off the road. Also, the car pulls to the right. Jensen mistakenly passes the lane to Meyer's farm and turns instead at the lane leading to the site of the old schoolhouse. He backs up and turns in Meyer's lane and pulls over a few yards down the road from the cellar.

Charlie, .22 in hand, orders the couple out. He walks them over to the cellar and tells them to go on down. Jensen goes first and then King starts, and all of a sudden Jensen comes running up the steps and pushes King out of the way. Charlie starts firing. Jensen keeps coming and Charlie keeps shooting, until Jensen falls back in the cellar. Charlie pushes the body the rest of the way down the steps, then goes back to the car and reloads the .22 . He returns to the cellar to finish Jensen off but gets scared and runs out and tells King to go down inside. He goes back to the car and, still scared, gets in the car, releases the emergency brake, starts it, and feels the car slide back into the ditch. He and Caril go back to the cellar, and he orders King to come out. Caril guards her with the .410 while he works on freeing the car. He hears a shot, goes to the cave, and sees that King is dead. Caril tells him she tried to run, so she shot her. He lifts King's body and carries it down to the bottom of the cellar stairs. He places the door over the cellar opening and goes to the school-house remains and gets a window frame and some boards and tosses them on top of the cellar door. He and Caril get Jensen's car out of the ditch using schoolhouse boards and the blanket from his car. He turns onto the county road back to Bennet and guns it. The pipes wrap up loudly. It's about 10:30 when he slows to turn right onto the main street of Bennet. They pass the cemetery on the left driving out of town. On the highway, Caril notices several schoolbooks in the back seat. Charlie tells her to toss them out. She does, one by one. Charlie has a change of heart; he's had enough of murder; he tells Caril he wants to turn himself into the law, specifically to his friend Sheriff Karnopp. Caril's got the .410 on her lap, the barrel pointing at him, and she says hell no, she's not going to give herself up and nothing's going to make her. With the barrel still pointing at him, Charlie gives in.

The APB is still out for the 1949 Ford, not Jensen's 1950 Ford. The two drive around Lincoln for a while, then to the Bartlett house in Belmont. Caril wants to get her makeup kit and little traveling bag that she forgot that morning. They stop about half a block away. The lights are on in the house and the street in front is full of police cars. Charlie turns the car around and creeps away. He drives through the heart of Lincoln and heads west over the O Street viaduct aiming for Hastings, a town roughly one hundred miles away. After a couple of hours on the road, Charlie changes his mind again, thinking it will be easier for the cops to spot Jensen's car in a small town, and drives back to Lincoln. Around 3:00 a.m., he parks at Twenty-Fourth and Van Dorn and they go to sleep. It's eighteen degrees above zero. Around 6:00 a.m., the couple wakes up in darkness. Charlie intends to find a place to hang out for the day, before they head out through the Sandhills for Washington that night. They drive around the neighborhood of South Lincoln looking for a house, and finally Charlie tells Caril to pick one. She points to a large white house on Twenty-Fourth and says, "There." Charlie parks down the block and waits for the man of the house to leave for work.

Caril

She and Charlie have walked about a mile down the county road when the headlights came around the curve. She is in pretty bad shape by then; Charlie has to hold her up by the arm, and even then she can barely pick up her feet. She is nervous and scared—she is convinced Charlie means to kill her like he killed Mr. Meyer. The car comes to a stop, and the window on the passenger's side rolls down. The boy at the wheel asks if they need help, and Charlie tells him his car is in the ditch a ways back. Could he get a ride into Bennet? "Sure," Jensen says, "get in."

Jensen says he'll take the guns, but Charlie insists they're not loaded, and Jensen lets it go. Charlie, with the .22, sits behind the boy, and Caril, with the .410, sits behind the girl.

As the car approaches Bennet, Charlie asks Jensen if he knows where a public telephone is, and Jensen says there is one but it usually doesn't work and he'll need to drive to the owner's house. Not a good idea. Charlie picks up the .22 and holds the barrel to the back of Jensen's head and tells him to keep driving. King stiffens in her seat. Caril, thinking Jensen is sure to meet Meyer's fate, begins to cry. Jensen protests and Charlie tells him to keep driving or he'll blow his brains out. "I don't think you'll do that," Jensen responds. "You want to find out, buddy?" Charlie asks him. His voice is loud and squeaky, something Caril has never heard before, and his face is angry and wrinkled like he'd just come out of a fight.

"Please don't hurt him," Caril says. Charlie tells her to shut up.

"Do as he says," Jensen says, "so we don't get hurt."

At Charlie's direction, Jensen turns the car around and heads back toward the schoolhouse remains and cellar. With the gun still poking the back of Jensen's head, Charlie tells him he's going to take his car. A little farther on, Charlie asks him if he has any money. "About four dollars," Jensen says. "Give it to me," Charlie orders. Jensen stops the car, takes out his billfold, turns around to look Charlie in the face, and holds it out. Charlie orders him to turn back around and takes the billfold. He hands his and Jensen's billfolds to Caril and tells her to take the money from Jensen's and put it in his wallet.

Caril can't move. She is shaking, scared. Frozen. Jensen tells her to do it so no one will get hurt. She still can't move. Charlie screams at her to take the money out, and this jolts her and she takes the bills out and puts them in Charlie's billfold and hands it back to him. She gives Jensen's billfold to King. Jensen seems calm and collected through it all. "Drive to the cave," Charlie screams. He's going to put both of them in there, pile some stuff on it, and leave. Someone will find them later. "Fine," says Jensen, "as long as no one gets hurt." During the ride, Charlie keeps the barrel of the .22 against the back of Jensen's head. The sawed-off barrel of the .410 is still pressed against Caril's stomach.

When Jensen pulls into the wrong lane, Charlie tells him to back up and go down the first one, with the mailbox. He stops ten or fifteen yards from the cave. Charlie tells his two captives to get out of the car. King doesn't move. Charlie yells at Caril to point the shotgun at King and get her out. Caril motions with the shotgun in the direction of the driver's door and tells King she'd better get out if she doesn't want to get hurt. King slides out of the driver's side. Charlie holds the .22 on them. Caril asks Charlie to please not hurt them; he tells her to shut up and get in the front seat. She crawls into the passenger's seat. The night is dark, with no lights visible. She can make out only the high bank of snow and the shape of some trees. She watches Charlie walk off with the teenagers, but they soon disappear in the darkness. For about ten minutes, she waits, fearful, knowing what's about to happen. She can't stop shaking. There are no sounds. Then she hears shots—two or three or more—and starts crying. She knows what he's done. She tries to move, to do something, but can't. Suddenly, Charlie is at the car, cursing that the boy had given him a lot of trouble and wouldn't die and saying he was going to leave him there. He opens the driver's door and sticks the gun in, and Caril feels sure he is going to shoot her. He lays the gun on the back seat, starts the car, and tries backing up. The car slides sideways off the road. With a blanket from the car, the two go to the schoolhouse remains and gather boards to stick under the car. While they're working, Charlie tells her that she has heard and seen enough; he is going to take her home to her family. After half an hour, they get the car back on the road. Charlie backs out onto the county road, and the car roars off. On the paved road back to Lincoln, Caril notices some schoolbooks on the back seat. If she throws them out, she figures, someone will find them and see the names inside and start looking for the teenagers and their car. With Charlie's approval, she tosses them out the window, one by one.

Back in Lincoln, Charlie drives to her house and comes to a stop on a road perpendicular to Belmont Avenue, half a block away, and from there they can see a police car with a red bubble on top and lights on in the house. Charlie says he's not going to let Caril off because she would tell the cops what he'd done. He circles around and stops a block away.

She thinks of running, but she knows that Charlie has the knife. The blade would end up stuck in her back. He drives west out of town, over the O Street viaduct. After an hour or so, Charlie turns around and, without saying why, drives back to Lincoln. It's the middle of the night, and he parks in front of a big house. Caril falls asleep. Early the next morning, Charlie parks a short distance up the block from a large white house. A few minutes later, a car pulls out of the drive. "There he goes," Charlie says, and starts the engine.

14

THE EVENING OF JANUARY 27, TWENTY-FOUR-YEAR-old reporter Del Harding was sitting at his desk at the *Lincoln Star*, Lincoln's morning paper, when he received a call from the night police reporter around 5:00 p.m. who told him that something was going on at 924 Belmont. Del jumped in his 1954 Oldsmobile and sped to the scene. He was the first reporter there, arriving just in time to see one of the bodies being pulled from the shed in the backyard. Men in overcoats and hats and a couple of state patrolmen were standing around in groups. Harding had only a few hours to get a story written in time to make the morning edition and to beat the *Omaha World Herald* and *Lincoln Journal*, both afternoon papers. He talked to the cops and called family members and neighbors and dug up some photos and put together a remarkably accurate story that ran under a large bold headline in the first edition Tuesday morning: BELMONT FAMILY SLAIN.

Beneath the headline was a line of tiny stars and the statement: "Tot And Parents Found Dead In Apparent Murder." Beneath that a sub headline read: "Daughter, Boyfriend Sought For Questioning: Couple Shot, Child Had Skull Fractures." Under that were separate photos of Marion, Velda, and a smiling Betty Jean Bartlett. Another photo showed the lawmen gathered around the shack, and another showed the house and the cluttered, junk-strewn backyard. Midway through the story is a photo of a smiling Caril Fugate with a finger to her cheek. At the very bottom is a photo of the note Caril had written and posted on the doorframe saying, "Stay Away Everybody is sick with the flu," and signed, "Miss Bartlett." A preliminary autopsy showed that the parents had died from bullets to the head and possible knife wounds and that the child had suffered a skull fracture. Starkweather's car was identified as a black 1949 Ford with license plate 2-15623. The grill had been taken out and the hubcaps were missing. Alerts to lawmen in six states had gone out. The two should be considered armed. Harding suggested a possible connection with the killing of a gas station attendant the previous December. Although the radio was carrying the story by 6:30 p.m. and TV later that night, Harding basically scooped everyone with the details. The only thing missing was a picture of Charlie Starkweather.

Lincoln awakes Tuesday morning, January 28, to the story of the Bartlett murders. The residents are startled. Only seven weeks earlier, a young man working at a gas station on Cornhusker Highway had been murdered in the middle of the night. Four killings in seven weeks? The photos of the dead child were particularly disturbing. The shock was ameliorated for many by the fact that the terrible crimes occurred on the north side of town, as well as the belief that by now the killers were long gone. While the residents were right that Charlie and Caril had left town, what they didn't know was that the couple had already returned and were at that very moment parked only a short distance up the block from a house in an affluent area of town, waiting for the garage door to slide up and a car to back out. The cops were two crime scenes behind.

15

THE TWO-STORY WHITE COLONIAL ON TWENTY-FOURTH Street was less than a block from the Lincoln Country Club. Houses on either side of the street were equally elegant, set on broad, well-landscaped, and nicely tended lawns. With drives leading to garages set back from the street, the colonials and Tudors and large ranches bespoke wealth and status. The Ward house faced east, and the double garage at the back of the house faced north, so you couldn't see the garage from the street. You could however, see cars parked outside the garage.

C. Lauer Ward, forty-eight years old and a Lincoln native, was tall and slender and an impeccable dresser. He was a highly successful businessman and well-liked figure in Lincoln society. He had graduated from the University of Nebraska, studied law at Harvard and the University of Chicago, and was a member of the Nebraska bar. Easily a millionaire a couple times over, he served as president of Capital Steel and Capital Bridge companies and sat on numerous boards of directors for local businesses. He was a personal friend of governor Victor Anderson.

His wife, Clara, fifty-one, was pretty with a round face and a lovely smile. She was also a graduate of the University of Nebraska, was very involved in community and church affairs. She served as the vice president of the Nebraska Alumni Association, the highest position a woman could hold in the organization at the time. Their one child, fourteen-year-old Michael (Mikey to her), was away as a freshman at the prestigious Choate School in Connecticut. The couple had two dogs, a Chesapeake Bay retriever, Queenie, and a small poodle, Suzy, Clara's lapdog.

The Wards' maid, Lilyan Fencl, fifty-one, known as Lil, adored by the neighborhood children for her sweet nature and baking skills, was deaf or at least hard of hearing. She had been with the Ward family for twenty-six years, beginning with Lauer Ward's parents and now with Lauer Ward and his family. She had a room in the basement.

The house was not on Charlie's garbage route, but it was close by. One classmate of Charlie believes that Charlie picked a house in the country-club area because it was the kids of wealthy families who had been the meanest to him in school. Another friend claims that he and Charlie had shoveled snow from the walk in front of the Ward house a few weeks prior, and that Mrs. Ward had given them five dollars. Charlie never showed any familiarity with the house or its occupants.

Around 8:30 a.m., Charlie pulls into the Wards' drive and parks. In the right or west slot was a 1956 Packard Patrician, usually driven by Clara Ward. The left or east slot is where the 1956 Chevy Bel Air just driven off by Lauer Ward had been parked. Charlie parks the black 1950 Ford behind the empty stall. He gets out of the car and leaves the garage doors open.

THE KILLINGS OF LAUER WARD, CLARA WARD, AND LILYAN FENCL
January 28, 1958

Charlie
Charlie tells Caril to stay in the car. He takes the .22 and walks to the back door of the house and knocks. A woman answers, and he walks into the kitchen, startling her. He begins questioning her and ordering her around but quickly realizes she's deaf. She picks up a notepad and pencil from the kitchen table and hands it to him. He writes on it: "Sit down and shut up." She sits in a small breakfast nook. He asks who else is in the house. "Mrs. Ward is upstairs," she answers. He tells her to continue making Mrs. Ward's breakfast, and in a few minutes Mrs. Ward comes into the kitchen in a nightgown and robe. She glances at the morning newspaper on the breakfast table. Gun in hand, Charlie tells the two women not to worry, he's going to stay there for the day, tie them up, and leave that night. Mrs. Ward says he can trust her and there's no reason to hold a gun on them. Charlie goes to the kitchen door

and motions Caril out of the car, tells her to bring the shotgun and his black leather jacket inside. Caril does as she's told, and Mrs. Ward gives her a cup of coffee. Caril drinks the coffee and goes into the library, off the kitchen and overlooking a rose garden, then leans the .410 against a wall and drops the jacket on a chair. Exhausted, she lies down on the couch and sleeps until 2:00 in the afternoon.

Mrs. Ward asks Charlie if the maid can do some ironing. Charlie says okay, and the maid retrieves the board and the iron from the basement. Around 9:30, a friend who lives across the street, Cordy Hallam, calls about a coffee that morning at 11:00. Mrs. Ward tells her she's not feeling well and won't be going. Then Mrs. Ward asks Charlie if she can get dressed, and Charlie says yes. She disappears upstairs. Around 10:00 a.m. she reappears in the kitchen in street clothes. Charlie sits on the stairs leading to the second floor, his rifle against a wall, watching, figuring. The agreement of trust appears to hold. Ms. Ward waxes the dining room table and then goes into the kitchen and begins cleaning the icebox. Charlie takes the radio from the kitchen and goes into the living room, leaving his gun at the bottom of the stairs. Caril sleeps. Mrs. Ward cleans the house. Around 1:00, Mrs. Ward asks Charlie if she can go upstairs and change her shoes. Charlie agrees to it, but after forty-five minutes he goes upstairs to see what the problem is. He looks into the bedroom at the top of the stairs on the left, then into the one at the right, and then the bathroom. He turns down the hall to the third bedroom, only to see Mrs. Ward about fifteen feet away holding a rifle. She takes a shot but misses. She brushes past him and heads for the stairs. Charlie takes the knife from his boot, throws it, and at fifteen feet sticks it in the middle of her back. She falls and he catches her under the arms. She's moaning as he drags her into the bedroom. He lays her facedown on the bed, and she says something that he can't make out. He dislodges the knife from her back, sets it on the bed, and goes down the stairs to find Caril awake in the library. He hands her the .32 and tells her to watch the maid, then goes back upstairs with the intention of putting a Band-Aid on Mrs. Ward's wound to stop the bleeding. But she is trying to get to the phone, so he moves it out into the hallway. He cuts up some sheets with the knife and ties her hands and feet and drapes a blanket over her. She asks what he's going to do next. He says nothing. He takes the Wards' .22 pump and goes downstairs, where he loads the rifle and sets it on the wall next to Meyer's longer, newer .22. He goes in the library and tells Caril what he's done, and she says, "Don't tell the maid or she'll go ape." He gives her a .22 and tells her to keep watch on her.

Around 4:30 p.m., Charlie goes outside to hide Jensen's car and prepare a getaway. He backs the Packard out of the right slot, turns it around, and points it down the drive toward the street. He moves Jensen's car into the Packard's slot but leaves the door up. Back in the kitchen, the phone rings constantly, and he writes a note telling the maid what to say. He ransacks the bedrooms, looking for another gun, anything, and takes a white shirt, a pair of gloves, and binoculars. He steals ten dollars and three packs of gum from the maid's purse in her basement room. He puts the white shirt on and tells Caril to change her shirt and get another jacket. It's about 5:30 p.m. and he's waiting for Mr. Ward to return, which he's been told would be around 6:00 or 6:30 p.m. The evening paper comes, and after reading it in the library he takes the front page off and gives the paper to Caril. He tells her to go upstairs, get the knife from the room where Mrs. Ward lies, and bring it down. Charlie gets pissed when she takes too long and goes to the bottom of the steps and yells at her. When she comes down, she says that the woman was trying to get away and either that she stabbed her or she wasn't sure whether to stab her or not—Charlie doesn't remember. She also says that the room stunk so she spread some perfume around.

Around 6:30 p.m., Charlie pulls the shades. He tries to fix the jammed-up shotgun. Unsuccessful, he takes Meyer's .22 and stands in the kitchen hallway and tells Caril to yell when the car comes in the drive. A few minutes later, Caril yells. He watches the headlights of the Chevy pull into the empty slot on the left of the garage. Mr. Ward comes in the kitchen from the garage, wearing a topcoat and hat, to find Charlie standing just inside with a gun. Charlie assures him there's nothing wrong, that they will only tie him up and take his car.

Mr. Ward says okay but immediately goes for the gun and gets ahold of it. Charlie pushes him down the basement steps. Charlie flicks on the light and sees him lying on the floor and looking up at him, the gun a few feet away. Charlie charges down the steps and both men get their hands on the gun. Charlie pulls it away. Mr. Ward grabs an iron off a nearby table and raises it over his head. Charlie cocks the gun and points it at him, and Mr. Ward drops the iron. He heads for the steps; Charlie tells him to slow down and he does, but halfway up he begins to rush up the stairs, and when he's only a step or two from the top Charlie raises the .22 and shoots him in the back. Charlie heads up the stairs, and Mr. Ward manages to take off for the front door. Charlie shoots him in the back of the head just as he gets the front door half open. Mr. Ward drops to the floor. Charlie reaches down, touches him, and asks if he's all right. The body jerks. Charlie goes through his pants looking for a wallet, without any luck. (Had he checked the breast pocket of Ward's suit coat, he would have found a wallet containing sixty dollars. He also missed a gold watch with a chain and locket containing a picture of Ward's son.) The body moves again, and he clunks it on the head with a poker.

When Mr. Ward first arrived, Caril took the maid into the downstairs bathroom. The two come out of the bathroom now and see the body, and the maid runs down the basement stairs. It's dark down there, and Caril tells Charlie the maid has a gun, so they encourage her to come up. Pretty soon, she does. Caril tells her that if she doesn't do what they say, she'll end up like Mr. Ward.

Charlie and Caril take Ms. Fencl up to the bedroom at the top of the stairs. Caril stands lookout at the front window while Charlie rips up the sheets and ties the maid's hands together and her feet together, then ties them to the bedposts at the top and bottom of the bed. She keeps moaning and groaning, so he tells her to shup up and puts a gag in her mouth. That doesn't do any good, so he puts a pillow over her head. He tells Caril to watch her, and he goes downstairs and loads the Packard with food, the shotgun, Caril's blue coat, and other items. He finds a tin of black shoe polish in the kitchen and stands in front of the bathroom mirror and rubs it into his hair. When Caril comes down, she rubs the polish into the back and sides. He changes from the blue cowboy shirt into a white shirt Caril has found in a closet upstairs. He gives the two rifles to Caril to take to the car. At 7:00 p.m., he shuts off the lights and they leave. He locks the house and closes the two garage doors.

Charlie pulls out of the Wards' drive and heads down Thirteenth Street through the middle of town and across Cornhusker Highway to Belmont, where he swings by Caril's house, sees the lights, and keeps on moving. They get on Highway 34 heading west toward Grand Island.

Caril

When Jensen's Ford pulls into the Wards' drive, Caril is totally exhausted. She hasn't really slept since they left her house, which was less than twenty-four hours ago but seems like forever. She's experienced three murders by now. Charlie parks in front of the empty garage space. He takes the knife, Meyer's .22, and the .32 pistol and tells her to stay in the car. He enters the house through the garage, and Caril can see him through a kitchen window. Half an hour passes before Charlie opens the kitchen door and motions her to come in.

Inside the kitchen, he is holding a gun on two ladies sitting at the table. He takes the shotgun from Caril and tells her to go into the room with a piano in it. She sits in a chair in the living room, and Charlie asks if she wants coffee. She says yes, and he brings her a cup. She drinks it, then takes the empty cup into the kitchen. When she tells Charlie she is tired, he tells her to rest in the library. She lies down on a davenport and goes to sleep. The next thing she remembers is Mrs. Ward bringing Charlie a plate of pancakes. She turns down an offer of pancakes herself and goes back to sleep. She wakes up hours later, still tired, and looks around for Mrs. Ward. She tries the door leading to the garden, but it's stuck. Then Charlie is there, holding her mother's bloody butcher knife in one hand. He tells her Mrs. Ward is dead upstairs. "How did you kill her?" she asks. "Stabbed her in the throat." He hands her the bloody knife and tells her to go in the bathroom and wash it off. She runs cold water over the blade and wipes it on her jeans. He tells her the blood upstairs is beginning to smell and to go sprinkle some perfume around. She finds a bottle of perfume on a dresser in one of the bedrooms but can't bring herself to open the closed door to where Mrs. Ward is. Instead, she sprinkles some perfume on the chair and rug outside her door. Downstairs, Charlie has found a buckskin coat belonging to Mrs. Ward for Caril to wear. At Charlie's instructions, Caril holds the .22 on the maid in the kitchen, but she writes her a note saying she isn't going to hurt her. Charlie tells her to stand by the window in the living room and yell when she sees the Chevy coming in the drive. If she doesn't, he warns, she'll get what Mrs. Ward got. Half an hour passes before the headlights come swinging in the drive. She hollers at Charlie, "He's coming!" and runs into the bathroom and shuts the door. She hears a shot and footsteps running through the house and a scream. She stands there, unable to move; she hears Charlie hollering her name but doesn't answer; and finally Charlie opens the door and berates her for not watching the maid. In the kitchen the maid is sitting at the table. Mr. Ward is lying on the floor by the front door, moaning. Charlie tells him to shut up. He bends down and searches his pockets. Charlie again tells Caril to keep the .22 on the maid. He asks the maid if she's made a phone call and tells her twenty or so gang members might be coming to the house and if anyone else comes to the door she'll be the first to die. Caril turns off the lights and, carrying the .22s and a flashlight, she and Charlie take the maid up the stairs to the third bedroom, which is dark. Charlie tells her to sit in a chair. Caril shines a flashlight around the room and looks out the front window while Charlie tears up a sheet and begins tying the maid's wrists. Caril suggests that rather than having the maid sit up all night in the chair, she might be more comfortable in the bed. Charlie moves the maid to the bed and finishes tying her wrists together and then to the bedposts. He does the same with her feet. The maid asks him several times to turn on the lights because she's scared of the dark. Caril is looking out the window to see if anyone is approaching when Charlie starts stabbing the maid with the butcher knife, more times than she can remember. The woman screams, and every time Charlie stabs her, she moans. He puts a pillow over her face. Caril hears a strange sound, and

Charlie tells her the maid has broken her hands loose from the bedpost. He complains that she's never going to die and tells Caril to shine the flashlight his way as he cuts her legs loose from the bedpost. He drapes a blanket over her. He orders Caril to shine her flashlight on him: the sleeve of his right arm is covered in blood. He tells her to find him a clean shirt. She goes to the closet in a bedroom at the end of the hall and finds a man's white shirt. They go downstairs to the bathroom; he takes off the blue cowboy shirt he's been wearing since they left 904 Belmont. He washes his arms and dries them with the blue shirt and tosses it on the floor. He puts on the clean white shirt. She washes the blood off the knife and wipes it on her jeans. In the kitchen, on the way out, the phone rings. Caril answers it. A woman asks how Mrs. Ward is doing, and Caril tells her she's sleeping. With that, they exit the kitchen door and get into the Packard. All three guns are on the back seat. They drive through the heart of downtown Lincoln and head west over the viaduct toward Grand Island.

Earlier in the day, Charlie had cut the photo of him and Caril sitting on a loveseat from the afternoon newspaper. He'd also cut out the photos of her family: mother, stepfather, and little sister. He'd told her that her family was missing—they were at the old people's house on Woodsdale—and the law must be looking for them. He hadn't let her read the paper. He'd stuck the clippings in his pocket.

It's Tuesday night, the twenty-eighth of January, and the murder toll is now nine bodies, although Charlie would say it's only seven or eight. Charlie swears that the maid was alive when they left the Ward house, and for all he knows Mrs. Ward was too.

16

WHILE CHARLIE WAS EATING PANCAKES AND CARIL was sleeping in the library and Mrs. Ward was waxing the dining room table and the maid was ironing clothes in the kitchen of the colonial on Twenty-Fourth Street, the countryside around Bennet was beginning to give up its dead.

The previous night, Monday the twenty-seventh, the Jensen and King families began to worry when Bobby and Carol had not returned by ten o'clock, which was late for a school night. Around midnight Robert Sr. walked to the King house, and he and Carol's brother, Warren, got in a pickup and began driving the town and country roads looking for Jensen's car, suspecting perhaps it had broken down. At 2:00 a.m., finding nothing, Warren called the Highway Safety Patrol. The missing person report went out at 3:15 a.m.

Around 9:30 that night, farmer Everett Bruening's dog began barking. He went outside but found nothing amiss. At 10:30, the dog set up another racket. Bruening was preparing to go outside again when he heard a car with loud pipes roar by on the road outside his house. His teenage son recognized the pipes: it was Bobby Jensen's car coming from the direction of the Meyer farm. Bruening wouldn't think about it again until the next day.

Elmer Boldt, the owner of the Champlain station in Bennet, received a call early in the morning of January 28 from Robert Jensen, who said his son and Carol King were missing. Boldt and a friend got in his car and, along with many other citizens of Bennet, scoured the countryside for any sign of the missing teenagers. When the back roads began turning to mush in late morning, he changed over to his four-wheel-drive pickup. Shortly after noon, he turned up the lane to Meyer's house and quickly spotted off to the left about a hundred yards a black 1949 Ford sunk in a field, nose up to the sky. He drove to a nearby farm and told a friend about the car, and the two of them drove back to the scene and stopped within a few yards of the vehicle. Boldt got out and walked up to the vehicle. He'd been hearing about the black Ford and the murders in Lincoln on the radio all morning, and he realized that the numbers on the plate matched. Boldt told his friend it was the Starkweather car, jumped in his pickup, tore out of the field, and sped back into town. He pulled into the gas station and called the Safety Patrol.

By 2:00 p.m., twenty lawmen from the Safety Patrol, the Lancaster County Sheriff's Department, and the Lincoln Police Department had descended on the Meyer farmhouse a mile up the road from where the car was found. News teams had picked up the story, and they arrived in numbers from Lincoln and Omaha. Curious locals gathered and shared what they'd heard. Word had spread that a man had been spotted near the farmhouse, so everyone assumed Charlie and perhaps even Caril were inside the house. Tracks of cowboy boots and a girl's shoes were spotted leading up the lane to the Meyer house. At the request of the cops, a few locals called the Meyer home, but none got an answer. The order went out to hold back until the tear gas arrived from Lincoln. Finally, a police car arrived with the gas and a loudspeaker stuck on the roof. An officer parked the car out of sight of the house behind a corn crib.

Reporter Del Harding was at the police station when the call about the Starkweather car came in. He took off in his Oldsmobile toward Bennet and spotted the Ford in the field as he drove up the lane. By then, the Meyer house was surrounded by thirty lawmen, all holding pistols or long guns. Assistant Lincoln police chief Eugene Masters called out over the speaker atop the car: "We know you're in there. We'll give you five minutes to come out with your hands up." Nothing happened. More time passed. Harding took his red bomber hat off, lest he become an unwitting target. Finally, after several more calls over the loudspeaker, two officers fired nine canisters of tear gas through the windows and waited expectantly for Charlie to come out either shooting or with his hands up. No one showed. When the gas finally cleared, a patrolman kicked in the door to the small building off to the side and found the body of August Meyer. The main house was empty.

Del Harding viewed the body lying flat on its stomach with the back of its head blown off, a trail of blood leading from the back porch to the small building. He took notes of the scene. Then a call came to go down the lane to a storm cellar next to the remains of an old schoolhouse. Two more bodies had been found.

Farmer Bruening was at the Meyer farmhouse when Meyer's body was discovered. He knew the Jensen boy and King girl were still missing, and he recalled the roaring of Jensen's car as it passed his house the night before. On a hunch, he walked back to the school remains and the cellar. The last time he'd seen the cellar door it was askew over the opening; now, it was sitting straight on top and was covered with a rubbish pile. He slid the door off and saw a pool of blood on the edge of the opening and blood-smeared steps leading down. At the bottom of the steps was a girl's nearly naked body. He ran back up to the farm and grabbed the sheriff.

Del arrived at the cellar along with the lawmen and other reporters. He looked down the cellar; at the bottom of the stairs was a girl's body. He could also make out the hands and feet of a man. Her body was bent in half. Her jeans and panties were bunched around her ankles, and her sweatshirt was pulled up over her head, revealing her breasts. Her thighs and buttocks were smeared in blood. Del had seen plane crashes with dead people and bodies of burned children, but nothing would haunt him like the image of that poor naked girl lying on top of her dead boyfriend at the bottom of the steps.

The news of the three bodies in Bennet hit the radio by midafternoon on Tuesday the twenty-eighth, and pictures made the TV evening news. The afternoon *Journal* covered it with photos in a late-afternoon edition. A low buzz of panic began infiltrating the nervous system of the capital city. Charlie and Caril were supposed to have left the city yesterday, for God's sake. They were figured to be well out of the state by now, but Bennet was only sixteen miles away. Cops all over the state—and six other states—were looking for them, but they were still in the area, killing people. Despite the descriptions of the car and its two inhabitants, the pair was driving around the area unseen and untouched, like ghosts.

Men left work early and went home. Wives drove to school to pick up their kids. Pleas went out for citizens to leave the keys in their cars so Charlie could take them without killing anyone and to leave their garage doors open so cars couldn't be hidden inside. Many people packed up their families and left town; some fled across the Missouri into Iowa. The coming of darkness brought a strange type of fear. The killers were loose, free and roaming. You were exposed with nowhere to run. Men loaded their rifles and shotguns and handguns and locked the doors.

The lawmen were two steps behind Charlie and Caril and facing in the wrong direction. Now, they figured the two desperados were likely still in the Bennet area, or maybe on the other side of the state line. Certainly not back home in Lincoln. The alert was still out for Jensen's Ford, now hidden away in the Ward garage. The lawmen began a search of the Bennet area, knocking on doors and searching abandoned barns and outbuildings. The *Journal* proclaimed Bennet to be a JITTERY ARMED FORTRESS. The locals feared "another onslaught" by the couple. "Thirty men armed with shotguns and rifles stopped in the local hardware for ammunition. They planned a 'foot-by-foot' search of the countryside for the slayers. Some men stood guard with rifles as others milked the cows. Most of the Bennet community stayed indoors with guns handy, although there had been no reported sightings of the two in the area." The party phone lines were jammed.

On the morning of Wednesday, January 29, the *Omaha World Herald* blasted:

FEAR ROUSES COUNTRYSIDE WITH
MULTIPLE KILLERS AT LARGE.

Bennet, Neb. *Terror stalked the countryside Tuesday night.* Farm houses became armed camps and grim-lipped men and women here, 16 miles southeast of Lincoln, burned lights far past the usual bedtime.

There was only one conversation topic, a gun-crazy teenage murder suspect and his 14-year-old girlfriend . . .

Horror mounted in Lincoln and throughout eastern Nebraska as dusk fell and the word got around that three more killings had been added to the triple murder discovered in Lincoln Monday.

Volunteer posses were formed.

As the night wore on the lights in the small town and farm houses continued to glow.

No women and children walked the streets.

Terror stalked the countryside.

A reporter for the *Journal* snuck in the Belmont house and stole a photo from on top of Caril's dresser. Charlie and Caril are sitting on a love seat shoulder to shoulder, looking like a pair of lovestruck teenagers. Caril, cute in short hair with a curl on her forehead, a purse in one hand, is wearing jeans and a plaid shirt, gray suede loafers and white bobby socks, a winter coat, and a smile of youthful innocence. Charlie, sans glasses, is wearing a jean shirt and jacket with the collar turned up, boots toed slightly in, and has a cigarette loosely gripped between the fingers of his left hand. His head is cocked slightly, and he's smiling at the camera like a mischievous rebel. Charlie's landlady, Mrs. Hawley, had taken the picture, and Charlie had given it to Caril. *The Journal* made a zinc plate and copied the photo, and the reporter snuck it back onto the dresser in Caril's bedroom. The photo ran everywhere, and from that moment on it wasn't just Starkweather; it was Starkweather *and* Fugate, or more commonly Charlie *and* Caril. Lincoln's very own shotgun-toting Bonnie and Clyde, as a *Journal* reporter would describe them a few years later.

FRED WARD KNEW his cousin Lauer to be a man of punctuality. He was seldom late, and if he was, he always called to check in. At noon on January 29, Fred arrived at the house on Twenty-Fourth Street. When no one answered his knock, he opened the front door with his key. Lying facedown on the floor, with his topcoat still on, was his cousin. Fred went inside and eventually up the stairs, where he found the bodies of Clara and Lilyan.

The law descended on the Ward house. The mayor, police chief, sheriff, district attorney, and numerous policemen, deputies, detectives, and patrolmen gathered to survey the latest tragedy. The commander of the Safety Patrol ordered all cars in the area to converge on Lincoln. The word hit the airwaves around 12:30. A TV station commandeered the living room of the Hallam house across the street. News photographers shot scenes of the bodies being carted one by one out of the house and down the driveway to the ambulances. Mayor Bennett Martin called for the city to be sealed off and for the police to conduct a house-to-house search.

The news blew up Lincoln. Panic whipped like wildfire across a dry prairie. Starkweather and Fugate had left Lincoln on Monday. That night they had killed three people in Bennet. *And now two days later they had come back to Lincoln to kill three more.* Nine bodies, and the cops had no idea where they were. There was no point to any of it. The killings were random. Meaning you or I could be next. If a man as distinguished and wealthy as Lauer Ward could be killed in his home by these two kids, who was safe? Starkweather was driving in and out of town right under the noses of the cops, who were always at least one massacre behind. No one even *saw* the killers. No one knew where they were now. Improvised and pointless roadblocks went up on a few of the many roads leading out of town. The governor, whose office Mr. Ward had just left before driving home the night before, called up the National Guard. Over two hundred soldiers, some in jeeps with mounted .50-caliber machine guns and others cradling submachine guns, began patrolling the down-town streets with the local police. Sheriff Karnopp sent out a call for the Sheriff's Posse, a group of Nebraska businessmen who rode horses in parades and gathered for various civic functions. When the call went out over the radio, some Lincoln men took it as a call *to form a posse,* and over a hundred men showed up at the county courthouse—several inebriated—with a variety of guns, ready to take on Charlie and Caril in a shootout. An AP photo shows four men carrying rifles or shotguns rushing down the steps inside the courthouse. Armed men walked the blocks of their neighborhoods searching garages and knocking on doors. "Just checking to see if you're all right in there," a voice would call after a couple knocks, which as often as not went unanswered. Men with rifles climbed up on their roofs. Several stood on top of St. Elizabeth Hospital. It was the lack of a pattern, a motive, a reason for the killings; it was Charlie and Caril's utter unpredictability; it was the idea that they could be in your garage at this very moment; it was the persistent failure of the lawmen to catch him—he struck in the night and disappeared ("hide and kill," one reporter called it)—that left people sweating in fear. Even the children. They saw the fear on their parents' and teachers' faces, heard it in their voices and became terrified themselves. Gun shops sold out of guns and ammo in hours. No one, big or small, powerful or poor, was safe. Anywhere. There was nothing you could do to get safe. Nowhere to go. No one to call. So you might as well stay right where you were—lock your family in a room in the basement and sit facing the front door with a shotgun on your lap through the day and night and pray like hell you saw the killers coming before they saw you.

Lincoln Police Chief Joe Carrol was not happy with Sheriff Karnopp's decision to call in the Sheriff's Posse to help in the search. Sightings of the Packard or Charlie himself were coming in from all over town. Lincoln had descended into the terrified land of Bennet, and with so many people running around with guns, drunk and sober, someone was bound to get shot. Several black 1956 Packards were run to ground, and the police picked up two short red-haired men and kept hold of them for hours before deciding they weren't Starkweather. One was fifty years old. One disturbed citizen chased a car down the street with a pistol believing the driver to be Starkweather.

Meanwhile, the Sheriff's Posse and the Safety Patrol conducted a farm-by-farm search for Charlie and Caril in the Bennet area.

17

CHARLIE AND CARIL WERE LONG GONE BY THE TIME the three bodies at the Ward house were discovered on Wednesday. In the dark of the previous night, the Packard had headed west out of town on Highway 34 for Grand Island. The two-lane highway gradually rose and fell through Seward and York. It was rich farmland, but in late January it had been abandoned to the elements. On either side of the road were empty fields, shorn of their fruit. Beneath the soil of some fields, grains of winter wheat, brought by the Germans immigrating from Russia and planted the previous autumn, were preparing to sprout as tiny green shoots in March. Tall grain silos with conical hats poked into the cloud-strewn sky.

Somewhere around Seward, Caril climbs into the back seat and takes off the blue shirt and puts on a red-and-white shirt belonging to Clara Ward. She tosses her shirt, Charlie's blue cowboy shirt, and the black-handled butcher knife out the window. Charlie sticks the straw cowboy hat on his head. Caril lays out a map of Nebraska on her lap, and she circles each town as they go through it.

Charlie pulls in at an all-night gas station and café at Grand Island, about one hundred miles west of Lincoln. He gets the gas tank filled and buys four cheeseburgers, fries, and coffee. He heads northwest out of Grand Island on Highway 2, which will lead him deep into the Sandhills, the high plains of Nebraska, the stunning 19,000-square-mile ocean of rolling waves of grass-covered sand. Hiding in the creases stand clusters of red cattle and thirty-foot metal windmills with angled blades turning constantly in the wind.

In Broken Bow, Charlie stops at the Bow Oil Company and has the gas tank filled. The owner and a few others in the station think he looks a little odd, driving the luxury black Packard, wearing a black leather jacket and a straw cowboy hat in midwinter. He asks the owner for maps, and the owner inquires which way he is headed, says maybe he can help with directions, but Charlie shakes his head and says, "I guess it really don't matter."

Back on Highway 2, heading northwest, around 3:00 or 3:30 a.m., Charlie falls asleep at the wheel. The car swerves into a ditch and jerks back up onto the road. Caril, who had been sleeping, is furious at Charlie for almost killing them. Charlie says a little sex would keep him awake, and Caril accedes. It doesn't work. Not too far down the road, Charlie pulls into a rest stop. They both fall asleep and don't see a state trooper who stops in to use the restroom. He checks the car out, but there is nothing out on it. Truck driver Maynard Behrends is also heading west when he pulls into the rest stop. He cannot see the sleeping couple in the car, but he jots down the plate number and drives on down the road, thinking he might come across them walking. Charlie and Caril wake up around 7:30 and drive a long stretch to Ellsworth, where they stop again for gas. The owner thinks the driver is acting jumpy and a little strange and calls the Safety Patrol, but nothing is done about it. Truck driver Behrends, now heading east from Alliance, spots the Packard with the two kids in it. When he arrives at Broken Bow, he calls the patrol to tell them what he'd seen. By then, it is too late.

Near Alliance, the hills flatten out into a rich fertile land ideal for growing sugar beets, corn, beans, and sunflowers. The Packard creeps through town in the weak winter light. Highway 2 swings north through rich farmland and then west for a few miles before heading north toward Crawford. Tall grain elevators line the railway tracks. To the west are the agate fossil beds, an area that would later be designated Agate Fossil Beds National Monument. The Packard crosses the Niobrara River, which runs east from Wyoming into Nebraska and across the Sandhills before joining the Missouri River at Lewis and Clark Lake.

The land begins to roll outside Marsland, and the crops are replaced by scatterings of black Angus cattle. A few miles north, in the Pine Ridge region, the barren hills are marked by strips and clusters of ponderosa pine. Off to the west are narrow canyons and tall bluffs of soft sandstone.

The road descends steeply into a forest of pines and eventually the town of Crawford, a few miles south of a site known as the Hudson-Meng Kill Site, where, nine thousand years ago, Native American hunters ran six hundred bison off a cliff. Charlie stops here for gas and stocks up on nine bottles of Pepsi.

In Crawford, Charlie and Caril swing west on Highway 20, the major road running east to west across northern Nebraska, and which stretches from Newport, Oregon, to Boston. A few miles west of Crawford, the highway cuts through Fort Robinson, the army fort built in 1874 in the midst of the Indian Wars. On their right as the Packard drives through the fort are the parade ground, barracks, and stables. To the left are the sites of the German POW camps and the jail in which Crazy Horse had been held and a plaque marking the spot of his death.

The road rises out of the piney valley onto rolling, grass-covered hills. This time of year, the countryside is a bleak array of brown and straw-colored grasses, with occasional dark green strips of ponderosa pines. Large haystacks, heavy with moisture, stand as a testament to last year's haying season. Occasional cabins dot the hillsides. About thirty miles west of Fort Robinson, around 12:00 or 12:30, close to the time when the bodies are discovered at the Ward house in Lincoln, the Packard crosses the border into Wyoming. The area is called the Badlands, but it's pretty much the same as the Nebraska cattle country on the other side of the border except for a range of blue hills off to the southwest in which real cowboy outlaws like Butch Cassidy and Jesse James and the Logan brothers once holed up. The railroad runs close to the highway, and long snow fences set at different angles atop the hills tell of the attempts to protect the highway from the blizzard winds. The sky is huge; flat-bottomed clouds wrap around 180 degrees; the blades of a windmill on top of a hill glint against the sky. The highway rises and drops in long, gradual hills and swings in long, gradual curves, as if it has all the time and space in the world. The fierce Wyoming wind rocks the black sedan on its wheels.

For some unknown reason, perhaps a celebration of some sort, Charlie slows down as he enters Wyoming. It takes him almost three hours to make it to Douglas, a small western town of 2,800, the seat of Converse County, about seventy-two miles west of the border. When he finally drives through Douglas, it seems to him like everyone in the town is staring at him and his fancy car. A police car drops in behind him and follows him for a few blocks before falling back. Charlie knows his time is running out. It is all happening as he had dreamed, but faster then he'd figured. Everything is closing in, like a trapdoor that starts falling when the animal moves toward it. There is only one way of escape, and that is toward the trapdoor. The faster he moves, the faster it seems to fall.

Over the radio comes the news of the three bodies found at the Ward house. Charlie begins looking for a new car. He notices a black Buick parked on the opposite side of the road close to the Natural Bridge Road turnoff, about twelve miles west of Douglas on Highway 20. He drives past and turns around and comes back and parks behind the Buick, headed east. He sees a man sleeping behind the wheel.

THE KILLING OF MERLE COLLISON
January 29, 1958

Charlie

Charlie gets out of the Packard and crosses the road with Meyer's .22 in hand. The Buick's windows are rolled up. He yells at the sleeping man and announces they are going to switch cars. The man says no, and Charlie shoots him through the glass, pumps the gun, and shoots again. The man says okay and rolls down the window, opens the door, gets halfway out of the car, and reaches for the gun. The two struggle for the weapon. Charlie manages to shoot him a couple more times before the gun jams. The guy has a lot of fight left in him, and Charlie calls for Caril to bring him the Wards' .22. Caril is already standing at the back of the car with the .22 in her hands. She begins firing. The guy is yelling that he has a wife and kids, and she yells back "too bad" and keeps shooting. She calls him all the names under the sun while she finishes him off. She is the most trigger-happy person Charlie's ever seen. She complains about all the blood on the front passenger seat and insists she isn't going to sit in it. A third car stops, and a man walks over and sees the body on the floor under the dash. In the middle of a struggle for the gun, Charlie spots a cop car coming to a stop not far away. He runs to the Packard and speeds off in the direction of Douglas.

Caril

Caril is tired and dirty. She has slept only a couple of hours the past few nights. She hasn't showered in two days, and other than Clara Ward's blouse she hasn't put on clean clothes since Monday morning. It's only been two days since then, but it seems like years. She had circled the towns on the map on their escape through Nebraska so it might help the law find them if they found the car.

Charlie passes a car parked on the other side of the road and turns around and stops behind it. He tells her he's going to get the car, grabs the .22, and walks up to it. She tries to start the Packard in an attempt to get away, but it was the type you started by pushing buttons and she couldn't figure it out. She hears some shots and knows what's happened. Charlie yells for her to bring the other gun, and she gets the other .22 and takes it to him. The driver's window is shattered and the door is hanging open. The guy inside is crumpled up and lying facedown on the floor. Charlie pushes the seat forward and tells her to get in the back. She slips in and Charlie gets in the front, but he can't start the car. He yells at the man on the floor for help. "Man, man, are you dead? Are you dead?" The man doesn't answer. Charlie finally gets the car started and drives across the road and pulls behind the Wards' car. They get out and grab stuff from the Packard and put it in their new car. Charlie drives a little ways, then stops and tells Caril he's going to move the Wards' car out of sight and to stay where she is. Back in the car, he can't get the emergency brake off. Caril sees a man walking up behind them and sticks her head out the window and motions with her hand and whispers for him to stay away. He keeps walking toward them. Charlie will kill him. Charlie gets out of the car with the .22 and tells the man if he can get the brake released, he won't get hurt. The man puts his hand down as if to grab the brake but instead grabs the gun and starts wrestling Charlie. Caril figures Charlie has finally found a man who can handle him, and as soon as the two men get clear of the door she pushes the seat forward, jumps out and runs. She sees a big truck with men sitting up high inside and another car, and she runs to it and jumps inside and tells the two men inside that the man in the road is Charlie Starkweather and he's just killed a lot of people and he has her parents and he is going to kill them and her too. Her story spills out of her all at once. The driver tells her she is safe and to quit crying.

18

ERLE COLLISON WAS THIRTY-FOUR, MARRIED WITH an infant son, and had served as a paratrooper in WWII. He drove this morning from Great Falls, Montana, to call on shoe stores in northern Wyoming. He had pulled over and was taking a nap when Charlie spotted his car by the Natural Bridge Road turnoff. Photos of Mr. Collison capture his body crumpled under the dash of the Buick with one shoe showing. The autopsy would show that he was shot more than nine times in the head.

Charlie's luck has finally turned on him. Joe Sprinkle, a six-foot-tall, twenty-nine-year-old land man for Sinclair Oil and Gas in Casper drives by and notices the Packard on one side of the road and the Buick on the other. He glances in his rearview mirror and, seeing someone get out of the Packard, figures there had been an accident. He turns around and parks behind the Buick. When he approaches the car, Charlie gets out and Sprinkle asks if he can help. Charlie brings a rifle out from behind his back and tells him to raise his hands and to help get the emergency brake released or he'll kill him. Sprinkle notices the dead man slumped on the floor. He fakes reaching for the emergency brake and instead grabs the rifle. The two struggle in the middle of the road. Sprinkle knows he's a dead man if Charlie gets the gun free.

At that moment, the trapdoor fell.

William Romer, a Natrona County deputy sheriff, was out on the road with a friend in the patrol car coming back from Casper when he happened by the Natural Bridge Road turnoff and saw two men struggling for a rifle in the middle of the highway. He jerked to a stop about seventy feet away and suddenly a girl jumped out of the back seat of the Buick and ran down the road to his car.

She screamed, "He's going to kill me. He's crazy. He just killed a man."

"Who is he?"

She struggled to say his name, clogged up in her throat, but finally managed, "Charles Starkweather."

Charlie looked up and saw the patrol car. He let go of the .22 and bolted for the Packard. Sprinkle walked to the edge of the road and tossed the rifle in a ditch. Charlie sped off in the direction of Douglas. Deputy Romer, with Caril in the car, took off in pursuit and called the Highway Patrol and told them Starkweather was headed for Douglas and to set up a roadblock. Romer whipped around and drove back to the crime scene. The patrol contacted Sheriff Heflin of Converse County and Douglas police chief Robert Ainslie.

Heflin, a tall man who wore satin cowboy shirts, a ten-gallon cowboy hat, snakeskin cowboy boots, a string tie, and a .38 on his hip, grabbed his .30-30 lever-action rifle from the jail and joined Chief Ainslie in the city police car. Ainslie, short and bespectacled, appearing more the high school principal than a lawman, drove west out of town. About five miles out, the lawmen met the Packard headed their way at close to one hundred miles per hour. Ainslie flipped the car around and took off in hot pursuit.

Starkweather maintained the speed until he hit Douglas. Red lights flashing, sirens wailing, the squad car followed him down Center Street, dodging in and out of traffic. Heflin leaned out the window and shot at the tires with his .38. Pedestrians ducked and scattered. Ainslie rammed the back of the Packard and locked bumpers. Charlie jammed the accelerator, and the Packard's bumper ripped loose. He took off heading back east toward Nebraska, hitting speeds up to 120 miles per hour. Heflin holstered the .38 and leaned out the window with the .30-30 in his hands. He ripped off twelve shots before blowing a hole in the Packard's rear window. About three miles out of town, the Packard disappeared in a dip for a few moments and then reappeared with brake lights flashing in the western sun. The car stopped cold in the middle of the highway, close to the fences of the Scott ranch, one of the biggest cattle and horse properties in the county. The two lawmen parked a hundred feet behind the Packard, crouched behind their open doors, and yelled at Charlie to come out. He appeared with hands at his sides. When he didn't put them over his head as ordered, Ainslie fired a shot at his feet and told him to lie down. Charlie appeared to reach for something in his back pocket, and Ainslie fired again. (Charlie was tucking his shirt in.) After a third shot, Charlie dropped to his knees and lay facedown on the highway. The lawmen cuffed him as he lay, then raised him to his feet. His ear was bleeding. "I'm shot!" he said. "You shot me!" (It would turn out to be a cut from a piece of flying glass from the rear window.)

"I would have shot you if I hadn't run out of ammunition," he bragged as the lawmen walked him to the car. He complained that the cuffs were too tight and said that if they didn't loosen them, he wouldn't say a thing. Heflin loosened his cuffs.

On the ride into town, Charlie told the lawmen: "Don't be rough on the girl. She didn't have anything to do with it."

THE LAWMEN AND reporters and lookers-on gathered in front of the Ward house were convinced Charlie and Caril were still in Lincoln. For three hours, the town sweated it. When word of the Wyoming captures reached Lincoln at 3:30, people put down their rifles and stepped out of their houses, unsure of where it all left them. They were safe now, at least, but who could forget how these two kids, in blood and mayhem, had terrorized the state? The city, even the state would suffer from cultural PTSD, and it would play out for years to come.

The *Omaha World Herald* lost it with the following headline: "Punk's Blood-Stained String Ends At 10 Dead With Wyoming Capture."

The lead sentence of the article read, "The crazy-killing career of Charles Starkweather, 19, ended Wednesday." Further on, the article refers to Starkweather as a "mad dog youth." Another article the same day referred to Starkweather as a "slayer" and "a killer," and a few days later a "bantam killer." Another reporter wrote: "Despite the biggest manhunt in the city's history, the killer and his girlfriend were always several hours—and several murders—ahead of authorities." All this before

Charlie had been anywhere near a courtroom. As his trial drew near, the paper referred to Charlie as "a trigger-happy kid" and "a confessed killer." When the trial started, the *Omaha World Herald* would head-line: "Mad Dog's Jury To Be Impaneled."

For Caril, her participation in the killings seemed almost a foregone conclusion: "Starkweather, Caril held without bond." (Caril is referred to her by her first name in all three Nebraska papers as well as the AP.)

The killing spree and the ultimate capture of Charlie and Caril was national news. *The Huntley–Brinkley Report*, NBC's evening news pro-gram since 1956, carried it night after night. Several foreign reporters, one from the *London Mirror*, showed up in Douglas. Lincoln was not only shocked at what had happened; it was embarrassed—perhaps even ashamed—in the national eye. Nebraska, the trustworthy, stable soul of America, was now front and center in a terrible swirl of depravity. The killers were natives. Self-doubt flourished. Who are we, really? Have we been fooling ourselves? A zebra who has escaped the claws of the swift leopard in a long chase will, when the chase is over, stand and shake for a minute or two to rid its system of the hormones and steroids fueling the flight. Lincoln would struggle to find a way, consciously or otherwise, to rid its system of the results of having lived in a state of terror-infused panic. The hysteria of the last forty-seven hours—the last *three* hours in particular—would linger like poison in the bloodstream. There were a few contrary voices. One young girl remembered the morning when the red-haired garbage man rescued a doll from a can and walked to where she was sitting on the lawn and gave it to her. An Everett Junior High teacher recalled Starkweather as a quiet youth who never caused any trouble at school.

Found in Caril's purse: a small padlock; a key chain; a pearl brace-let; a gold heart engraved with "Charlie and Caril"; two silver chains, one with a gold cross; a car-key holder; pancake makeup; nail clippers; a Script fountain pen; a change purse; five lipsticks; one match; a black eyebrow pencil; and thirteen cents.

19

REPORTER DEL HARDING'S GRANDMOTHER LIVED four blocks away from the Ward house; Charlie was her garbage man. At the Ward house in the early afternoon of January 29, he thought how easily it could have been her that was killed. When news of the capture of the two fugitives hit, the *Star* and the *Journal* chartered a private plane to fly to Douglas. Harding grabbed his camera and flash attachment, drove to the airport, and jumped on board. He was the first reporter on the scene. Sheriff Heflin told him to go on into the jail and get a good look at Charlie and take some pictures. Charlie, still in Lauer Ward's white shirt, now splattered with blood from the nick to his ear, stood in his cell and scowled back at him. Harding snapped away. Within a few hours, the tiny jail was flooded with reporters. Heflin gave them access to Charlie's cell. One picture shows Charlie sitting at a small table and eating dinner. One reporter yelled out: "Why did you kill all those people, Charlie?" He answered with his own question: "What would you do if they was coming at you?" One reporter wrote that Charlie stood in his cell and banged on the bars and shouted, "Where's my girl? Where's my girl?" An AP story began:

> This fellow Starkweather doesn't look like the kind of guy who could kill 10 people. Not until you look into his eyes. They look wild. Starkweather was sort of slouched on a bunk when I talked to him. He wore Levis and [a] crumpled white shirt with blood stains on it.

Charlie now had to play out the rest of his life's story. His fervent dream of dying in a shootout with cops in front of his girlfriend had been set up to happen on the road between Douglas and Casper. The cop showed up in his car, and his girlfriend was right there at his side. True, his girlfriend had run to the police car, but the real problem was that he'd had no firepower. One .22 had jammed, and the other Caril had emptied into Merle Collison. He had Betty's .32-caliber pistol but had never been able to find any ammo for it. So he ran. When the bullet shattered the rear window and the glass nicked his ear, he realized that the next bullet might take him out. He would be a coward shot while running. And he was probably right. Deputy Romer, commenting on Starkweather's complaining about the blood, said that, "He (Starkweather) was just as yellow as we thought he would be." An outlaw cowboy with useless guns and whose girlfriend has gone over to the law, shot in the back while running away, was not the right ending.

There was another way out: Confess to everything. Confess even to a crime the law had no idea you committed. Take a little pride in your work; stand straight with shoulders back and look into the cameras. Heflin testified that Charlie was "friendly" on the ride back to Douglas. Sheriff Karnopp, from Lancaster County, would remark after talking with Charlie in the car on the ride back to Lincoln that he had never seen a vicious killer talk so casually about his crimes. He was "cool as a cucumber." The look on Charlie's face whenever he faced the press would baffle reporters, leading one to describe it as a "quizzical smile." The fact is, Charlie was not unhappy with the turn of events. The road to glory would not end with a shot to the head; it would stretch out for weeks, months, even a year, and his face and the story of his crimes and his death would be implanted in history. He would write a book on his life. Maybe movies would be made about him. He would be James Dean with the guts to act out his alienation and hatred. He didn't fear death. He awaited it. Viewed in this light, even banging on the bars of his cell and screaming for Caril could be seen as part of the show.

So Charlie set about confessing. He stated early on that he would be happy to meet and talk with county attorney Elmer Scheele and Sheriff Karnopp about what he'd done. Before that happened, he wrote a letter to his mom and dad:

(The Letter to His Parents)

In a way i hate to write this or maybe you will not read it but if you will I would like to have you read it, it will help a lot.

I'm sorry for what I did n a lot of ways cause I knew I hurt every-body and you and mon did all you could to rise me up right and you always help me when I got in bad with something. But this time i would like you not to do anything to help me out. i hope you will understand, i know my sister and brothers even nom that this will take a long time before people stop looking at them in a funny way. So it would make me happy if everybody will go on just like anything didn't happen. the cops up here have been more than nice to me but these dam reporters—the next one that come in here he is going to get a glass of water, but dad im not real sorry for what i did cause for the first time me an Caril had more fun, she help me a lot, but if she comes back don't hate her because she had not a thing to do with the killing. All we wanted to do was get out of town. tell everybody to take care. Chuck. P.S. tell Bob Von-Bruck to think of some body besides him "he help to cause this."

Charlie was more specific about his crimes in a lengthy statement written and signed that same evening at the urging of County Attor-ney Dixon, referred to as the Douglas Jail Confession. He wrote that he arrived at the Bartlett house around 1:30 p.m. on January 17. He got into an argument with Mrs. Bartlett, and she told him not to see Caril anymore. Charlie said something about Robert Von Busch and his wife, and Mrs. Bartlett slapped him three times. He slapped her back and she screamed. Mr. Bartlett came running into the room and hit Charlie. Then he threatened Charlie with a hammer. Charlie ran into the bed-room, grabbed his brother's .22, and shot Mr. Bartlett. Mrs. Bartlett came in holding a knife. Charlie shot her as well. Betty Jean was scream-ing, so he hit her.

Caril came home about 4:00 p.m. He "told her a line that they were somewhere." He meant to tell her about her parents, but the day went by so quickly he never got around to it. He took his brother's .22 to a friend's house, found the .410 belonging to Mr. Bartlett, and sawed nine inches off the barrel. After Pansy Street threatened to come back with a warrant, he told Caril to "come on," grabbed the .410 and the revolver, got his car from a friend's house, and drove to Bennet. His car got stuck in August Meyer's drive, he and Caril walked up to Meyer's house, and he asked Meyer to help pull the car out. Meyer agreed and went back inside to get his overcoat.

The statement does not mention the shooting of Meyer. About King and Jensen, Charlie wrote only that he didn't want to shoot either one. He drove into and out of Lincoln and eventually back again. He and Caril slept in the car that night. He chose the Ward house as a place to hide out during the day.

Mrs. Ward and her maid were frightened but agreed to "be nice." About two o'clock that afternoon, he went upstairs to see what Mrs. Ward was doing and she shot at him. Charlie threw his knife and it stuck in Mrs. Ward's back. He tied her up and left her on the bed. He also tied up the maid and told Caril to tie her to the bed. He was waiting behind the kitchen door with a .22 when Mr. Ward came in. Ward struggled with him, got ahold of the rifle for a second, and then Charlie got it back. Charlie shot Mr. Ward when he tried to flee. Charlie and Caril headed to Washington in the Wards' Packard. When they left, there was "only one dead person in that house." He stopped by the Buick on the side of the road and woke the driver. The man said he "would not do any wrong," but he grabbed for Charlie's gun and Charlie shot him "about three or five times."

Thus, according to Charlie in this statement, Caril was not at home when he murdered her parents and little sister. She was not involved in the killing of Carol King, Robert Jensen, or Lauer Ward. He does not accuse her of killing Clara Ward or Lillian Fencl but states that they were both alive when he and Caril left the house. Having admitted to stabbing Mrs. Ward, Charlie could be implying that she hadn't yet died

from the wound when they left. The same suggestion could also apply to
the maid: he had stabbed her, but she was still alive when they left. Or he
could be suggesting that Caril killed both of them. The latter would be
somewhat odd because it directly contradicts what he wrote in his letter
to his parents: that Caril had nothing to do with the killings.

In fact, the first story Charlie told about the killing spree, known
as the Ward Letter, was also a confession. Found in his pocket, the note
was folded and inserted inside an envelope addressed "for the law only."
Charlie claimed to have written the note while sitting at the table in the
Wards' kitchen. He figured both he and Caril would soon be dead, and
it was meant to be a posthumous note to the world about the killings.
It is written in his handwriting, but the narrator almost incoherently
switches back and forth between himself and Caril.

This is for the cops or law-men who fines us. Caril and i are writing this so that you and every body will know what has happem.
On tue.day 7 days before you have seen the bodys of my non, dad
and baby sister, there dead because of me and Chuck, Chuck came
down that tue.day happy and full of jokes but when he came in
nom said for him to get out and never come back, Chuck look at
her "and said why" [and] at that my dad got mad and begin to hit
him and was pushing him all over the room, then Chuck go mad
and there was no stopping him, he had his gun whit him cause
him and my dad was going hunting, well Chuck pill it and the the
[drawing of a bullet] came out and my dad drop to the foor, at
this my mom was so mad . . . she had a [drawing of knife] and was
going to cut him she Knot the gun from Chucks hands, Chuck
just stood there saying he was sorry he didn't want to do it. i got
Chucks gun and stop my mon from killing Chuck. Betty Jean was
about 10 steps fron her, he let it go it stop some where . . . Chuck
had the [drawing of a knife] so he was about ten steps from her,
he let it stop some where by her head. me and Chuck just look at
them for about 4 hours then we wrapped them and pull them out
in the house in back. my sisters and everyone else we not believed

this but it's the true an I say by god then me and Chuck live with each other and monday the day the bodys were found, we were going to kill ourselves, but Bob VonBruck and every body would not stay a way and hate my older sister and bob for what they are they all ways wanted me to stop going with Chuck show that some kid bob Kwen could go with me. Chuck and i are sorry for what we did, but now were going to the end. i feel sorry for Bar, to have a ask like bob. i and Caril are sorry for what has happen. cause i have hurt every body cause of it and so has caril, but i'm saying one thing every body that came out there was luckie thre not dead, even Caril's sister.

Chuck S.
Caril F.

So far we have kill 7 person.

The letter and both signatures were in Charlie's handwriting. Charlie explained this by saying that Caril dictated the letter to him. One theory is that Charlie was simply fooling with the law. As shown by his letter seeking employment and, later, his memoir, Charlie knew how to put a sentence together. He knew how to put a paragraph together. The jumbled tenses and disjointed phrases and misspellings seem to be almost intentional, as if the writer was attempting to scramble the head of the lawmen who would read it. He certainly couldn't have believed it would be taken seriously as a confession by Caril. Finally, it's difficult to conceive that a double suicide was the way Charlie wanted to bring his dream-wrought saga to an end. Cowboys and outlaws did not kill themselves.

20

The Douglas County jail is in the basement of the two-story brick county courthouse a block off Central Street, which also houses city hall. Sheriff Heflin and his wife, Hazel, who served as the jail matron, lived in an apartment above the jail. In midafternoon January 29, Hazel Heflin came down the stairs from her apartment to find a deputy sheriff and a young girl waiting for her. The girl was nervous and shaking and very dirty. Her face was streaked with tears and she appeared in shock. The deputy left and the matron had Caril, now officially in her custody, sit on a couch. The girl, whose hair was pinned up and who was wearing a silver cross around her neck, was crying hysterically; Mrs. Heflin could make no sense of what she said. She kept picking at a hanging thread. Sheriff Heflin called the doctor, who showed up quickly. He gave the girl a strong dose of the sedative Phenergan. The three sat on the couch and talked a little. Mrs. Heflin brought a cup of soup and held it while Caril drank. The girl talked, but nothing could be made of it. It was more mumbling than words. She refused to let anyone touch her, even to let the doctor examine her.

The girl went to sleep in one of the cots in the women's ward upstairs. Matron Heflin stayed up all night to keep an eye on her charge, who finally awoke around 8:00 or 9:00 the next morning. The matron managed to get her to wash her face and made her breakfast. Caril cried and screamed for her mother and her little sister over and over and wondered why they didn't call. Mrs. Heflin told her the phones were busy and that Caril could try them later. The girl smelled bad, and Mrs. Heflin tried to get her to take a bath, but Caril refused to take her clothes off because she wanted to be ready when her family showed up for her. At one point, the girl asked if she could see Starkweather, and Mrs. Heflin replied she doubted it. The doctor stopped by again and gave Mrs. Heflin four more sedatives and told her to give the girl one pill every four hours.

The jail was in chaos. Sheriff Heflin had flung open the doors to the press, and reporters were prowling the building and bunching up outside Charlie's cell taking pictures and shouting questions. Newsmen were trying desperately to sneak inside and snap a photo of Caril. Mrs. Heflin chased them out of her kitchen more than once. The next morning, with the press peeping around every corner, Mrs. Heflin spent as much time as she could with her charge; the girl was still afraid and insisted that her keeper stay with her.

Charlie was booked, and photographers captured the sullen, almost-handsome killer in rimless glasses, wearing handcuffs, his victim's white shirt now splattered with his own blood, eyes downcast, cigarette stuck between his parted lips, the pure murderous James Dean.

A photo of Caril coming into the sheriff's office to be booked shows a tiny, bedraggled waif in white majorette boots and black jeans, wearing Mrs. Ward's red-and-white shirt and suede jacket, arms several inches too long for her, a red kerchief on her head, her face tense and pale. Caril sobbed while being booked and interrogated. Witnesses said her eyes were surrounded by puffed red circles like she'd been crying for days. When Del Harding saw Caril leave the jail the next day, he was shocked at how tiny she was and wondered how she could have committed such horrible murders.

Over seventy-five reporters and photographers with their pads, recorders, flash cameras, and floodlights descended on Douglas that first night. A local motel sold out forty-three rooms by dinner. The town switchboard increased from two to seven operators, and it could take up to thirty minutes to get an open line. Reporters resorted to planes, trains, and automobiles to get their film to their stations. The *Casper Star-Tribune* reported that the jail "was surrounded by a mob of thrill seekers." Photos show a crowd of people three and four deep around the jail entrance.

The lawmen from Lincoln arrived in Douglas the next morning in an Air National Guard C-47. At the head of the contingent was county attorney Elmer Scheele and sheriff Merle Karnopp. Their first task was to get Charlie and Caril out of Wyoming and back to Lincoln. With the killing of Collison in Wyoming, that state could enforce a claim to Starkweather for murder in Converse County. Although there was a death penalty in Wyoming, Governor Simpson opposed it and had made it clear that no one would be executed on his watch. But you couldn't count on that—there could be another governor in a year or two who would execute a convicted Charlie, and that would deprive Nebraska of the right to work out of its nightmare by trying and executing Charlie, and perhaps even Caril. Charlie, a home-grown boy, had killed nine (the count would soon rise to ten) Nebraskans. He needed to die on Nebraska soil. County Attorney Scheele had already filed first-degree murder charges against Charlie and Caril for the killing of Carol King, a necessity to seek extradition. The federal government filed charges against both Caril and Charlie for unlawful flight to avoid prosecution.

The delegation of Lincoln lawmen met with Douglas lawmen for several hours on the morning of the thirtieth to sort out the issues. County Attorney Dixon initially stated he had already filed first-degree murder charges against Starkweather for the murder of Merle Collison and intended to try Starkweather in Wyoming. Sheriff Heflin argued that Starkweather and Fugate were his prisoners and he didn't intend to give them up. Governor Simpson told a reporter that if Charlie were tried and given death, he would commute the sentence, but that he would "sign extradition papers in a jiffy." Dixon, hearing this and also feeling bad for the many Nebraska victims, agreed to the extradition. Several times during the meeting, Mrs. Heflin came through the apartment shooing enterprising reporters out of her home. Reporters from *Time* and *Life* and all the wire services were among them. Heflin, now aware of the circus that would accompany any trial in Douglas, also agreed to the extradition of their two captives. Governor Simpson signed the papers.

County attorney Dixon and Natrona County deputy Romer met with Caril in her cell and explained to her the extradition process. Several times she asked them what they thought she should do. Dixon handed her a telegram from her sister, which read:

Tell everything you possibly can. Will help you when
you return. Our home is always open to you. We
love you very much.

Bob and Barbara Von Busch.

Caril asked Romer again what she should do. He told her it was
good advice and that she should cooperate fully with the authorities.
She agreed to sign the extradition waiver.

Dixon and Scheele and Caril met later that day in the Heflin apartment with local justice of the peace Harry Wise. Scheele explained to
Caril that she was in serious trouble and that charges would be waiting
for her when she returned to Lincoln. She signed the extradition papers
nonetheless, and when the process was over she asked Scheele whether
her parents were dead. Scheele replied, "Don't you know?" After Scheele
left the room, Caril turned to the justice of the peace and asked him if
her parents were dead. He told her they were.

Elmer Scheele was forty-six years old and a graduate of the University of Nebraska Law School. He was a former FBI agent who had
been elected county attorney four years earlier. He was generally considered a hard-nosed but fair prosecutor. A heavy smoker—he would die at
age fifty-six of cancer—he wore nice suits and his dark hair was neatly
slicked back. He looked at the world through horn-rimmed glasses. He
was known for handling only one case at a time, and he was methodical
and thorough in trial preparation. He had a short temper, and some saw
him as a bit cold, but he had a good track record of convictions. Almost
from the beginning, Scheele was convinced of Caril's participation in
the murders, and he was determined after visiting the Bartlett crime
scene to seek the electric chair for Charlie.

In fact, when Scheele introduced himself to Starkweather in the cell
in the Douglas jail on the morning of January 30, he told the prisoner
straight out that he was going to do everything in his power to send
him to the electric chair. Charlie seemed amused by the remark. He

signed the extradition paper without hesitation, telling Scheele that it was okay with him because he "didn't like the smell of gas," referring to Wyoming's use of the gas chamber. When Charlie learned that Karnopp had come to the jail, he asked to see him, and when Karnopp appeared, Charlie greeted him as a friend and asked after his son Dennis, whom he knew from school.

Lieutenant Eugene Henninger of the Lincoln Police Department wanted to interview Charlie in the jail. Heflin objected, insisting that Starkweather was *his* prisoner. Henninger told him there might be other bodies and possibly live victims in Lincoln and that they needed to get the information from him. Heflin gave in.

Henninger gave Starkweather a pack of cigarettes and sat on the other side of the bars taking notes for two hours. Henninger remarked to reporters afterward that he hadn't taken a written statement from Charlie but that he had learned enough to tie him to nine deaths. Charlie was "cooked and primed" for a full statement. Charlie had wanted to know: "What are people saying back home? What are the headlines? What's the television saying about me? Have you seen my folks? What are they saying?"

Henninger gave out one damning, inflammatory detail to the reporters: Charlie told him he had committed an unnatural sex act on Carol King after she was dead. While Starkweather told him Caril had been a hostage, the investigation so far indicated that she was involved in the Nebraska deaths; if she was a hostage, there had been many chances to get away.

Natrona County deputy Romer added to the weight of public evidence piling up on Caril. He told reporters on the afternoon of January 30 that Caril was in a high state of excitement when she got in his car and told him she had been a hostage, that the Bartlett home in Lincoln was the headquarters for a group of two or three teenagers who with Starkweather planned to rob a Lincoln bank but that the other boys chickened out; and that "she had 'seen' all nine murders in Nebraska." Caril "finally wound down" and became "unintelligible."

So, less than twenty-four hours after the arrests, the state was pro-
claiming it had evidence indicating the guilt of both Charlie and Caril
for murder. The press gladly ran with the story.

Scheele was determined to get his defendants back to Lincoln on the
thirty-first. Both Caril and Charlie refused to fly on the C-47. Scheele
and Karnopp came up with a plan: Wyoming officers would transport
the suspects in separate cars that evening across the state line to Gering,
Nebraska, about 130 miles southeast of Douglas. The two would spend
the night in the county jail. Nebraska Safety Patrol and Lincoln police
cars would meet the party in Gering that night, and the next morning
the officers would drive the suspects the rest of the way to Lincoln.

The route from Douglas to Lincoln is essentially the Oregon Trail in
reverse. The North Platte flows from Douglas to Scottsbluff/Gering and
southeast to the town of North Platte, where it joins the South Platte
flowing from Colorado to become simply the Platte.

Kindly Matron Heflin was assigned along with her husband to ride
in the car with Caril to Gering. She had gone to the "welfare" that afternoon to get some fresh clothes for Caril, but the caravan took off at
6:00 p.m., before she had a chance to get her charge into the bathtub and
cleaned up. Mrs. Heflin would say to the press, and testify in court, that
she did not believe Caril knew at the time of her capture that her parents
were dead. By the time Caril reached Gering, Mrs. Heflin had given her
the last of the four sedatives.

Sheriff Karnopp, worried that Charlie might try to escape, put the
cuffs and ankle chains on his prisoner in the Douglas cell himself. He
also wrapped a carrying chain around Charlie's waist, to which the cuffs
were linked, although he was still able to raise his hands high enough to
smoke a cigarette. Caril was never restrained. Matron Karnopp would
wind her hand through her arm and body and grasp her wrist while
escorting her.

The caravan headed west on Highway 20 and then turned south on
85 to Lingle, a small ranch town along the Platte. The road crossed miles
of ranch country, rolling hills with swaths of pine trees and occasional
outcroppings of soft, pale-yellow sandstone. A few miles east of Lingle,

ruts made by the settlers' wagon wheels as they headed toward Oregon are easily visible. The Platte angles southeast out of town and through fields of corn, sunflowers, and alfalfa. Passing through villages spaced about ten miles apart, the road and the North Platte cross the border into the panhandle of western Nebraska.

The town of Scottsbluff sits right across the river from Gering, in the shadow of the Scotts Bluff National Monument, and is the namesake of the area. The sandstone formations breach the sky in high ridges and towering formations like Chimney Rock.

Karnopp and Henninger were in the car with Charlie. Cars of reporters and photographers from around the country followed the caravan to Gering. On the ride there, Sheriff Karnopp had questions for Charlie, and Charlie gave his "buddy" lots of answers. Karnopp told the excited gathering of reporters on arriving in Gering the evening of January 30 that Charlie had admitted to killing eleven victims. He gave them Starkweather's oft-quoted line: "Since I was a child I always wanted to be a criminal, but not this big a one." In the car, Charlie went through the killings one by one. After killing the Bartletts, Starkweather held Caril hostage in the Bartlett home until Monday. They left after Pansy Street showed up and said she was going to call the police. He killed August Meyer when Meyer greeted him at the door of the farmhouse with a gun in his hand. He marched Jensen and King to the storm cellar and shot the boy when he tried to escape. He then shot Carol King. He denied performing an unnatural sex act on her. Starkweather told Karnopp that he shot Lauer Ward and fatally stabbed Clara Ward and Lilyan Fencl. The "young slayer," as the *Journal* called Charlie, told him that Caril had no part in the slayings.

Starkweather startled Karnopp and Henninger with the story of his first victim: Robert Colvert, the twenty-one-year-old gas station attendant found dead with his head blown open on Superior Street in north Lincoln on the early morning of December 1, 1957. Charlie claimed that he hadn't meant to kill him, but that after he had driven Colvert into the country at gunpoint, Colvert grabbed at the handkerchief over his face, so he had to shoot him.

The caravan made it to Gering by 10:30 that evening. Caril was si-lent on the trip—not surprising, given her sedative consumption. The parade of cars was met by a gaggle of local citizens, reporters, and flash-ing cameras. Mrs. Heflin handed Caril off to the county-jail matron, Hazel Warwick, the wife of the Scottsbluff County sheriff. Caril asked Mrs. Warwick if her parents and sister were dead. She told her they were. Caril ate a dinner of bacon and eggs in her cell. A doctor was called, and he gave her a shot of Carbatrol, an anti-seizure medication. Charlie was also given a dinner of bacon and eggs and when asked by Karnopp if he was tired and wanted a good sleep, he replied, "I slept like a log last night."

Sometime in the night, Charlie stood on the toilet in the cell and scratched out in pencil on the wall what would be known as the Gering Jail Confession:

Caril is the one who said to go to Washington state.

by the time any body will read this i will be dead for all the
killings then they cannot
give Caril the chair to

From Lincoln Nebraska they got us Jan. 29, 1958
1958 kill 11 persons (Charlie kill 9) all men
(Caril kill 2)
11

To the left of the message Charlie drew a heart, with an arrow stuck through it. Inside the heart is scrawled, "Charlie Starkweather and Caril Fugate." The final comment was circled: "they have so many cops and people watching us leave I can't add them all up." Perhaps Charlie meant to refer to the fact that his scratching incorrectly indicated nine men and two women, when in fact there were five females and six males (in-cluding Colvert). Charlie never denied the writing on the wall.

Fear of Charlie Starkweather and Caril Fugate had seeped from the

Missouri River more than five hundred miles west to the Wyoming state line. When news reached Scottsbluff that Starkweather and Fugate had been captured in Wyoming, the fear receded, until the locals learned the next day that Charlie and Caril would be coming to town and held in the county jail in Gering. Now, Charlie was among them, in their town, and they feared, given all else he had gotten away with, that he might manage to escape the old jail and start killing people. Not until he was well on his way to North Platte the next day did the two towns begin to relax.

For the trip to Lincoln, Sheriff Karnopp and Lieutenant Henninger rode in a car with Charlie, while Matron Karnopp and two officers rode with Caril. Charlie was still wearing the blood-stained shirt of Lauer Ward, and Caril was still wearing the suede jacket and red-and-white blouse of Clara Ward. The caravan left Gering at 10:42 a.m. for the 394-mile trip to Lincoln. There was a light snow swirling over the highway. State troopers were stationed at various locations along the route. People in small towns on the way gathered in their winter coats and hats on the sidewalks of main streets to see the young killers pass through in the caravan of police cars. "It was like a parade," the sheriff would say.

Within a few hours, both the sheriff and his wife had obtained damaging statements from their charges. The *Star* reported that Charlie told the sheriff that in fact Caril was not a hostage; he did not hold a gun on her and tell her what to say when people came to the Bartlett house. On their escape from Lincoln to Douglas, "she could have gotten away but she didn't try."

Mrs. Karnopp said Caril asked if her folks were dead. When Mrs. Karnopp did not answer, Caril asked her, "Who killed them?"

"Don't you know, Caril?" Mrs. Karnopp responded.

Caril did not answer but was quite talkative, describing the death of August Meyer and telling of the day spent in the Ward house. She told Mrs. Karnopp that the newspapers had said the three bodies had been shot where they were found, but actually they had been shot in the house and carried outside. "Which bodies?" Mrs. Karnopp asked, to which Caril replied, "Mr. Meyer was shot in the house and then drug outside." Caril fell silent and spent her time twisting Kleenex into little dolls.

The highway from Gering swung south and east following the Platte River for 174 miles to North Platte. North Platte is a hub of the Union Pacific Railroad, which hauls to market cattle from the Sandhills and the produce from the farms of central Nebraska irrigated by the Platte and the Ogallala Aquifer. Buffalo Bill owned a cattle ranch outside North Platte.

During WWII, the army used the rail line to transport soldiers trained on the West Coast to the East Coast to be shipped to the front in Europe. The people of North Platte learned that a trainload of North Platte boys was coming through on Christmas Day, 1941, and the women made cookies, cakes, and sandwiches and pots of coffee to serve during their brief stopover. It turned out it wasn't their boys on the train, but the women served the soldiers anyway. The North Platte Canteen was born. From that day until April 16, 1946, women from towns all over Nebraska volunteered to meet every troop train coming through. On troop days, cars and trucks from around the state arrived early at the station carrying cakes, pies, baskets of fried chicken, doughnuts, pickles, cookies, dozens of fresh eggs, loaves of freshly baked bread, oranges, ham, popcorn balls, cupcakes, and sandwich meat. Cartons of cigarettes and stacks of cash were placed on side tables. Coffee was served in china cups. One photo shows two women rushing alongside the moving train and passing baked goods through the windows to the soldiers. Thousands of women from 145 towns in Nebraska served over six million soldiers passing through on troop trains.

The caravan left North Platte on Highway 30 and traveled ninety miles farther east to Kearney, where the line of cars stopped at a roadside park for a picnic lunch. Caril stayed in the car, glaring at Charlie and drinking a coke. Caril held one of the Kleenex dolls up for Charlie to see and wrung its neck.

On the afternoon of January 31, the caravan headed out of Kearney on Highway 30 to Grand Island, where three days earlier Charlie had turned north into the Sandhills. The land is flat and blanketed in corn fields. Many of the roads turning off the highway are dirt or gravel.

Telephone poles next to the road march in an endless straight line over the horizon. The temperature in Grand Island was 30 degrees.

Here, Highway 34, the main road to Lincoln, swings east from the Platte, which heads up to Columbus and Fremont before swinging back down to flow into the Missouri. The caravan moved swiftly over the one hundred miles from Grand Island to Lincoln. A black-and-white Safety Patrol car met the caravan a few miles outside Lincoln to guide it safely through town on a back road.

The press coverage of the spree began four days earlier, on Monday, and reached a roar on Wednesday night after the bodies were found at the Ward house and Charlie and Caril were taken into custody. Almost without exception, the papers and TV were on board with the prosecution. Based on Henninger's and Karnopp's statement, the papers felt free to convict Starkweather on the spot, and while not explicitly convicting Caril, their references to her suggested, to say the least, an active involvement in the crimes. The *Journal* headlined: "Killer, Caril on Road to Slaying Scenes." The *Star* referred to "the stocky red-haired gunman Starkweather and teenage girl companion." One *Star* headline read, "Police doubt Caril," and it quoted Lincoln police chief Joe Carrol as saying he had grave doubts about Caril's story of being held hostage because she had "ample opportunity" to get away from Starkweather during the eight days. On January 30, the *Los Angeles Times* quoted Karnopp as saying Starkweather had admitted to eleven deaths and that "The Slayer Wanted to Be Somebody." *The New York Times* reported that Nebraska had obtained custody of Starkweather and Fugate and was returning them to Lincoln. The *Casper Star-Tribune* referred to Starkweather as the "bandy-legged little gun toter."

Chief Joe Carroll, forty-eight, was a legendary figure in Lincoln. He was a big, burly Irishman with a booming voice who smoked cigars and told great stories. He would slap the back or put his hand on the elbow of whomever he was talking to. He was appointed chief in 1941, at age thirty-one, and had run a tight ship ever since. When the hunt for Starkweather was on, he was reported to have sat at his desk one day, slapped a clip into a submachine gun, and said, "I want that boy!" He would later tell a reporter that Caril was a good actress but that there was no way she was going to "wiggle out" of the murder charges.

The string of black-and-white patrol cars arrived in Lincoln around 10:30 p.m. The first stop was the Nebraska State Penitentiary, built in 1876, a massive, gray-walled structure with glassed-in guard towers on Highway 2 south of town. Guards and reporters were jostling for position in front of the administration building when the caravan pulled in. A reporter had run a cable through a window, and the driveway was lit up in harsh floodlights. The pen didn't have a death row, and the county jail wasn't set up to handle a famous prisoner, so it had been decided to keep Charlie in a cell in the hospital ward. He would be isolated and under twenty-four-hour guard. When the first car stopped, Karnopp got out the back door, followed by Charlie and a state trooper. According to Mrs. Karnopp, Caril waved and smiled at the reporters as her car pulled to a stop.

Charlie, still in Lauer Ward's blood-speckled white shirt, his hair yet streaked with black Shinola, stood still for a moment in the bright lights. A cigarette hung from the corner of his mouth and his face was composed in a sullen smile. The reporters yelled at him to look in their direction. Karnopp nudged him forward and he walked up the steps with, according to one observer, "swaying shoulders" and an "exaggerated swagger." (Which could have just been the result of his bow legs.) As Caril's car pulled away, a reporter shouted, "Blow us a kiss, Caril!"

Nebraska state law prevented a juvenile from being held in the same county jail as adults. Lincoln had no facilities for juveniles. So, after being booked and processed at the Lancaster County jail, Caril was taken to the Lincoln State Hospital, where she would be placed, according to the superintendent, in a locked ward with other "mild type mental patients." Caril was confused about where she was and why. She became fearful when she saw another woman receiving electric-shock treatments. This hospital would be Caril's home for the next eleven months.

21

ON FRIDAY, JANUARY 31, WHEN THE CARAVAN WAS heading across the plains, August Meyer was laid to rest in a cemetery outside the Trinity Lutheran Church in Walton, a small town near Bennet. A joint funeral was held for Robert Jensen and Carol King at the Community Church in Bennet, where they had both been members and Carol had sung in the choir. Six hundred people attended. The funeral for Velda, Marion, and Betty Jean Bartlett was held at a mortuary chapel in Lincoln. Pansy Street lay little Betty Jean in the arms of her mother because, it was reported, she didn't have enough money for a third casket. The family was interred in Wyuka Cemetery in Lincoln.

Mike Ward, a slight, dark-haired boy, had returned to Lincoln in the company of David Gracey, the former minister of Holy Trinity Episcopal Church. A service for the Wards was held on Saturday, January 31, at Westminster Presbyterian Church with an estimated 1,500 mourners in attendance. The couple was interred in Wyuka Cemetery. Several months later, Mike returned to the Choate School. For many years he refused all entreaties to talk about his parents, their murders, Charlie Starkweather, or Caril Fugate.

A funeral service for Ludmilla Lilyan Fencl was held on Friday in Wahoo, a nearby small town settled by Czechs and Germans in the years following the Civil War. Lilyan's family, like most Czechs, were farmers. Lilyan was considered a timid and gentle soul by those who knew her. A knock on a neighbor's door on Saturday morning was likely to be that of Lilyan in her apron with a plate of cookies or jar of jam in hand. A relative would say that there had been no need to kill her; if Charlie had stuck her in a closet, she would have remained there quiet and still.

When news of Starkweather's confession to the murder of Robert

Colvert hit the Lincoln media on Friday the thirty-first, the uproar was loud and bitter. The town turned its fury on the Lincoln Police Department. If the cops had nailed Charlie for Colvert's murder, ten people would still be alive. The cops had over seven weeks to catch Starkweather, and there were at least two witnesses who had given information to the police that pointed to Starkweather. The cops had bungled the Colvert killing, just like they had bungled the ten subsequent killings. To quell the uprising, mayor Bennett Martin announced he would appoint a special investigator to look into the matter.

III

THE TRIALS

22

C OUNTY ATTORNEY SCHEELE HAD DONE A REMARK-
able job of returning Charlie and Caril to Lincoln little more
than forty-eight hours after their capture in Wyoming. By 8:00
p.m. on the night of January 31, both were safely under lock and key in
the capital city. Keeping up the pace, Scheele wanted to have both Charlie and Caril arraigned on Monday, February 3. But he needed to rethink
his charges. Charlie had admitted to eleven murders. If the physical evidence matched up, he could be tried for any of the murders; some would
be easier to corroborate than others, particularly if he ended up claiming insanity. While Charlie was the big dog, Caril had to go down as
well. She hadn't admitted to a thing, and so far he had no solid evidence
linking her to the killing of Carol King, with which he had charged her.
The only apparent way to link her other than through supposition and
inference was either through her or Charlie's mouth.

On Saturday, February 1, Scheele, in the company of Karnopp, Lincoln psychiatrist Robert Stein, and court reporter Elmer Shamburg,
took Charlie's statement in an office in the penitentiary. After getting
Charlie to agree that he was answering the questions freely and voluntarily, Scheele led him through the murders one by one, starting with
Robert Colvert. After Colvert, Scheele turned to the Bartlett murders
on Tuesday, January 21. Charlie stated clearly that Caril was not in the
house when he went inside at approximately 1:30 p.m. Later in the questioning, he added that Caril didn't get home until around 4:00 p.m., well
after the murders. He told her that her family was being held hostage by
the old couple on Woodsdale, where he kept his Model A.

Turning to the killing of August Meyer, Scheele asked whether Caril
knew her parents were dead when the two left for Bennet. Charlie replied, "No, I don't believe she did," adding that he hadn't told her they

were dead. He claimed he shot Meyer in the back of the head with the .410 after Meyer had taken a shot at him with a .22 from the porch. He also shot the dog when it wouldn't stop barking. It was about 8:30 that night when he ordered Jensen and King from the car and into the cave. Caril stayed inside the car. He told the boy to go down into the cellar, which he started to do. But then the boy came "flying up" and pushed King out of the way and came for Charlie. He shot him, and the boy fell back into the cellar. The girl at the top of the steps began screaming, and he shot her. He shoved her down the steps and put the door and some brush on top of the cellar. He denied ever touching her body in a sexual way. He returned to the car, to find Caril now sitting in the front seat.

At this point, Charlie seemed to have cleared Caril of any direct role in the killing of Jensen and King. Scheele did not ask him any questions about a robbery of Jensen in the car ride back to the cellar. It seems highly unlikely that, if Scheele had known about one, he would have failed to develop the facts in this statement.

In Charlie's statement on the Ward killings, he testified that Caril held a gun on the maid when he went outside to move the car and when he shot Lauer Ward, and that she warned him when Ward pulled into the driveway after work. She also held the gun on the maid when they took her upstairs and he tied her up on the bed. Caril kept watch on the maid while Charlie loaded up the car and dyed his hair black. Charlie denied stabbing the maid and said he only flung the knife at Clara Ward's back after she took a shot at him. He also denied stabbing Lauer Ward. Both Clara Ward and the maid were alive when he and Caril left the house. But still, at the Ward house, he wasn't sure if Caril knew her parents were dead. He cut out pictures from the paper and gave them to her, except the ones of her family, which he threw in the wastebasket.

Thus, as matters stood on February 1, 1958, Charlie implicated Caril in aiding and abetting in the killing of Lauer Ward by warning him (Charlie) when Ward came home. But if Caril denied it, Charlie's word alone, which was already shifting like the tides, would be shaky grounds for a conviction.

Likewise, Charlie's denial that he stabbed Lilyan Fencl and Clara

Ward and his insistence that they had both been alive when he left the house at the most merely pointed the finger at Caril for their murders: somebody else killed them. Even shakier grounds for a conviction. The prosecution's best shot at convicting Caril of murder lay with Caril herself.

At 6:00 p.m. that day, Scheele held a press conference at the prison. The Sunday edition of the *Journal* and *Star* headlined: STARKWEATHER REPEATS MURDER CONFESSIONS. Scheele read a statement saying Starkweather had readily confessed to ten murders in Nebraska, but he didn't give any details. He noted that Starkweather had been visited earlier in the day by his parents, who brought him several packs of cigarettes.

The Sunday edition of the *Star* continued to link Charlie and Caril as partners in crime when it referred to Douglas as the place "where Starkweather and his girlfriend were captured—after another murder."

Caril was teetering on the edge of the precipice of the legal system. It was getting ready to pull the fourteen-year-old eighth grader in and subject her to a male-dominated process that was totally unprepared for dealing with a fourteen-year-old girl. Her mother and stepfather and little half-sister were dead. So her sixteen-year-old sister and her biological father and his wife were her only advisors on how to proceed in a system that had already charged her with first-degree murder, which could bring her death, and they advised her to cooperate. She had not spoken to a lawyer, and one would not be provided until after she was questioned extensively and taken to court for a plea hearing.

On the morning of February 1, Caril met with Dr. Vance Rogers, assistant chief of police Eugene Masters, Dr. Coates, deputy county attorney Dale Fahrnbruch, and Mrs. Karnopp. For roughly two hours, Fahrnbruch asked Caril questions, which, according to Mrs. Karnopp, Caril answered "willingly." The next morning, February 2, Caril first met with Fahrnbruch, Mrs. Karnopp, and Dr. Coates, for about half an hour. A second meeting was held at around 2:00 p.m. that day, this time attended by Caril, Fahrnbruch, William Fugate and his wife, and Caril's sister Barbara. Fahrnbruch explained that they were going to take Caril's statement, that she could tell her side of the story, and advised her to tell the truth. Her father and stepmother agreed with the prosecutor and urged her to do the right thing and tell the truth.

After these preliminary meetings, Fahrnbruch took Caril's formal on-the-record statement that night from 8:00 to 10:30 p.m. and the next day, Monday, February 3, from 12:30 to 1:30 at the state hospital. The result of these two meetings was the famous 166-page statement (the Statement) which would serve as the basis for two new charges to be levied against her. In the Statement, Caril in effect tied the noose for those who would put it around her neck.

On February 3, 1958, the county attorney filed new complaints against Charlie and Caril, both of which charged two counts of first-degree murder:

Count I Murder in the First Degree alleged that on January 27, 1958, Caril Ann Fugate (Charlie Starkweather) did unlawfully, feloniously and purposely and of her own deliberate and premediated malice kill Robert William Jensen contrary to the form of the Statutes made and provided and against the peace and dignity of the State of Nebraska.

Count II Murder in the First Degree alleged that on the same date Caril Ann Fugate (Charlie Starkweather) did unlawfully, feloniously and purposely kill Robert William Jensen in the perpetration of a robbery.

Count II is what is normally described as the felony murder rule, which holds that a person who commits a felony when a death occurs is guilty of murder whether involved in the murder or not. The state need not prove the person's intent to commit the crime; it need not prove that the person committed or had anything to do with the murder; only that a death occurred during the commission of the felony. Thus, in a robbery situation, where one robber shoots and kills the owner of the store being robbed, the driver of the getaway car can be charged with felony murder. If the storekeeper kills one of the robbers during the course of the robbery, the remaining robbers could also be charged with felony murder. Under Nebraska law at the time, the penalty was the same for felony murder as it was for straight murder. The jury chose between death and life in prison; neither the judge nor the prosecutor could take death off the table. (In 1988, the U.S. Supreme Court held in *Enmund v. Florida* that the death penalty could not be imposed for felony murder if the defendant did not kill, or attempt to kill, or intend to kill.)

In the Statement, Caril, by her own words, made it possible for the state to convict her of first-degree murder without putting a weapon in her hand or even participating in any manner in the actual murder of Robert Jensen. The Statement would also get her in a lot of trouble having nothing to do with the killing of Jensen.

Fahrnbruch asked Caril whether anything other than the car was taken from Jensen and King before they were shot:

A. Yes, there was $4.00.

Q. And how did that come about?

A. Well, Chuck asked them if they had any money, and the boy said yes, he had $4.00, and handed his billfold to Chuck, and Chuck handed his billfold and the boy's billfold to me. I took the money out of the boy's billfold and put it in Chuck's, and handed Chuck's billfold back to him, and handed the boy's billfold back to the girl, because he asked me to.

Q. And was that the only thing that was taken at that time?

A. Yes.

There was the felony: an armed robbery. Taking four dollars from Jensen's wallet and putting it in Chuck's wallet, while the two held guns on Jensen and King.

Although it can't be established as fact, it seems likely that the prosecution learned of the robbery in the "practice" sessions prior to the formal statement.

A few hours after the statement was completed on February 3, Caril was taken to the district court for arraignment. Under Nebraska law, Caril would be entitled to a court-appointed lawyer only *after* the preliminary hearing. Until then, she was on her own.

At 10:30 that morning, Charlie was arraigned on identical charges. He pled not guilty. Charlie had confessed to all the murders at one time or another, and he planned on claiming self-defense. He made it clear that under no condition would he allow his lawyer to claim he was insane at the time of the crimes. "No one remembers a crazy man," he would tell Reinhardt. But given the evidence and the circumstances, a not-guilty-by-reason-of-insanity plea was his only chance of avoiding the chair. People were shocked that he would prefer to be electrocuted rather than be found crazy.

People didn't understand Charlie. He was ready to die. He expected death. He welcomed it. It was the proper and fitting end to his story. He would tell the lawmen that he did what he did because of a hatred that had built up inside him, and there was undoubted truth to that. But he wasn't angry when he shot August Meyer. He had an understanding, a covenant, with the ambiguous gray form that appeared in his window, in his dreams and when he was awake. The end might have arrived a little sooner than he'd figured, but he had held up his part of the bargain.

After Charlie's plea, Scheele held a press conference and laid out in considerable detail most of Charlie's confessions. Scheele explained to the press that he had decided to charge Caril with the murder of Robert Jensen, but as for the charge of killing Carol King, which he had filed earlier, he was going to "let it sit awhile." Under the headline "Teen Killer Tells Dad 'Caril Held Gun,'" the *Star* reported the next morning that Charlie told his dad that Caril had held a gun on the maid in the Ward house.

In response to a question about the widespread rumor that Caril was pregnant, Scheele shot it down: Matron Karnopp had told him that Caril was having her period on the day of the caravan from Gering to Lincoln.

The superintendent of the mental hospital reported that Caril was so dirty when she got to the institution that they "chucked her" in a bath and scrubbed her clean, but she was doing pretty well, particularly given the intensive questioning she had undergone. He added somewhat gratuitously that while Caril was not psychotic, there were some funny mental things going on and he would be highly skeptical of any statement by her that she was a hostage.

On the Monday of her arraignment, students at Whitter Junior High raided Caril's locker looking for souvenirs.

THE COUNTRY'S SHOCKED fascination with the story only grew with the arraignment and pleas. Papers large and small around the country covered it. Many papers carried the AP or UPI stories, while some papers in larger cities, such as *The Kansas City Star*, the *San Francisco Examiner*, and the *Chicago Tribune*, wrote their own pieces. The AP reported that "The swaggering little outlaw, head lowered and smoking the inevitable cigarette, entered the vintage Lancaster Courthouse at 10:40 a.m." In one story, the AP referred to Charlie as "a pint-sized red head," "a bow-legged gunman," and "a bantam killer." The AP also ran a headline stating that "Caril Could Get Chair," as if she had already been found guilty. *The New York Times* incorrectly reported that "Starkweather Enters Plea to One of Eleven Charges." (He entered pleas of not guilty to the only two charges brought against him.) A favorite photograph of Charlie in the early stories was of him in his black leather jacket, collar up, cigarette hanging from mouth, hands cuffed in front of him, head down, standing in his blue-and-white cowboy boots with the butterflies on the tips. By the arraignment, Charlie was wearing prison clothes—a chambray shirt, denim jacket, and pants—and work boots without laces. (His several requests to be allowed to wear his treasured cowboy boots to court had been denied.) His "flame-red hair" had been cut, but he still had managed to brush it up on the sides and twist one or two locks down over his forehead.

After his arraignment, Charlie was taken into Sheriff Karnopp's office and photographers were allowed to come in and take pictures.

Starkweather, cigarette dangling from his mouth, smiled for the shots and muttered a few comments. Security was immense when Charlie was brought to or from court. The law had real fear that someone would shoot him. Snipers stood on surrounding rooftops. Plainclothes cops worked the crowds. Some thought that the cops paraded Charlie around so much in order to convince the citizenry that he was not still on the loose.

A few papers looked back briefly at the case of Howard Unruh, a twenty-nine-year-old WWII vet from Camden, New Jersey, who in 1949 shot to death thirteen people in twenty minutes while walking through his neighborhood in what became known as "The Walk of Death." Unruh was diagnosed with schizophrenia and found unfit to stand trial and died in a mental hospital at eighty-eight.

The world waited for news of the sensational trials of the two crazed teenage killers who left a trail littered with bodies young and old, male and female, poor and wealthy, throughout the heartland. Pens were poised. Fingers hovered over keys. Red lights on TV cameras blinked brightly. Chet Huntley or David Brinkley frequently updated the story on the evening news, handing it off to the eager reporters at the Omaha affiliate to fill in the details. The local stations gave it daily coverage.

The *Chicago Tribune* noted that Scheele had recounted in detail the part of Charlie's confession that implicated Caril in the killing of Robert Jensen. Scheele was leaving no stone unturned in his effort to undercut Caril's hostage defense and portray her as an active participant in the crimes. (Current legal parlance would describe his actions as an attempt "to poison the jury pool.") Scheele also told the press that he asked Caril if she wanted an attorney but that she declined one.

Caril appeared for her arraignment at 3:30 in the afternoon of February 2, accompanied by her father and stepmother and sister Barbara. In a dark blue skirt, white sweater, black wedges, and white bobby socks, Caril still wore the tan suede jacket of Clara Ward. She pled not guilty, and her preliminary hearing was set for March 13. She smiled and blew her sister a kiss as she was driven away in the police car taking her back to the hospital. On February 5, Caril straightened up a little. On the informal advice of two local attorneys recruited by her father, she refused to sign the Statement. The UPI carried the headline "Fugate Girl Refuses to Sign Spree Accounts." That is, Caril refused to affirm the crimes to which she had previously admitted.

23

DISTRICT COURT JUDGE HARRY SPENCER WOULD CON-
duct the trials of both Starkweather and Fugate. Spencer, who
had immigrated to the country from England in 1907 as a boy
of three, had attended the University of Nebraska Law School. He had
run for election as a Republican twice as a county court judge and twice
as a district court judge, winning each time. There were four district
court judges, and they rotated among the four courtrooms. In 1958,
Judge Spencer was assigned to the criminal court. He was generally considered a hard-working, competent, fair-minded judge.

Judge Spencer called John McArthur, one of the most experienced
and respected criminal-defense attorneys in the Nebraska bar, and
asked him to represent Caril Fugate. McArthur, forty-seven, who grew
up in Broken Bow, felt that it was his duty to represent indigent defendants and accepted on the spot. Sometimes likened to Atticus Finch of
To Kill a Mockingbird or even Abe Lincoln in the courtroom, McArthur
was tall and thin and carried himself with a sort of quiet dignity. He
had a very soft, deep voice, which he never raised. His arguments were
clear, cogent, and well articulated. He sometimes worked a half-dollar
between his fingers as he addressed the court or the jury. The judge officially appointed McArthur to represent Caril on February 15, some
seventeen days after she had been taken into custody. McArthur had a
son, Jim, fifteen at the time, who was his father's greatest admirer and
who would attend as much of the hearing as he could. Minutes after the
appointment hit the airwaves, Jim picked up the home phone and heard
the first of many threatening calls.

Judge Spencer appointed Clement Gaughan (pronounced "Gone"),
fifty-four, and Wiliam Matschullat, fifty-two, to represent Charlie.
Gaughan, a gruff, heavyset Irishman who loved cigars, liquor, and

chewing tobacco—he kept a spittoon in his office—was a good old boy in Lincoln's political and legal circles. In those days, you could buy hard liquor only by the drink at a private club, so Gaughan bought a bar on the outside of town; gave memberships to his friends, city officials, lawyers, bondsmen, lawmen, and assorted cronies; and drank and played cards most evenings with them. He was the city's unofficial public defender, regularly accepting court appointments, and represented many poor people charged with crimes. (He would later become Lincoln's first official public defender.) When notified of his appointment by Judge Spencer, he was reported to have said: "I can't pull rabbits out of a hat, but I'll do what I can." His problem was, of course, that his client had already confessed at one time or another to all eleven murders, although in his formal February 1 deposition, Charlie had confessed to only nine of the eleven murders (excluding Clara Ward and Lilyan Fencl). His claim of self-defense was absurd, particularly when you considered the killings of the little Bartlett girl and Bobby Jensen, who was shot six times, three behind the right ear, two in in the ear, and one above the ear, all within a four-inch circumference, and August Meyer, who was shot in the side of the head with the .410. His only defense was not guilty by reason of insanity. Gaughan's client would have none of it. He was not crazy then, and he was not crazy at the time of the killings. Charlie would fight him every step of the way on that.

McArthur's first task was to try to get Caril's case moved from district court to juvenile court, where the maximum penalty was confinement to the Geneva Girls Training School until she was twenty-one. He filed a motion on February 19 seeking to have the case transferred to juvenile court. When the motion was denied in county court and subsequently in district court, he filed a writ of prohibition in the supreme court to restrain the county court judge from proceeding with the preliminary hearing. The court denied the motion, and the case was appealed directly to the Nebraska Supreme Court.

The appeal to the supreme court would result in a delay of Caril's trial, which was unfortunate in a way. The state would put Charlie on trial in May, and his version of who killed who and why would receive massive publicity and lie unrebutted for six months. Paul Douglas, one of the prosecutors and later state attorney general, stated his belief after the trial that Lincolnites were 100 percent against Caril. All the prosecution had to do was show up. Their only concern was that one juror would hold out and hang the jury.

Meanwhile, mayor Bennett Martin had to deal with the growing fury at the Lincoln Police Department. On March 9, he announced the appointment of a special commission to select an independent investigator to review the police conduct in the case. The commission appointed Harold Robinson, a former FBI agent who worked for the California Department of Justice. He promised to have his report in the mayor's hands on March 23.

24

DEATH FOUND CHARLIE IN THE MIDDLE DAYS OF FEB-
ruary. She reminded him of their deal: He would go out in a
blaze of glory, yes, but he would not go out alone. He would be
joined by his girl, Caril. This would seal their lives, their love, forever.
On the other side they would find the happiness that had eluded them
in this life. Charlie would never be alone; that had been promised him.
In his cell, he smoked and worked on his memoir and drew pictures and
read the Bible, more than willing to bet whatever he had that he would
meet James Dean on the other side, in the strangely comforting fires,
with Caril at his side.

So Charlie began telling new versions of the killings. His first on-
the-record shift was February 27, under the guidance of deputy county
attorney Fahrnbruch and Detective Henninger. If true, this statement
pinned Caril to the wall like a butterfly. Charlie arrived at the Bartlett home about 1:30 with the intent of going hunting with Mr. Bartlett,
carrying the .22 and the two rug scraps Mrs. Bartlett had asked him to
bring. In a short time, Mrs. Bartlett told him to leave and not come back.
He told her to go to hell, and she slapped him several times in the face.
He left and drove around the block for about ten minutes, then returned
to get his brother's .22 and "find out what the hell was going on." Mr.
Bartlett and Charlie got into a fight, which ended with Mr. Bartlett grabbing Charlie by the neck and kicking his ass out the back door. (Hard
enough that it still hurt three days later.) Charlie drove to Hutson's store
and called Watson Brothers Trucking Line and told the woman who
answered that Mr. Bartlett was sick and wouldn't be coming to work.
Around 2:30, he got his car from the house and drove it to the Griggses'
house, where he left it. Back at 924 Belmont, he knocked on the front and
back doors and no one answered, so he sat on the back porch and waited

for Caril. Around 4:00 p.m. he heard Caril come in the front door and begin arguing with her mother. Charlie went inside and began arguing with Mrs. Bartlett, who, among other things, accused him of getting Caril pregnant. She slapped him, he hit her back, and she yelled. Mr. Bartlett came in the room, picked him up, and started carrying him to the front door. Charlie wrenched loose, and the two of them struggled. He got away, picked up his gun, stuck a shell in it. Mr. Bartlett came at him with a hammer, and Charlie cocked the rifle and shot him in the head. Mrs. Bartlett came in the room with a black-handled knife with a curved blade and threatened to cut Charlie's head off. Caril jerked the gun away from Charlie and told her mother she was going to blow her to hell. Charlie got the gun back, put a shell in it, and shot her mother in the head. When she didn't go down, he hit her in the head with the butt of the gun; when she still didn't go all the way down, he smashed her skull again. All the while, the little girl was in the kitchen screaming, so he brought the butt of the gun down on her head. She kept screaming, so he threw the knife at her and it stuck in her throat. Mr. Bartlett was still moving, so he took the butcher knife and stabbed him in the throat. The man kept moving, so he stabbed him three more times. Caril went into the living room and sat on the couch. They talked about what to do, then watched television for a while. He began cleaning the place up. He put Betty Jean in the sink because she was bleeding, then found a small cardboard box with garbage in it and stuck her in there. He wrapped Mrs. Bartlett in a blanket and rug and took her and the baby to the outhouse. He wrapped Mr. Bartlett in a blanket and green construction paper, took the screen door off its hinges, and drug him outside to the chicken shack. He went back in and started cleaning up the blood again. Caril stayed in the chair watching TV, and he walked up to the store and bought three bottles of pop and a bag of potato chips. They ate the chips, watched television, and played gin rummy, at which he "beat the hell out of her." He fell asleep in the chair, and she fell asleep on the couch. In the ensuing days he had sex with her every night and morning and twice on Sunday, when no one came to the house.

Charlie admitted that he shot both Jensen and King at the cave. He pulled the girl's jeans and underpants down with the intent of "screwing her," but it was "colder than hell" and he "couldn't get to the point." So he left her there.

Charlie's story regarding the killing at the Ward home was pretty much the same as earlier, except now he said he told Caril to go up to the bedroom and wash the knife he had thrown at Clara Ward, and she was up there about five or ten minutes, and when she came down she said either that she had stabbed the maid or she should have stabbed her. Caril told him later in the car that the maid just wouldn't die.

On its face the statement is not particularly convincing. It is clear throughout the deposition that the three men (Karnopp, Fahrnbruch, and Starkweather) had met earlier that afternoon and had gone over the story in detail. On the record, Fahrnbruch and Henninger coached Charlie frequently to get the correct responses. In the end, Charlie refused to tell them why he had changed his story.

But now the state had evidence, shaky as it might be, that Caril was at the Bartlett home when Charlie killed her parents and little sister, thus blowing the guts out of the hostage defense, which depended completely on Caril not knowing that her family was dead. While Charlie still took credit for the murder of Carol King, he made it clear that he stabbed Clara Ward only once and didn't stab the maid at all. Autopsies show that Clara Ward was stabbed seventeen times and that Lilyan Fencl was stabbed at least twelve times.

Fahrnbruch also obtained a verbal statement from Caril making herself into a murderer. On February 7, after her preliminary hearing but before McArthur's appointment as her counsel, Fahrnbruch and Dr. Coates met with Caril, who "willingly and without hesitation" answered his questions. Fahrnbruch memorialized the meeting in a memo to Scheele. Among other things, Caril said that at the Ward house, she had ordered the maid around, telling her to sit up, stand up, and quit talking. In Wyoming, when Charlie was standing at Collison's Buick, he hollered for her to bring him a gun from the Packard, which she did. On the highway, either to Hastings or Douglas, Charlie told her that he was tired but that "if he could have a piece of ass," he could drive on. They stopped and had intercourse. They also had intercourse once or twice on the road after leaving the Ward house. Fahrnbruch got what he wanted: Caril and Charlie had sex in a way that didn't sound like rape but more like lovemaking. Consensual. More importantly, previously she had admitted to warning Charlie of Lauer Ward's arrival, before he was killed, and to twice holding a gun on the maid, who was later killed. In the interview she admitted that she brought Charlie the .22 that he used to shoot Collison. *Three more felony murders.* If needed.

At the institution, which was a series of grim-looking four-story brownstone buildings and a spacious lawn with a few scattered trees, Caril had her own room in the locked receiving section of the main building. It had a bed, sink, toilet, and desk with a lamp. The staff found her quiet, pleasant, and helpful. She volunteered every day to help change beds and clean rooms. But things with Caril weren't as they seemed. In late March, an aide found in her bedside table a letter she had written to her mother. In uneven, crooked handwriting, she wrote in pencil:

Dear Mother:

Please come and sea
me. I am very lonely hear.
Barbara, Bob has been
out to sea me so has
dad I miss Bill and dot.
Please come out and bring
Betty Jean. I want to sea
her. Winnlen has been out
to. But I want to sea
you. Please come out. I am
fine but I want to come
_____. I am afrade to
be alone. Tell daddy I said
___will you come out and

take me home. I don't really
like it hear. Every body is
good to me. But there is
no body my age her just old
people. I wish Billy was
hear. Mother please come
and get me. Or I will come
and get you. I want to be
with you and betty and
daddy to. I know you love me.
But if you really love me
take me away from hear and
take me home with you.
You know how I ____so
I am asking you to come
Please. All the people are
so strang. I don't thank
they like me a all. So please
come as soon as you can.

                            Love Your Daughter
                            Caril Fugate

                            Lincoln State
                            Hospital

CHARLIE SMOKED CONSTANTLY in his cell. He chatted with the two
guards seated outside his cell and watched stories about himself on television. He drew sketches on his sketch pad. One of them was a carica-
ture of Gaughan, whom, along with his parents, he had come to despise.
At his attorney's insistence, Charlie was meeting with six psychiatrists

and psychologists in preparation for an insanity defense, even though he continued to insist that he was sane and that all the killings were in self-defense.

Gaughan took extensive notes of his initial conversations with Charlie, and while some are dated, others are not, and they are not in good order. As was becoming his habit, Charlie would say one thing here and the opposite there. It appears that the first set of notes were taken on February 15. Gaughan writes that Charlie stated that he "screwed the hell" out of Carol King and also "in her behind," and that he "pinched her tit." Elsewhere in the notes, Charlie denies any sexual contact with King and denies sticking anything inside her.

Of considerable interest is Charlie's reference to a black wooden-handled knife. He describes it as around ten inches long and having edges on both sides and says that he sharpened it at the Bartlett house. His prints would be on it, he said, although he hadn't seen it since leaving the Bartlett house. At another point, he seems to indicate that the knife would be on a shelf or on the floor in the Bartlett house. This knife is most likely the same one Caril refers to as her mother's black-handled butcher knife, which was taken from the house. It would also most likely be the knife used in the mutilation of Carol King.

Other Gaughan notes indicate that Charlie stated he stuck his penis in Caril Fugate's anus, and that on the road from the Ward house Caril told him "the maid just wouldn't die." In Charlie's first telling of the Bartlett killings, Caril is not present. When she comes home at 4:00 p.m., he has already killed the parents and the little girl and cleaned up the house. He tells her that her family is away. In the second version, he kills the three family members *after* Caril has come home from school. She is a witness to all three murders. In this telling, he pushed Carol King down the cellar stairs after shooting her and then placed the door on top of the cellar.

In notes dated March 2, Charlie told Gaughan that after killing Jensen and King, he and Caril drove back to Lincoln and the Bartlett home to get Caril's piggy bank, her cosmetic bag, and some oranges and other food but that they passed on by when they saw police cars at the house.

After the Jensen and King killings, Charlie told Caril his oil was low and he needed "some." She responded that he had already had his for the day. Charlie denies stabbing Clara Ward after putting her on the bed and says that he never touched the maid. His odd claims continue: he and Caril approached Jensen's car parked alongside the road, and when they opened the door Jensen and King were having sexual intercourse. At one point, he denies hitting the baby in the head with the rifle; at another he describes the blows to her head in some detail. In all his versions, he never varies from the fact that he shot and killed Carol King. He states again that he pulled her blue jeans and panties down and "inserted his penis into her privates." When he left, she was lying on her back about five steps from the top. On another day, he denies "having intercourse with the King girl." The inconsistencies and contradictions continued on. Attorney Gaughan came to see all this shifting and contradicting positively: he could use it to bolster his insanity defense.

25

THE MEDIA COVERAGE GREW EVEN MORE INTENSE. The local papers, radio, and TV stations covered daily events. Feature stories about the various characters in the saga appeared in the Lincoln and Omaha papers. AP coverage ran nationwide. The networks gave the story play as facts developed and courtroom proceedings got underway. The images of Charlie and Caril on the love seat, of Charlie with his black leather jacket on, of Caril drinking a bottle of pop, of Charlie walking into the courthouse with his famous amused-yet-surly look on his face, seemed everywhere. Other famous cases like the Lindbergh-baby kidnapping and murder or the Rosenberg treason trials had been well told in words and stills. TV brought these people into your home. Into your living room.

Life magazine headlined the story. In its February 10, 1958, issue, which had a photo of actor Ralph Bellamy as FDR on the cover, Charlie was featured as the second article in the table of contents. Over a photo of him as a good-looking young man, the headline demanded: "What Made Charlie Kill?" Inside was a four-page spread with thirty photographs, several of which were appearing for the first time. A few of his paintings were shown, including one of his younger sister, Laveta, whom he supposedly cared for very much. She used to clean his room regularly, and he always offered to pay, but she refused the money. Next to the painting is an attractive photo of Laveta with a gold cross around her neck. As for why Charlie killed, *Life* was only able to quote Reinhardt: "Here was a totally defeated ego which had no satisfactory anchorage in social life. Socially he was an empty man. The only way he could become important was to kill." One popular photo shows Caril sitting on a cot in the Douglas jail, in Clara Ward's red-and-white blouse, a breakfast tray on her lap, eyes looking plaintively upward at her visitor.

Time magazine ran an article on Charlie and Caril on February 10. It discussed Charlie and the killings in the hyper-dramatic fashion of a tabloid detective magazine: "Home again and locked in a special cell at the Nebraska penitentiary, Chuck himself showed signs of realizing that in the end the world had beaten him. He had been gay and insolent earlier; now, in ultimate defeat, he blinked his myopic eyes and became sullen and silent."

On March 23, Harold Robinson submitted his report to the mayor and city council. He had been charged with investigating police activities in regard to the Colvert and Bartlett killings. A thorough, unbiased report would have fueled the outrage over police conduct in investigating the crimes; this one seemed designed to placate the town. The report talks condescendingly about the long view, the medium view, and the short view of policing. In this analysis, the police are seldom, if ever, to blame. In the long view, it is the people in the community who are to blame for any failures because, after all, the police come from and are members of the community and also the community is responsible for funding and setting salaries for cops. The high turnover of officers and the lack of training is the fault of the citizens of Lincoln. (In fact, recruits received no training in Lincoln; they walked a beat for two weeks with another officer and then were given a weapon and their own beat.) Only three officers in Lincoln were assigned to night patrol.

In the medium view, Robinson heaps praise on the police for "clearing" thirteen murders in the prior ten years and two months. Of the thirteen, six were the murders of the Bartletts, the Wards, and Lilyan Fencl. In fact, "clearing" the murders was not the result of anything the Lincoln police did. Five of them were "cleared" when Charlie confessed after his capture in Wyoming by Wyoming lawmen, and the murderer of Lilyan Fencl was never proven. According to Robinson, the Lincoln police were also deserving of praise because they had almost eradicated prostitution in town.

In the short view, which was supposed to be the focus of the report, Robinson cleared the police for failing to identify and arrest Starkweather after the Colvert murder and before the Bartlett murders, a period of fifty-seven days. The police did not connect Charlie to the Colvert murder in any manner until he confessed to it in Wyoming. One excuse was that the police didn't have a mug shot of Charlie to show people who might have identified him. However, Robert McClung, the previous attendant at the Crest Service Station who had known Charlie for seven months but didn't know his name, testified that he told an officer about a man who frequently hung around the station and slept in his car and bummed cigarettes, "a young redhead who had a peculiar walk, as though he had straddled a barrel." While McClung didn't know the name of the redhead, he knew where he worked. The redhead often slept in his car at the station, and he would ask McClung to wake him around 4:30 a.m. so he could run his garbage route, which he worked with his brother. Another employee described to police a redhead who loitered around the station and drove a light blue '49 Ford.

If the cop interviewing McClung had asked him if he knew where the redhead worked or the type of work he performed, McClung would have told him he was a garbage man. There were four garbage companies in Lincoln in 1957. Charlie was working with his brother Rodney at Niederhaus Refuse, where he had worked before. Unless there was more than one short, bowlegged, red-haired garbage man at Niederhaus, a phone call to the company would have surfaced Charlie's name and address in minutes.

McClung also knew that Starkweather had previously worked at Western Newspaper Union and would have told the officers that if asked. A single phone call to the company would also have come up with Charlie's name and address. (Not long after the murder, Charlie stopped by Western Newspaper and joked with his old workmates about having committed the murder. He also kidded that Caril was pregnant.)

Although the lady at the thrift store did not know Charlie's name, she described him as short and having "fiery red hair." Very close to the description McClung gave the deputy. If one cop had read both reports and seen the references to a red-haired man—one who hung around the Crest station and another who came in the store day after the killing and paid the thrift store owner ten dollars in silver—maybe the cop would have focused on redheads and gone back to McClung and asked him if he knew where the redhead worked. But no one made the connection.

When identified, Charlie would immediately have become a prime suspect, and there was plenty of circumstantial evidence pointing to him as the killer. He had been locked out of his room for nonpayment of rent, but on December 2 he paid his landlord his rent in full. He bought clothes at a thrift store on December 2 with roughly ten dollars in coins, and the owner would most likely have been able to identify him. Paper coin wrappers similar to those found at the station were found in Caril's room. Shortly after the murder, Charlie changed the tires on his car, painted it, stripped it of hubcaps, and ripped out the grill. While Charlie did not admit to Caril that he had killed the station attendant, he told her he was present at the murder scene.

The police would most likely have obtained a search warrant for Charlie's room shortly after picking him up. One can only speculate as to what would have been found, but the facts show that Charlie was struggling with Colvert when the first shot was fired, and it would seem possible that, at that range, blood would have splattered on Charlie's clothes and perhaps boots. Similar shotgun shells might also have been found in his room. The coin wrappers that he later gave to Caril might have still been in his room at the time of the search. In fact, given what we know about Charlie's motivation, he might well have confessed on the spot or after a brief interrogation.

Whether or not Charlie would have been arrested and charged with Colvert's murder, it is difficult to imagine that given his status as a prime suspect the events of January 21 to 29 would have played out as they did. If he were not in jail, he would have been under intense investigation and most likely observation. If one of the sheriff's deputies had asked Robert McClung if he knew where the short guy with red hair and the '49 Ford worked, Caril would very likely have finished junior high at Whittier; she might even have continued on to high school and eventually attended a community college to study to become a nurse. In a year or two Bobby Jensen and Carol King might have married and raised a family in Lincoln. In early June, Mike Ward would have flown home from prep school for the summer and been greeted warmly at the airport by his parents. August Meyer and Lilyan Fencl would likely have lived out their lives in peace.

Robinson had the temerity, the arrogance to blame McClung for not offering the information as to where Charlie worked to the officers on his own initiative.

Robinson attributed the failure of the two uniformed police officers who went to the Bartlett house on Saturday night to go inside the house or check the outbuildings to the fact that the officers considered the call a "domestic conflict." There was nothing in Caril's behavior or her explanation that everyone in the house had the flu to arouse their suspicion. As for the detectives who went in through the rear window of the Bartlett house with Pansy Street on Monday morning, January 27, their job that morning, according to Robinson, was mainly to placate Pansy Street. To get her off their backs. There was blood splatter on the walls, on the dresser, and on both sides of the kitchen door frame; a nine-inch sawed-off shotgun barrel sat on the piano; a hacksaw lay on the kitchen counter; a cut of rope lay on a chair; spent 22 shells were scattered about on the floor; boxes of .22 shells and .410 shells sat on the dresser top; the back screen door was missing, and the door frame had recent pry marks. Nonetheless, there was "no cause" for the detectives to investigate further, such as taking a quick—a few minutes at most—look in the outbuildings. The detectives figured the occupants had gone somewhere for a few days, despite the fact that their car was still sitting in the driveway, as it had been for the previous six days. Robinson placed blame for the subsequent murders on Rodney Starkweather, Robert Von Busch, and Guy Starkweather for not alerting the police earlier to Charlie and Caril leaving the Bartlett home.

Assuming that the detectives had checked the outbuildings and found the three bodies by 11:00 a.m., and assuming that the same time elapsed from finding the bodies to the call going out on the police radio describing the car and the occupants as it did later in the day, the call would have gone out at 12:10.

From 10:00 to 1:30 Charlie was in Lincoln, picking up his car, getting gas, changing a tire, picking up wheels, and getting his transmission fixed. At around 1:30 he showed up at Tate's, where he had a tire repaired and went in the café to pick up hamburgers ordered by Caril. So Charlie was in the Lincoln area for roughly two hours after the radio call would have been broadcast. From Tate's he drove about six miles on the highway before turning off for Bennet, when he would have been subject to the eyes of the Safety Patrol. A rough estimate from the time of the radio call to when he turned off the county road on the lane to the Meyer farm would be close to three hours. County, state, and city lawmen would have been on the lookout for a black '49 Ford with its grill and hubcaps missing for these three hours, and given the nature and number of the murders it's safe to assume that the officers would be on heightened alert. And one shouldn't forget that Charlie returned to Tate's at around 5:30, just when the sun was setting, after having killed Meyer. Certainly, well before this time news of the murder and the description of the car and its occupants would have hit the air waves of Lincoln stations KFOR and KLIN as well as the local TV news and possibly a late edition of the *Journal*. While one can't know what would have happened if the detectives had found the bodies at 11:00 in the morning, rather than 4:34 in the afternoon, the odds of capturing Charlie before he killed again would have to have been substantially higher than when the first broadcast hit the police radio at 5:43 p.m., after he had long since left town and murdered August Meyer.

Nonetheless, Robinson found in his report that the police handling of the crimes was adequate and "showed no laxity." He found the actions of the detectives at the Bartlett house before the bodies were discovered to be commendable. He concluded that "fate" was on Charlie's side in the string of murders, and he recommended higher wages for officers and a number of administrative changes.

The mayor declared that the report gave the city a "clean bill of health." Chief Carrol said the report made him happy. As weak and biased as the report was, it served its purpose: to distract the fury of the citizenry from law enforcement and shift it back to the perpetrators of the crimes. Even the press went along with it. From that moment on, the lawmen were essentially blameless.

26

WHILE SCHEELE HAD A GOOD CASE AGAINST CARIL on the felony murder of Robert Jensen, he was convinced, as were most if not all of the lawmen involved, that Caril was herself a murderess. On the morning of February 2, with Scheele's approval, Karnopp asked Caril if she would like to see Charlie. "He's been asking about you every time I meet with him. How about it?" Caril responded that she was "scared to death of him" and never wanted to see him again.

"Well, Starkweather might not believe that if I tell him, so why don't you write to him and tell him you don't want to see him, and I'll give him the note later on," Karnopp suggested. He gave Caril a pencil and piece of paper. She wrote, "Charlie I don't want to see you. I'm afraid of what I might do." Karnopp took the note and gave it to Charlie, for the purpose, some would insist, of turning him against her. In *The Twelfth Victim: The Innocence of Caril Fugate in the Starkweather Murder Rampage*, the authors argue that the note was one reason Charlie changed his story in late February to implicate Caril in the murders.

Charlie wasn't finished. On March 28, he wrote a note addressed to Scheele:

Dear Mr. Scheele:

i'n writing this at ny own free will and well sign it when done. It would take too much paper to tell why i changed my mind of what happen in Caril f part of Killings of Carol King? i Know my folks can tell you why i'n writing this. When i Kill the boy out at the cave by the school house, he drops on the steps and landed on the floor in the cave. the King girl never ran or said anything i told her to stay right were she ws i gone on dowm into the cave and Carol King was standing right where I left her. "i think she was Shock" i went to the car to get a flash light Caril Fugate was sitting in the front and with the .410, i gone down into the cave and was down there about 15 or 25 min. then I got scared and ran and out of the cave and told King to go on down she was about the 2'd step and ran to the car, i ws so dan scared i back into a dichd. we got out of the car to see what happen, i and caril went on back up to the cave and i told carol King to come on up. i gave the .22 cal to caril fugate and told her to watch her, gone on back down to the car and was on the side jacking the car body up, then i heard a shot an ran back to the cave, caril said that King started to run and had to shot her. caril went on to car and got in it. i put the King girl in the cave, on about the 2 or 2 step from the top. the rest is in the statement i gave you. when we got the car out i and caril walk up to the cave and past the door and some boards on the opening of the cave, if there is any details you would like to Know about the King case come out or asked ny folks to asked ne, and i'll tell you. and the nan that got Kill in wyoing, caril and I both shot hin! My writing is a little of a mess, but i hope you can read it.

The statement is so absurd on its face that one must wonder if Charlie meant it to be taken seriously or whether he was intentionally fooling with people's minds for his own amusement. After shooting Jensen and pushing him down the stairs, Charlie went down into the cellar for fifteen or twenty minutes while King, after having watched her boyfriend get shot in the head six times, simply stood at the top of the steps and waited? Charlie got scared of something and ran up the stairs and told King to go down the stairs, which she did, and she stayed there while he tried to get the car out of the ditch? He came back and told King to come back on up and she did? He intended to leave the scene of a murder with a witness still alive? Not exactly his style.

On April 9, Charlie sent another letter to Scheele, and this one was a little more coherent. He didn't mind being convicted of doing something he did, he said, but he'd be damned if he'd go down for something he hadn't done. After shooting Jensen, and pushing him down the cellar, he returned to the car and reloaded the .22. He went down in the cellar to finish Jensen off but became scared and ran out and told King to go into the cellar. He ran to his car and, still scared, tried to back it out of the ditch. Then he and Caril went back to the cellar, and he told King to come out. Caril guarded her while he went back to working on freeing his car. When he heard a shot, he went back, and Caril told him King had tried to run, so she had shot her. He "lifted" King's body and put it in the cellar.

As for the unfortunate shoe salesman, Collison, in Wyoming, Charlie wrote that after he'd shot Collison two or three times, his rifle jammed and he called for Caril to bring the other .22. She brought the rifle, but rather than give the rifle to him, she began shooting Collison herself. When Collison cried about his wife and kids, Caril told him, "That's too damn bad," and she continued to shoot. Charlie noted that "caril fugate was the (most) trigger happy person i ever seen." The press, enthralled by the image of Caril as a trigger-happy young moll, ran with this description.

On May 9, Gaughan would read the April 9 letter aloud to the jury in Charlie's trial. The press blared the charges the next day. His allegation that Caril had killed two people stood essentially unrebutted in the public mind for almost six months until her own trial, at which time it was repeated.

The theory that Caril's note to Charlie angered him to the point where he would accuse her of criminal conduct makes some sense, except that it misses one fact: Charlie still loved Caril. He told Reinhardt this. He wrote it in his memoir. He turned on Caril to ensure that she would join him in the execution of his covenant. Charlie must have figured no jury would send a young girl to death unless she had at least committed murder herself, such as stabbing a maid to death in her bed. (He was undoubtedly right.) On February 7, Charlie had written the following letter to Caril:

Dear Caril:

How are you? "ok, I hope"
They said I cannot see you
till they get done talking to you
so I'm hoping I can see you then
that is if you would want to see me.
You never did let me know
if you hate me. "Well I think i know
but you could tell me" i would
like to know something, that is did
you think i would have killed
you when we got to Washington.
i told you i could not shoot you
if i had to, besides if i was have
done it a long time ago. and one more
thing i would like to know, these
things you were saying when
we were on the road, like when
i ask you if you hate me, and
I think you know what the rest of
these were, was you just giving me
a line or what was you?
the sheriff said i couldn't see you
at this time so i'm writing to you i
would like to know if you would or would not
like to have me write to you. if you don't
want me to write to you i will not do it.
I'm sorry about your mom, dad and little sister
but please believed me I just didn't (i sorry i can't
tell you.) I'm going to write one
letter to you if you want it or not
I'm not going to write it at this time,
but when you read it i think

you will understand about a
lot of things. i hope to get the hot
seat for what i did, and not life
cause i'll do everything i can
to get out of here, one way or
another i'm going to get it.
write back if you will. "please."

    Chuck
    p.s. you know dam well i would
    never shoot you, even if you
    had a gun on me.

This reads more like a forlorn love letter than a hostile missive from a mad, jilted lover. The April letter could also have been a simple taunt to the prosecution. It wouldn't be surprising. Charlie was stage-managing his own ending, and he was enjoying himself. He knew the nature of his exit, and the manner of it didn't bother him. The specifics had been written into the script a long time ago, and he had no fear of them. He confessed to the murders within hours of his arrest, then slowly began to undermine the confessions, sowing confusion and chaos. One day Caril was a hostage and had nothing to do with any of it, the next day she could have left whenever she wanted, the next she was there when he killed her family, the next she killed King, and finally she killed King, her little sister, the shoe salesman, and even, most likely, the maid. He was like a shifting shadow. Who knew what he would say on the stand? Some days he was jaunty and cocksure, with a new hairdo, rattling his chain when he came into court, smiling cockily at the observers. Other days he seemed moody and on edge. Charlie walked from the courtroom one day during his trial and right into the flash camera of a crouched Des Moines photographer. Charlie swung his left hand into the camera, which smacked the photographer in the face and knocked him back against the wall. The next day, at the request of Guy Starkweather, Sheriff Karnopp arranged for Charlie to stop in the hallway and apologize to the photographer. "No hard feelings?" the photographer asked, as the two men shook hands. Charlie nodded, said, "Next time, I'll kick you in the head." Some press played the comment as a jest; others wrote it as a murderer's threat of violence. The picture of the two men shaking hands was centered on the front page of the next day's *Star.* If you're on the way to the chair and you don't give a shit, you're a free man. You can do anything you want and read about it the next day.

Charlie scratched the statement on the wall of the Gering jail about him killing nine people and his girlfriend killing two as if he were a teenager bragging about bowling scores. He added up the murders wrong to make the story even weirder. This guy couldn't even count the dead victims! The tortured syntax, misspellings, change in writing styles, and missing words in the Ward Letter and in his March 29 letter to Scheele nailing Caril as a killer were likely in that manner on purpose and were meant to tease and provoke and confuse. He knew how to write clearly and with better spelling, as shown in his memoir and the letter seeking a job, and even in the aforementioned letter to Caril. He wanted readers to shake their heads and wonder about who he thought he was fooling. He was having fun. Nothing could hurt him. There was only one absolute constant: out of all the things he might be, crazy wasn't one of them.

He even tried giving his memoir a literary touch. His opening paragraph reads:

The sun was out, and the sky was as clear as water, but it was cold and windy on January 27, 1958 at Casper, Wyoming, the day Caril and I Viciously and unlawfully slayed Marle Collison.

On another page he wrote:

. . . warm flooding sunlight, and looking up my neck would ached from the constant strain while my neck would be bent back as I gazed above and between the jagged limbs, and branches of greenish, brown, and yellowish foliage, into the sky of mile, and miles, of undiscover, unknown, previous existence, and the more

I sat and gaze into the far miles of the sky a wave of something
would come over me, something like directness and frankness,
in a fascinating world away from that of non-committed civiliza-
tion, such as a gust of unexpected wind.

Charlie gave Scheele what he wanted in his two letters, not because
he had come to hate Caril, but because he still loved her. He needed her.
To go with him.

27

CARIL'S CASE WOULDN'T BE SET FOR TRIAL UNTIL THE courts had resolved the issue of her transfer to juvenile court, which wouldn't be until summer. Charlie's trial was set for May 5. Until then, the press and the community occupied themselves on puzzling over two questions: Why did Charlie become a killer? And what could have been done to prevent it?

The Lincoln papers searched in vain for something in Charlie's early years that could have or should have tipped off authorities. They found he had gone to Sunday school 122 times from 1944 to 1954 and that he had no record of behavior problems in school with either teachers or counselors, or any contact with juvenile authorities, either formal or informal. How can you prevent something if there are no signs? This became the question. (Charlie would admit to attorney Gaughan in some detail that he and Robert Von Busch in fact stole numerous cars over several years. They took the cars to a friend's garage and stripped them for parts.) You could always point the finger at the family, and one minister sermonized that rather than his father taking his son to the country on Sunday morning to practice shooting, he should have taken him to church. (Guy Starkweather would complain later that he was tired of being blamed for everything. "What could I have done?") But the facts were that Charlie came from a relatively stable home with a working mother and a disabled, alcoholic father and six siblings, none of whom had shown any antisocial tendencies and all of whom Charlie got along with. Although Helen would make a famous statement on the stand that of her seven children, she had six problems and one catastrophe, she later wrote in a letter to the press that she didn't mean it as it sounded. All of her children were unique, and she loved each one of them. Even

Charlie. Charlie wrote in his memoir that he shined his shoes each morning before going to school to please his mother.

The spotlight shifted to the inadequacy of the social systems to deal with juvenile crimes, lack of sufficient guidance counselors in schools and social workers and trained juvenile probation officers, etc. Or perhaps it was the community at large. Lincoln had become a big city, and the small-town collectivity of monitoring and correcting social behavior had evaporated. The disapproval of neighbors or the congregation didn't mean anything anymore.

There was the larger community, the culture, now suffused by decadent elements such as rock and roll, in particular Elvis Presley, street gangs, drag racing on city streets, and a general if not hostile disdain for the social mores of the time. Guys wearing T-shirts with packs of Luckies rolled up in the shoulders, greasy hair brushed back into ducktails, sometimes cut short on the top or with a curl flipped over the forehead, beltless pants hanging low in the back, a hot chick always close by, hanging out at drive-ins or roller rinks. The "tough girls" from the poorer sections of town were part of that scene, but some of the nice middle-class girls were now wearing too-tight sweaters, frequenting the drive-ins, and roaming the streets in their fathers' Oldsmobiles. The school board in Crete, a small town twenty miles west of Lincoln and the home of Doane College, responded to the rising decadence by banning the wearing of sideburns and black leather jackets to high school.

The *Orlando Sentinel* wrote in 1970 that Charlie was the First Antihero, and that he was followed by Mao Tse-tung, Ho Chi Minh, Che Guevara, and Eldridge Cleaver. The writer must have been taken with Charlie's sullen looks and the amount of violence he perpetrated. But while Charlie dressed the role of the alienated, sullen rebel, and looked eerily like the most famous one, James Dean (who was five foot eight), and who smoked constantly, and drag raced his car on city streets and got in fights and had a girlfriend, he wasn't rebelling against the conformity and materialism of the growing middle class, where everyone seemed to look and think and act alike; he wasn't egged on by *Blackboard*

Jungle to bang up against the law. Charlie's unique rage, which showed itself mainly in his fighting—shaking frightfully before he waded in, fists high and cocked, fueled by shame over his physical characteristics and vicious childhood bullying—had mutated into a magnetic fantasy of the outlaw gunning for his last showdown, not to puncture or punish society but simply to walk violently down the path before him and to become more in death than he had ever been in life.

28

ON MAY 5, 1958, CHARLIE CAME TO TRIAL ON TWO first-degree murder charges in the killing of Robert Jensen. Less than three and a half months had passed since he had been charged with the murder, but everyone—the prosecution, the defense, the people of Nebraska, certainly the press, and probably even Charlie himself—was ready for the show to begin. There seemed to be little if any doubt in anyone's mind about the outcome: Charlie had confessed to all eleven murders, hadn't he? Charlie's insistence that he killed only in self-defense was ludicrous, of course. There was no possibility of a guilty plea in exchange for the prosecution taking the death penalty off the table. A prosecutor would say later that the state's only concern was whether the jury would give Charlie death, but if it didn't, they had other charges set up and ready to go. Charlie was going to be convicted, and Charlie was going to die. That was it. It had only to play out properly in the public eye. There would be television coverage every day of his comings and goings, and the papers would run photos and highlights of the testimony. The show ran regularly on the national evening news.

Chet Huntley introduced the story on the NBC evening news: "Nineteen-year-old Charles Starkweather and his fourteen-year-old girlfriend made national headlines. They were responsible for eleven murders in two states." You see how Charlie *and* Caril had become bound into one killer. The entity was "responsible" for eleven deaths. (No one ever linked Caril to Colvert's death.) If that weren't enough, the NBC local affiliate's Floyd Kalber locked it up tighter when in the broadcast he referred to Caril as "Charlie's fourteen-year-old accomplice." Some newspapers weren't quite so obvious; they referred to Caril as Charlie's "companion" or as his "girlfriend" that "accompanied him on the bloody spree."

Kalber told how Gaughan, Charlie's attorney, had handed out to the press a photo of Charlie's pencil scratchings on the jailhouse wall in Gering, the ones that stated, "Charles kills nine, all men, Caril kills two, all girls." Kalber noted that Charlie had his math wrong: there were "six men, four women, and a baby girl." The photo got great play in the press on the day Charlie's trial began. Gaughan was willing to serve Caril up on a platter in his attempt to save his client's life.

Despite Charlie's robust and continuous insistence that he was not crazy and would not plead insanity, Gaughan was proceeding full bore down that path, well aware that it was the only chance to save his client's life. His strategy, as shown in the trial, is questionable but clear: show Charlie as so bloodthirsty and mentally sick and delusional and cruel that the jury has to conclude that he must have been insane when he killed. Proof of such a state of mind would not likely meet the test for legal insanity in Nebraska, yet through that door Gaughan would walk a string of murders for which neither Charlie nor Caril were ever charged. Guy Starkweather, Charlie's father, said Charlie would rather "face the music" than be declared insane. To Gaughan, it didn't matter what Charlie wanted—if he and his associate decided that an insanity plea was best, they would enter it. Which is the first thing he did Monday morning, May 5, over Charlie's disapproving glare. "Innocent by reason of insanity," he told Judge Spencer.

At 9:58 that morning, Charlie arrived at the courthouse in a pink-and-white sheriff's car (deputies drove their own cars, identified by a whip antenna on a rear fender and a portable red light on top). Snipers crouched on rooftops, and six armed deputies guarded the "mass murderer" as he stepped from the car. Several plainclothes cops mingled in a crowd of about fifty people. Wearing a tan suit, white shirt, red tie, and black shoes, his hair trimmed but still with a flip curl in front, cuffed hands chained to a wide leather belt, ten pounds heavier than when he was arrested, Charlie smiled broadly to newsmen as he climbed the steps to the entrance. Behind him a step or two, Karnopp, with a cigarette in his mouth, held on to another chain attached to Charlie's waist belt. A phalanx of armed deputies lined the hallway.

The courthouse was a massive four-story sandstone building with a tall bell tower in the center and turrets on each corner. It sat in a two-block complex a few blocks south of O Street, and behind it on the northwest corner stood the county jail, a two-story whitewashed building that also served as the residence of Sheriff Karnopp and his wife, the jail matron, who received a per diem for cooking for each inmate, a not-uncommon practice in those days. From the courthouse entrance, a set of steps led to the second floor, and a right turn led to Courtroom One, known as the criminal courtroom, the largest in the building. The judge sat high on the bench, looking down at a long, polished wood table at which both counsel for defense and the prosecution sat (and at Charles's trial, either his mother or father most days as well, a highly unusual practice), and behind them, the jury box and the spectator section. The witness chair was next to the judge. The tin ceiling was ten feet high, and from it hung a line of fluorescent lights. The windows were eight feet high. The spectator seating was rows of pew-like wooden benches. The only ventilation was provided by a huge fan at the back of the room. The judge decided when the fan was to be turned on or off and in what direction it was to be pointed. When a hard rain fell, the beating on the windows sometimes grew so loud the proceedings had to be halted. In warm weather, the windows were opened in hopes of a little breeze.

The wooden benches held seventy-two spectators. Seventy-five chairs were added to seat the 147 potential jurors to be called. Well over one hundred news organizations from around the country had filed for accreditation, and the judge set aside an area next to the jury box for them. Officials had set up a press room on the third floor. The room was specially wired for what the reporters called "on-the-spot coverage," meaning live broadcasts, which was a new and big deal.

During jury selection, Charlie was described as looking bored, chewing gum, and glancing casually about as if he were at a community gathering. He sat at the counsel table with his two attorneys and his mother. At a table behind him sat Karnopp and a deputy. The selection process, designed to obtain twelve fair and unbiased jurors, was tedious because a good many of the jurors were well versed in the facts of the case from their endless repetition in the press. Eighty prospective jurors were interviewed, and half were eliminated because they admitted they would not be able to dismiss their biases or opinions about Charlie's guilt or innocence.

The *Star* printed the photographs, addresses, and employment of the final twelve jurors: four housewives; employees of a hospital, a railroad, a bookstore, a rubber plant, and a department store; and a carpenter, salesman, and electronic specialist. Spectators were seated for opening statements. There would be no cameras, and the court made it clear there was no saving of seats; if you left during the hearing, the next person outside got your seat. There was a stirring in the courtroom when Charlie entered and had his cuffs removed at the counsel table, required before the jury came in the courtroom to avoid the implication of guilt cuffs might suggest. The six armed deputies lining the walls would seem to raise the same implication. One deputy said they weren't as worried about what Charlie would do but rather that "somebody would try to get to him."

The attorneys gave opening statements on May 8. In his opening, Scheele told a relatively simple story of the killing of Bobby Jensen. After working in his father's store until about 6:00 p.m., Jensen stopped by a gas station, filled the car with gas, and ordered four retreads. After dinner, he left to pick up Carol, telling his folks they would be home early, and the two went for a ride.

Scheele continued that nineteen-year-old Charlie Starkweather and fourteen-year-old Caril Ann Fugate, who had been going together for more than a year, had left Caril's parents' house about midday, carrying a .32-caliber pistol, a .410 shotgun, and a hunting knife, all wrapped in a blanket. They stopped at a gas station and bought shells for the .410 and a .22. They drove to the farm of August Meyer, near Bennet, but got stuck in his drive. Starkweather took the rifle (he had picked up in the Meyer house), Caril held the .410, and they began walking down the road to Bennet. Jensen and King pulled over in his 1949 Ford and asked if they needed help. Starkweather said they needed a ride into town. Jensen said he would take the guns, but Caril Fugate told them not to worry because the guns weren't loaded. Starkweather told Jensen to drive to the storm cellar. On the way, Starkweather told Jensen to take his wallet out and give it to Caril. Caril took the money from Jensen's wallet and put it in Starkweather's billfold. At the storm cellar, Starkweather ordered Jensen out of his car and down into the cave. As Jensen was descending the steps, Starkweather shot him six times in the back of the head with the .22. All six shots penetrated the skull within a four-inch diameter.

Scheele was careful not to mention the killings of Meyer, King, or the other victims. He also instructed the jury that Starkweather was presumed sane. He did not say whether he would be asking for the death penalty.

In his opening, Gaughan told the jury that this case was not about *who* shot Jensen but *why* that person shot him. Charlie would take the stand and tell you he shot Jensen in self-defense, but the defense was actually insanity. The defendant was delusional at the time of the killing; it was a diseased or defective mind he was either born with or acquired. Little things were more important to him than big things, such as his desire to wear his favorite cowboy boots to court as opposed to his utter lack of concern that he was on trial for his life. He'd suffered an injury to the head a few years earlier and was subject to severe headaches. He was so opposed to the allegation of insanity that he would not let doctors run tests to see if there was any brain damage. His client was not the brightest boy in the world. In fact, Charlie was of subnormal intelligence. He moved from second grade to fourth grade without actually passing. IQ tests showed that he was one step above idiocy. "Now, I'm not claiming he's an idiot. The defense will be insanity."

During Scheele's opening, Charlie chewed gum and rocked back and forth on the back legs of his chair, seemingly following the prosecuting attorney with interest. When Gaughan spoke, however, Charlie bit his lips and grasped the edge of the table. To one reporter, it looked like the defendant was going to come up out of his chair and jump his attorney. Another wrote that the flush in Charlie's face as he left the courtroom after Gaughan's opening matched his red hair. His mother, who sobbed quietly during the description of the killing, was also visibly upset by Gaughan's description of her son.

The first witnesses would be called the next morning.

29

I N A MURDER CASE, IT IS A COMMON PRACTICE FOR THE
prosecution to begin with a description of the murdered person.
Bring the person alive for the jury, let the jury see him, feel him,
before the defendant kills him. On May 9, Scheele began with Robert
Jensen Sr., Bobby's father, who described his son as an all-American
small-town boy, a kindhearted, God-fearing youth who played high
school football until his childhood polio brought him down. Having
to wipe his eyes frequently, Mr. Jensen told of the evening of January
27, when his son didn't return home from his date with Carol King.
How they went looking for him through the night and attended his and
Carol's funeral a few days later. He identified his son's watch and wallet
and high school jacket. Bobby's photo was passed among the jury.

Although Carol King was not a victim in this case, Scheele brought
her alive as well. Warren King, Carol's brother, described his sister as
a very bright student—always at the top of her class—a well-rounded
Christian girl who was a cheerleader and volleyball player and member
of the church choir and Youth Fellowship. She did not plan to go out that
evening because she had a very bad cold. And then Robert called around
7:30 and said he had something he wanted to talk to her about.

Having set up the killing, for the next several days Scheele wired
into place all the small necessary pieces of the story: the attendant and
owner of the gas station in Bennet; the engineer who described the lay-
out of the roads around the storm cellar and Meyer's farm; the photographer who took aerials of the area; the man who found the discarded
schoolbooks along the highway; Homer Tate, owner of the gas station
on Highway 77 where Charlie and Caril stopped twice on January 27; an
employee at Tate's; the farmer who pulled the 1949 Ford out of the ditch;
the Bennet resident who spotted Charlie's car in the field; the farmer

who discovered the bodies in the storm cellar; the state trooper who identified the schoolbooks and Charlie's car; the state trooper who took photos of the Meyer farm and the cellar and the Ward residence; the pathologist who performed the autopsy on Robert Jensen; the deputy sheriff who took photos of the crime scene and Jensen's body; the deputy sheriffs and state patrolmen who found cartridge shells at the scene. On and on it went. Even with the windows open, the unair-conditioned courtroom was stifling by noon. The jurors were fanning themselves. The men in the courtroom, with the exception of the attorneys and the defendant, removed their jackets.

The only controversial testimony came from Deputy Sheriff Romer, who testified that when Caril jumped in his car on the Wyoming highway, she told him she was a hostage and she did not scream that Charlie was crazy. Sheriff Heflin testified that in the police car after his capture, Starkweather told him to go easy on the girl because she "had nothing to do with it." Sitting in the audience, listening intently, taking mental notes, was John McArthur, Caril's attorney, anticipating the day he and his client would be onstage.

Cross-examining Heflin, Gaughan began his bizarre attack on his own client to demonstrate his insanity. First, he got Heflin to repeat several times that while he was in the Douglas jail, Starkweather showed no remorse for his heinous criminal acts. He then introduced through Heflin the Ward Letter, in which Charlie admits to killing the Bartletts and in which Gaughan said that Caril supposedly wrote, "Betty Jean was yelling so loud I hit her with the gun about ten times."

The extra-large headline on the front page of the *Star* the next morning shouted: 'CARIL BEAT BABY'—LETTER.

A sub headline in only slightly smaller letters read: "Note Blames Girl In Fatally Clubbing Sister."

The press was shocked: the defense attorney was convicting his client of crimes he wasn't even charged with, and he was busting Caril for murdering her little sister. (The paper failed to mention that of Charlie's ten statements, this was the only one in which he blamed Caril for her sister's death.) In the gallery, McArthur was surprised, if not shocked himself. He had never seen the letter and was sure Caril wasn't aware of it either. Gaughan also introduced into evidence the "Letter to the Parents," which Charlie wrote the night of his capture. Both letters were read aloud to the jury. Look at what he did, he seemed to be saying; be repelled, be repulsed by him, and then ask yourself if such a person could possibly be sane.

To close out the prosecution's case, Scheele read aloud to the jury in a long drone those portions of Charlie's typed confessions relating to the murder of Bobby Jensen, in which Charlie admits pumping bullets into Jensen until he twisted around several times and fell down the steps into the cellar.

The bailiff hustled over several times with a small paper cup of water for Scheele during his reading. When the outside racket grew too loud, the calm, methodical county attorney paused and waited for the noise to recede.

30

ON MAY 14, THE TIME HAD COME FOR THE DEFENSE. Gaughan needed to raise a reasonable inference that his client was insane at the time he murdered Jensen. Once the reasonable inference was raised, the burden shifted to the prosecution to prove the defendant was sane. For determining sanity, Nebraska adopted what is commonly referred to as the McNaughton rule. In 1843, a man named McNaughton attempted to kill British prime minister Robert Peel but instead shot and killed his secretary, Edward Drummond. Doctors testified that McNaughton was psychotic at the time of the act, and he was acquitted on the grounds of insanity. The acquittal caused a sensation, and the House of Lords in England directed the Lords of Justice of the Queen's Bench to fashion a rule for the insanity defense. The Lords of Justice declared that

> The jurors ought to be told in all cases that every man is to be presumed to be sane, and . . . to establish a defence on the ground of insanity, it must be clearly proved that, as the time of the committing of the act, the party accused was laboring under such a defect of reason, from disease of the mind, as not to know the nature and quality of the act he was doing; or, if he did know it, that he did not know that what he was doing was wrong.

Under this rule, the defendant is declared legally insane either if he did not know the nature or quality of his act or if he did know the nature and quality of his act but did not know that his act was wrong. In an oversimplification, the first element could refer to a man with schizophrenia who was so delusional at the time he cut a person's head off that he did not realize he was in fact cutting a head off, and the second element could be met if the man understood that he was cutting a head off but did not realize that cutting a head off was wrong. The challenge is to point to some defect or disease of the mind to demonstrate either of the two elements. Gaughan would try to prove that Charlie suffered from a defect of the mind that left him delusional at the time of the murders. To establish this, he would call two psychiatrists and one psychologist to testify and present evidence showing that (1) Charlie believed all the killings were in self-defense, (2) he showed no remorse after any of the killings, (3) he often imagined things that weren't true, (4) he had headaches from brain damage from getting whacked in the head by a baler, (5) he wasn't very smart to begin with, and (6) only a crazy person could commit a string of such terrible crimes.

All of which was pretty thin gruel for a finding of a mental defect or disease that would leave Charlie so delusional he either wouldn't know he was killing Jensen when he shot him six times in the head or wouldn't know that it was wrong to shoot him six times in the head.

Gaughan told reporters he would put his client on the stand, even though he had no idea what he would say, hoping, apparently, whatever he said would further the case of insanity. Gaughan had been battling not only with Charlie but with his parents as well, neither of whom liked Gaughan or the insanity defense. Guy Starkweather had been encouraging family members not to speak with the attorney or his associate. The Starkweathers apparently didn't want the family name stained by an insanity claim. For Charlie, his life would come to a pointless, miserable end if he were found insane or crazy.

Gaughan needed to clear away more underbrush. An optometrist testified that in 1954 he examined Charlie and found him to be myopic with 20/200 vision, which meant at twenty feet he could see what someone with normal vision could see at two hundred feet. He corrected him to 20/30 distance vision, almost normal. The owner of the Western Newspaper Union, where Charlie had worked from 1955 to 1957, testified that Charlie was the "dumbest" employee he'd ever had and that in fact he was "retarded." Other employees were nice to him because he was "weak-minded." But he could do the work and he did as he was told. A manager testified to an incident in January 1957 in which Charlie was hit in the head with the handle of a bailing machine, which required three stitches over his left eye. One employee testified that at various times after he quit work, Charlie had come to the building and remarked that he and Caril were married or that Caril was pregnant. Mrs. Rose Griggs, whose daughter Barbara was married to Rodney Starkweather, testified about Charlie dropping his car off at her house on January 21, picking it up with Caril at about 10:30 on the morning of January 27, and dropping off Rodney's .22 on Saturday the twenty-fifth. Reporter Del Harding testified that when he called Deputy Romer the night of the capture, Romer told him that when Caril came running to the car, she screamed, "Charlie is crazy. He's going to kill me." Eight friends and associates of Charlie were called to the stand to testify that Charlie had been having headaches but that he had not acted unusual or shown any remorse after December 1, 1957, the point of which was to suggest that Charlie's lack of remorse after killing Robert Colvert showed that he was insane.

Older brother Rodney Starkweather testified that Charlie had been fired from his job as a garbage collector because he caused too much trouble with customers and other drivers. He also said that Charlie complained of having headaches once or twice a week and liked to make things up, like saying he had a chrome-plated motor for his Model A.

Gaughan came up well short in his attempt to show Charlie was of subnormal intelligence. Public schools guidance-director Jules Humann testified that the only intelligence test given to Charlie by a psychologist showed he had an IQ of 91. An average IQ is between 90 and 110. Further, Charlie had scored 100 on reasoning ability and 84 on verbal skills, indicating, among other things, that he could think things through and see consequences. Humann testified that Charlie repeated third grade because of low grades. His grades remained poor the second year, and he was put on "special adjustment" in fourth grade. At Irving, he was promoted from sixth to seventh grade; his grades there were low but sufficient to pass from seventh to eighth. He transferred to Everett for ninth grade and was placed in a room for "slow learners." He competed ninth grade, although ranking in the bottom quartile. His odds of completing high school, had he attempted—he did later take one night class at Lincoln High—would have been slim. His "citizenship," or behavior, was satisfactory in all grades. He was never reported to the central office. In sum, Charlie's intelligence came in as "dull normal"; his behavior, on the surface anyway, wasn't that much different than a lot of Lincoln boys who preferred cars and girls to school.

The next day, May 15, the word was out that Charlie himself was going to testify and that his confessions were going to be read into the record. In the hopes of proving him insane, Gaughan was going to seal him up tight as Nebraska's first mass murderer.

First, Robert Von Busch, Charlie's buddy for four or five years before he married Caril's sister and who was a fighter himself, took the stand to testify that Charlie regularly got in fights after he transferred to Everett. Charlie also imagined things that never happened, like he had dates with girls he didn't have, or that his aunt was dead when she wasn't, or that he lived in Texas as a cowboy or sheriff. He did some strange things, like laughing loud at Von Busch's mother's funeral, or trying to get his brother to date Caril after he broke up with her, or asking the same question a dozen times. One thing about Charlie: If someone wanted trouble, and even if they didn't, he would give it to them. He had an explosive temper.

In the Ward Letter and the Douglas Jail Confession, Charlie tried to lay some blame for the murders on Von Busch because he and Caril's sister tried to break the couple up so a friend of Bob's could date Caril. Von Busch only hinted at this motive in his testimony.

Helen Starkweather, small and frail, red-haired like her son, wearing a brown cardigan over a blue dress, unsteadily took the stand. Charlie, wearing a lightweight, open-collar summer shirt, put his elbows on his knees, dropped his head in his hands, and stared at the floor during the entire forty minutes of his mother's testimony. She said in a low voice, which broke occasionally, that although Charlie might have had something wrong with him at the time of the killings, he didn't now, and it was wrong for the attorneys to try to prove that he did. In her view, the lawyers should have first claimed self-defense and then insanity as a secondary defense. She told how Charlie had severe headaches after the baler accident. When asked if there was anything she would like to add, she said that Charlie was a different boy after he met Caril. "Just after he went with Caril, his family was pushed behind and his life centered around her. She seemed to have a hold on him." Charlie had told her he was sorry for what he'd done. He was good at covering up most of his true feelings, except anger.

When Gaughan asked her if it was true Charlie wasn't the brightest boy in the world, she objected and said it was a hard question to ask a mother about her son. Gaughan backed off. After her testimony, she told a reporter, "I know I shouldn't say this, but I want to thank Mr. Scheele from my heart for showing that Charlie isn't all that bad." She later came clean in a comment to a psychiatrist: she would rather Charlie be executed than "locked up in some insane asylum where they could never see him."

Charlie followed his mother to the stand. He threw the world a change-up pitch: it came in slow and outside. Gone was the half smile, the cocky attitude. Instead, the young man appeared calm and unruffled. He sat relaxed on the stand with his legs crossed and answered questions softly and succinctly. "Yes, sir." "No, sir." Without his rimless bifocals, he had to squint at his questioners. His mother smiled at him from the table, but it was unlikely he could see her well. He told how his schoolwork was not very good because he didn't listen to the teacher half the time and he couldn't make out the blackboard the other half. Yes, he began fighting at school. The fights increased to one every two or three weeks, and by the time he reached junior high it was almost one a day. He told about getting smacked in the head by a two-by-four while working on a farm as a boy and getting hit in the head again by the baler about a year and a half earlier. About his headaches, he would say only that he had them about every other day and they could last half a day and be quite painful. A little lightness fell on the scene when Gaughan asked him:

"Do you trust anybody in this world beside your mother, Charlie?"

"A little bit."

"Well, I think you trust me a little bit now, don't you?"

"No."

Charlie identified the April 9 letter he had written to Scheele. Gaughan asked him why he killed all the people, and Charlie replied, "The ones I killed? Self-defense." If they hadn't threatened his life, they would all be alive. All of them. With that, Gaughan suddenly concluded the questioning, leading one reporter to wonder what the point of it was. Apparently, the point of it was to get the April 9 letter into evidence and before the jury. On redirect, Gaughan asked him about a statement he made in the letter about being mad at Caril at the storm cellar:

"What were you mad about, Charlie?"

"What she did."

"What is that? And what did she do there?"

"She shot Carol King."

"She shot Carol King?"

"Yes, sir."

Gaughan then completed the prosecutor's work by reading the April 9 letter to the jury. A casual observer might easily conclude that the person on trial that day was not Charles Starkweather but rather Caril Ann Fugate.

Gaughan called to the stand Robert McClung, the gas station attendant who had befriended Charlie over several months but never learned his name and who had the good fortune to quit a few weeks before December 1. McClung allowed Charlie to sleep in his car at the station because he felt sorry for him. He woke him at 4:30 so he could make it to the garbage route, which he worked with his brother. Charlie had big plans to build a fancy hot rod, but he had to borrow a quarter for a pack of cigarettes, and his conversation was pretty much limited to cars and racing at Capitol Beach, although he told him one night about a fight he'd had with his father that he seemed quite upset about. McClung saw Charlie as someone who needed a little help in life, a decent job. In a much-quoted statement, he described Charlie as "self-schooled on comic books and living in a shell."

Gaughan decided to offer into evidence Charlie's five-volume February 1 confessions to the murders. Scheele, in an abundance of caution, objected to the confessions as irrelevant. Gaughan replied only that "These are all part of one simulated act and that the jury should know the whole facts." The exhibits were received into evidence, and Gaughan proceeded to read all 376 pages of them into the record. During the recitation, Charlie slept for two hours with his chin on his chest. Court was recessed halfway through until the next morning.

ON MAY 16, the shock of the allegation that Caril had killed Carol King led the news. Although the defendant had taken the stand and confessed to the crimes with which he was charged, as well as several others, the headlines were about the April 9 letter and Caril:

CARIL KILLED TEENAGE GIRL the bold headline read in the *Sioux City Journal* over an AP story. The sub headline read: "'Most Trigger Happy Person He Ever Saw' Starkweather asserts."

The *Star* headlined that Charlie had testified and claimed the killings were self-defense, but the sub headline read: "New Letter Says King Girl Killed by Caril Fugate."

The *Lincoln Journal* ran with the headline "Starkweather Insists He Didn't Kill Miss Fencl." The clear implication being if he didn't kill her, who did?

Perhaps the most sensational and irresponsible reporting was done by the UPI. Under the headline "Starkweather Claims Girl Killed Woman," the article, relying solely on Charlie's statement in his February 27 confession that he hadn't stabbed the maid and that he had sent Caril upstairs to get the knife stuck in Mrs. Ward, led with: "Caril Fugate, 14, knifed a woman to death as she lay on a bed with her hands and feet tied to a bed post, a confession read at Charles Starkweather's murder trial indicated today."

John McArthur gave his take on his client's former boyfriend: "I think Charles Starkweather will do anything to increase the spectacular character of this trial. This appears to be the high point of his life and he's really enjoying it."

Guy Starkweather was referred to by some in the press as a dandy; he showed up one day in a gray suit, red tie, and a new black ten-gallon cowboy hat, cocked a little off to the side. He was usually amenable to answering questions. But he had been dodging the sheriff's subpoena for two days, before a deputy finally found him at home the previous night at 11:40. On the stand, he told about the fight he and Charlie had about Caril Fugate driving the car in which the two of them slapped each other and Charlie fell through the window. About the crime spree, he could say only that Charlie had become a different boy after he met Caril Fugate. His son got stubborn and told him he was tired of being told what do.

"Do you think your son is crazy, Mr. Starkweather?" Gaughan asked him.

"He had never done anything to act crazy to me."

He did admit, however, that during the crime spree he was worried Charlie might end up coming back to shoot him.

And yes, his son knew the difference between right and wrong, and yes, he knew what he was doing when he did things. The killings were a matter of bad judgment.

The court recessed until 9:00 a.m. Monday morning. The only witnesses remaining were the six psychiatrists, three for the prosecution and three for the defense.

31

MAY 19 SAW THE BATTLE OF THE PSYCHIATRISTS. Matschullat had trouble finding psychologists or psychiatrists in Lincoln who would testify for the defense. The Menninger Clinic in Kansas City, often referred to as the Mayo Clinic of psychiatric hospitals, said they would love to evaluate Charlie, but they would need him in residence for at least two weeks, which was an absurd notion. There was no way the state of Nebraska was letting go of Charlie Starkweather for an hour, much less two weeks. However, Matschullat finally found his experts.

Clinical psychologist Nathan Greenbaum and psychiatrist John O'Hearne, both from Kansas City, interviewed Charlie together for eight hours in April. Greenbaum also interviewed Charlie the night before his testimony for two hours. Greenbaum came right to the point in his testimony: Charles Starkweather suffered "from a severe mental illness of such a kind as has influenced his acts and has prevented him from using the knowledge of right and wrong at the time of the commission of the act." He was suffering from a "severe warping of the emotional faculties which leaves him unable to experience feelings the way other people do." In fact, he was devoid of basic feelings toward other people. "People do not mean anything to him. A person is no more than a stick, a piece of wood to this boy. And this is one of the symptoms of a very serious disease of the mind."

Another element showing a sickness or defect in Charlie's mind was his lack of capacity for control. In normal people, there is a space between the desire to act and the act, a pause for reflection on the consequences. Charlie's mind short-circuited this process. "The moment the impulse comes upon him, he acts immediately. He is unable to stop." Thus, he would not be able to premeditate a crime, such as robbing or shooting Robert Jensen. This lack of impulse makes Charlie exceedingly dangerous and violent, and had Greenbaum examined Charlie six months prior to the spree, he would have detected it and sought to have him committed to an institution.

When asked about the possible cause of such a mental illness, the doctor essentially pleaded ignorance. They can diagnose such conditions, but as far as the cause of them they simply didn't know. Charlie could have been born with the condition. "We simply don't know enough about what the causes are." Essentially, Charlie was like a primitive animal whose appearance of domestication is only a thin crust, and once the creature "tastes blood, it breaks through and a wild rampage occurs or a primitive impulse comes back." Charlie, in other words, had a "primitive mind." A human life meant much less to him than his automobile.

Psychiatrist John O'Hearne found that Charlie suffered from a mental illness that prevented him from feeling like an ordinary person. Charlie was not capable of premediating the murder or robbery of Robert Jensen. The stress was simply too much, it flooded in on him, and he couldn't feel like a normal human being. He was a frightened animal trying to escape. "I don't think he has ever become a human being. Yes, he walks around in the body of a human being, but the thoughts and feelings are not there like they are in an ordinary person...I don't think he has ever learned to be a person." Thus, Charlie would not know that killing Robert Jensen was wrong before he did it, and neither did he have the ability to control his actions. "Pumping bullets into a human body makes not much more difference to him than pumping them into a rabbit." Once, when O'Hearne had mentioned the murder charge and his possible death, Charlie simply laughed.

ON TUESDAY, MAY 20, the last of the defense expert witnesses to testify was Dr. John Steinman, a Lincoln psychiatrist. His opinion was similar to that of the first two doctors. Starkweather had a diseased or sick mind, in part based on the finding that he goes from impulse to action without any deliberative process. Some people, like Hamlet, deliberate too much and are indecisive and unable to act. Others, like Starkweather, are short-circuited and proceed immediately from impulse to action. The short-circuit is the disease of the mind. Starkweather's ability to evaluate the consequences of an act of violence was nonexistent in moments of stress. When he shot Jensen, he did not have the degree of reasoning necessary to realize that it was the wrong thing to do.

With that, the burden shifted to the prosecutor to prove that Charlie was sane. Scheele's first witness was Charles Munson, a clinical psychologist who worked at the Lincoln State Hospital. He interviewed Charlie at the penitentiary on five separate occasions, during which he administered eight different tests. None of them revealed any brain damage. In fact, Charlie scored 110 on the Wechsler Adult Intelligence Scale, which is the high end of normal or average. Based on the tests and interview, he determined that Charlie was not psychotic and was legally sane on January 27 when he robbed and killed Jensen.

Dr. Edwin Coats, a neuropsychiatrist and assistant superintendent at the hospital, examined Charlie and found no evidence of brain damage or that he suffered delusions or hallucinations. He found Charlie to be "a cooperative, pleasant young man" who "readily admitted to the crimes with which he was charged." He was "well-oriented" and showed no hostility toward him or others. He was, however, "immature." His intelligence was slightly above average, but his judgment was poor. And he still had the remnants of a slight speech defect. Coats found him to be legally sane on January 27, 1958. He knew the difference between right and wrong, and he knew what he had done was wrong. Charlie was, in his view, suffering from an antisocial sociopathic disorder. He did not have a diseased or defective mind. In fact, a person who cooperates with doctors seeking to have him found sane and being hostile to those declaring him insane and who wants to be executed for his crimes so he can be a hero is in and of itself indicative of a sociopathic personality disorder. Not insanity.

The last to opine on Charlie's sanity was Dr. Robert Stein, a highly respected Lincoln psychiatrist. He agreed with the other two prosecution witnesses that Charlie did not show any evidence of a brain disease or psychosis. His conclusion was that "Charles had a personality disorder characterized by emotional instability, considerable emotional insecurity, and impulsiveness that would fit into an antisocial personality disorder." He was legally sane. He knew the difference between right and wrong and knew what he had done when he killed Robert Jensen. He was totally capable of premeditating and planning the murder and robbery of Jensen. In response to specific questions regarding Charlie's IQ, Dr. Stein excluded Charlie from being an "idiot," which has a range from 25 on down, or an "imbecile," which has a range from 25 to 50, or a "moron," which has a range from 50 to 70, or a "borderline," which has a range from 70 to 90. The only ranges higher than Charlie's were "superior" and "genius." He noted that Charlie had considerable feeling and affection for his mother and that he swore he would never use the vulgar language or have such negative feelings as Caril Fugate used and showed in front of her mother. Dr. Stein found Charlie to be a cooperative, friendly, and cheerful young man.

During much of the testimony, Charlie appeared to be staring at his feet. He would straighten up and flip through the pages of a textbook entitled *Manual of Psychiatric Case Study*. His mother, complaining of a headache, left the courtroom during the afternoon recess and did not return. At one point, Charlie bet Dr. Steinman a pack of cigarettes that he would "get the battery charge," meaning the chair. When he suggested to Gaughan that "Scheele is trying to burn me," Gaughan responded in amazement, "You're just realizing that?"

The evidence was finally in. Everyone was exhausted from the tedious, verbose testimony of the mental-health guys. Hours filled with words like *monomania, neurological damage, brain lobes, paranoia*, and *hypothalamus* had thickened the warm air until it was hard to breathe. Now, after two and a half weeks, the script had wound out; the parts had been well played; the final scene was waiting in the wings. Tomorrow morning the lawyers would tell the jurors what to make of it, and then the judge would tell the jurors how to think about it.

—

AT 9:00 A.M. on Thursday, May 22, Fahrnbruch opened the closing statement for the prosecution by reciting the evidence on the robbing and killing of Robert Jensen. In turn, Matschullat stressed that the evidence and expert testimony showed that Charlie was not responsible for his actions. He quoted several times from the Bible, causing Starkweather to wisecrack after the lawyer sat down, "You would make a good preacher." Gaughan gave an impassioned speech for Charlie's life, comparing his own early years with that of the defendant, striding back and forth, voice breaking, insisting that "But for the grace of God I could have been sitting in that chair." They need not worry about the defendant ever getting loose on society again because "Even an act of Congress will not take him out of there [the mental hospital]. The society that has spawned this young lad has set up rules for the insane." He described the electrocution process if the jury sentenced him to death, and, his face stained with tears, his voice shaking, he said, "Ladies and gentlemen, I ask you for the life of Charles Starkweather."

Scheele told the jury he could deliver an emotional appeal as well if he chose to, and he held up the photos of the bodies of Robert Jensen and Carol King, and he mentioned what he had seen on the August Meyer farm and in the chicken coop and outhouse in the Bartlett backyard. The facts were the facts, and Charlie had confessed to both charges. Don't be hoodwinked by the insanity plea, he urged; while Charlie wasn't normal, the doctors said he was legally sane. Scheele told the jury that for the first time in his four years in office, he was asking for the death penalty. It was necessary in this case to ensure that Starkweather was never released on society again.

Judge Spencer instructed the jury on the law. They had a range of options: on each charge, they could find Starkweather guilty of first-degree murder (premeditated and with malice aforethought) and sentence him to death or life in prison; or they could find him guilty of second-degree murder (without premeditation); or they could find him guilty of manslaughter (negligent homicide); or they could find him innocent; or they could find him innocent by reason of insanity.

The jury deliberated for close to three hours before retiring to the

Lincoln Hotel for the night. The next morning the jury deliberated for five and a half hours before signaling a verdict. The attorneys and families were notified, and Charlie was brought from the jail to a packed courtroom.

Charlie was usually escorted from the pen to the courthouse in the sheriff's car followed by two patrol cars. Ten police officers met the caravan when it arrived. When he left, Charlie always exited the courthouse through the north entrance. But on this day, a restless crowd had gathered at the courthouse early, and Karnopp was worried about its reaction if Charlie was not convicted and sentenced to death. His plan was that if anything short of death was handed down, he would walk Charlie out the basement door on the south side of the building. The officers would stand in their regular positions to avert suspicion.

In a white shirt with cuffs rolled up, gray slacks, and hair trimmed but brushed up and over, Charlie sat slouched in his chair as the foreman handed the verdict to the clerk. He looked at the floor as the clerk read: Guilty on both counts of first-degree murder. Sentence: death.

The jury had deliberated for six hours and twenty minutes. The first vote had been twelve to zero to reject the insanity defense, which left the penalty. The next vote was nine to three in favor of death, two women and one man holding out for life. The third vote was eleven to one for death. By 2:30, the vote for death was unanimous.

After the verdict was read, Charlie yawned, said something to his attorney, and smiled back at his buddy Sheriff Karnopp. He looked anxiously at his mother as she fled into the judge's chambers. Her sobs could be heard in the hallway for close to half an hour. His father, asked later for his reaction, said only, "The Lord giveth and the Lord taketh away."

The wires, radio, and television stations had the conviction and penalty on the air within minutes of the verdict. The *Journal* beat the *Star* and the *World Herald* with an extra edition late that afternoon. Papers all over the country and around the world carried the AP version on the front page the next morning. One photograph showed Charlie being led on the chain by Karnopp to the sheriff's car, a cigarette dangling just left of center in his mouth, lips slightly open, past a gathering of spectators, mainly young men, several with their shirt sleeves rolled up, to Karnopp's Oldsmobile. Charlie was looking down at two boys no older than six or seven, who were looking up at him in awe.

"I presume Charlie got what he wanted," Gaughan told one reporter. Another asked him if Charlie was going to testify in Caril's trial. "That's up to Charlie," he said. "Some days he insists Caril is going down with him, and other days he says he will not testify against the girl." He opined that he thought the prosecution had an open-and-shut case against her without Charlie's testimony, based solely on her 166-page statement.

In the hallway, Charlie commented to reporters, "Yes, that verdict was fair. I don't think they tried me for Jensen. They tried me for the whole thing." As for why he didn't fight harder, he said, "If I want to make my atonement with God by being electrocuted, that's my business."

Leaving the courthouse after the verdict, Guy Starkweather was heard suggesting to his wife and Rodney, "We ought to go someplace and eat a big, fat steak."

32

ONE DOWN AND ONE TO GO. THERE WAS A BRIEF moment of intense relief in Lincoln and the entire state that Charlie Starkweather was going to die in the electric chair. It didn't undo the trauma, but at least it showed that Lincoln could do what needed to be done, whether you called it revenge or justice or something else. There was remaining business, of course. Lincoln would overwhelmingly agree with Warren King, Carol King's brother, when he said that from the family's perspective, the story was far from over. Caril Fugate must still come to trial. According to the UPI, Warren said, "And we all feel in the back of our mind that she killed Carol."

All eyes turned to the Nebraska Supreme Court. Oral arguments were scheduled for June 6 on the question of whether Caril would stay in district court and be tried as an adult, where she too could receive the death penalty, or whether she would be transferred to juvenile court, where the maximum sentence was seven years, until her twenty-first birthday.

Charlie had indeed got what he wanted. An image of him strapped in the electric chair would be the perfect ending to his story. He had done what he could to not suffer death alone. "She shot Carol King," he said loud enough for the world to hear. She was "trigger happy."

And he was not done screwing with the head of the society that had trashed him so badly. He found God. In a Bible-study book, he wrote a note to his younger brother Greg:

> Thank you for letting me read your book there's a lot of pictures in it and it's a very nice book. But when you get older read the Bible it tells more about the Lord from the frist of his life to the end of his life but do not think there is an end in the life of the Lord because there is no end, he is all the way alive! to help you.

Read the Bible for me if you would. i know there is a lot of dry stuff in it. but it's the care of all Religion but there's a lot of everyday wisdom in it to, and I think you will like it. and do this for me to, be nice to Mom and Dad. Did all you can to help your mother. OK

Your brother,
Charles

The note was in Charlie's handwriting and dated March 9, although the press did not get it until the day of the conviction. Charlie would make similar comments to criminologist Reinhardt, who, along with everyone else, declined to take them seriously. Reinhardt quoted him as complaining, "Jesus wouldn't let me be treated the way I was treated."

Charlie's formal sentencing was held in front of Judge Spencer on June 6, the same day Caril's case was argued before the Supreme Court. Dressed in a long-sleeved yellow shirt, pinstriped black wool trousers, and black loafers, back in handcuffs, Charlie sat in the jury box between Sheriff Karnopp and another deputy. His father, the only family member present, was in the row behind him. Charlie sat calmly, occasionally shifting in his chair or shuffling his feet. Only a few spectators were present.

The court first disposed of Gaughan's motion for a new trial, which consisted of seventeen alleged errors. The principal alleged error was that the jury had erred in finding Charlie sane. Matschullat argued that Charlie was paranoid, as evidenced by the fact that five of his victims were shot from behind, and that the jury was influenced by passion and prejudice when shown the photos of the dead body of Jensen and the nude Carol King. After telling Scheele it wasn't necessary for him to respond, the judge denied the motion. He asked Charlie if there was any reason why the sentence should not be imposed at this time; Charlie looked him straight in the eye, shook his head vigorously, and said, "No." Without further comment, the judge sentenced him to die in the electric chair between 6:00 a.m. and 6:00 p.m. on December 17, 1958.

When Charlie asked him to repeat the date, he did so, and Charlie nodded. (This was cause for a ridiculous headline the next morning in the *Star*: "Starkweather Told Twice: 'You Must Die December 17.'")

When asked by a reporter if Charlie understood what was happening to him, Gaughan gave his take on his client: "Well, I don't know but Charlie is the type of fellow who hates us all and if he can't kill us all he'd just as soon leave us."

Guy Starkweather stated to a reporter, when asked how his son was doing, "There's still hope."

On Sunday, June 8, papers around the country carried an article written by Reinhardt in which he tried to explain why Charlie had done what he did. His analysis was of little help. Several of his facts were wrong, and his findings regarding Charlie's motivation sounded more like something from *True Detective*. He wrote things like, "A remorselessly power-mad ego drove Starkweather to kill." He called Starkweather a "maniac" and said that he was afflicted with a poor, defeated ego and that he turned to guns because they were a short road to power. "He had all that life had to offer: a girl to use, a gun to shoot, and power that could be tasted."

Of more value is Reinhardt's recollection of what Starkweather said to him. In one of their sessions, Charlie declared that he still loved Caril and had to hold on to her at all costs. "Caril and I get along just fine," he said. "She does whatever I tell her to do." Reinhardt wrote that Charlie told him, "I would be glad to go to the chair tomorrow if I could have Caril on my lap." In truth, the statement revealed quite clearly Charlie's motivation behind the whole murder spree.

On July 3, the Nebraska Supreme Court issued its ruling and held that the statute in question did not require that juveniles be tried in juvenile court. The two charges of first-degree murder against Caril would stay right where they were. If convicted, the jury would sentence her either to life in prison or death. Her trial was scheduled to begin on October 27.

33

THE LINCOLN STATE HOSPITAL WAS A COLLECTION OF three-story tan brick buildings on 154 acres southwest of Lincoln. The largest building, Old Main, was eighty-eight years old and housed 385 of the 1,600 patients at the facility. On March 9, the roof of Old Main caught fire. The sprinklers on the top floor were turned off for the winter so the pipes didn't freeze. Caril lived in the receiving unit of the building, which was not affected. In the news coverage of the fire, an attendant described Caril as showing a lot of poise but explained that it wasn't "a poise that comes with maturity and culture, but a shell-like quality that goes with ignoring rather than facing issues." He added that the older patients in the unit did not show Caril the same maternal care they usually showed mentally ill children.

At the hospital, Caril played cards, did jigsaw puzzles, watched TV (her favorite shows were *Abbott and Costello* and *The Thin Man*), and read the schoolbooks her stepmother brought on her visits. The superintendent explained to the press that Caril wasn't an oddity at the hospital; they had dozens of murderers there. He described Caril as a good patient who followed the rules and volunteered to wash sheets and make beds. She was the best seamstress in the ward, and in addition to sewing her own clothes she repaired the clothes of other patients. She received no treatment or counseling of any sort during her eleven-month stay.

On July 31, Caril had a small party at the hospital in celebration of her fifteenth birthday. Her stepmother and sister, the only guests, joined her for ice cream and cake. Her stepmother gave her a new light blue cotton dress. A few days later, Caril, wearing her new dress, left the hospital for the first time since February for a visit to the dentist. She appeared happy and in good spirits and told the dentist and his assistant that she had gained twenty pounds at the hospital. She added that she spent her days visiting with other girls in the ward and her evenings playing gin rummy, at which she almost always lost. She was locked in her room at night, although she had a TV and radio.

The news of the birthday party drew a bitter letter to the editor of the *Star*. A Bennet resident noted that Bobby Jensen would have turned eighteen on July 31 but the only gifts he received were a basket of gladioli and a bouquet of garden flowers placed at his grave site by "remembering hands."

In mid-August, Caril was transferred without explanation from the receiving unit to a new high-security building, which had more attendants, more restrictions, and security windows. The thirty-five other patients had all been transferred from the Women's Reformatory in York, which meant they were mentally ill criminals. They were all over twenty-one, which would appear to violate the state law prohibiting housing a prisoner under sixteen with adults.

As the days of summer passed, Caril clung to the belief that when her case finally came to trial, she would be found innocent. Her counsel, John McArthur, now joined by Lincoln attorney Merill Reller, was not so sanguine. He knew the intensity of the feeling in Lincoln against his client, and he wasn't sure a jury could be found in the city that would acquit her. McArthur was convinced beyond any doubt that his client was innocent, and he intended to fight for her every step of the way. He could have filed a motion for a change of venue, but Nebraska law at the time provided that venue could only be changed to a contiguous county, which in this case would accomplish nothing.

In 1966 the U.S. Supreme Court threw out the conviction of Cleveland osteopath Sam Sheppard for the murder of his wife in 1954 on the grounds that the massive, pervasive, and prejudicial publicity surrounding the case prevented Sheppard from receiving a fair trial consistent with the Fourteenth Amendment. The three Cleveland papers repeatedly called for his prosecution, and during court proceedings reporters walked freely around in the courtroom, creating a "carnival" atmosphere. The hostile publicity in Caril's trial did not rise to the level of that in Sheppard's trial, but a strong argument could be made that the restriction on a change of venue to adjoining counties was unconstitutional on its face as depriving Caril of a right to a fair trial.

McArthur filed a motion for a rehearing with the supreme court on the juvenile court ruling, which the court denied on September 27, 1958.

The court had set Caril's preliminary hearing for September 30. Although McArthur intended to waive the hearing, it was necessary for Caril to appear and indicate that she understood her right to the hearing and agreed to waive it. She appeared in the courtroom in the light blue cotton dress, a cardigan sweater, and black shoes. She wore no makeup, and her hair had been cut short and was in curls, which made her look older. The haircut angered McArthur. He said that her hair had been cut on purpose so that a jury would be not be deciding the fate of a cute eighth grader wearing a ponytail but a "an older looking girl with short, bobbed hair."

Caril was faring no better in the public eye now than she had when she was returned from Wyoming some eight months earlier or during Charlie's trial in May. The papers referred to her as Starkweather's "sidekick" or his "companion" on the bloody trail through Nebraska and Wyoming, only occasionally mentioning her claim that she was a hostage. The UPI referred to her as "an accused murderess" and an "overgrown school girl."

Enter Ninette Beaver, a reporter for KMTV in Omaha, an affiliate of NBC. She covered the story from the very beginning and would in some ways become a part of the story herself. She had landed an interview with Starkweather's parents on Thursday, January 30, and another one on Saturday, February 1. The latter was shown in its entirety on the evening news. Del Harding, the *Star* reporter, would state that of all the reporters covering Starkweather and Fugate, only Ninette Beaver and a UPI reporter believed Caril to be innocent. (The only hint of empathy expressed in print for Charlie came from *Journal* reporter Marjorie Marlett, who wrote that Starkweather had expressed deep and hopeless remorse for his crimes.) Beaver had cultivated a relationship with John McArthur and tried for months to get him to agree to an interview with Caril. She pointed out the terrible image Caril had in Lincoln, which, after all, was where the jurors would come from. Finally, McArthur and Reller agreed to an interview on two conditions: it would be in a press conference format, and only Beaver would be allowed to ask questions. The other reporters protested the arrangement, but it was this or nothing. The interview/press conference was held at the state hospital on October 17.

In her book *Caril,* coauthored with B. K. Ripley and Patrick Trese (Lippincott 1974), Beaver recounts how much like an average teenage girl Caril seemed when they first met a few minutes before the interview, although she was surprised at how tiny her subject was. Caril blinked her blue eyes and smiled widely. Standing next to McArthur's son Jim, the same age, they seemed just like two average teenagers. When told she would soon go on camera, Caril giggled, "Ooh, I'm so nervous . . . I just know I must take a terrible picture." When Beaver admired Caril's sweater, Caril smiled up at Beaver and Reller. "Thank you," she said. "Mr. Reller got it for me. I told him blue was my favorite color and he gave me this sweater and skirt."

Sitting next to the reporter at a table cluttered with mics, Caril looked like a little doll. Beaver was shocked by the transformation of "the friendly little girl she had met just a few minutes before . . . into a hard-faced, angry young woman . . . who spoke in a clipped brittle voice." When Caril insisted on her innocence and described Charlie as "crazy," her face tightened. "Her jaw was set and her eyes were hard." When asked if she thought about the possibility that she might die in the electric chair, Caril looked straight into the cameras and floodlights and replied, "Yes, I have. And I don't really believe that I have anything to worry about. The Lord knows I'm innocent, and I know it, and the people who are involved know it, too."

The AP wrote that Caril answered questions "crisply and firmly with no show of emotion." Bobby Jensen's mother watched the interview. She was struck by how "very, very cold her eyes were," projecting an "unfeeling look" she would never forget. The interview was played on *The Today Show* the next morning.

In ten days, Caril Ann Fugate, age fifteen years and almost three months, would be the youngest girl in the United States to stand trial for first-degree murder.

34

O N MONDAY, OCTOBER 27, 1958, NINE MONTHS TO THE
day after she and Charlie fled her parents' house at 924 Belmont Avenue, Caril Ann Fugate emerged from the state mental
hospital to answer to two charges of first-degree murder in the death
of Robert Jensen. Was she a "helper" or a "hostage"? was how the *Star*
put it. The AP wondered: "Was Caril an accomplice of her stubby bow-
legged lover during a January bloodletting that shocked the nation?"
The jury would be "death qualified," meaning they would be able to im-
pose the death penalty if warranted.

Caril Fugate was never evaluated by a psychologist or psychiatrist
or even interviewed by a social worker or counselor prior to her trial.
Caril swore in her Statement, in her testimony, and later on radio and
television programs that she was not in love with Charlie when "the
trouble" began. She had broken up with him on Sunday, she insisted. It
was over. She never wanted to see him again. However, on Tuesday, the
last day she went to school, she told Charlie's younger brother, Bobby,
who was in her class, that she missed Charlie and asked him to tell his
older brother to come over. She testified in her trial that she had broken up with Charlie and gotten back together with him a lot of times
(like most teenagers). In her bedroom was found the famous picture
of her and Charlie on the love seat, and in her purse was a gold locket
inscribed "Charlie and Caril" on the back with a heart. She testified in
her Statement that on the road to Wyoming, she told Charlie that she
loved him. Twice. She also testified that they had sex at least once, and
maybe twice, on the road after leaving the Ward house. One of the first
questions she had for Mrs. Heflin in the Douglas jail was whether she
could see Charlie. Finally, she admitted to cutting out the photo of her
and Charlie on the love seat from the newspaper and putting it in her

pocket. The photo was found in her possession when she was taken into custody outside of Douglas. You can be terrified of someone and love them at the same time. Charlie had become obsessed with Caril, which, twisted as it might seem, was still a form of being special to someone. One fight on a Sunday afternoon was not going to untangle her from the likes of Charlie Starkweather.

The world was watching: Charlie's conviction and sentence had been almost a foregone conclusion, but Caril's situation was different. No one could place a gun or a knife in her hands in the death of Bobby Jensen. She had a defense: she was a hostage, not a murderer. She had gone along with Charlie out of fear for her family's life as well as her own; she had been in a state of shock the entire time without the capacity or means to pull off an escape. In the eyes of the law and society, she was a little girl, a child, in the thrall of an adult male.

The evidence of guilt, to the extent it would matter, was fairly thin; no one knew if Starkweather would come from his death cell to testify against her, and without him, the only evidence linking her to Bobby Jensen's death came from her own mouth, the infamous Statement, which might be excluded. If Charlie didn't testify, if the Statement was excluded, if any evidence of the other nine murders was excluded, a conviction would almost as a matter of law be ruled out. But this trial wasn't as much about facts as it was about emotions. The big dog was now down and out, but there needed to be a clean sweep of the alley if there was to be any hope of a recovery from the soul-shaking trauma. As for her defense that she was a hostage, that could be dismissed by the many, many, opportunities she had to escape and didn't.

Caril showed up for the first day of jury selection happy that the trial was finally underway and firmly convinced that she would be found innocent. Security around and inside the courthouse was light. Only a few observers showed. She wore a light blue blouse and blue plaid skirt and no jewelry or makeup. Now in glasses, with her hair in tight curls, she barely resembled the little waif brought into the sheriff's office in Douglas almost ten months earlier. She sat at the long table between her two attorneys, McArthur and Reller. Unlike Charlie, who chewed gum and rocked in his chair during the selection process, Caril sat perfectly still and concentrated on the lawyers and prospective jurors. Out of an initial panel of two hundred prospective jurors, thirty-four were selected to be questioned in depth. Three were excused for cause because they had an opinion on her guilt or innocence strong enough to prevent fair deliberation. In an odd moment, McArthur asked Caril if she would like to ask the prospective jurors any questions. She declined. On Wednesday, a jury of seven men and five women were selected: a city street employee, two salesmen, three housewives, a meat buyer, a school teacher, an automotive-firm employee, a university instructor, a welder, and a dairy farmer. Once again, the *Star* printed the jurors' pictures, names, and addresses.

In his opening statement, McArthur referred to Caril as "this child" or "this little girl." He warned the jurors that Caril saw things he and they would never be called upon to see and that they must always keep in mind that what Caril did during "the bloodletting was pursuant to the reasoning of a fourteen-year-old child with the memory of a gun stuck in her head." And yes, Caril was going to take the stand and tell her story. She wouldn't have it any other way. Scheele stressed that "Caril had opportunities to escape her captor, but instead willingly and actively accompanied and assisted him in the things he did ... particularly on January 27."

The first and second day of testimony was pretty much a rerun of the opening of the Starkweather trial: Robert Jensen, Warren King (Carol's brother), Dr. E. D. Zeman (pathologist), Dennis Weaver (engineer), and four men from Bennet involved in finding the car and the bodies.

The *Ames Daily Tribune* headlined its UPI story the next day with "Caril Fugate Stony Calm as State Begins Its Case." The last paragraph read: "The defendant showed her usual composure, fixing a stare on Jensen as he tearfully testified about his son. The same unwavering gaze was directed at each witness."

The first witness of significance was deputy sheriff William Romer, the lawman who on the afternoon of January 29 happened on the scene of Starkweather and Sprinkle fighting in the middle of the road between

Casper and Douglas. The key to Caril's hostage defense is that she didn't know her family was dead. She claims that she absolutely believed Charlie when, after sticking a rifle in her face and slapping her around, he told her that members of his gang had her parents and little sister in a house and that if she tried to get away, he would make a phone call and have them killed. If she knew that her family was dead, then the hostage defense would fall apart, which means that, given the many opportunities to escape, she could only have been Charlie's willing accomplice from then on. Thus, anything pointing to the fact that she knew her parents were dead at the Bartlett house, regardless of her actual participation in a murder, was damning; anything supporting her belief that they were alive supported her hostage claim.

Romer testified at the trial that when he pulled up to the scene, a young girl came running toward the police car and jumped in the back seat. She appeared to be in a state of shock. The specifics of his testimony are critical. Q is Scheele and A is Romer:

A: She said, "he's going to kill me, he's going to kill me. He's already killed one man."
Q: And was she crying at the time?
A: Yes sir, she was.
Q: What did you ask her when she told you that?
A: I asked her who was going to kill her.
Q: What did she say?
A: She didn't answer me. She just kept saying "He's going to kill me." And then I asked her her name. And it was about then— she kept crying; and then she told me it was Charlie Starkweather who was going to kill her.

Later, the following questions and answers:

Q: What did Caril Fugate say to you, Mr. Romer?
A: She told me she had seen Starkweather kill ten people.
Q: Did she say who she had seen him kill?

A: Yes sir, she did.

Q: And what did she say?

A: She said she had seen him kill her mother, her step-father, her step-sister, a boy and a girl, a farm hand, three other people.

Q: Did Caril Fugate tell you any of the details of the killing of the three people she had witnessed?

A: Yes sir.

Q: Including the death of her father and mother, her step-father, her mother and step-sister?

A: Yes sir.

Q: Did she say whether or not she had been present when her mother, step-father and stepsister had been killed?

A: Yes, sir.

Romer testified that Caril was crying hysterically until the moment the word came over the radio that Starkweather had been captured. Then she stopped crying and talking. She was clearly afraid of Starkweather as long as he was on the loose.

For some reason, on cross-examination, McArthur had Romer repeat the details of what Caril told him she had seen:

Q: Would you tell the jury what she said about it?

A: Yes sir. She said that her mother had been in an argument with Charles Starkweather and had slapped him, and he started to hit her when the stepfather interfered and at that time he killed her stepfather and then killed her mother, and killed her step-sister.

Q: Anything else about that?

A: Do you want the details of what she gave me?

Q: Well in reference to that particular matter if she said anything else.

Q: Yes sir; she told us how the baby was killed.

A: Well, that's what I'm wanting to know, what she said about it and what happened.

Q: She said that the baby was crying, and that Starkweather took
the barrel of the gun and pushed it in the throat of the baby.

Caril denied to a friend that she ever told Romer that she had witnessed her family's murder; she said that his testimony was a lie. If
his testimony carried weight, it could prove highly problematic to the
hostage theory, particularly when coupled with the evidence on the numerous opportunities for Caril to escape.

The speculation in the press about Starkweather's possible appearance intensified. Gaughan still had no idea if his client would testify
against Caril. In Charlie's own trial, and in the press, he had nailed her
for at least two murders, and possibly three if you include Clara Ward,
four if you include Betty Jean, five if you include Lilyan Fencl, and in
this case he could tie her directly into aiding and abetting the Jensen
murder. If he wanted to.

The prosecution was definitely working on him to take the stand,
and according to the book *The Twelfth Victim*, written by Caril's Lincoln attorney John Stevens Berry and Ohio attorney and friend Linda
Battisti, Scheele was aggressively shaping Charlie's testimony to make
Caril into a cold-blooded murderer. If true, the effort wasn't really necessary. Charlie's fantasy was his reality. It had been from the beginning.
It could only end by him walking into the cool fires with his girlfriend
at his side, or even sitting on his lap. He would do what he had to do to
make that happen.

The week closed with the testimony of the man who pulled Charlie's car out of the ditch, the man who found the bodies in the cave,
the man who found the car in the field, and that of Sheriff Heflin of
Converse County. He recounted the tale of chasing Charlie through the
Badlands and shooting at him with his .30-30 until he finally came to a
stop, and then shooting at the ground between Charlie and the car when
he started to return to it and Chief Ainslie shooting the ground between
his feet again. Finally, Charlie flattened on the ground with his hands
behind his back, before taunting the officers that he would have gone
down shooting if he'd had any ammo. On cross-examination, the sheriff

stated twice that on the ride back to Douglas, he asked Charlie about the killings and Charlie said Caril had nothing to do with them.

At one point, McArthur was making an objection to a question and Judge Spencer interrupted him: "John, you're talking to yourself. I can't hear you." At which point McArthur raised his voice. On several other occasions during the trial, the judge directed questions or statements to "John."

The prosecution offered into evidence the shocking picture of the mutilated nude body of Carol King bent in half, thighs smeared with blood. McArthur objected vociferously and argued that the photo was inflammatory and was totally irrelevant since Caril was not charged with any crime against Carol King. Despite the seemingly obvious validity of the objection, the judge allowed the photo in. It was passed among the jury. Several jurors visibly winced when the photo reached them. Caril had never seen it. She noticed a juror look up from the picture at her with disgust.

Scheele spent the next few days setting the pieces in place: Lincoln police; Lancaster County deputy sheriffs; Sheriff Karnopp; a ballistic effort from the FBI agent who tied the three weapons used in the slayings to the bullets taken from the bodies and casings from the scene; several witnesses who stopped by the house during the week in question and were told by Caril that everybody inside had the flu; the owner of Hutson's grocery store, who testified that Charlie made phone calls on Tuesday, January 21, and Friday, January 24; and a Lincoln cop who testified two officers went to the Bartlett house on January 25 after complaints by Robert Von Busch and Rodney Starkweather. Critical testimony came from Virginia Robson, an employee of Watson Brothers Trucking, who testified that she saw Marion Bartlett at a Safeway store on her lunch hour around 1:15 p.m. on January 21. He looked fine at the time. A secretary at the trucking company testified that she had received a phone call right around 2:00 p.m. from a man who didn't identify himself but said that Mr. Bartlett wouldn't be coming to work that afternoon because he was ill. In his trial, Starkweather admitted making this phone call, which indicates that Charlie had either killed Bartlett or decided to kill him between approximately 1:30 and 2:00 p.m. for the apparent purpose of forestalling anyone from coming to the house to check up on Bartlett when he didn't appear for his 6:00 p.m. shift.

Mrs. Griggs testified that Charlie dropped his car off at her house around 4:00 or 5:00 p.m. on the afternoon of January 21. The next Saturday he stopped by and returned Rodney's .22 that he had borrowed on the twenty-first. He came back on Monday with Caril Fugate to fix the tire on his car and take the vehicle. Rodney testified to lending his brother the .22, going to the Bartlett house on Wednesday to get it back and being turned away by Caril, going to the house on Saturday with Robert Von Busch and being turned away again by Caril, and going to the house again with Von Busch on Monday, January 27, when they discovered the bodies. A cop described visiting the Bartlett house on Saturday with another policeman and being turned away by Caril; two employees of the Champlain gas station recounted how Charlie and Caril came to the station for transmission grease on the morning of January 27; the owner and an employee of Tate's gas station testified to Charlie and Caril's two visits on January 27; the waitress inside Brickey's Café testified that Caril was alone inside the café for ten minutes.

The courtroom received a jolt on the morning of November 5. The judge announced that the state would call Charles Starkweather to the stand the next morning. People started gathering outside the courthouse three hours before court opened.

Charlie was at his best. Dressed in a light gray suit, white shirt, and print tie, he walked across the room to the witness chair next to the judge. His hair had been trimmed, although it was still oiled and brushed up on the sides and back into a ducktail. He wore his round rimless bifocals with a gold nosepiece along with the familiar amused, quizzical look on his face.

Waiting for court to begin, he laughed and chatted with the new prison warden and the court reporter. On the stand, he lowered his head a little and looked around, everywhere except at Caril. She was nervous and agitated when Charlie first came in, but she soon settled down and held him in her steady gaze.

Charlie answered Scheele's questions in such a low voice the judge admonished him to speak up, and Charlie said it was because the shirt was so tight and he would like to unbutton it. The judge told him to loosen his tie and unbutton his shirt. In his demeanor and speech, Charlie was a polite young man. His answers were brief and to the point. He and Scheele were there to get the story told correctly, and he didn't want to come across to the jury as angry, or vengeful, or, worse yet, a mad man. (He commented to one reporter that Gaughan's insanity defense had ruined his reputation.) As he recounted the murders, he could have been talking about a trip to Kansas City for a ball game. Clearly, the questions and answers had been rehearsed.

Charlie told pretty much the same story he had told to the prosecutors on February 27. After Bartlett kicked him out of the house, he went to the grocery store and called Bartlett's place of work to say he wouldn't be coming in. He returned to the Bartlett house around three and sat on the back porch. Caril came home around four, and after listening to her and her mother argue he went inside. He got into an argument with her, she slapped him, he slapped her back, Mr. Bartlett came at him with a hammer, and he shot him in the head with the .22. He then shot Mrs. Bartlett. In this telling, he threw a knife at Betty Jean but that was all. After the killings, Caril watched TV for four hours while he removed the bodies and cleaned up the house. During the six days they were in the house, he was gone frequently, sometimes for more than three hours at a time. He never tied Caril up when he left.

In the courtroom, Caril's composure broke when Scheele read aloud Charlie's statement about killing the Bartletts. Tears slid down her cheek and off her chin. Her hand rose to her mouth. The AP wrote that "she clenched a handkerchief in one hand, swallowed, put her hand to her face once and regained her composure with hardly a movement."

Scheele walked Charlie through the day of Monday, January 27, when Charlie and Caril left town after numerous stops and finally drove to August Meyer's farm and the various times the cars got stuck. Charlie testified that Caril knew how to shoot—and had in fact shot—both a rifle and a shotgun.

The rest of Charlie's testimony for that day pretty much matches the April 9 letter for the details of the killing of August Meyer and Jensen. The shooting and mutilation of Carol King's body was not mentioned.

After returning to Lincoln and sleeping at Twenty-Fourth and Van Dorn, Charlie parked in the Wards' driveway. Charlie went inside and left Caril in the car with the .410 for at least half an hour, at which point he motioned her in. Charlie's story of what went on in the house for the next 11.5 hours is not dissimilar from his February 27 story in many respects. He testified to the many instances in which Caril had the opportunity to escape or seek help: the several times he was upstairs for ten or fifteen minutes and she was downstairs with her own weapon, and vice versa; when Caril was watching the maid with the .22; when he went outside to turn the car around. He testified that around 6:30 that evening Caril called out to him that Mr. Ward was pulling into the driveway. Charlie told about cutting photos and articles from the two daily newspapers and the taking of money from Mrs. Ward's pocketbook and ten dollars from the maid. Scheele directed him several times to raise his voice. Direct examination ended without any testimony on the killing of Mrs. Ward, the maid, or Carol King, although Charlie managed to slip in that he had shot Lauer Ward.

On the face of it, Charlie's testimony was devastating, at least as far as proving the crime of felony murder. While holding a gun on King, Caril took money from Robert Jensen's wallet and put it in Starkweather's. The felony of robbery occurred in the course of events leading to Jensen's murder.

McArthur's cross-examination of Charlie was long and arduous. It was a strange configuration: Charlie became antagonistic when he tired of McArthur's asking him a question he didn't like and would say to him, "There you go again." Or "I already answered that." McArthur, ever the gentlemen, explained why he was asking the question again, and one time Charlie simply refused to answer any further questions on a topic. At one point, in order to identify the shotgun, he rose from the witness stand and began to walk to the table where the three weapons lay, before being stopped by McArthur. It was a weird, scary moment in the courtroom; everyone knew the gun was empty, but it was the killer's tool, and what if a shell was stuck inside?

McArthur spent considerable time on the Meyer, Ward, and Collison killings, to no obvious purpose other than perhaps to show what a monster Charlie was. He read aloud from Charlie's letter to his parents on January 29, in which he describes killing the Bartletts before Caril got home. He read aloud from the February 1 statement in which Charlie also says Caril was not at home during the killings, that he was hiding behind the door when she came in, and that he told her that her parents were being held hostage at the "old people's house." Twice Charlie dismissed these earlier statements as "hogwash." He was only trying to protect Caril. As for how he felt about Caril now?

Q: What is your present attitude toward Caril Ann Fugate?

A: I don't dislike her.

Q: I beg your pardon?

A: I don't dislike the girl.

Q: Well, do you have any feelings for her one way or another?

A: It don't make no difference.

Q: Does it make any difference to you whether she's dead or alive?

A: It don't make no difference to me.

Charlie had taken his glasses off for cross-examination and refused McArthur's suggestion that he put them on. There was no one in the courtroom he cared to see, although he admitted he was able to see Caril.

As to whether he was worried that Caril was going to sound the alarm while they were on the road, Charlie said, "I wasn't worried about her talking. She wasn't going to talk. I didn't think about what she might have done because I knew she wouldn't talk." "Mentally," he claimed, "I'm as sane as anybody."

The AP reported that Caril kept a "frozen, fixed stare" on Stark-weather but that Starkweather did not look at her as he testified she was in the home when he killed her family.

While Charlie testified about the killings, a probate judge in a courtroom one floor down ruled that the estate of Betty Jean Bartlett, consisting of $782.75, would be split between Caril and her sister Barbara. Presumably, a share of the properties and monies of the parents devolved to Betty Jean when her parents were killed and then went instantly to her sisters when she was killed a minute or so later. That same day, Gaughan and Matschullat argued in front of the Nebraska Supreme Court that it should overturn Starkweather's death sentence and order him held for life in a mental institution.

35

S CHEELE WAS ABOUT READY TO PLANT THE SWORD. HE would lay the groundwork to enter the now-famous and never-seen-by-the-press Statement. It was this Statement, if allowed into evidence, that would force Caril to take the stand. It was this Statement, seen by many as a confession, that might force her to admit to a felony murder; it was this Statement that many argued showed her to be as cold-blooded as her boyfriend.

But first, Scheele sought to weaken Caril's credibility before the jury by entering into evidence an oral admission that she had been present in the Bartlett house when Charlie killed her mother, stepfather, and little sister. Jail matron Gertrude Karnopp took the stand and testified in detail on what Caril told her in the car on the drive from Gering to Lincoln on January 30, the day after her capture.

"Is my family dead?" Caril asked Mrs. Karnopp.

"Why, Caril, don't you know?"

Caril didn't answer.

"Don't you know, Caril?"

Caril then began talking freely about the murders. She recounted the killing of Meyer and getting picked up by the two teenagers. She told of taking some money from Jensen and him driving to the cave, where Charlie killed them both. She told of what happened at the Ward house, in particular the killing of the maid in the upstairs bedroom. She talked about her family, that she didn't care for her stepfather because he was too strict, and of a fight between Charlie and her mother, and how her sister Barbara would not want anything to do with her when she returned. And then Caril talked about "how the papers said that those three bodies were found where they were shot, but that they weren't shot outside, they were shot in the house."

Ms. Karnopp asked her which three bodies she meant, and after waiting a second, Caril said, "Mr. Meyer's body was shot in the house and drug out there." Caril refused to say anything more. Mrs. Karnopp asked her why she said three bodies if she was talking only about Mr. Meyer, and she stayed silent. Mrs. Karnopp identified three newspaper clippings that Caril had taken from her jacket pocket and shown to her and which later had been taken from her jacket at the mental hospital.

Moving to the Statement, Scheele asked Mrs. Karnopp about a "conversation" with Caril on the morning of February 1, in the presence of herself, Dr. Coats, assistant police chief Eugene Masters, Dr. Vance Rogers, and Dale Fahrnbruch. Fahrnbruch had questioned Caril for around an hour. Mrs. Karnopp, her husband, Fahrnbruch, and Dr. Coats next met with Caril at 11:00 the next morning for about half an hour. At 2:00 that afternoon, she and Fahrnbruch met with Caril, her sister Barbara Von Busch, and her father and stepmother. Mrs. Karnopp testified that Fahrnbruch told Caril he would like to take a statement from her, that she should tell her side of the story, and that charges could be filed against her. Her father and stepmother urged her to tell the truth and do the right thing. It was agreed that a formal statement would be taken that evening at 8:00 p.m. That questioning lasted until 10:45. The on-the-record questioning was continued the next day from 12:00 to 1:30 at the hospital, after which Caril was taken to court to be arraigned. All in all, Caril was questioned for at least six hours and twenty minutes over a period of two days. She was questioned again by Fahrnbruch on February 7 for approximately half an hour.

In the questioning, Mrs. Karnopp reminded Scheele that she and her husband had spoken with Caril around 8:00 a.m. on the morning of February 2, at which time Sheriff Karnopp obtained a note from Caril to Charlie saying she did not want to see him and that she was scared of him. The sheriff subsequently passed the note on to Charlie.

On cross-examination, Mrs. Karnopp admitted that on the road from Gering to Lincoln, Caril told her that she had done what she did because Charles had taken her folks someplace and something would happen to them if she didn't.

McArthur developed the record for what would be perhaps his strongest attack on the admission of the Statement: the absence of an attorney. Mrs. Karnopp testified that on the initial meeting on February 1, Fahrnbruch told Caril she had a right to an attorney. Caril's response was that she didn't have one. The interrogation proceeded the next day and night and the next afternoon without any attempt to provide her an attorney. Here is a fourteen-year-old girl charged with a crime that could lead to her execution if convicted, McArthur argued, and yet the state proceeded to interrogate her for over six hours without her speaking to a lawyer. When Mrs. Karnopp stated that it was normal process for the person to get their own attorney, McArthur asked her how a fourteen-year-old girl in the confined custody of the state was supposed to arrange for a lawyer. Well, Mrs. Karnopp responded, she did have Dean Bolshein from the University of Nebraska Law School and William Blue from Legal Aid. But that was *after* the statement had been taken, wasn't it? Yes. *After* Caril had damned herself, she had a lawyer. These two lawyers, faced with a fait accompli, could only tell her not to sign the statement (but they did allow her to read and verbally correct it, which would seem to have almost the same effect as signing it). And then, even after Caril obtained legal representation, Fahrnbruch questioned her on February 7 and 11 without notifying her attorneys of the interrogation.

McArthur turned to the three "practice sessions." He pointed to several pages in the transcript in which Fahrnbruch was asking questions that could only be answered "yes" or "no." In other words, he was feeding Caril the facts in the questions, to which she then agreed (and would hopefully repeat later on the record).

The prosecution had the burden of proving that Caril's "confession" was given freely and voluntarily and was not obtained by coercion, intimidation, or promises. Mrs. Karnopp testified that Caril had answered the questions freely and without hesitation, although she did appear at times to be mixed up.

Fahrnbruch had arranged for Dr. Coats, who had testified in Charlie's trial, to be present at each of the interrogations. Contrary to Mrs.
Karnopp's testimony, he testified that the first session on February 2
lasted from 9:45 a.m. to 2:00 p.m. At this meeting, Caril was cooperative, friendly, and "she answered the questions without embellishing
them or going into great detail, and there didn't seem to be any question
but what she knew what she was saying." She did not appear frightened
and answered the questions without hesitation.

The 8:00 p.m. interrogation was held in Coats's office and transcribed by Audrey Wheeler. Coats testified that although at times Caril
was a little mixed up, she answered the questions freely and voluntarily.
She knew what she was saying and was oriented and in contact with
reality at all times. She appeared the same to him on the February 3
questioning. She appeared rested and well oriented to her situation. He
was also present at the meeting on February 5 in which Caril refused to
sign the Statement. Once again, Caril was polite and appeared to know
what she was doing. As to her behavior as a resident at the hospital, Caril
was cooperative, pleasant, and very quiet, and she always followed the
rules. (He mentioned one exception, which might have been the incident
in which a youngster on the grounds spotted Caril in the second-floor
window and hollered up: "What do you think of Charlie now, Caril?"
Her shouted reply: "I hope they fry his ass!")

Coats testified that at the February 2 meeting, Caril initially said she
didn't want an attorney because she wouldn't be able to pay for one, but
once it was explained to her that she wouldn't have to pay a lawyer, she
changed her mind and said she did want one.

SCHEELE THEN CALLED Audrey Wheeler, the court reporter who transcribed the interrogation on the February 2 evening meeting and the
noon meeting on February 3, which together would result in the Statement. She produced notes of a conversation between Fahrnbruch and
Caril that took place after the interrogation on February 3. Fahrnbruch
questioned Caril about a conversation between her and Scheele in Wyoming. The notes read that Scheele told her she could have a lawyer if

she wanted one but that Caril denied that she told him she didn't want one. "I did not know what he meant at that time by that. I thought he meant by the district attorney." When asked if she wanted a lawyer, she responded, "Yes, but who would take it?"

At that point, Scheele offered the Statement into evidence. Although there was no specific ruling on the voluntariness of the Statement, McArthur objected on numerous grounds, stressing that the Statement refers to different and unrelated offenses, i.e., nine other murders. In the Statement, Caril is questioned and talks about not just the killing of Jensen but the murders of King, Meyer, Clara Ward, Lilyan Fencl, Lauer Ward, and Merle Collison. The danger, of course, was that the jury would in effect try her on all these crimes as well as the one she was actually charged with. Prosecutors frequently attempt to introduce "uncharged conduct" or "similar acts" supposedly to show a pattern of criminal conduct on the defendant's part. Thus, the prosecution in Harvey Weinstein's New York trial was allowed to introduce the testimony of three women who claimed he sexually assaulted them (but for which he was not charged) because of the similarity between his assault on them and the sexual assault for which he was charged. In the Starkweather case, it was never clear why the judge allowed in the testimony regarding these other incidents of uncharged conduct.

The press had heard about the Statement but had never seen it. They knew snippets of Caril's side of the story but nothing more. This is how the Statement went.

Seated at the table in a conference room of the state hospital were deputy county attorney Dale Fahrnbruch, Dr. Coats, jail matron Gertrude Karnopp, and Caril Ann Fugate. Off to the side sat stenographer Audrey Wheeler. It was a few minutes after 8:00 p.m. by the time the questioning began. Caril had been watching TV and was a little tired but said she was willing to go ahead with the questioning.

Fahrnbruch began the interrogation not with the killings in the Bartlett house or Jensen and King but with the shooting of August Meyer. Caril hesitated: "I'm all mixed up now. I don't know whether I can tell it straight or not now." Fahrnbruch encouraged her to tell it as best she could, and she told the story of the 1949 Ford getting stuck in the drive to Meyer's farmhouse and going down in the "bomb shelter." Charlie hung up a lantern in the shelter and loaded the .410 (Caril referred to it as a .45 shotgun), and after half an hour they left and began walking to the farmhouse. A dog started barking, and Mr. Meyer came out the back door of his house. After Chuck explained to Meyer that they needed his horses to pull his car out, Meyer turned to go back in his house. Caril was walking behind Chuck. He raised the gun, pointed it at Meyer's head, and shot. Meyer's body fell on the porch. Chuck grabbed him by the feet and dragged him inside a building a short distance away. She tossed his hat inside.

Inside the house, Charlie ransacked the place, looking for "a gun" and five hundred dollars in cash. He found three guns, one of which was a .22 rifle but which Caril referred to as a pistol. Charlie made a meal of cookies and Jell-O, which she refused. While telling how they returned to the car and finally got it unstuck, Caril loses track of what happened next. "I don't remember," she tells Fahrnbruch as he presses her. He suggests that they next went to a filling station, and she agrees but then gets the course of events confused. When they left Tate's, they headed for a "hide-out," but they went back to the farm. Caril gets mixed up again on when they got stuck and unstuck. Fahrnbruch leads her into the story of Charlie and a farmer, Howard Genuchi, getting the car unstuck and the return to the farmhouse. She volunteers a very damaging fact:

A: We got out of the car and started walking towards the house. I had the rifle [shotgun] then.
Q: You had the rifle then?
A: Yes.
Q: Was it loaded?
A: Yes.

At the farmhouse, they both got scared and left after a few minutes. They started walking toward Bennet when a car pulled over and picked

them up. Charlie, with the shotgun, sat behind the driver. She sat behind
the girl in the passenger seat with the .22. Charlie eventually told him to
drive to the cellar and threatened to blow the man's head off.

Fahrnbruch asks Caril what they took from the couple besides the car:

A: Well, Chuck asked them if they had any money, and the boy
said yes, he had $4.00, and handed his billfold to Chuck, and
Chuck handed his billfold and the boy's billfold to me. I took
the money out of the boy's billfold and put it in Chuck's, and
handed Chuck's billfold back to him, and handed the boy's
billfold back to the girl, because he asked me to.

Jensen parked close to the cellar.

A: Chuck told the boy to get out, and I pointed the gun at the girl.
I put it on the seat back, like that [indicating], and told her to
get out.
Q: You mean you pointed the gun at the girl and told her to get
out?
A: Yes. I just waved the gun across the seat like that [indicating].
Q: What did you tell her at that time?
A: I told her to get out.
Q: Why did you do that, Caril?
A: Because he told him to get out.
Q: He told the driver to get out?
A: He told them both to get out.
Q: Then you told the girl to get out?
A: Yes.

Charlie walked the two teenagers to the cellar and Caril moved to
the front seat. Shortly, she heard two or more shots, she wasn't sure how
many. About half an hour later, Charlie came out of the cellar and put
an old door over the cellar opening. He got in the car and it slid back
into the ditch. Through the use of boards and blankets, they managed to

extricate it and headed for Lincoln. They drove by Caril's house, spotted some cars in front, and took off for Hastings. At this point, Caril gets very confused about the course of events and mixes up stopping by the old couple's house (the Southworths') and the Ward house. But it doesn't matter; Caril has completed the elements of the felony murder when she described the killing of Jensen and King.

Fahrnbruch proceeded on to the Ward killings to poke around for inconsistencies and to tie Caril down on the facts of those three killings, most likely in case a decision was made to file additional charges against her while also getting more negative uncharged conduct evidence before the jury. He scored early when she told him she waited in Jensen's car with the .410 on the floor in back for half an hour after Charlie went inside the Ward house alone. When Charlie motioned to her from the kitchen door, she went inside with the gun and his black jacket. She walked into the living room, had a cup of coffee, and fell asleep on the couch until midafternoon. She awoke when Mrs. Ward served Charlie pancakes. She refused the offer herself. She went back to sleep, and when she awoke Charlie told her he had stabbed Mrs. Ward in the throat and she was dead upstairs. He told her not to tell the maid. She agreed, saying that if the maid knew "she would go ape." He handed her a knife and told her to wash it off in the kitchen, which she did. It wasn't the hunting knife but her mother's kitchen knife: "straight on one side and curved on the other." Charlie complained about the smell of blood and told her to go upstairs and sprinkle some perfume. She found a bottle in a dresser and sprinkled it on a chair and rug outside the bedroom, although she did not go inside.

Caril then makes another damning admission:

Q: Now Caril, did you ever have a gun in your hands while you were in the Ward house?

A: Yes.

Q: And what gun did you have in your hands?

A: The .22.

Q: And was that loaded at that time?

A: Yes.

Q: And what did you do with that gun, Caril?

A: Pointed it at the maid.

Q: Why did you do that?

A: Because he told me to.

Caril also admitted that she heard on the radio in the Packard about three bodies being found in Lincoln. A baby girl was not mentioned.

Charlie told her to watch out the living room window for Mr. Ward, who, according to Mrs. Ward, would be returning around 6:00 or 6:30. When she spotted the late-year Chevrolet pulling in the drive, she hollered at Chuck. She then went inside the bathroom and closed the door because she knew what was going to happen. All she knows about the killing of Mr. Ward is what Charlie told her. When she came out, the maid was sitting in a chair against the wall and Mr. Ward was lying by the front door moaning. Chuck gave her the .22 and told her to hold it on the maid, which she did. Chuck was carrying the .22 he got from Mrs. Ward, and the two of them escorted the maid up the stairs to one of the bedrooms and sat her in a chair. Charlie tore up a sheet and began tying her wrists, and Caril suggested he let her lie on the bed because she was going to get tired sitting up all night. He tied her hands to the bedpost and her feet to the end of the bed. The maid asked several times for them to turn on the light because she was afraid of the dark.

Q: Then what happened?

A: I was looking out the window, and he started stabbing her, and she started screaming and hollering.

Q: How many times did he stab her?

A: I don't know.

Q: Do you know what he stabbed her with?

A: My mother's kitchen knife.

Q: Did he say something while he was stabbing her?

A: I don't know. He put a pillow over her face.

Q: Did he stab her more than once?

A: Yes.

Q: Would it be more than twice?

A: Yes.

Q: How do you know that Caril?

A: I heard it. Every time he stabbed her, she moaned.

Q: How many times did she moan?

A: Well, more than five.

Q: Was she laying face down on the bed, or face up?

A: Faceup.

She heard the maid tear her hands loose from the bed while Charlie was stabbing her. When he was done, he declared he didn't think she was ever going to die. He covered her up with a blanket. Then he told Caril to shine the flashlight on his arm. "There was blood stains all over his shirt; all over the cuff of his shirt" on the right arm. He told her to find a clean shirt for him, and she found a white shirt in a closet. In the downstairs bathroom, "He took his shirt off and throwed it on the floor and started washing his arms, and then put the white shirt on." While he was cleaning up, she washed the knife in the kitchen sink. She wiped the wet knife on her black jeans. They got some food, she put on her black jacket, they turned off the lights and left the house through the kitchen door. Right before she left, she answered the phone and told the lady caller that Mrs. Ward was sick.

Fahrnbruch turned to a critical piece of evidence: the newspaper clippings from the *Star*, which were on the kitchen table when Charlie and Caril arrived, and the *Journal*, which was delivered in the afternoon. Sitting at the kitchen table, Caril helped Charlie cut out the picture of herself and Charlie sitting on the love seat in his landlady's room. "I had my white majorette boots on." He cut out some of that picture and she cut out the rest. She first said that either she or Charlie cut out the pictures of her mother, stepfather, and little sister, and then she decided that he and not she had cut them out. Then she wasn't sure: "I think he cut them out, or I think I cut them out." He did cut out the picture of his car, but he wouldn't allow her to see the rest of the paper.

Caril and Charlie had turned out the lights and left. On the road out of town, Charlie told her to change her clothes, and she put on the red-and-white blouse and the buckskin jacket belonging to Clara Ward. She threw her old blouse out the window. On the road west out of town, Charlie got tired and pulled over. They had sexual intercourse in the car and then got back on the highway and headed west. Fahrnbruch has Caril go over the killing in Wyoming, although he doesn't ask her if she took the .22 to Charlie when he called for it or if in fact she had killed Collison.

Fahrnbruch then turned to the critical issue in the case: Was she home when Charlie killed her family? She explains how when she came home from school that day around 3:30, Charlie was standing behind the front door with a gun in his hands. He told her to sit down on a chair. She had noticed the car in the drive and asked where her folks were. At the old lady's house, he said, and if she did what he told her, they wouldn't be hurt. She told him she didn't believe him. He told her to change her clothes, which she did. She asked him if she could talk to her folks, and he said no, they were all right. They sat on the davenport and watched TV until it went off the air. In the morning, people started coming to the house, and he told her to get rid of them. She goes through the litany of visitors: Bonnie, her friend; the bread man; the landlord; the egg lady; her stepfather's boss and a little boy; Rodney and Robert Von Busch; her sister; her sister and Robert Von Busch; Laveta (Charlie's sister); her grandmother Pansy; and the police. She told them they couldn't come in because everyone inside had the flu, then wrote a note to that effect and put it on the doorframe. When she saw the two cops coming to the door, she woke Charlie and told him, and he said to get rid of them. She didn't let them or anyone else in because Charlie said he would shoot anyone who came in the house.

Caril admitted she had plenty of opportunities to leave. When Charlie left at night, he tied her up with a dish towel or pieces of rope cut from the clothesline running across the living room, but during the day she often went outside to get the mail from a box at the end of the drive or to feed the dog by herself. She could have left in the cab with her sister and her husband. She could have walked away with the cops when they came to the door, but she didn't. She did try to warn Laveta that Chuck was in the house and her parents were being held hostage, but Laveta didn't get it. She told her grandmother that she would have to leave if she didn't want her daughter to get hurt.

Around 10:50, Caril grew tired and the interrogation was terminated. It resumed the next day at 12:00 p.m. at the state hospital. Fahrnbruch asked her about her experience hunting or shooting guns with Charlie, and she said they would go hunting but that while Charlie hunted rabbits, she plinked at tin cans. She doesn't understand the difference between a shotgun and a rifle.

Then Fahrnbruch turned to series of questions about Caril and Charlie's sex life that were designed to show that the relationship was more one of lovers than hostage and hostage-taker. It was clear that she and Fahrnbruch had gone over this in some detail before.

Q: Did he at any time put his penis up to your sexual organs?

A: Yes.

Q: And did he stick it in very far?

A: No.

Q: Did he put it in slightly?

A: He didn't put it in an inch.

Q: He put it in less than an inch?

A: Yes.

Q: He did put it in, but less than an inch, is that right?

A: Yes.

Q: What was the reason he didn't put it in further?

A: It hurt.

Q: And did you tell him that it hurt?

A: Yes.

Q: And what did he say?

A: He stopped.

Q: And how many times did that happen, Caril?

A: I think twice.

Q: Now then Caril, you told me previously that he also put his penis in your rear end, is that right?

A: Yes.

Q: And on how many occasions did that happen?

A: I think about twice.

Q: On different occasions; different nights?

A: I think so.

Q: Now Caril, do you know how far he put his penis in your rear end?

A: No.

Q: Did it hurt, Caril?

A: Well, I would say yes.

Caril stated that she had sexual intercourse with Charlie in the car on the road west to Wyoming when they had pulled over to sleep. She also told Charlie more than once on the road that she loved him, but only because she was afraid he might kill her.

One time, when she and Chuck were having an argument in the Bartlett house, Charlie threw a gun at her and told her to go ahead and shoot him.

Q: And what did you say?

A: I told him, don't be silly.

On November 10, Scheele read all but fifteen pages of the Statement aloud to the jury. The deletions were the description of Charlie stabbing the maid, Caril washing the knife used to kill the maid on her black jeans, and the sexual activity of Charlie and Caril in the house and in the car on the road to Wyoming.

After the reading, the AP headlined, "Contradictions in 'Hostage' Story May Hurt Caril's Case." It pointed out the contradiction between Caril's statement that she had told Charlie she loved him out of fear he might kill her and her admission that she had lied when she said that. The AP noted that "Twice during the reading of the statement Caril broke into tears. But she wept so quietly only those sitting near her detected it." Charlie was described as Caril's "bow-legged companion." The *Journal* blared at the top of page 1 that "Caril 'Waved' King Girl From Car With Shotgun."

Assistant police chief Eugene Masters, who was present at the February 2 interrogation, testified that while Caril might have been a little nervous, he was "amazed at how calm she was for a fourteen-year-old girl who had gone through what she did." The AP wrote that when Masters described finding the three bodies at the Bartlett house, Caril cried for the second time in the trial.

McArthur filed a motion to dismiss the charges on the grounds that there was too much time between the felony—taking the money from the wallet—and the killing of Jensen for it to be considered one transaction or event. The motion was denied.

The court recessed for Veteran's Day. The defense would begin on Wednesday. Caril would be the first witness.

36

MCARTHUR HAD HIS WORK CUT OUT FOR HIM. HIS main problem was that by her own words, Caril had just condemned herself for two things in particular: holding a gun on Carol King and "waving" her out of the car, and holding a gun on the maid and telling her what to do. Both women ended up dead. She also admitted to warning Charlie of the policemen coming to the Bartlett house and alerting him to the arrival of Lauer Ward's car at the house. Whether charged or not, this looked like a lot of bad conduct. And as for her hostage defense, her Statement established there were plenty of opportunities for her to flee her captor.

In a blue dress, nervous, looking a little older in her glasses, Caril took the stand and sat primly with her hands folded in her lap. Her feet just touched the floor. McArthur attempted to put a human face on the defendant through her own words, to present her as a young schoolgirl who got caught up in something or someone way beyond her ability to handle. She was fourteen, halfway through eighth grade. She could identify the president, the former president, the governor, but not the mayor of Lincoln. She'd been on one vacation to the Sandhills in her father's car but had never been to Omaha or the Missouri River. She got along fine with her mother and adored her little sister, for whom she would do anything. Her stepfather had "his ways," but they got along. He gave her a spanking shortly after he and her mother were married for refusing to put the mop away, but that was the only time. Her face didn't change expression as she talked, and her answers were clipped, strangely flat. McArthur coaxed her gently, trying to get her to relax. She identified all the main participants in the courtroom by name, including the judge, except for Scheele. As for this trial, she had learned only at the last minute that Starkweather was coming to testify against her. McArthur asked her how she felt when she saw Charlie come into the courtroom. Her eyes flashed. "I was scared to death." She had known Charles Stark- weather (which is what she called him on the stand) for a couple years (which meant she was a little over twelve when they met).

McArthur turns back to her family.

Q: How did you feel when your baby sister was born?
A: I felt like a million.
Q: What were your feelings toward that little girl?
A: I would do anything for her.

McArthur had Caril identify a number of family photos showing Caril with her mother and siblings and one of Betty Jean opening a Christmas present of dishes that Caril had given her. The photos were passed among the jurors. Caril liked to roller-skate, ride her bike, and dance, and she did a lot of babysitting for the five children of Virginia and Sonny Von Busch. She'd wanted to be a nurse ever since she could remember because she liked children so much. She knew she had to get an education beyond high school.

Caril had been going with a boy named Dick when Charles Stark- weather butted in and ran him off. During the six months before the "trouble" began, she and Charles had spent almost every evening to- gether. She thought he was a decent boy. He treated her nice, and he was never mean to her. He took her to shows, the Runza Drive-In, and horseback riding in Pioneers Park. The whole Starkweather family were nice people.

McArthur directed her to the "trouble." The jury had just heard her tell the story through Scheele's reading of her Statement. It had now been eight months since she made it, but what she said now had to be consistent with what she said earlier. She told how Charles came over the Sunday before "the trouble" while she and her mother were washing clothes and began accusing her of going out with another boy behind his back and repeating all sorts of nasty things. She told him she never wanted to see him again. Charlie asked her if she was telling him never to come back, and she said yes, she was. Her mother told Charlie to leave the house. He turned red in the face, knocked his hand on something, and left.

McArthur directed Caril to the night one week later. It was cold and windy, she said, the trees were rustling, the roads were clear, but there was snow on the embankments and in the ditches; she and Charles were walking away from the Meyer farm, and she carried her dad's .410, which was broken from Charlie's having smashed it on Meyer's dog's head, and Charles carried Meyer's .22 rifle, her mother's pistol, and her mother's knife, behind his back, wedged between his pants and shirt. She was so tired and cold Charlie had to hold her up while they walked on the road leading down from the farmhouse to the road to Bennet. A few minutes on that road and a car came around the corner and stopped, and the driver, a boy, told them to get in and that he would drive them to Bennet but he wanted the guns. Charles told him they were not loaded and kept them. There was a girl in the passenger's seat, and Caril sat behind the girl with the shotgun on her lap, while Charlie had the .22 pointed at the head of the boy. Once in Bennet, Charles told the boy to turn around and head back into the country, and when the boy said he didn't think Charles would do anything, Charlie assured him he would blow his head off. Caril, who said nothing, was scared; she believed Charles would kill all of them. Charlie was talking in a high, squeaky, and very loud voice, and his face was all wrinkled up like he'd just been in a fight. He asked the boy if he had any money, and the boy said he had four dollars, and at a stop sign he took his wallet out and handed it to the girl, who handed it to Caril, who took the money out and returned it to the girl and placed the money in Charles's wallet, then gave him the wallet back. Charlie told the boy to drive to the old schoolhouse; he was going to leave them in the cave and take the boy's car. The teenagers talked about their friends at school. The barrel of the shotgun lay on Caril's lap, the stock was on Charlie's. The boy stopped the car not far from the cave. Charles got out and told the boy and the girl to get out; the boy got out, but the girl didn't move. Charles told Caril to point the gun at the girl and ordered her to get out.

McArthur handed Caril the .410 shotgun, and she demonstrated for the jury how she waved it at the driver's door and told the girl to get out, whispering to her that she'd better do it if she didn't want to get hurt. Caril was scared Charles was going to shoot the teenager if she got out the passenger door, thinking she might run away, but the girl slid out the driver's side. Caril begged Charles not to hurt them—she'd just seen him kill August Meyer with a shotgun blast to the back of the head—and he told her to shut up and get in the front seat. She laid the gun on the floor in back and crawled over the seat and onto the passenger's side. She watched as the teenagers and Charles, carrying the .22, walked away from the car. She was scared stiff, trying to believe that Charles was going to put them in the cellar and cover them up for someone to find, like he said he would. She sat shaking for about ten minutes, and then she heard the shots, two or three of them, and she started crying because she knew what he'd done. She had no place to go.

A: Well, I just couldn't move. I was just froze stiff.
Q: Did you know where you were?
A: No, sir, I did not.
Q: Did you know where the nearest house was?
A: I knew where Mr. Meyer's house was.
Q: Would you have gone up there if you could?
A: No, sir.
Q: Did you know where any other house was around there?
A: No, sir.

Next:

Q: Why didn't you run away?
A: I couldn't move after I heard the shots . . . I was froze stiff.

She didn't think of taking the shotgun and shooting Charles with it; she didn't know how to use the gun, and she had never killed anyone. When he came back, he shoved the .22 in the door, and she thought he was going to shoot her, but he dropped it on the back seat. He backed the car into a ditch.

Here, McArthur interrupted Caril and told her she was talking a little fast, her words were running together, and she needed to slow down a little.

Charles and Caril jacked the car up, put boards from the old schoolhouse and blankets under the wheels, and after half an hour got it out. Charles said he would take her home to her family because she had seen and done enough. She insisted that the only reason she took the money from the boy's wallet was because Charles Starkweather told her to; if it were just up to her, she would never have touched it.

Caril told the jury about the trip back to Lincoln and when she threw the schoolbooks out the window as a sort of trail for the cops to follow, and she told them about stopping a block or so from her home on Belmont Street and seeing the police, although this time she added that she thought about jumping from the car but was scared about getting stuck in the back by Charlie's knife.

Caril was exhausted. The court was recessed, and it was agreed that she would be recalled at a later date. McArthur told the press he would put her back on at the close of his case. If it was a strategic decision designed to allow Caril's testimony to sit uncontested in the jurors' minds, it was a risky one; Scheele's cross-examination would be the last the jury heard from the defense.

McArthur next called Dr. Zeman, the pathologist who had testified in Charlie's trial, to testify to the cause of death of Carol King, although it is not immediately clear why, or how, this would help Caril's case. Zeman testified that a bullet entering King's skull behind her right ear pierced her brain, killing her. There were also brush or burn marks on her back from having been dragged. He then testified to "rather copious bleeding from the vagina." An examination showed several smaller wounds and one deep "puncture wound in the cervix and into the rectum caused by a sharp instrument." (Although he didn't testify to this fact, his report noted she had also been sodomized.)

On cross-examination, Scheele handed Zeman the knife, and Zeman opined that he didn't see how this knife could have caused this wound, which was three inches deep and three-quarters of an inch wide. The knife didn't fit the wound; the wound was sharp, incised and pointed on both sides, and was wider than three-quarters of an inch. What he appeared to have meant by "pointed on both sides" was that it was sharp on both sides, like a dagger.

The only apparent purpose of the defense calling Zeman to testify about the knife wound was to show what a monster Charlie was; the problem was that it also gave some credence to the widely believed theory that Caril had attacked King's genitals with a knife in a fit of jealousy after finding Charlie having sex with her corpse at the bottom of the cellar.

McArthur also read into the record the testimony of psychiatrist Dr. O'Hearne given in Charlie's trial, which said that Charlie was insane, in order to impeach his credibility as a witness and also perhaps show what a nightmare it was for Caril to be in his thrall on the murder trail. Charlie, after all, while he walked in a human body, was not really a human being.

Odell Hanson, a reporter for the AP, gave Caril a fair shake in the next day's story. He referred to her as "an attractive fifteen-year-old brunette," without describing her as a "companion," former "sweetheart," "girlfriend," or "lover" of convicted mass murderer Charles Starkweather. He wrote of her sitting in the witness chair with "her hands folded in her lap, her voice generally firm" in one article and "poised and generally calm" in another. He told how she nearly broke down while identifying pictures of her mother and sister Betty Jean. He gave equal weight to her hostage theory, recounting it in detail, as opposed to the *Omaha World Herald*, who led with the headline "Caril's Hopes Fading."

The *Star* ran a story by Nancy Ray headlined "Caril Reserved, Emotionless During Testimony." Caril, she said, was "a bright spot of color in the drab courtroom in the witness chair wearing an electric blue sweater and skirt." Ray described her voice as "almost a monotone, neither rising or falling" whether she was talking about Starkweather's threats to kill her parents or her feelings when the shots from the cellar told her Starkweather had killed the teenagers. Caril was "wearing no make-up to break the striking paleness of her face," and the only time she lost her composure was when the Bartlett slayings brought tears to her eyes. In comparison with the testimony of "her fiery-haired, fiery-tempered ex-boyfriend, Caril Ann Fugate's words seemed like one of those in a trance."

In the morning session, a shotgun blast echoed throughout the halls of the courthouse, startling the people in Courtroom One. A deputy sheriff had been placing an item in an evidence locker when he bumped a loaded shotgun and it fired. He wasn't hurt, but the blast blew a hole in the top of the locker.

The defense continued with two friends of the Wards testifying that Clara and Lauer Ward were in their forties and in good physical and mental health, the point being to wonder how could Caril, a diminutive fourteen-year-old girl, be expected to escape Charlie's grasp if these two healthy adults could not. Then came friends and relatives to testify about Caril's love for her baby sister. Forest Hutson, the owner of the grocery store where Charlie went to make his phone calls, testified that Caril "seemed to think the world of the baby." She was "very well-behaved and quiet" and her stepfather was a good provider "who went out of his way to treat the children alike. If one child got something, he made sure the other ones did too." Caril often spent her money on things for the baby, and when she came in by herself, she was always quiet and well-behaved, "very lady-like."

Dot Fugate, Caril's stepmother, testified that Caril always brought her baby sister with her when she visited and it was obvious how much the two loved each other. She had visited Caril at least once a week at the hospital, and Caril had accepted the restrictions and was cheerful and never complained. When Dot brought her things like candy or a jar of pickles, she gave them to the other patients. As for Charles, he was always polite and quiet when he came over with Caril, but she couldn't say she ever liked him. The defense did not put William Fugate, Caril's biological father, on the stand, undoubtedly because of his previous child-molestation convictions that would likely be brought up by the prosecution if his testimony was at all helpful to Caril.

Macie Smith was in charge of Ward A-3, women's maximum security, Caril's home at the state hospital. She testified that Caril was very friendly and cooperative and always did whatever she was asked. Although she was not allowed off the ward for recreation, she played cards, embroidered clothes, and typed and read magazines in her room. On the last day of October, Caril weighed in at ninety-one pounds.

Pansy Street, Caril's grandmother, pretty much repeated her testimony from Charlie's trial. Caril looked "awfully white" and appeared to be signaling a warning as she refused her entrance to the house on Monday morning. She said, "Go away, Grandma, go home Grandmom, oh, Grannie, go away, Momma's life is in danger if you don't go away." While she talked, Caril backed up and seemed to be pointing her finger at something in the corner as a warning. Mrs. Street screamed at her to let her in to speak with her daughter. When Caril refused, she got mad and said she was going to the police station for a warrant.

Mrs. Street testified that after she went through the house with the detectives she was so certain of trouble that when she returned to work at the café, she asked her boss to keep the radio tuned to news reports. She testified as to what a good man Mr. Bartlett was and how much Caril loved Betty Jean. When the baby came along, it was like Caril now had a live doll to play with and take care of.

Here, Caril bowed her head and cried openly for several minutes.

Virginia Von Busch, who had employed Caril as a babysitter for her five children, broke into tears as she talked about how much Caril loved her children and how much the children loved Caril, "and still do," she added, bringing Caril to tears again.

Katherine Camp owned a thrift shop where the Bartletts shopped on occasion. The two older girls would pick out their clothes, and Mr. Bartlett would pay for them. When he told them nicely that they might have to wait until next week to buy an item, Caril was respectful and obedient. Both girls seemed to idolize their baby sister and were quite proud of her. Mrs. Camp also sold Charlie clothes on December 2, the day after he killed Colvert, and she got suspicious because he bought more than usual and paid in ten dollars' worth of silver. She contacted the police and told them the story. She did not know the boy's name, but told the officer who responded that he had "fiery red hair." They showed her mug shots of young men with red hair, but none were of him.

McArthur next called a critical witness: Hazel Heflin, the matron in whose custody Caril was placed when she was brought to the Douglas jail. If believed, she would cast serious doubt that Caril had told Romer in considerable detail about witnessing her family being killed. Mrs. Heflin described how dirty and unkempt Caril was when she first saw her and how she was shaking and appeared to be in shock. At one point, Caril was crying and screaming for her mother and baby sister and wondering why they didn't call her. She was mumbling and was basically unintelligible. Caril did not mention anything about her family members being killed or discuss anything about the killings. Mrs. Heflin would later state that she, like her husband the sheriff, believed Caril was innocent.

Barbara Von Busch was nervous on the stand. She testified shakily that on Saturday, when she and her husband and baby approached the Bartlett house, Caril appeared in the doorway, looking very white. She hollered at them not to come in because everyone had the flu. Barbara said she wanted to see her mother, and Caril told her several times she needed to leave or her mother would get hurt. When she and her husband returned to the cab, Caril came out and said she was sorry she was cranky but that their mother could get hurt if she didn't leave. Caril ran back in the house crying.

Bob Von Busch told almost the same story as his wife, except he gave a vivid description of what Caril looked like when she came to the door: "She looked like she had been awful run down, had her housecoat on, and her hair looked like it hadn't been put up for a week, and she looked pretty rough." When Caril came out to the cab, she warned them about possible harm to her mother if they didn't leave, and then she started crying and ran back in the house and closed the door behind her. Von

Busch returned that night with Rodney, and Caril again refused to let him in: "Please don't try to get in, my mom's life will be in your hands if you try to get in." From there, he and Rodney went to the police station, where the captain told him to quit bothering his in-laws.

Caril was taken back to the hospital during the lunch recess, and on her return she walked up the stairway at the back of the building to the sheriff's office on the second floor. Her few remaining relatives, particularly Barbara, often joined her in the office during recesses. One afternoon, when leaving the courthouse for the lunch break, a determined photographer attempted to hurdle a fence to get a good picture of her and fell flat on his face. She laughed at the incident and was still chuckling as she got in the sheriff's car a few minutes later.

A reporter reminded prosecutor Scheele in the hallway that he hadn't sought the death penalty for Caril, and Scheele replied that he had never contemplated the death penalty but that he still had an open charge on Caril Fugate for the murder of Carol King.

McArthur ended his string of witnesses midafternoon on Friday. Caril returned to the stand, wearing a dark blue dress trimmed in white at the collar and sleeves. She walked confidently to the witness chair with her chin up. She testified that the last class on Tuesday afternoon, January 21, was square dancing, and when school was out she rode a bus and walked the last few blocks home with her friend Bonnie. She entered the front door of the house, only to find Charles Starkweather standing there with a .22., which he stuck in her face. "Sit down," he ordered, and when she asked about her family, he slapped her in the face and pushed her down in the rocker. When she started to get up, he slapped her again and pushed her down. She had never seen him like this. "Are you crazy?" she demanded, at which point he screamed at her never to say that again. "Where is my family?" she asked again and again, and he told her if she'd shut up, he'd tell her: they were stashed away at the old couples' house, where his gang was keeping an eye on them. The gang was also keeping an eye on this house, and if Caril didn't cause a problem, her family would be coming home. She made some coffee and had a cup while Charlie sat in the rocker talking to her and rubbing a cloth on a gun on his lap. Eventually, he turned the TV on and they watched it until it went off the air at midnight. She slept on the couch.

Caril swore that Charlie never left the house during the day and that when he went out at night, he tied her with kitchen towels or clothesline he had cut from the ceiling. When people came to visit, he told her to not let them in or he'd shoot them. When Rodney showed up, he told Caril to get rid of him or he'd kill him. "Your own brother?" she asked. "Yes." She put up a note on the door telling people to go away because everyone inside had the flu, and she signed it Miss Bartlett, Betty Jean's nickname, which was meant to tip people off. She told of all the people coming to the door, including her sister and brother-in-law, whom she got angry with and followed out to the cab, and her grandmother, who screamed to see her daughter and finally left to get a warrant. She felt then, and she felt now, that there was never an opportunity for her to get away from Charlie without someone getting hurt. Had she known her parents and little sister were dead, she would have taken more chances. At the Griggses' place, where they went to get his car, he told her not to say anything to Mrs. Griggs or he'd kill the whole family. At Tate's Conoco, he told her to go inside Brickey's Café and get some hamburgers, and said he'd be watching her, and she knew he had a knife and gun. She didn't sneak out the back door because she didn't know where it was, and she was there only for a few moments. She was tired and nervous and hungry and worried about what he would do to her family if she didn't do as he said.

At the Ward house, Caril claimed she tried several doors in the living room to get out but that she couldn't open them. When she was washing off the knife Charles used to kill Mrs. Ward, she thought of stabbing him but realized he was stronger than she was. He also told her that if she didn't warn him about Mr. Ward coming home, she would get what Mrs. Ward got. She stayed in the bathroom, scared, until "Charles Starkweather found me."

On the clippings, Caril was a little bit clearer this time. She cut out the picture of her and Charles, with his help, and he cut out the photos of her mother, little sister, and stepfather. He showed the photos to her but would not let her read the articles. He told her to put the clippings in her shirt pocket, which she did, but she never read them. She had an interesting theory as to why the photos were in the paper: Charlie had said her family was being held hostage, and she figured the authorities were looking for them.

Caril admitted that she had become suspicious of Charlie's story by this time. She also admitted to hearing something on the radio about what had happened to her family. She denied taking the .22 to Charlie at the Collison scene. She ran to Romer's car when she saw Sprinkle put his hand on the gun because she figured Charles had finally run into a man "who could take care of him." She was so excited when talking to Romer that she tried to tell him everything, about how he had killed the young ones, the teenagers, plus the farmer and the people in the Ward house and "that man," meaning Collison, but she never said she had seen him kill her family. She said Starkweather "had" her family. "It just came out of me, all at once," she said, and she was crying the whole time.

During her testimony, she became tired and mixed up and still thought she had been held in the Casper jail rather than the Douglas jail, although she agreed to take McArthur's word that it was Douglas. At the Douglas jail, she refused to take a bath because she thought her family was coming for her and she wanted to be ready. In the Gering jail, she was told her family was dead, and on the ride the next day to Lincoln she kept asking Mrs. Karnopp if her parents were dead, but she didn't really believe it until she saw her sister in Lincoln the next day.

On cross-examination, Scheele needed to avoid badgering or bullying the fourteen-year-old girl while at the same time showing her to be an aider and abettor of murder, a true "companion" or, better, an "accomplice" to Starkweather in his killing spree. He began by going over the extradition process, and Caril conceded that she came back voluntarily. There had been one breakup with Charles Starkweather, but they were back together when he came to her house on January 19. Scheele obtained his first damning admission when Caril admitted she told Charlie to leave and not come back all the time.

The four Chrisman sisters who settled along Lieban Creek in Custer County, Nebraska, in the late 1880s. FROM LEFT TO RIGHT: Hattie, Elizabeth, Lucie, and Ruth. Each sister filed homestead claims and built her own sod house.
(Nebraska State Historical Society, Solomon Butcher collection)

House at 924 Belmont Street
(Nebraska State Historical Society)

Caril Ann and her sister Betty Jean
(Nebraska State Historical Society)

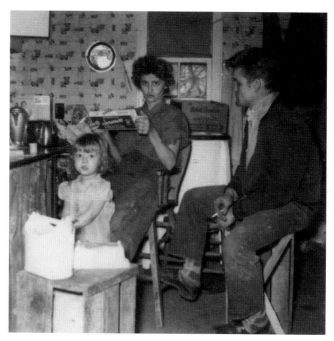

Starkweather, Velda, and Betty Jean in the Bartlett kitchen
a few weeks before the killings
(Courtesy of Maria Diaz)

Two photos of Charlie and Caril in a photo booth. Date unknown.
Note the change of appearance.
(Lancaster County, Nebraska)

Charlie's 1949 Ford
abandoned in field
on the night of
January
21, 1958
(Lincoln Journal Star)

High school yearbook
photos of Bobby Jensen
and Carol King
(Getty Images)

The cellar on the farm where Carol King and Bobby Jensen's
bodies were found
(Nebraska State Historical Society)

Ward house
(Lincoln Journal Star)

Starkweather, still wearing Lauer Ward's shirt, and
Sheriff Karnopp at Douglas jail after his capture
(Shutterstock)

Caril and Deputy Sheriff Bill Romer arriving at the Douglas County
courthouse shortly after the killing spree ended
(Casper College, Chuck Morrison Collection)

Caril leaving the courtroom in a matron's grip after the jury found her guilty of first-degree murder in November 1958
(Courtesy of Del Harding)

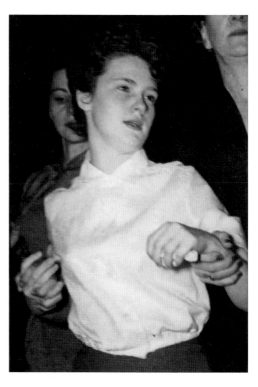

Guy and Helen Starkweather
(Lincoln Journal Star)

Charlie locks eyes with boys leaving courthouse after
receiving the death sentence *(Lincoln Journal Star)*

Caril in front of a mic at a press
conference prior to her trial in the
fall of 1958 *(Courtesy of Del Harding)*

Caril one year before her release
from the reformatory
(Courtesy of Jackie Crawford)

A gathering at a motel in York, Nebraska, after the showing of the movie *Badlands* in a local theater prior to its release in 1973. FROM LEFT TO RIGHT: director Terrence Malick, Jill Jakes (Malick's wife), Caril Fugate, Martin Sheen, Jim McArthur, and John McArthur *(Courtesy of Jim McArthur)*

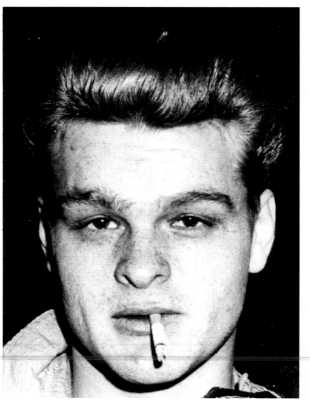

Charlie Starkweather in 1958 after his arrest (Lincoln Journal Star)

Q: You had those kind of spats pretty frequently, didn't you?

A: I told him that all the time.

If so, then her claim that she had broken up with Charlie once and for all on Sunday, January 19, and was therefore unlikely to have accompanied him on the murder spree voluntarily, was seriously weakened.

Scheele turned to the opportunities she had to escape. The first stop at Tate's, she was alone in the café for several minutes, and while she came close to handing the note in her pocket to the waitress, she didn't because Charles Starkweather had said he would be watching her.

Caril was consistent in her defense: every time she did something that made her look complicit, like holding the gun on the maid, or sprinkling perfume upstairs to suffuse the smell of Mrs. Ward's blood, or rifling through Mrs. Ward's purse for money, or warning Charles Starkweather of Mr. Ward's turn into the drive, she did so because Charles Starkweather told her to do so. Twice Scheele asked: "You took the money from the boy's wallet and put it in Chuck's wallet?" And twice she responded: "Yes, but Charles Starkweather told me to." Caril also made it clear that Charles threatened to kill her if she didn't do what he said, and she testified that Starkweather had her mother's pistol in his pocket and knife in his belt, as well as Meyer's .22 most of the time after killing him. She did what she did under threat to her life.

Scheele then questioned Caril about the savings account card signed by her and Starkweather in October, again to show their ongoing commitment to each other. Caril said that Charlie told her he had been tossed from his car dragging [racing] and wanted the money in the account to go to her in case he was killed.

Scheele returned to the killings at the cellar on the lane to the Meyer farm.

Q: When Charlie stopped the car at the cave, they got out and you stayed in the car?

A: He told me to, yes.

Q: And did you point the gun at the King girl and tell her to get out of the car?

A: Charles Starkweather told me to point the gun at her and get her out, yes.

Q: And did you do it?

A: Yes sir.

In Jensen's car at the Ward house driveway, she sat in the car for twenty minutes, with her father's shotgun in back.

Q: You brought the jacket and gun into the house, correct?

A: When he motioned me, yes.

Q: And part of the time you were watching the maid with one of the loaded guns?

A: He told me to, yes.

Q: And you did that?

A: I did what he told me.

She also shone a flashlight on the maid in the upstairs room while Charlie stabbed her to death because Charles told her to. She held a gun on the maid upstairs because Charlie told her to. There were times when Charles was upstairs and she was downstairs alone, but she couldn't see where he was and he said he'd always be watching her.

Q: You held the loaded gun on her [the maid] downstairs, didn't you?

A: He told me to.

Referring to Charlie's shirt being splattered with blood after stabbing the maid, Scheele asked:

Q: Did you look for a clean white shirt for him to wear?

A: He told me to, yes.

Q: So ... you did look for a clean white shirt for him to wear?

A: I was scared he'd kill me if I didn't.

Q: But you did do that?

A: He told me to.

Q: Did you do it?

A: Yes.

He asked about the knife.

A: He gave me the knife and told me to wash it off.

Q: And did you do that?

A: I was scared he'd kill me if I didn't.

Q: And did you do it?

A: Yes, sir.

Q: And what did you do with the knife?

A: He took it.

She admitted to helping clip pictures of herself and Charlie from the *Journal.* Charlie kept the pictures of her parents and sister in his pocket and later told her to put them in her shirt pocket. She did not read the clippings. All she ever looked at were the pictures from the front page. Yes, she might have shown the clippings to a man in the jail when he said he was sorry about her parents. Scheele showed her another envelope of clippings, and she said she had never seen them.

Scheele returned to the aiding and abetting.

Q: The two of you in that car, in Mr. Ward's car, proceeded on across the state of Nebraska, right?

A: What do you mean?

Q: After leaving the Ward house did you and Chuck ride in Mr. Ward's car all during the night?

A: I didn't want to.

Q: But did you?

A: Yes.

Scheele turned to a key piece of evidence on the hostage claim: her conversation with Deputy Sheriff Romer.

Q: And what did you tell Romer?

A: I told him I'd seen him [Charlie] kill Mr. Meyer, and these three people at the other house. I told him he'd killed a man, a woman, and these two young teenagers, and this man in Wyoming.

Q: And did you mention any number?

A: No, sir.

Q: Did you tell Mr. Romer he'd killed ten people?

A: No, sir, I didn't mention it.

Reaching the end of his questioning, Scheele returned to the "old lady's house" on Woodsdale where Charlie worked on his car and where he told Caril he had stashed her parents and sister with his gang. She was sitting in the car while Charlie grabbed two wheels from the garage.

Q: Well you know he went back behind the house into the garage and got some wheels and put them in the car, don't you?

A: He went up to the house, yes.

Q: Did he go behind the house?

A: I don't remember.

Q: You stayed out in the car?

A: He told me to stay there and not to leave.

Q: But you did stay in the car?

A (continuing): and he said if I did, I'd get shot.

Q: But did you stay in the car while he was in the garage?

A: He told me my family was in the house and if I tried anything they'd get hurt.

Q: But do you understand my question; did you remain in the car during the time that he was back in the garage?

A: Yes, sir.

Q: And he did bring some wheels out and put them in the car at that time, didn't he?

A: Yes, sir.

Q: Did he make more than one trip in order to do that?

A: I don't believe so.

Q: And then during the time that you were sitting out there in the car at that time you thought that's the very place where your family was, didn't you?

A: Yes, sir.

Q: Did you do anything or make any effort to go up to that house while he was out in the garage?

A: He told me to stay there and not to leave.

Q: But did you make any effort to go up to the front door of that house while he was in the garage?

A: I didn't want my family to be hurt, no.

Q: Did you make any effort to do that?

A: No, sir.

Q: Did you say anything to Charles to please let you go in the old lady's house when you were out there that day?

A: Yes, sir. I wanted to get in.

Q: You did ask him that?

A: Yes, sir.

Q: So you could see your family?

A: Yes.

Q: How long were you alone in your car there when he was back in the garage?

A: Just a few minutes.

Q: And he had no loaded gun in his possession during the time he was away from the car, did he?

A: He had my mother's knife and my mother's small gun.

Q: Did you leave with him, Caril?

A: Against my will, yes.

Q: But you did leave with him?

A: Against my will, yes.

Q: And even after you left the Wards' home while you were on the way to Wyoming, did you tell Chuck Starkweather that you loved him?

A: Yes, I did; I was afraid he was going to kill me.

Q: And did you kiss him?

A: No, sir.

Q: You never did that?

A: No, sir; he kissed me.

Q: He kissed you?

A: Yes, sir.

"That is all," Scheele said, and he sat down. He was modulated and polite in his questions, and while he pushed Caril a little here and there, he was never overly aggressive or rude. If anyone became antagonistic, it was the fifteen-year-old girl on the stand, although Scheele never managed to really rattle her or get under her skin. She looked him directly in the eye the entire cross-examination. He could have been rougher, tried to make her out to be a liar by pointing out that in the Statement she had said explicitly that Charlie had never threatened to kill her and admitted to having lied in Wyoming when she said he had. And he didn't ask her about having sexual intercourse with Charlie on the road from the Ward house to Wyoming or in her bedroom at home. He ended instead with her confession of love for and a kiss from the killer.

Caril's constant need to explain her behavior didn't help her, but her answers didn't directly contradict her answers on direct or her Statement. McArthur decided to leave well enough alone. He told the judge he had no further questions for Caril.

The AP headline the next morning read, "Caril Clings to Story Didn't Know Family Was Slain."

Charlie was following his girlfriend's trial. He had not abandoned his fantasy—his reality, really—of walking to his death with Caril at his side. He invited his persecutor, prosecutor Elmer Scheele, to visit him in prison. On a note to the prosecutor, he scribbled: "If you have time I would like to see you. It's about the Wards." Signed "Chuck."

Scheele didn't visit Charlie, so Charlie wrote another note: "Tell E.S. he knows where to find me. I am ready and raring to go." Signed, "Charles Starkweather." When Elmer still didn't visit him, he began writing notes. He said that Caril was upstairs alone on three occasions at the Ward house, and he included a numbered list of her reasons for being upstairs: (1) to retrieve the bloody knife he had stuck in Mrs. Ward's back, and (2) to get a suitcase, but at (3), he left a blank space, indicating he didn't know what she was doing the third time; perhaps killing the maid?

In his notes to Scheele, Charlie attacked Caril personally, calling her a liar and an ungrateful child who cursed her mother ("go to hell") and stepfather loudly when she didn't get her way, and claiming that she was constantly spanking the kids she was babysitting. She lied when she testified that she told Carol King to get out of the car so they wouldn't get hurt; when she was holding the gun on the girl, what she said was, "Go on, get out of the car." She was lying when she said that he told her he would shoot anyone who came in the Bartlett house; when she testified that he pointed the gun at her when he got in the car (after shooting Carol King) (seemingly an admission that he had in fact killed King); when she testified that he told her the .410 he gave her at the Meyer farm was broken; when she testified she pleaded with him not to hurt Jensen; when she said Charlie told her he would kill her if anyone came in the house; when she said she was hiding from him in the bathroom after he shot Mr. Ward. In fact, it was Caril's idea to kill August Meyer. She had Charlie's hunting knife, which she apparently carried in her boot, and she swore that if she got close enough, she would stab him with it. He wrote:

> She said I was angry, excited, shaky, nervous, his face was angry, mean, all wrinkled up. some of that may have been right, but not all of it, and what I can't understand is she said she was watching me, cause I know she wasn't, cause I didn't trust Caril to far, and I

was glancing at her every now and then, and not once can I recall did Caril take her eyes of Carol King. Caril had the .410 right behind Carol King's head at all times.

I did tell Caril in a nice way if she would watch for Mr. Ward, but I did not tell her if she didn't she would get what Mrs. Ward got.

Caril new that murder charges were against her because we heard it on the car radio many times and when she did hear she said she didn't care because I was taking the blame.

I (Charlie) came over on the Monday night before the killings, and Caril's stepdad gave her the devil because she hadn't gone to school, and Caril said she was so mad "she could kill him."

We had the radio on in the car all the time, because then we could tell we were still ahead of the police. We heard they searching every home. One reason we left Lincoln. Also T.V. at Ward's in the library was on and Caril heard some thing she did not like—I do not know what—she turned it off. When I went to turn it on she got mad—turned it off—unplugged it and shut down TV.

Charlie wrote that Caril was always telling him to leave her house and not come back. He'd get to his car, and she would come running out and tell him to come by the next evening. She would tell her mom she was going to stay at her sister's apartment and instead spend the night with Charlie. Caril was always accusing him of running around with other girls.

In a three-page typewritten statement, Charlie wrote that on the road back from Bennet to Lincoln he told Caril he wanted to give himself up because he was tired of running, but Caril, who had the shotgun lying across her lap, barrel pointed right at him, said she was not giving up and nobody including him was going to make her. "The shotgun and her words convinced me." Under threat, her persuasion, and her crying, Charlie changed his mind and carried on.

On it goes. In Jensen's car, Carol King thanked Charlie for not being abusive, and Caril got jealous and stuck the shotgun an inch from King's nose and said, "'Turn around and keep your mouth shut.'"

"Carol King looked at me with a look more like she had to do as she said or not. I said 'She's the boss, better do as she says.'"

All in all, Charlie wrote a total of ten letters, many of them apparently written just before or during Caril's trial. Many corrected small things, like Caril's testimony that she liked to roller-skate when she didn't, or that she referred to her mother as "mama" when she sent her grandmother away, which she never did, or that she had bought the collie dog for four dollars. One letter indicated that Charlie had urged Scheele to file conspiracy charges against McArthur apparently for defamation. Scheele politely declined.

A few things are absurd on their face. Charlie wrote that Caril hated Bob Von Busch so much for trying to break her and Charlie up that she swore she would have shot him when he came to the Bartlett house if Rodney hadn't been with him. When Bob and Barbara and the baby showed up at the house in a cab, Caril grabbed the rifle and said she was going to shoot Bob until Charles jerked the rifle away from her and said, "Don't be dumb." No one had ever suggested that Caril had access to or walked around the Bartlett house with the .22 (or the shotgun, for that matter). And it was Charlie who hated Bob, not Caril. It seems more likely that Charlie himself was fantasizing about blowing his fighting buddy away.

Charlie wrote that the tops of his blue-and-white cowboy boots got splattered in blood in the Ward house. As they were driving away, up Twenty-Seventh, Caril wetted her handkerchief with her tongue and wiped the blood from the boots.

Caril could also be very manipulative.

Caril is also a very good actor, for some reason she can cry whenever she wants to—like she did to me when she wanted something—she may try it in the courtroom to get people on her side and feel sorry for her, but behind those tears she is laughing, because many a time she wanted something from somebody and could not get it and she would cry as though she was a little baby and after she got what she wanted she would laugh at them behind their backs.

Perhaps in all these letters Charlie was trying to convince Scheele to seek death for Caril for the Jensen murder, or perhaps he was setting Scheele up to charge Caril with another murder, a more gruesome one—the head shot and the knife puncturing of the genitals of Carol King—that would get her the chair if she didn't get it for Jensen's murder.

Or perhaps Charlie, once again, was just having fun.

37

JUDGE SPENCER SET ASIDE ALL OF WEDNESDAY, NOVEMber 18, for closing arguments. By agreement, each side would get 2.5 hours. Scheele would go first, then McArthur, then Scheele a final time.

Trial lawyers are essentially salesmen. The jury is their customer. Their product is a story. Here, they say, here's what really happened; my story is backed up by facts and logic, as opposed to that of my competitor, whose story is so full of holes and contradictions it's simply unworthy of belief. I'm going to give you the highlights now; then I'll lay out the details for you through testimony and exhibits. In closing, they say, Now you know the story, just as I told you, and certainly you can see it is the truth, the only truth honest, intelligent people such as yourself could find.

Scheele began by insisting that he was not enjoying telling (and selling) the story of this fourteen-year-old girl and what she did, just as he was sure the jury wasn't enjoying listening to it. One would not think that an ordinary fourteen-year-old girl could be capable of such conduct. But this was no ordinary fourteen-year-old. She knew the difference between right and wrong and had to be made to realize that you can't go on an eight-day murder spree without paying the price. Her statements and testimony established her complicity in the killing of Robert Jensen, as had her conduct, appearance, and demeanor in the courtroom. She was an accomplice, a willing accomplice. Step by step, Scheele methodically walked the jury through the eight days of the horror story, beginning on January 21 and ending on January 29. Caril was at her home on 924 Belmont and watched as Starkweather killed the three members of her family. She had plenty of opportunities to flee. Remember the two policemen? Charlie was asleep when they came knocking; Caril could easily have walked right out the door with them, but she woke Charlie up instead. Just as she could have gotten in the cab with her sister and brother-in-law and drove off to safety. And there was the afternoon when several people came to the door and Charlie was on the far side of town visiting a relative. Well, she wasn't tied up that day. She was free to leave. The note to the police that she wrote in the car in the shop—she could have given that to a gas station attendant or the waitress in the café. Not to mention the twenty minutes she sat in Jensen's car in the Wards' driveway while Charlie was inside the house. Caril decided to "escape" only when "the jig was up." Scheele did not fail to mention the kissing scene in the car on the way to Wyoming after the killings in the Ward house. As for the penalty, he told the jury, he was "perfectly satisfied" to leave that up to them.

Caril wept silently as Scheele recounted the crimes.

The tall, lean defense attorney rose slowly and removed his glasses. He looked tired. In his dignified manner, he spoke calmly to the jury: They were talking about a girl. A fourteen-year-old girl. Not a woman. Not an adult. A girl. The prosecutors, Elmer Scheele and Fahrnbruch, did not see Caril. They had never seen her. "They see Lucrezia Borgia, or one of the witches from *Macbeth* when they see Caril." Ordinary fourteen-year-old girls were giddy and played with Hula-Hoops. Not this one. She was obedient and gullible. The jury couldn't convict her on the word of a hopelessly insane madman. Eleven people had already died at his hand; "Will you add one more?" he demanded. McArthur argued that the prosecution brought and tried the case out of a terrible prejudice; they were burning and cringing under stinging criticism for their handling of the investigation, and this prejudice made it necessary to hang guilt on this girl. The Lincoln Police Department was a dead-letter office. Caril was a scapegoat for their failures. And what did the jury expect of this fourteen-year-old girl? Ten victims, grown men and women, like Marion Bartlett and Merle Collison and Robert Jensen and August Meyer and Lauer Ward, couldn't handle Charles Starkweather, and they expected this little girl to? The fact was that Caril's physical and mental ability to escape was gone after she saw Starkweather shoot Bennet farmer August Meyer on January 27. As for her 166-page statement, McArthur advised the jury to be very suspicious of it. It had been edited; questions had been deleted. Essentially, what they had here was a little girl in the hands of a maniac. If they took Starkweather's testimony out of the evidence, the prosecution's case was gone.

McArthur insisted that "The shock of witnessing Starkweather's killings reduced Caril to a 'piece of putty' with no more ability to resist than a three-year-old child."

In his rebuttal, Scheele told the jury that Mr. McArthur was using one of the oldest tricks in the book: when you have no defense, you criticize the police.

The jury was excused at the end of the day. The judge advised them to bring their bags the next morning, for they would be sequestered in the Lincoln Hotel if deliberations ran into the night. The jury reconvened at 9:00 a.m. on Thursday morning, November 20.

By law, a jury is charged with determining the facts of the case; that is, they decide which story to accept, or sometimes they will write their own story. The judge instructs them as to the relevant provisions of the law and how to apply them to the facts they have determined. The reading of the instructions in this case took forty minutes.

Many of the instructions are stock, such as the presumption of innocence and burden of proof. As to the first charge, that Caril actually murdered Robert Jensen, the judge instructed that to convict Caril of this charge, the jury must find that she killed him with deliberate malice and premeditation (whatever that might mean). If the jury found that she aided and abetted Charles Starkweather in the killing of Robert Jensen, she would also be guilty under the first count. Or the jury could find Caril guilty of second-degree murder, which has no requirement of premeditation or deliberation. On the second count, murder in the perpetration of a robbery, the jury needed only to find that "the defendant intended to rob Robert William Jensen and that Robert William Jensen was killed during the perpetration of that act." The judge also gave a somewhat-circular instruction on the reliability of Charlie's testimony: "Great care and caution should be used in weighing his [Starkweather's] testimony. You will scrutinize it closely in the light of all the evidence in the case, and you will give to it such weight as you may think it is entitled to have, keeping in mind the credibility of such witness."

As the defense requested, the judge gave an instruction on the voluntariness of Caril's actions:

> Duress may be defined as an unlawful restraint, intimidation or compulsion of another to such an extent and degree as to induce such other person to do or perform such act contrary to his will and inclination. If the evidence shows that the defendant did the things with which she is charged under duress, it is your duty to find the defendant not guilty of any degree of homicide under both the First and Second Counts.

The judge also instructed the jury that the defendant was not on trial for failure to run away from her killer companion, for not giving an alarm, or for not trying to prevent the offenses. And he told them that merely being present while a murder is committed does not make a person an accomplice to it. He gave the case to the jury at 10:01 a.m.

After the judge declared a recess, Caril lingered at the defense table in the courtroom with her sister Barbara and lawyer Reller, to whom she had become quite attached. He had brought a stack of fan mail, and she and Barbara were reading the letters. He hadn't shown them to her before because he didn't want to upset her. The little gathering ended when Sheriff Karnopp came in the courtroom and reminded Caril it was time to return to the state hospital. "There's a brave little girl," Reller commented to a reporter.

Caril was cheerful about her prospects for acquittal. The people at the hospital were nice, she told Reller, but she would be glad to leave there. Reller also anticipated an acquittal. Not so McArthur. The people would not be denied their pound of flesh.

At 9:40 that night, the jury quit deliberating and went to the Lincoln Hotel. The jury returned at 9:00 a.m. the next morning to resume deliberations.

The jury bell rang at 10:30, after a total of nine hours of deliberation.

Within moments, newsmen and locals filled the courtroom. Photographers clogged the hallway. Caril, who had been waiting in the sheriff's office with her sister and grandmother, appeared pale in a white blouse, bright blue skirt, and bobby socks. She walked in the courtroom briskly with her usual impassive look and tight mouth. She moistened her lips and stared at the jury as they walked in and were seated. At 11:10 the foreman stood and read the verdict: "We the jury . . . do find the defendant, Caril Ann Fugate, guilty of murder in the first degree on Count 2 and do fix the penalty at life imprisonment."

Caril broke into quiet sobs at the word "guilty." Her body convulsed as she buried her head against Reller's shoulder. He put his arm around her. "I'd rather be executed," she managed. "But they couldn't because they know I'm innocent." Her sobs filled the courtroom. Her family in the first row was also in tears. Caril's sobbing continued for ten minutes, until finally Reller was also crying. "I wished he had killed me too so I could be with my mom," she managed. Charlie got off easy, she would later say. His suffering ended when he died.

"By necessary inference," Judge Spencer intoned over the weeping, "Caril was found not guilty on Count One."

The judge asked Caril if she understood the verdict, and she nodded her head. As the judge thanked the jury for their service, she fell into sobs. After the jury was excused, her grandmother and sister gathered around her. "I'm not guilty," she insisted in tears. Pansy Street consoled her that we didn't always understand God's will and it would turn out all right for her in time. "Keep your chin up," she said. Caril embraced her sister and pleaded, "Don't leave me."

Mrs. Karnopp and another woman held Caril up by the arms as they escorted her from the courtroom and down the hall jammed full with newsmen and photographers to the sheriff's office. She was dry-eyed and composed when she walked to the sheriff's car half an hour later. Her sister and grandmother rode in the back seat of the car on the drive to the state hospital.

On Monday, Superintendent Spraddle told a reporter Caril spent the weekend quietly and without incident.

38

CARIL'S CONVICTION WAS ANNOUNCED ON RADIO AND TV and splashed across the front pages of newspapers of cities and towns small and large across America. The *New York Mirror* ran a headline almost half of the front page that read, "We Stay in Berlin: Ike." On the bottom half of the front page was a photo of Caril after the verdict, looking balefully into the camera, with a side note: "Caril wept uncontrollably when the verdict was announced. They made a mistake . . . why didn't they give me the chair?' she cried." The AP proclaimed that "bobby-soxer Caril Ann Fugate heard herself condemned to prison for aiding and abetting Charles Starkweather on a killing rampage last January."

Scheele proclaimed himself satisfied with the verdict. McArthur said he was shocked and surprised at the verdict and planned to appeal. Attorney Matschullat opined that he felt the verdict was a bit harsh, given that Caril was in the custody of a madman (Starkweather, his client) when the murders took place. Mrs. Jensen, Bobby's mother, declared that Caril should have received the death penalty. Mabel King stated that Caril was as guilty as Starkweather, but that she was satisfied with the verdict as long as Caril never received parole. The general sentiment in Bennet was that Caril should have been sentenced to death.

One juror didn't find Caril particularly credible. It seemed that she had been coached too much by McArthur. "She sounded like a broken record," the juror said. "She kept repeating two or three statements over and over again," such as "Charlie told me to do it." The juror also recalled the many chances that Caril had to get away but didn't. The juror hoped that if Caril really was innocent, some proof could be found for a new trial to prove it.

The morning of the verdict, Starkweather returned to his cell from a visit with his mother at 11:00 a.m. He got his lunch tray, put on his headphones, and was listening to the radio when he suddenly stood and walked to the bars. "Caril was convicted and got life imprisonment," he said in a low voice to one of the guards sitting outside his cell. After finishing his lunch, he told the guard that he felt "real sorry for Caril."

A few days after her conviction but prior to her sentencing, there was a brief glimmer of hope for Caril. A few days before the trial, one of the jurors, H. A. Walenta, from Crete, had bet a dollar with one of his hunting buddies that Caril would get the chair. It was a big story—a juror bets on the outcome of a trial. And while she didn't get the chair, she was convicted. McArthur filed a motion for a new trial. He pointed out that Walenta hadn't mentioned the bet in voir dire and that any bet, no matter how small, should cause the verdict to be set aside.

On the face of it, it seemed like a good shot. Everyone in the Fugate camp, including Caril, was optimistic. Jurors are supposed to enter the trial with open minds, and this one was so sure of Caril's guilt that he had bet she would not only get convicted but also be sentenced to death. One problem was, of course, that he lost his bet. In an affidavit, Walenta stated that the bet was casual and he had forgotten about it until reminded of it after the trial. The jury foreman swore that Walenta had never mentioned the death penalty in deliberations. The person who reminded him of the bet said Walenta appeared to have forgotten about the bet when he told him.

On December 20, 1958, Caril appeared in court to be sentenced. First Judge Spencer denied the motion for a new trial, finding that juror Walenta had dismissed the wager from his mind and was not motivated by it. Caril stood in front of the judge, hands clutched behind her back. He read aloud:

It is hereby adjudged and decreed that the defendant Caril Ann Fugate, being 15 years of age or upward, be and she is hereby sentenced to imprisonment in the State Reformatory for Women in York, Nebraska, for the period of her natural life and shall pay the costs of this prosecution taxed at $291.30.

After the hearing, Sheriff Karnopp drove Caril to the mental hospital to pick up her few things and then drove her to the Women's Reformatory in York, about sixty miles west of Lincoln. There, she would be
held in an isolated, closed setting for seven months, until her sixteenth
birthday.

IV

GUILT OR INNOCENCE

39

CHARLIE AND CARIL STOOD CONVICTED OF MURDER within ten months of the slaughter of the innocents. The day of her sentencing, December 21, when asked if she had anything to say, Caril proclaimed her innocence. At York, she was allowed no visitors over the holidays and had no contact with other inmates. For the next seven months, she spent all but an hour or two a day in her cell alone. It would be ten years before she could seek to have her sentence commuted.

While the community closed the chapter on Caril, Lincoln understood that the town would never be the same, in its own eyes or in the eyes of the world, and that this would go far beyond the simple reality that from now on household doors would be locked and car keys pulled from the ignition. The days of paralyzing fear were now threaded into the nervous system of the community, and it knew without thinking that even Charlie's execution would not allow for a full recovery, as if the slaughter had never happened. The 1950s were gone for good.

Caril Fugate, now fifteen, was alive and was going to stay alive. The system would not kill her, and she wasn't going quietly into the night. Her lawyers filed motions arguing she had not received a fair trial and listed seventy-seven errors made by the court. The lawyers insisted she had been bullied into making the Statement, and they would carry that claim to the U.S. Supreme Court. A reasonable estimate would be that 90 percent of the city agreed with chief Joe Carrol that Caril was every bit as guilty of the murders as Charlie Starkweather. Yes, she was only fourteen at the time, a child, really, but that concern was ameliorated by the fact that she wasn't put to death. It turned out the jury went at their process backward: first, they decided they weren't going to execute her, and once that was in hand, they decided she was guilty of felony murder in the death of Robert Jensen.

The questions raised about her role in the spree would not go away, and they grew even more intense as time passed and she and Charlie were portrayed somewhat glamorously in movies, songs, TV shows, and countless articles and books. The image of the tiny girl with her dark brown ponytail, in her "white majorette boots," as she called them, or "baton twirler boots," as the cops called them, knifing and shooting people to death at the side of her crazy James Dean–looking boyfriend proved irresistible. But even for some of those condemning her, the questions gnawed: Was justice done? Or was it vengeance? Did Caril receive a fair trial? Is she guilty or innocent?

The latter two questions are separate and distinct. The issue of a fair trial deals with the process of the criminal justice system as it attempts to determine the question of guilt or innocence. Did the government play by the rules? The second question asks, Do the facts prove that she is guilty of the crime? It would be futile, of course, to attempt to retry today the case as it stood then with the same facts and laws. It is possible, however, to bring the judicial decision-making process in modified form to bear on the old and newly discovered facts and to apply new laws and knowledge about the brain and trauma to sort out the answers to both of these questions, as if Caril were on trial for first-degree murder today.

40

THE WORKINGS OF THE CRIMINAL JUSTICE SYSTEM are seen as a search for the truth. While some legal minds argue that the process does not establish the truth but only what the evidence did or did not prove, for the person on the street that is a semantic game. If a man is convicted, it means he's guilty. If a man is acquitted, it means he's innocent. In the factual determination of guilt or innocence, the system has many safeguards against the workings of an overzealous and powerful government. Two of the most important protections are the presumption of innocence and the requirement of proof beyond a reasonable doubt, both of which the Supreme Court has determined are required by the Constitution. Both are incapable of a clear or definitive articulation. One trial lawyer says that a defendant coming into the criminal courtroom is cloaked in a presumption of innocence. Proof beyond a reasonable doubt means that you must have a conviction of guilt unshaken by time; you won't look in the mirror tomorrow morning or a year from now or five years from now or even on your deathbed and wonder if maybe the defendant was innocent. Some courts consider both principles so sacrosanct and unknowable that they prohibit the lawyers from trying to explain them to the jury.

This was the 1950s. The government, at least the law enforcement and judicial systems, in Nebraska and most of the country was respected as basically competent and honest. Police were looked up to, trusted, and obeyed. Judges were black-robed gods. One of the most popular TV shows of the day was *Dragnet*, starring Jack Webb as the smart, straightforward, and upstanding Sergeant Friday. There weren't any shows like *Training Day*, where the cops are the criminals. To put it simply, when you got in trouble with the law, it was most likely because you'd done something wrong. The mere fact that you were sitting at the defense table

might be enough to rebut or at least neutralize the presumption of innocence. Lincoln may have lost its innocence in the cold days of January
1958, but not its faith in the criminal justice system and its main players.

There wasn't a person in the juror box who could look at the hard-
faced girl sitting in front of them and wipe their mind clean of all they'd
heard and seen in the past eight months about her and her role in the
shocking rampage.

In taking a fresh look at Caril's guilt or innocence, it is helpful to
proceed through the murders in the order they occurred.

MARION, VELDA, AND BETTY JEAN BARTLETT

No lawmen ever seriously suggested that Caril participated in the murder of her mother, stepfather, and little sister. The question was: Was she
present for their killing? Did she witness the shooting and knifing of her
parents and the skull smashing and knifing of two-year-old Betty Jean?
If she did, then her claim that she was being held hostage for the safety
of her family was a lie. And if that was a lie, then her failure to run away
when given opportunity after opportunity was sufficient to wind her in
as an active participant in the terrible carnage. If she was there for the
killings at 924 Belmont, how could she explain not leaving with the two
cops who came to her house when Charlie was sleeping? Not getting in
the cab with her sister and brother-in-law? Not fleeing from Jensen's car
in the drive of the Ward house after Charlie had gone inside? If she came
home *after* the killing, then her hostage story, while still a little shaky,
could hold some water. It would mean that the first time she learned
that her boyfriend was a killer was when she saw him blow the head off
August Meyer on the porch of his farmhouse for no apparent reason,
and everything happening after that moment would have to be viewed
in that light.

Most criminal cases involve a dispute of facts, and most of the disputes involve two or more competing stories of what happened. One
witness says the light on the second floor was on. Another says the light

was off. Sometimes, one of them is telling the truth and the other is lying. But not always. Sometimes memories fail or change. In our case, however, someone is lying and someone else is telling the truth. Either Charlie killed her family *before* Caril came home, or he killed them *after* she came home. She either witnessed their murders or she didn't. There is no in-between. In such a case, it is the trier of fact's job to determine who is telling the truth, to decide which of the two versions of events is most worthy of belief, and thereafter accept it as fact.

In making judgments of credibility, the jury is frequently instructed to use their common sense and to bring their life experiences to bear on the question. The jury should also observe the demeanor and conduct of the witness on the stand and consider any corroborating evidence, any prior inconsistent statements, or any motives or reasons for the witness to tell the truth or lie. There is another factor, a highly subjective one: Which version "sounds like the truth"? The court's jury instructions often attempt to encourage this sort of consideration by suggesting jurors are free to use their intuition in deciding factual disputes. This can be a scary idea, since it allows the jurors to essentially rely on anything they feel like relying on in choosing between truth and a lie. But admitting that fact-finding is a somewhat subjective process is simply acknowledging that any perceived reality itself is subjective, since by definition it is cycled through the mind of the perceiver. Jurors would do it even if they weren't so instructed.

In some cases, the jury also considers and determines facts not directly in issue. If I were sitting as the judge in the case, I would find initially that Charlie Starkweather set out for the Bartlett house on 924 Belmont in the early afternoon of January 21 with the full intention of killing Marion Bartlett. Less than two days earlier, Caril told him that she did not want to see him anymore. Marion Bartlett had previously accused Charlie of getting Caril pregnant and had told him to stay away from her. In his testimony, Charlie admitted that out of all the murders he committed, the one person he did not feel bad about killing was Marion Bartlett. Betty (Velda) Bartlett also told him not to come around again, but the stepfather—the male—was the ultimate obstructionist. Charlie's death-seeking fantasy of him and Caril roaming in hell free was foreclosed as a reality as long as Marion Bartlett lived.

On January 21, after finishing the garbage route with brother Rodney around 1:00 p.m., Charlie drove to Rodney's house to borrow his .22. He told Rodney he had a date to go hunting with Marion Bartlett later that afternoon. He told the same story in his statements and on the stand: he was going hunting with the hated stepfather. This story defies belief. The two men bore intense animosity toward one another. Neither was the sort to make a good-will gesture toward the other. Bartlett wanted Charlie gone from the house, gone from his stepdaughter's life. An attempted reconciliation with Charlie by going hunting with him would have no appeal and serve no purpose. Even if Charlie had asked him to go hunting, it is highly unlikely he would have agreed. Marion Bartlett was not a hunter. He did not have a hunting license. He did not talk about hunting. Charlie shot rabbits with a .22. Marion's only gun was a .410, which could shred a rabbit if you got close enough to hit it. While Caril knew the gun was in the house, she had never seen the weapon out of its case.

Marion Bartlett normally went to work at Watson Brothers Trucking at 5:30 or 6:00 p.m. He often went shopping with his wife in the morning and slept in the afternoon. It seems more than unlikely that he would have agreed to cut his sleep short to go hunting with anyone, much less Charlie.

Charlie testified he took the .22 inside the Bartlett house with him. Why, if you were going to drive somewhere to go hunting with another person, would you take the rifle inside the home of that person? Wouldn't you leave it in your car at least until you found out which vehicle would be used for the hunting trip? The only readily apparent purpose for taking the rifle inside would be if you intended to use it. With the Colvert killing, Charlie had tasted blood, as one psychiatrist put it, and he liked it. It was the door to eternity.

This finding is important for one reason: Caril didn't normally get out of school until 3:15 and usually didn't make it home until around

4:00 p.m. So Charlie knew she wouldn't be home for at least two and a half hours when he went to her house. This finding alone would be insufficient to establish with certainty that Caril was not home when Charlie stabbed and shot her family to death, but it certainly is considerable support for Caril's insistence that she wasn't there for the killings: her presence wasn't part of Charlie's plan.

The prosecutor relied heavily on Charlie's testimony to establish that Caril was present when he murdered her parents and sister. As set forth earlier, Charlie's numerous oral and written statements were wildly inconsistent in most all respects, but particularly on the key fact of whether Caril was in the house when he killed her parents. He made four oral statements to lawmen shortly after his arrest in Wyoming, and in none of them was Caril involved in the killings. That first night he wrote in the Letter to His Parents that she was not at home when he killed her family. He wrote in the Douglas Jail Confession that same night that Caril was not involved in the killings. In the caravan from Douglas to Gering the next day, he repeated to Sheriff Karnopp that Caril had nothing to do with the crimes. Detective Henninger's notes state that the next morning Charlie told him that Caril was not home when he killed her family and that he had killed Jensen, King, Lauer Ward, Clara Ward, and Fencl. Only in the police car from Gering to Lincoln did his story begin to change when he told Karnopp that in fact Caril was not a hostage and could have left anytime she wanted. In the Ward Letter, found on him at the time of his arrest, he accused Caril of killing her baby sister and Merle Collison, and on the jailhouse wall in Gering he had written that Caril had killed six women. But the first two written and four oral statements *after the arrest* indicate that either Caril was not home or that she was not involved in the killings.

In his first formal statement, taken on February 1, Charlie stated *twice* under direct questioning by Scheele that Caril was not present at 924 Belmont when he killed her parents and sister. Asked again whether Caril knew her parents and sister were dead when they left the house on January 27, Charlie replied that no, she didn't. It was not until the February 27 statement that Charlie placed Caril in the house at the time of the killings, and even then he did not accuse her of directly killing anyone. (It wasn't until March 28 that he claimed Caril had shot Carol King and finished off Merle Collison with a .22.) Lawyer Gaughan's notes show that Charlie first told him Caril was not in the 924 Belmont house at the time of the killings, but that he later said she was there, then again that she wasn't.

It would be hard to imagine a witness entitled to less credibility than Charlie Starkweather. He was not only a convicted murderer on death row at the time of his testimony but also an admitted liar. He told McArthur on cross-examination that his earlier statements to the law and in his letters that Caril was not present for the murders were all "hogwash." His story about Caril's role in the course of events changed almost every time he told it.

A fact finder sometimes informally relies on a rebuttable presumption to the effect that when a person gives conflicting statements, the one given most closely in time to the event is more likely the truth. This is particularly true when the event in question is startling or traumatic. The law recognizes an exception to the hearsay rule when the statement given is an "excited utterance"; that is a statement made by a person in response to a startling or shocking event. The theory is that a spontaneous statement after a shocking event is likely to be trustworthy because there was no opportunity for the maker to plan or think about what to say. In our case, Charlie was coming off a killing spree of seven people in less than forty-four hours. Whether he decided to implicate Caril in the killings because of Caril's note given to him on February 2 by Sheriff Karnopp, which seems unlikely given Charlie's February 7 love letter to her, or because he came to realize that if she did not die, the fantasy would be defeated and his vision of a much-anticipated death in a sun-blaze of lead-striped glory would be greatly diminished, is not critically important. What is important is that given almost a month to reflect on Caril's role, he changed his story. Now he put her in the Bartlett house for the killings.

Charlie testified that after Bartlett kicked him out the front door, he drove to Hutson's store and called Watsons Brothers Trucking and told a woman who answered that Mr. Bartlett wouldn't be in for work that day because he was sick. He returned to the house and waited on the back porch for around an hour and a half for Caril to return.

A woman who took the call at Watson's verified that the call came in around two o'clock. Another witness said she had seen Mr. Bartlett at the grocery store between 1:30 and 2:00. So under Charlie's version, he returned to the house shortly after 2:00 p.m. and waited on the back porch, playing with the dog, until Caril returned around 4:00. Only then did he go inside and kill three members of the family.

The obvious problem here is the notion that Charlie would call the employer *before* he killed Marion Bartlett. Charlie had a wildly explosive temper, and he admitted that he decided to kill Bartlett the moment he kicked him out the front door. Charlie was in a rage, his gun was handy, he had bullets in his jacket pocket, and yet instead of going inside and killing his tormentor, he drove to the store to call Mr. Bartlett's employer to say he would not be coming to work. Rather than turn back into the house, he thought ahead about a consequence of killing him— that someone might come to the house looking for him—and decided to first deal with that problem. A contract killer might think ahead like that, but not Charlie. Charlie's rage was never far below the surface; his hatred was always bubbling hot. Being humiliated by a kick in the butt from his girlfriend's stepfather would serve to mix the ingredients into plastique. And yet, after being kicked out the front door, and after deciding then and there to kill him, he calmly drove to the store and made the phone call? The more likely version is that, if he was in fact kicked out, he turned back into the house, perhaps engaged Mr. Bartlett in an argument, perhaps a scuffle, and at some point grabbed his .22 and shot him, as he had always planned. The killings would have been over at the latest shortly before 2:00—after Mr. Bartlett returned home from the store and before Charlie made the call around 2:00—a good hour and forty-five minutes before Caril returned home.

Even if Charlie had made the phone call before killing the Bartletts, why would he then return to the house and sit on the back porch for an hour and a half? His rage would only have been fueled by the passage of half an hour since the boot on his backside. The picture of Charlie sitting calmly on the back porch in thirty-degree weather, playing with the dog, his rifle only a few yards away, and bullets in his pocket, for an hour and a half waiting for his girlfriend to come home so he could go inside and kill her stepfather in front of her is so contrary to all the known facts as to, as lawyers like to say, strain credulity.

On the other hand, Caril was, by most objective standards, a credible witness on the question of her presence in the home for the murders. With some exceptions, her trial testimony of what happened inside the Bartlett home stayed close to the Statement.

In the Statement, Caril appears somewhat naive and basically unaware of the jeopardy she is in. In answering questions about Charlie's weapons, she describes her stepdad's gun as a .45-caliber shotgun and the .22 rifle as a .22 pistol. She admits to being mixed up on the order of events and allows herself to be led through the facts by Fahrnbruch. Only a few hours earlier, her father and sister had advised her to cooperate and tell the truth, and she appears to be doing her best to do as told. She responds to questions simply and straightforwardly; there is no evasion or ambiguity in the answers, no hostility or antagonism toward her interrogator.

Interestingly, Caril freely admits to various behaviors or conduct that are extremely harmful to her claim of innocence. This serves to enhance her overall credibility: If she were lying or covering up, why would she so readily admit to highly incriminating conduct? For example, in the Statement she readily admits to holding the .410 on Carol King and waving it toward the door as she orders her out of the car, and she readily admits to taking the money from Jensen's wallet and putting it in Charlie's. Why would she admit to something as damaging as taking the .22 out of the Packard in Wyoming and running it over to Charlie if at the same time she was lying about knowing that her parents were dead? She told in detail about waking Charlie up when the two police officers came to her house and lying to them about everyone inside having the flu. She admitted to having opportunities to leave the house on the several occasions when she went outside to the mailbox.

She admitted to holding the gun on the maid in the Ward house and to alerting Charlie to Mr. Ward's arrival at the house.

She makes a particularly damaging admission when she admits to carrying the loaded .22 as she and Charlie were walking from Meyer's house to their car. This is the first time in the Statement that a gun is placed in Caril's hands, and she placed it there herself.

As discussed, at one point she even admits to having lied to investigators:

Q: Caril, I understand that you have made the statement that he [Starkweather] was going to kill you when you got to the state of Washington. Have you made that statement?
A: What do you mean?
Q: Out in Wyoming, did you make that statement?
A: I think I did.
Q: And is that a true statement?
A: No.
Q: Can you tell me why you made that statement?
A: No. I was scared.

This exchange also shows quite clearly the amount of preparation the prosecution had engaged in prior to questioning Caril on the record. Fahrnbruch clearly knew the answers to the questions before he asked them.

At another point, Fahrnbruch asks Carl about her stepfather's .410 and the fact that Charlie had sawed off the barrel:

Q: What were you doing while he was cutting this gun off?
A: I was asleep, and I woke up when he finished cutting it.
Q: What did you say to him about cutting off the gun?
A: *I told him my dad was going to be mad about it* [emphasis added].
Q: What did he say?
A: I don't know.

If this statement is true, then Caril obviously believed at the time that her stepfather was still alive. For her to have on the spot concocted a lie that would serve to demonstrate that she believed her family was still alive would require an incredibly quick and clever mind.

Does her testimony have the ring of truth? As discussed earlier, this highly subjective standard plays consciously or otherwise into many if not most credibility judgments. In finding that Caril's Statement sounds like the truth, I also weigh it against the credibility of the maker of the only other version, Charlie Starkweather. If true, his version would show Caril to be not only hateful but an out-and-out monster. She would have watched him kill her stepfather, shoot and smash her mother's head with a rifle butt until she fell on the floor, smash her baby sister's skull twice with the rifle butt, and whip a hunting knife into her throat to stop her crying. She would then sit and watch TV while he wrapped up and removed the three bodies and stuffed them in outbuildings and afterward cleaned up the blood in the house. And then the two of them would have hung around the murder house for six days watching TV, having sex, and drinking pop and eating potato chips while her family lay bundled up and frozen outside only yards away. Nothing supports such a psychopathic personality. Indeed, the facts show that Caril dearly loved her mother and cherished her baby sister. No facts, other than those offered by Charlie in later statements, indicate a coldheartedness sufficient to cause her, after witnessing her family's bloody execution, to turn to their killer and ask calmly, "What do we do now?" and settle in to watch TV.

Perhaps Caril was a multiple personality: the quiet, kind Caril who loved children and wanted to be a nurse versus the stone-cold Caril who killed innocents without remorse. However, by definition a multiple personality switches back and forth between the various personalities as circumstances change, and Caril was only the killer Caril one time, for eight days. One could always argue that for some reason she froze in the personality of the kind, child-loving Caril and never switched back to the killer.

All of this must be weighed against the evidence showing that Caril in fact knew her parents were dead, most of which consists of statements made shortly after her arrest. On January 30, 1958, deputy sheriff Bill Romer told the press that after getting in his car, Caril said that "she had seen all *nine* murders in Nebraska" (emphasis added). His testimony at trial was much more specific; he testified not only that Caril said she had seen Charlie kill *ten people* but that she had listed them in close to perfect order: "her mother, her step-father, her step-sister, a boy and a girl, a farm hand, three other people." She had gone into detail about the killings: her mother had gotten into an "argument with Charles Starkweather and had slapped him, and he started to hit her when the stepfather interfered and at that time he killed her stepfather and then killed her mother, and killed her stepsister." On being pressed by McArthur, Romer said Caril told him that "the baby was crying, and that Starkweather took the barrel of the gun and pushed it in the throat of the baby."

There are several problem's with Romer's testimony. First is that the number of deaths witnessed by Caril has increased from nine to ten. The second pertains to all the additional facts Caril supposedly told him after she got in the car. By his own words, Caril was crying and not making much sense. It took her a while before she could even get Starkweather's name out, and yet she was also able to give him some detail on the *identity* of the ten victims.

Nine months had passed from the time of Caril's capture to her trial. Romer was a deputy sheriff in Casper at the time, and the *Casper Star-Tribune* carried many stories that walked through the rampage victim by victim with names and identities, and many articles mentioned Romer by name. In her groundbreaking work on memory, Dr. Elizabeth Loftus, a professor at the University of California, Irvine, has shown that memory is a process and not a thing; it is a reconstruction that can easily be affected by post-trauma events and the acquisition of new information. (*The New Yorker*, April 5, 2021.) It is not unreasonable to suggest that, having been directly involved in the rampage, Romer would have read many of the stories, particularly because he was frequently mentioned in them, and unconsciously wove a few of them into his memory of events. This possibility is reinforced by Romer's statement at the trial for the first time that Caril told him Charlie stuck the barrel of the gun down the baby's throat. Where did this come from?

Romer's version of events does not mesh with the testimony of Mrs. Heflin, the jail matron in Douglas. She testified that Caril was in a state of shock and was not making any sense when she came into the jail. The girl cried and screamed for her mother and sister and asked why they hadn't called her. In fact, Caril asked several people if her parents were dead. When she asked Scheele, he said, "Don't you know, Caril?" Caril also asked Hazel Warwick, her jail matron in Gering, if her parents and sister were dead, and Mrs. Warwick told her they were. Caril showed clippings of her parents to the doctor who visited her in the Gering jail and asked him if they were dead. County Attorney Fox testified that in the discussion at the Wyoming jail about waiving her extradition rights, Caril specifically asked Justice of the Peace Wise if her parents were dead, and the judge replied they were.

Caril's accusers often pointed to Mrs. Karnopp's statement to the press and her testimony at the trial about what Caril told her in the police car on the road to Lincoln. Caril talked in some detail about her stepfather, her older sister, and the fight her mother had had with Charlie. At one point, Caril asked Mrs. Karnopp if her parents were dead, and when Mrs. Karnopp didn't answer immediately, Caril asked, "Who killed them?"

Mrs. Karnopp responded, "Don't you know, Caril?" Caril said that the newspapers stated that the three bodies had been shot where they were found, but that actually they had been shot in the house and carried outside. "Which bodies?" Mrs. Karnopp asked, and Caril, after waiting a moment, replied, "Mr. Meyer was shot in the house and then drug outside." Mrs. Karnopp asked her why she said three bodies if she meant Mr. Meyer, and Caril looked out the window and did not answer.

It is difficult to give much weight to Caril's statement—if she made it, which she denies—that the newspapers were wrong when they said the three bodies had been shot where they were found. On the afternoon of her capture, Caril had been given a sedative strong enough to knock her out for seventeen hours. The next day she took four additional sedatives, and that night she was given a shot of the drug Carbatrol in the Gering jail. It's remarkable she was able to string two sentences together on the ride to Lincoln. By this time, at least three people had told her that her parents were dead, and the county attorney had warned her that murder charges awaited her on her return to Lincoln. It would seem wrong to rely on this statement as probative evidence that she had seen her parents killed. The fact was she had just been talking about the August Meyer killing, and Meyer had been dragged from the porch where he was shot across the snowy ground and into a small outbuilding nearby. Given this and her considerable consumption of sedatives at the time, I would give little, if any, weight to this single sentence.

Finally, no newspaper of record had at the time—or ever, for that matter—suggested that her parents had been shot outside the house. In his numerous confessions, Charlie always said the killings happened inside the house. The forensic evidence also indicated that the murders had been committed in the house.

We also need to look at Caril's version of events, in which she explained that she was held hostage by Charlie's threat that he would kill her parents and sister if she tried to escape. According to her, he said he had them stashed at the Southworths' house in Lincoln (where he stored his Model A), and that the people holding them were his gang, and that his gang was going to rob a bank. He told her that he had convinced her family through a threat of some sort to leave and go to a house across town, where they would be kept by his gang, who would kill them on Charlie's order if Caril tried to escape.

Implausible? Highly. It sounds like the story of a child trying to lie their way out of trouble. Caril testified that she didn't believe Charlie's story at first, but the more she challenged him and asked to see or talk to her parents, and the more he refused, the more she eventually came to believe his story. Keep in mind that Caril has always said that she entered the house on Belmont to find Charlie standing behind the door with a gun in his hand. In his initial telling of the story, Charlie also stated he held a gun on Caril when she came in the house.

Caril was fourteen at the time of the killings. Current research shows that the cognitive wiring of adolescent brains is far from complete. Cognitive wiring is what allows a person to think things through, to foresee the consequences of certain behavior, in essence, to reason. A brain of an adolescent girl is more developed in the right side, or the emotional part of the brain, than the left. Caril said she was scared for the lives of her parents, while Charlie, whom, in her own obsessive, destructive way, she was still in love with, held a gun on her and threatened the lives of her family. McArthur asked the jury to put themselves in the shoes of a fourteen-year-old girl, which was of course impossible. But still, the jury could ask: What was the girl supposed to do? Take her father's .410 and shoot Charlie while he lay asleep in her bed? Simply walk out of the house and down the street? And go where? The police station? And tell them what? And risk, however improbably, the lives of her parents and sister?

Finally, Caril's testimony that she was in actual fear for her parents' life is corroborated by several family members who testified that when they came to the house, Caril told them in effect that they had to leave or her mother could be hurt or that her life would be in danger.

In summary, there is simply no reliable evidence that Caril was at home when Charlie killed her family. When one throws out Charlie's testimony as simply too inconsistent and unreliable to be entitled to any significant weight, the case against her on this issue collapses. There are no other facts pointing to her presence in the house. All we have left is common sense and her testimony. So, were I the fact finder, I would find that Caril was not in the house when her parents were killed. When she left the house on 924 Belmont with Charlie on the morning of January 27, she believed that her family was still alive.

AUGUST MEYER

Charlie had a plan when the couple left 924 Belmont in the aftermath of Pansy Street's screaming insistence that she was going to get a warrant to enter the house. He was going to drive to the farm of family friend

August Meyer outside of Bennet. He needed money and he needed weapons. He had returned the single-shot .22 to Rodney, which left only the sawed-off .410. His weapon of choice was a .22. He knew that Meyer had a .22 rifle, and he'd heard that he had around five hundred dollars in cash and a bunch of new clothes in his house. On the way to Bennet, at Homer Tate's Conoco station, he bought one box of shells for the .410 and three boxes of shells for a .22 rifle he didn't have. He fully intended from the outset to kill August Meyer and take his rifle and his money.

The light was fading when Charlie turned off the county road and up the lane to Meyer's farm. The noon sun had melted the snow into a muddy slush, and he drove only a short distance before the Ford was mired. After failing to get the car out, he and Caril walked over to the cellar to get warm. They went down the steps, hung a lantern, and stayed for about ten minutes. In that time, according to Caril, Charlie opened the box of shells and *loaded the .410*. They left and began walking up the hill to Meyer's house. His dog barked as they approached. Meyer appeared on the porch, there was a discussion between the two men, and, according to Caril, Meyer turned to go back in his house. She was walking behind Charlie. He raised the shotgun, pointed it at Meyer, and blew the back of his head off. Meyer's body fell on the porch. In later statements, Caril was uncertain whether she actually saw Charlie shoot Meyer or heard the shot and looked and saw him dead on the ground. Charlie says she was around the corner when he shot Meyer. What is consistent in her statement and testimony is her reaction to the scene: She "froze." She couldn't move. She would say that she saw herself screaming but couldn't hear the sound of it. She saw only the blood and the body with the back half of its head missing and watched silently as Charlie dragged the body from the porch across the ground and into the small building. At Charlie's direction, she picked up Meyer's blue plaid hat and tossed it in the summer kitchen.

Caril was never implicated in any fashion in the murder of August Meyer.

BOBBY JENSEN

Having found that Caril was not at home when Charlie murdered her family, and that she had nothing to do with the murder of August Meyer, the analysis turns to the next murders and the actual charges against her: count one, first-degree murder; count two, first-degree murder, Robert Jensen killed in the course of a felony. The first charge was never proven; even Charlie, the prosecution's star witness, testified that Caril did not shoot or aid and abet in the shooting of Jensen. (As noted, the jury did not convict or acquit Caril on this charge. The judge's failure to send the charge back to the jury for a decision on count one might have been out of a fear of subjecting her again to the possibility of the death penalty.) In order to prove the felony murder charge, the state needed to prove each and every element of the offense beyond a reasonable doubt: that is, that she had taken the money from Jensen's wallet and put it in Starkweather's wallet and returned the wallet to Starkweather and that Jensen had subsequently been murdered. A failure of proof of any of these facts would, or should, doom the charge.

Charlie testified that Caril had robbed Jensen. In her Statement, Caril detailed the passage of Jensen's wallet to Starkweather; Starkweather's passage of his and Jensen's wallet to her; her taking money from Jensen's wallet, putting the money in Starkweather's wallet, then returning Starkweather's wallet to him; and passing Jensen's wallet to King. In both her testimony and her Statement, she stated quite clearly that the idea for the robbery was Starkweather's. (Charlie said it was her idea.)

Most defendants don't testify in their defense. The rubric is that it's simply too risky. But Caril had no choice: The prosecutor had read her Statement aloud to the jury. The Statement on its face was sufficient to show her participation in the robbery. This forced her to tell her story to the jury. Whether the Statement should have been admitted into evidence is dealt with in a later chapter, but if the Statement had been excluded, Caril would not have taken the stand, and the sole evidence against her would have been Charlie's testimony, which, under even the most generous formulation, could not be sufficient to establish her guilt beyond a reasonable doubt.

But assuming the Statement is in evidence, Caril's admission dooms her unless there was an explanation or mitigation of some sort. There was one: duress. McArthur mentioned coercion and duress in his opening statement, and Caril had always insisted that she did what she did out of fear for herself and her family. In an instruction, the judge defined duress as "an unlawful restraint, intimidation or compulsion of another to such an extent and degree as to induce such other person to do or perform such act contrary to his will and inclination." In this case, that would mean that if Charlie intimidated or compelled Caril "contrary to her will and inclination" to rob Jensen, then she was innocent of any degree of homicide.

41

C ARIL'S MENTAL STATE AT THE TIME THE CRIMES were committed would be the key to her defense of duress and coercion were she brought into the judicial system today under the same circumstances as in 1958. The defense would immediately take a number of steps to determine her mental state at the time of the robbery and murder of Robert Jensen. The defense would undertake an extensive history of her childhood, looking for sexual, emotional, or physical abuse in her household. The defense would retain one or more psychiatrists to determine if a clinical diagnosis of post-traumatic stress disorder (PTSD) was appropriate. The doctors would conduct extensive interviews with Caril. Caril would take the PCL-5, which is a self-administered checklist of possible PTSD events as well as a list of possible symptoms. Caril would also fill out a questionnaire called the Dissociative Experiences Scale, which is designed to measure the possibility of dissociation as a reaction to traumatic experiences. The psychiatrist would have administered neuropsychological tests to reveal deficits in memory or other brain abnormalities.

In 1995, imaging techniques started being applied to the brains of patients with possible PTSD. The scans showed the discrepancies between a brain with PTSD and one without PTSD. Several brain scans will indicate damage to the amygdala, hippocampus, and prefrontal cortex as well as increased cortisol levels in the brains of people with PTSD. The impact of PTSD on the brain has been shown by scans to affect memory, specifically deficits in what is called the verbal declarative memory function, which is the processing of names, dates, places, facts, events, and the like. Given that Caril's life would be at stake, the psychiatrists would today almost certainly administer these brain-imaging techniques to her.

In the trial, the defense would call the psychiatrists as expert witnesses to testify that in their opinion, Caril suffered from PTSD and a dissociation disorder. The experts would be asked to relate these conditions to the concept of duress and coercion.

To begin with, the experts would explain to the jury that the primary function of the brain is to ensure survival. Inside the organ are two structures the size of almonds, called the amygdalae. Usually referred to in the singular, the amygdala sits deep in the brain and is part of the autonomic nervous system, which is, in short, a surveillance system designed to ensure the survival of the human. The amygdala has several functions, but perhaps its most important function is to serve as an alarm system to threats from the outside. It receives input from the five senses through the thalamus and is constantly scanning for any sign of a threat. The route from the thalamus to the amygdala is short, allowing the amygdala to process any threats obtained through the senses rapidly and send a danger or warning signal.

The frontal lobes of the cortex sit right behind the forehead and eyes and perform the executive functions of the brain. They process information from other lobes of the brain and integrate it into a single experience of the world. The cortex is in charge of planning actions, anticipating responses, and absorbing information from the world to adapt behaviors. In other words, it makes sense out of things. It says, "If you do this, that will happen. If you don't want this to happen, don't do that." It provides for language and abstract thought. It is also the seat of empathy. The neocortex also inhibits excessive reactions to sensory data.

The thalamus also sends the warning signal to the cortex, but the amygdala receives the information first and is able to react before the cortex has processed the information. So, when a bed frame falls off the roof of the car twenty yards ahead of you on the interstate, you are able to react "automatically," by swerving out of the way, without even thinking. If you took time to think about it, you would smash into the frame. The amygdala is set up to react before the cortex even knows of the danger. If the bed frame does not in fact move but only bounces a little under the straps, the cortex will process that and downplay the danger.

When the amygdala senses danger, say a figure lurking in a doorway a few yards down the sidewalk, it reacts quickly through the central
nucleus, which is wired tightly into the sympathetic nervous system,
which consists of neurons hooked up to almost every organ in the body.
The amygdala sets up the fight-or-flight-or-freeze response; it is able to
instantly tell the sympathetic nervous system to slow or increase heart
rate and respiration and to activate or deactivate muscles. It signals the
hypothalamus to release cortisone and adrenaline from the adrenal
glands, which are located on top of the kidneys. The adrenaline boosts
energy, increases heart rate and breathing, and numbs pain. The cortisol
provides the energy to react. All this before the cortex—you—knows
what's happening. In fact, the amygdala has the power to override the
activity of the cortex. In those instant reactions, it is in control of the
brain.

The freeze response originates in the primitive or reptilian part of
the nervous system, an example of which is a lizard standing stock-still
on a rock for hours, or a rabbit going immobile when a dog wanders by.
This is also called the immobilization response. In the polyvagal theory, developed by Dr. Stephen Porges, the freeze response is described
as shutting down or collapsing the nervous system when it deems escape (flight) or struggling (fight) to be hopeless. Dr. Porges directs attention to the vagal nerve and a branch of it called the dorsal vagal,
which takes charge when the danger seems overwhelming and leaves a
feeling of numbness or "not here." He states that there is a hierarchy of
responses to a threat: the first response is to escape/flee or fight, and this
originates in the sympathetic branch of the nervous system. If struggle
or escape seems hopeless, the system reverts to the reptilian response of
immobilization. To survive, it shuts down the nervous system. This entire process is beyond awareness or conscious control and happens in an
instant. There is no thinking.

Stress hormones flooding the brain can cause a rapid loss of prefrontal cognitive functions, such as thinking, planning, or reasoning in the
face of the threat. They impair the brain's ability to organize experiences
into logical sequences. Intense responses such as hyperarousal increase

while processes of planning and decision-making decrease or cease altogether. It explains why some victims of sexual assault have difficulty explaining the decisions made during the assault. The prefrontal cortex is so impaired, the victim is unable to strategize or plan an escape. There is also evidence that if the stress is prolonged, the hormones can begin to have pathological consequences, interfering with cognitive functioning and even causing brain damage. The prefrontal cortex, as well as the hippocampus, may be altered by stress. A stress-induced shutdown of the cortex by the hormones might allow old fears to resurface. Studies on rats show that if the hippocampus is not able to control the release of stress hormones, the rats are unable to learn and perform tasks and memory failure occurs.

When escape seems impossible and the outcome unavoidable, then extreme survival reflexes will take over. One of those extreme responses may be dissociation. One of the consequences of dissociation is depersonalization, or a loss of feeling.

In 1958, psychology was a clinical inquiry, a treatment process. Psychology was not particularly interested in the why of a particular disorder. It could diagnose and it could describe and it could treat. But it could not, and seldom attempted to, provide an understanding of why the person was the way the person was.

The experts would testify that in the 1960s, psychiatry began to focus on childhood trauma, with the publication of such books as *The Battered Child Syndrome*. The mental disorders of soldiers returning from the Vietnam War brought a focus on the impact of battlefield traumas and post-traumatic stress disorder. In the 1970s, in large part due to feminist influence, studies began to focus on the effect of childhood physical and sexual abuse on adults, and over time the field expanded to include the effect of the impact of traumas experienced as adults. In the 1980s, the theory of dissociation hit the popular culture in concepts such as repressed memories and multiple personalities. In the fifth edition of the *Diagnostic and Statistical Manual of Mental Disorders*, the three primary dissociative disorders are (1) dissociative identity disorder (previously known as multiple personality disorder), (2) dissociative amnesia (previously known as repressed memories), and (3) deperson-alization/derealization disorder.

Dissociation is defined most simply as a separation of consciousness from memory, emotions, and perceptions of self and body. The individual disconnects from memories and feelings. Some see it on a continuum, at one end being simple daydreaming and the other end being a splitting of consciousness from feelings in order to survive an intolerable emotional experience. A child being sexually abused dissociates from the experience because it is too painful to experience emotionally. Primary symptoms of dissociation are emotional detachment, the sensation of being physically detached from the body, and a numbness. In *The Body Keeps the Score*, Bessel van der Kolk describes dissociation as resulting in "feeling lost, overwhelmed, abandoned, disconnected from the world . . . helpless, trapped and weighed down." Dissociation can result from a single trauma or repeated traumas. It can be a learned response in that a child can learn to split from her body when she hears her bedroom door open and her father come in the room at night. The trauma setting up dissociation can be something as basic as prolonged abandonment and neglect, repeated instances of physical abuse by a parent, or a single instance of being raped. Dissociation can lead to post-traumatic stress disorder (PTSD).

Today, childhood trauma, particularly sexual and physical abuse, is often seen as a contributing factor to eating disorders, bipolar disorders, borderline personalities, sociopathology, schizophrenia, depression, and so on. The expert witnesses would testify on the concepts of trauma and dissociation, as well as evidence on the effects of being abused as a child, the nature of dissociation and PTSD, and more specifically the impact of witnessing violence committed on others.

The experts would explain battered woman syndrome. This psychological condition, first described by Lenore Walker in the late 1970s in a book of the same name, refers to a woman who has suffered repeated cycles of abuse in an intimate relationship. The condition can result in symptoms similar to PTSD, including depression and a sense of being defeated that can lead to what is called "learned helplessness," or psychological paralysis, which leaves the woman unable to leave her abuser.

While Caril was not the classic battered woman, the reasoning of the courts in allowing evidence of past abuse in to establish the condition is relevant in our case. Courts have held that battered woman syndrome falls both within the duress defense and a claim of self-defense, and that evidence of past abuse and violence is admissible to prove the claim. Under current law, the elements of the duress defense are that (1) the defendant or a third party was under an immediate threat of death or serious bodily injury, (2) the defendant had a well-grounded fear that the threat would be carried out, and (3) the defendant had no reasonable opportunity to escape the threatened harm. The issue is whether, in establishing these three elements, the evidence must be subjective or objective. Is the reasonableness of the fear or belief based on the objective-reasonable-person standard, or is it based on the mental or psychological condition of the woman at the time? If the latter, then the defense is entitled to introduce evidence of past physical or mental abuse to meet the standard.

In *United States v. Lopez*, 913 F.3d 807, 822–23 (9th Cir. 2019), the court found that objective reasonableness was not the standard and that a woman's experience in terms of the three requirements was admissible; that is, that the jury could consider the particular circumstances of her fear in determining the reasonableness of her belief in the threat, the harms intended, and her inability to escape:

> This court has long recognized that a defendant's particular situation includes consideration of past experiences. See *Johnson*, 956 F.2d at 898 ("Fear which would be irrational in one set of circumstances may be well-grounded *if the experience of the defendant with those applying the threat* is such that the defendant can reasonably anticipate being harmed on failure to comply.") [Emphasis added.]

The court also applies the principles of battered woman syndrome to item number 3, the reasonable opportunity to escape.

Moreover, battered woman syndrome evidence is relevant in assessing whether a defendant had a reasonable opportunity to escape from the coercing party. As seen above, this inquiry often focuses on why the defendant did not call the police at the first opportunity. (See, e.g., *Kuok*, 671 F.3d at 949; *Contento-Pachon*, 723 F.2d at 694; *Nwoye*, 824 F.3d at 1133.) Experts on BWS, however, have explained that:

The battered woman's perception of viable options for stopping the violence and abuse by any means is not only shaped by her own prior experience with violence, but also influences her future actions in response to violence. The perception or understanding of whether there are options available that would end the violence is based largely on what has actually been learned through experience.

The court specifically held that expert testimony that the woman had a well-grounded fear, even were it not objectively based, that she would be harmed if she failed to commit the illegal act demanded of her and that she had no reasonable opportunity to escape is relevant and should be admitted. The vast majority of state and federal courts allow evidence of battered woman syndrome into the record to substantiate a claim of duress in the commission of a crime.

While the courts have held in the past that duress was not a defense in a murder case, the clear weight of authority now is that battered woman syndrome is a defense to murder. The reasoning behind these cases could well be applied to the case at hand.

In 1958, there was no psychiatric theory of duress that would allow evidence of past physical or sexual abuse as a child or as an adult or other traumas to mitigate or excuse a defendant from the charge of murder. There were no mental health professionals learned in the theory of trauma or fight, flight, or freeze, or PTSD, through which Caril's behavior could be viewed, because there were no such theories.

With the assistance of experts, these concepts could be applied today in an effort to determine the guilt or innocence of Caril Fugate.

Accepting the earlier finding that Caril was not at home when Stark-weather murdered her family, the first notice she had of violence was when she walked in the house to find Charlie standing behind the door with a rifle in his hand. He told her to sit down and slapped her when she hesitated. He told her he had her family hostage and that if she tried to escape, he would, with one phone call, have them killed. Given her previous history with domestic violence as a child, she could easily have learned to dissociate from what would have been a scary scene, such as when her father was strangling her mother. There is a concept in trauma psychology called "the sitting duck." Someone who has dissociated before is more likely to dissociate in the future or is more vulnerable to doing so.

The evidence would show that the prefrontal cortex isn't fully developed until the early or mid-twenties. Adolescent girls are more likely to react from the emotional or limbic part of the brain. Given this, the idea that Caril might have been truly frightened by the gun and Charlie's threats is highly credible. The fact that she was at the time in love with Charlie would only heighten the fear. As each killing occurred, she would become more vulnerable to the belief that she would herself be killed if she attempted to leave. It is not a big leap to include in the second element of duress a "reasonable belief" in the truth of Charlie's threat to kill her mother, stepfather, and little sister if she tried to escape. Defense experts would be offered to establish that after the murder of Meyer, Caril suffered from ongoing "psychological paralysis."

Acute stress disorder (ASD) is found in the *DSM-5*. This disorder can result from exposure to a single traumatic event. It often results in intrusive memories, changes in mood, the impairment of daily functioning, emotional numbing, or existence of an emotional blank slate. It can also result in immediate dissociation. Acute stress disorder usually surfaces between three days and two weeks after the trauma. It can progress into full-blown PTSD.

In our case, Caril did not meet all the parameters of ASD, but she certainly satisfied several of them. Her trauma can properly be seen as continuing every day, and she believed her behavior could determine whether her family lived or died. She seemed to acquiesce in Charlie's definition of the situation. She got rid of all visitors, failed to run when she had the chance, and essentially was very compliant—all the while in the ongoing fear for her parents' and little sister's lives, as well as her own.

The discussion of ASD shows that given her circumstances and childhood abuse, Caril could have been subject to the impact of an ongoing trauma, and it also points out that were the case tried today, under the reasoning of battered woman syndrome cases, experts could be called to testify as to whether in their opinion Caril was suffering from ASD and what the impact of the disorder might have been on her ability to think through her situation and freely make her own choices.

Caril saw Charlie's plan to drive to the Meyer farm as a visit to a friend. She and Charlie had been hunting there the previous fall. Caril might have wondered why Charlie loaded the shotgun in the cave and carried it with him on the way up the road to the farm, but at this point, if the previous findings are accurate, she had no inkling that Charlie had in fact killed anyone. But when Meyer turned to go inside the farmhouse, Charlie raised the .410 and shot him in the back of the head. Caril saw him lying facedown on the porch with blood flowing from his skull. She would say that she "froze" at the sight. She saw herself screaming but no sound was coming out. This is classic dissociation language, before there was such a thing called dissociation.

What fourteen-year-old girl wouldn't be both terrorized and terrified at such a scene? Was she next? Applying current brain science to the facts, an expert might testify that the amygdala would have signaled the danger to the cortex and at the same time pumped adrenaline and cortisone into it to energize and equip the brain to fight, flight, or freeze. Before the cortex could make a decision, the amygdala determined that Caril had no ability to fight Charlie or to flee him, so it kicked in the freeze response and shut down or overrode the cortex. She dissociated. She separated from her body. In their *Report to the Department of Justice Canada* (2019), Dr. Lori Haskell and Dr. Melanie Randall wrote that a person who has dissociated "often has the perception of things as unreal and report that they are unable to make sense of what is going on. Dissociation can be automatic for people who were traumatized earlier in life. Victims describe their experience as feeling like being on autopilot. Others report trance states, feeling in a fog or in a dream, and that they don't feel their bodies."

Caril followed Charlie from room to room as he searched the Meyer house and came up with some money and three rifles. She watched him load the .22 he had just found. She told Charlie she wanted to get out of there. As they left, Charlie shot the barking dog with the newly acquired .22 and it ran off into the brush.

The ongoing trauma maintained or even grew in intensity. The fear would not have diminished. She had no choices. She was stuck. Where was she going to flee on a dark, cold night in the rural countryside? How far would she get before Charlie shot her in the back, just like he had Meyer? The amygdala would have perceived an ongoing threat to her very survival and would have continued to pump adrenaline and cortisone into the cortex, signaling a freeze and disabling the thinking processes. She was carrying the shotgun as they walked down the lane to their car, but there was no thinking and assessing going on; she was stuck in the place of fear and immobilization. Even if she'd had her wits about her, who's to say that she would have been able to raise the shotgun and shoot Charlie? Psychologist Sharon Stanley describes this state of mind in her book *Relational and Body-Centered Practices for Healing Trauma*:

> A person who perceives suffering but immediately becomes disembodied and dissociated from feelings of terror and horror never connects the reality of the suffering to his or her higher cortical wisdom, empathy and compassion. If fear and terror are disembodied, suppressed, repressed, or dissociated, the neural energy may become "stuck," leading to a numb depression and immobilization.

Thus, the expert defense testimony would show that after Meyer's murder, Caril would likely have been in a numbed or immobilized state.

In this condition, she would have been compliant to Charlie's demands. This is a condition that would meet the definition of duress: a complete loss of the ability to think and assess and choose a rational course of action. Free will, or, as they say today, free agency. She was at Charlie's mercy. She was in a trancelike state, and if the cortex were signaling any strategy, it would have been compliance and passivity.

The felony murder charge alleges that Caril committed a robbery in the course of the murder of Robert Jensen. The first element of proof is the robbery. In her Statement and in her testimony, Caril admits that she took money from Jensen's wallet and put it in Charlie's. Earlier, when the boy doubted if Charlie would really do anything, Charlie had threatened to blow his head off. He was talking in a high, squeaky, and very loud voice, and his face was all wrinkled up as if he'd just been in a fight. Only a few hours earlier, he had in fact blown a friend's head off for no apparent reason. Given these facts, Caril was in no shape to refuse to take money from Jensen's wallet and place it in Charlie's wallet. The danger was stark and overwhelming. Her ability to refuse was nonexistent. She was under duress.

The prosecution would certainly call experts challenging the theory of trauma-induced duress, as well as its application to Caril's case. Psychiatrists for the prosecution would be given the opportunity to interview and evaluate Caril. They would attempt to portray Caril not only as not traumatized but also as an active participant in the murder of Robert Jensen and possibly others. Perhaps they would even diagnose her as a sociopath. On the face of it, however, the facts seem clearly to fit within the accepted theory of duress due to a trauma-induced paralysis or dissociation.

So, were I the judge in Caril's trial today, I would find that her participation in the robbery of Jensen was made under duress and coercion. Since there was no evidence of her actual participation in the murder, this would result in her acquittal on both the murder and felony murder charges.

In reaching the decision to admit the expert testimony, and in deciding on Caril's ultimate responsibility, I would point to several recent Supreme Court cases that recognize the disabilities of youth. These cases rely on brain science and concepts of child development to establish their findings that juveniles should be afforded special treatment under the law. In *Thompson v. Oklahoma* (1988), the court barred the execution of persons under fifteen as cruel and unusual punishment under the Eighth Amendment to the Constitution.

In *Roper v. Simmons* (2005), the court held that imposition of the death penalty on a person under eighteen at the time of the crime was unconstitutional as cruel and unusual punishment. In reversing *Stanford v. Kentucky*, the court held that (1) a juvenile's susceptibility to immature and irresponsible behavior means that "their irresponsible conduct is not as morally reprehensible as that of an adult," (2) a juvenile's vulnerability and comparative lack of control over their immediate surroundings means juveniles have a greater claim than adults to be forgiven for failing to escape negative influences, and (3) the fact that juveniles still struggle to define their identity means it is less supportable to conclude that even a heinous crime committed by a juvenile is evidence of irretrievably depraved character. The court relied on a range of behavioral research, expert opinion, and sociological and psychological studies in support of its findings that juveniles have diminished culpability and greater prospects for reform due to the above three factors. The amicus curiae brief filed by the American Psychological Association referred to research and expert opinion on the characteristics of youth such as impulsivity, risk-taking, peer orientation, temporal perspective, *and vulnerability to coercion and false confession.*

In *Miller v. Alabama* (2012), the Supreme Court held that sentencing a juvenile to life without the possibility of parole was also unconstitutional as cruel and unusual punishment. The court relied on studies showing that relatively few adolescents develop "entrenched patterns of behavior" and pointed to the possibilities that "his deficiencies will be reformed" and that "incorrigibility is inconsistent with youth." In other words, society shouldn't give up hope on kids. More specifically to our point, the court held in *Eddings v. Oklahoma* (1982) that "in assessing a minor's culpability, the background and mental and emotional development of a youthful defendant *must be* considered."

These cases show that today the statute under which Caril was prosecuted would be held unconstitutional both on the grounds of her age and the fact that the only alternative to the death penalty was life without parole. It also shows that the court is now welcoming, if not insisting on, testimony regarding the youth's background and upbringing in sentencing, which in our case, were it tried today, would open the door wide for expert testimony and research on the impact of trauma on the vulnerability of a minor to be coerced into illegal behavior.

42

ALTHOUGH CARIL WAS NOT CHARGED WITH KILLING Carol King, the prosecution and most of Lincoln believed she was involved one way or another in Carol's murder. It was the initial charge drawn up by Scheele, and he was prepared to bring her to trial on the crime if the Jensen charges failed. Charlie also claimed that Caril had killed the maid and stated she was "the most trigger happy person i ever seen" in killing Merle Collison. In weighing the guilt or innocence of Caril Fugate, it is beneficial to look at the evidence of her guilt or innocence in these other cases.

CAROL KING

First, of course, is the fact that, other than Caril's own words, the only known evidence of her participation in the murders of King, Mrs. Ward, Collison, or Miss Fencl are the statements of Charlie Starkweather. As shown, Charlie's words are worth very little. His statements are notoriously inconsistent and contradictory, and he lied constantly and unabashedly. The March 29 letter nailing Caril for the murder of King comes across as nonsense; the April letter cleans up the charge a little but still makes little sense. Charlie is running back and forth from the cave to the car because he is "scared" of something and leaves King standing alone at the cave for several minutes? He returns and leaves Caril to guard King at the entrance to the cellar? Caril, on her own, decides to shoot King in the side of the head with the .22 because she is running away? Did Charlie really intend to leave her alive as a witness? Charlie's two letters are so close to gibberish that one must wonder if in fact he was toying with the prosecutor and the system for his own amusement.

Nothing points to Caril's involvement in the murder. Her fingerprints do not show up on Meyer's .22, which was used in the killing of both King and Jensen. Some people have suggested that Scheele had other evidence on Caril for the King killing but that he repressed it because of its sensitive nature. I uncovered nothing in my research to back this up. The fact that a knife had been used by someone to cut into King's cervix and rectum would seem about as sensitive as you could get. There is also no evidence pointing toward Caril's use of a knife at any time.

Observers point to Caril's behavior in Jensen's car as evidence of her participation in the murder of the teenagers. In her Statement, she testified to holding the .410 in her lap on the drive to the cellar. When Charlie ordered the teenagers out and told her to tell the girl to get out, she waved the .410 toward the driver's door. This conduct could be seen as either aiding or abetting the murder or as a felony murder, since threatening someone with a gun is a felony and Carol King died soon after the threatening. She did this, she would later testify, because she thought otherwise they might all get killed. In the few hours since Charlie had killed Meyer, she would not have recovered from the trauma of witnessing the murder. Her cortex would have been affected by the explosions of adrenaline and cortisol. There was no signal that the danger was over and she could begin to relax. And even if there had been, it takes time for the hormones to clear the cortex. One author wrote that if adrenaline and cortisol are not worked out of the system, they can continue to affect the ability of the cortex to function.

I would find, applying the expert testimony to the facts, that Caril was still under duress during the car ride and when the car came to a stop at the cellar. She did not participate in the killing of Carol King. When she realized that Charlie had killed two more people, the impact increased the reaction of the amygdala to the heightened danger and left her in something like a separated, trancelike state.

LAUER WARD, CLARA WARD, AND LILLIAN FENCL

Three people were killed at the Ward house. Charlie admitted to killing one, Lauer Ward, but claimed that Clara Ward and Lillian Fencl were alive when he and Caril left on the evening of the twenty-eighth. He told of throwing the knife into Clara Ward's back as she was running away from him, and that he had returned later to tie her up, but he insisted that he never touched her. And while he tied the maid up, he had not harmed her.

After his capture, Charlie told both Sheriff Heflin and Sheriff Karnopp that Caril had nothing to do with the murders. More specifically, he told Karnopp he had killed all ten people. However, in his Douglas Jail Statement, he said that only one person was dead when they left the Ward house. In his transcribed statement on February 1, he said that he had tied up the maid and had left Caril in charge of her while he blackened his hair and loaded the car. When Caril came down the stairs later, she said either that she had killed the maid or that she should have killed the maid. Much is made of the fact that when he was asked in his February 1 statement if he'd killed the maid, his response was: "Why, ain't the maid alive?" The question seemed to some to resemble a "spontaneous statement" and was therefore entitled to some weight. One could ask, why would Charlie admit to killing Lauer Ward and six other people but deny stabbing Clara Ward and Lilyan Fencl unless it was true?

Nothing ever said by Charlie is entitled to be taken as the truth. Here, he lied when he stated that he did not stab Lauer Ward. The autopsy showed that Mr. Ward had been stabbed at least once in the back. Charlie's claim that he had hit Ward in the head with a fire poker was also disproven.

Further, Charlie's statements are not direct evidence that Caril killed either or both of the two women. At most, they provide an inference to be drawn of Caril's guilt. But one has to be careful in basing any finding of fact on an inference; in this case, the inference is far too weak to justify finding beyond a reasonable doubt that Caril killed the two women. It was not corroborated by any evidence, forensic or otherwise.

The autopsies also raise some interesting questions about these two murders. Clara Ward was found on the floor with six deep stab wounds in her back, one in the throat/neck, and two in the back of the neck. Tiny Caril Ann Fugate would have to have been in a powerful homicidal rage to drive a knife through the back and neck of Clara Ward eight times, and then turn her over to stab her in the throat/neck. Charlie testified that he had so much trouble stabbing Marion Bartlett in the chest as he lay on a hard floor that he had to smack the handle with his fist to drive the blade through the bone, and Charlie was in a full-blown rage at the time. What could have stimulated such a rage in Caril to give her the will and strength to stab this nonthreatening woman over and over and over with such lethal viciousness? Mrs. Ward had given Caril a cup of coffee and offered her pancakes. When Caril awoke from a nap, she took the coffee tray from the library into the kitchen. However, Mrs. Ward had pulled a gun on Charlie and, according to Charlie, taken a shot at him. (No bullet holes in the walls or ceiling were found.) He also caught her trying to make a phone call from the bedroom. Recall that Rodney Starkweather testified and others have agreed that when Charlie shot the .22 while hunting, he might kill a rabbit with the first shot but then keep on shooting until the gun was empty. To a disinterested observer, it would appear that of the two, Charlie was far more likely the one in the homicidal rage. Clara Ward would be his fifth homicide in roughly twenty-four hours.

The same questions arise in the accusation that Caril killed Lilyan Fencl. Fencl was found to have been stabbed three times in the chest, deep enough to collapse both lungs, stabbed once in the right ventricle of the heart, and stabbed three times in the stomach. If killing her were the point, certainly two stabs in the chest would have done it. But the killer kept on stabbing her. While it is frequently suggested that Caril killed King in a jealous rage, there has never been a serious suggestion as to why Caril would have stabbed Lilyan Fencl at all, much less seven times in the chest, heart, and stomach.

In her Statement, Caril gives a very detailed and vivid description of Charlie stabbing Fencl on the bed. He kept stabbing her and she kept moaning, until finally he put a pillow over her head. (Later she would add that as he was stabbing her, he screamed, "Die! Die! Die!") She told of Charlie's arm being covered with blood afterward and him telling her to get a new shirt, which she did (and which was confirmed by Charlie).

And of Charlie washing his arm off in the downstairs bathroom, putting on the new shirt, and telling Caril to wash the blood off the knife. Caril even recalled wiping the knife on her black jeans. Could Caril have concocted every vivid detail in these scenes to cover for her killing the maid? Possible, but how likely does it seem, given the absence of any motivation or mental state that could have given rise to the compulsion to kill her?

Charlie was obsessed with knives. He threw one constantly into the wall of his room and the walls of the Bartlett house. He carried the bone-handled hunting knife in his boot. He stabbed Marion Bartlett several times in the chest with the kitchen knife to finish him off. He threw the kitchen knife into the back of Clara Ward and into the throat of Betty Jean. He stabbed Lauer Ward in the back with it. Charlie carried the kitchen knife between his jeans and back. Other than in one comment by Charlie, a knife was never placed in Caril's hands in the entire series of events. No forensics showed her prints on a knife. Finally, the notion that Charlie would have knowingly left two witnesses alive in the Ward house doesn't match his modus operandi.

Both Caril and Charlie testified that they threw clothes out of the car on their way out of Lincoln after the Ward killings. Charlie told Detective Henninger that he threw out his blue cowboy shirt with snaps on it because it had blood on the sleeves. He said that Caril threw out her blue striped shirt to avoid being recognized, not because it had blood on it. The sheriff's department made numerous attempts to locate the clothes. On February 2, two deputies searched culverts, ditches, bridges, shrubs, and state trash cans on Highways 2 and 34 west and 15 south to Highway 6, without any luck, reporting that the clothes might be under blankets of snow. On February 21, one deputy walked four miles east on Highway 15 and drove another four miles east checking ravines, culverts, and ditches for the clothes and a possible knife Charlie said he might have thrown out, without any luck. On April 19, a few weeks before Charlie's trial was to begin, the famous Sheriff's Posse was organized to search ditches along both sides of the highway. Eighteen men on horses split into groups of two and were assigned stretches of five miles out and five miles back on the highways leading west and north, so that forty-five miles of highways were searched on both sides. No clothes were found, but a four-and-one-half-inch black bone-handled hunting knife was found in a ditch. A memorandum indicates it was to be sent for serology testing, but no mention of it is included in the investigative records.

The clothes could have been important evidence in determining who killed Clara Ward and Lilyan Fencl. If blood were found on Charlie's shirt sleeves, as he indicated, it could have been matched against the blood types of both women, who had different blood types. The FBI found blood on the left sleeve and left shoulder of Charlie's jacket, but the amount was too small for grouping. Blood spots on his jeans and cowboy boots were also too small. The FBI found blood on the left rear portion of Caril's coat, but it was also too small for grouping. If Caril's shirt showed no blood, it would have been evidence, given the number and fury of the stabbings, that she had not murdered the women. If Charlie and Caril's clothes were available today, blood on the shirts could be tested against the DNA of Ward and Fencl. While the presence or absence of Fencl's or Ward's blood on either Charlie or Caril would not have definitively established their guilt or innocence, it certainly would be entitled to considerable weight in making that finding. However, the clothes as well as the vast majority of the exhibits in the two cases are nowhere to be found.

Caril's hostage explanation has two serious problems: her admission that she held the gun on the maid on two occasions and that she notified Charlie when Lauer Ward pulled in the driveway. These incidents could, in fact, set up separate charges of felony murder in the deaths of Ward and Fencl. However, the expert testimony on the impact of the three earlier murders on Caril's ability to think and sort out her options and act independently would also be brought to bear here. The defense experts would point out that Caril had seen Charlie kill one man and knew that he had killed Bobby Jensen and Carol King, all without provocation. The amygdala's scanning of her environment could only make her situation seem more dangerous and continue to send signals to release more hormones. Any ability to formulate and execute an escape plan or protect herself would be so weak under these circumstance as to be nonexistent. The safest path to survival, the reptilian brain would signal, was passivity. Compliance.

Perhaps the biggest evidentiary problem for Caril was the newspaper clippings. In her Statement, she said that she had asked the maid for scissors to cut out the photos. Either she had cut out the photos of the two of them on the love seat or Charlie had, or they both had. She wasn't sure who had cut out the pictures of her parents and little sister, but she had seen them. In her testimony, she said that she cut out the picture of the two of them on "the chair" and he cut out the pictures of her mother, stepfather, and little sister. He showed them to her but wouldn't let her read the rest of the paper. She thought maybe the photos were in the paper because her parents were missing and the authorities were looking for them. She put the photos in her jacket pocket. And she might have shown the photos to a man in the Gering jail when he told her he was sorry about her parents. Even if Caril did see and read the clippings at the Ward house, that knowledge cannot be imputed back in time to the previous murders.

Caril admits that she had become suspicious about the condition of her parents, mainly because Charlie wouldn't let her see or talk to them. She had also heard something about them on the radio in the Packard on the way to Wyoming. Charlie said he thought she knew something was wrong in the Ward house. By this time, Charlie had killed six people in roughly twenty-four hours. Caril undoubtedly sensed that something was wrong, that maybe her parents were dead, but it is not at all clear at that point that she would have had the cognitive ability to sort through and concretize the facts in such a manner as to enable her to formulate and execute an escape. In the *Report to the Department of Justice Canada*, Haskell and Randall describe the experience of freezing in rape victims:

> Freezing feels a lot like depression, in that we feel numb and apathetic, with little energy or motivation. We do not find pleasure in anything and tend to get "brain fog"—our higher cognitive

processes shut down and we are unable to plan or focus, and our memory becomes patchy or even non-existent. We might watch a whole film just staring at the screen with no idea what is happening and no memory of it afterwards. We can experience derealisation and depersonalization—states of being so disconnected from our body and the world around us that we feel like we do not exist and that nothing is real.

Caril had most likely come to some sort of realization or at least serious suspicion that her parents and sister were dead. After being taken into custody, she asked almost everyone she came into contact with if her parents were dead. This would seem to show a traumatized, disorganized mind rather than the mind of a person who had a clear memory of seeing her family murdered eight days earlier. If in fact she had known they were dead for eight days, this questioning would have been an elaborate ruse to help establish that she in fact did not know of their deaths.

43

THE PEOPLE CONVINCED OF CARIL'S GUILT POINT TO
her failure to take advantage of the many opportunities she had
to escape, such as her failure to leave with the cops when they
came to 924 Belmont, or to ask for help when she went inside Brickey's
Café for hamburgers, or to walk away when Charlie left her sitting in
Jensen's car in the Wards' drive for half an hour. The defense made a
strategic mistake by arguing both that she didn't try to escape because
she feared for her family's lives—that is, the hostage defense—and also
that she didn't try to escape because there were no opportunities to.
Either you didn't run because you were scared for your family's lives
or you didn't run because you didn't have the chance. By stressing that
Caril was tied up every time Charlie left the house and that she wrote a
note asking the police for help, the defense presented a picture of Caril
wanting to run if only she'd had the opportunity, while Caril herself
admitted that she had numerous opportunities to escape. It downplayed
her basic hostage defense that she didn't run out of fear for her family's
lives. The lack-of-opportunity-to-escape defense was so easily destroyed
that it left the hostage defense—the stronger of the two at that point in
time—as a seriously weakened backup defense.

If the case were tried today, the failure—or rather the inability—to
escape would most likely be the primary focus of the defense. The idea
that a fourteen-year-old girl whose boyfriend had threatened her with a
gun, who told her he would kill her family if she tried to escape, and who
had used a shotgun to blow the head off a friend in front of her, would
have had the cognitive capacity to plan and execute an escape from the
killer on a farm road in the cold and dark would be challenged by expert
testimony on the impact of severe and repeated trauma on adolescent
brains, as discussed earlier.

Consider the case of Elizabeth Smart. She was fourteen, the same age as Caril, when she was taken from her bedroom by a religious vagrant in Salt Lake City in June 2002. She was raped repeatedly and threatened with murder and the murder of her family by him and another woman over the nine months she was held captive. In this time, she and her captors took the bus, visited grocery stores, ate in restaurants, attended a party, and traveled outside Salt Lake City several times, and she did not raise an alarm. One day, the three of them, wearing white robes, headdresses, and veils, were seated in the public library in San Diego when she was approached by a plainclothes detective. He flashed a badge and asked if she was Elizabeth Smart. Her female captor clamped a hand on her leg under the table, and Elizabeth did not respond. The detective asked her to remove her veil. Her male captor told the detective that she was his daughter and asked why, if she were the girl, would she just sit there? The detective left.

After her rescue, one question permeated the media: Why hadn't she run? Had she developed some sort of affection for her captors? She had to answer the question of why she hadn't tried to escape time and again, and it bothered her. She insisted it was not Stockholm syndrome—she had not developed affection or come to care for her captors. It was intense fear and intimidation. Throughout her captivity, she was afraid for her life and the lives of her family. Her captor threatened to kill her or them if she screamed or tried to escape. She did not answer the detective because she was convinced in "her fourteen-year-old mind" that her captors would kill her first and then her family. Smart explained that the intimidation "left her feeling hollowed out and paralyzed." In her memoir, *My Story*, she wrote: "I am the living dead. I am nothing but a shell." Her words, like those of Caril, are the words of dissociation. It is the language of trauma-induced incapacity.

A recent example of what appears to be incapacity to act in the face of threat can be found in the case of the murder of four students on the second floor of a house in Moscow, Idaho, in January 2023. All four students were stabbed to death in their beds in the middle of the night. A probable cause affidavit for the arrest of Bryan Kohberger stated that a fifth student, identified only as D.M., was asleep alone in a bedroom on the first floor. Around 4:00 a.m., D.M. awoke to the sounds of what she thought was one of the male students playing with her dog. She then heard the student say "There's someone in here." She looked out the window, but saw no one. Later she heard crying from one of the rooms and a voice saying "It's OK, I'm going to help you." She opened her door and saw "a figure clad in black clothing" and a mask walking toward her. The man was athletically built with bushy eyebrows. He walked past her toward a sliding door while she "remained frozen in place." She went into her room and locked the door. She eventually called the police at 11:58 a.m. that morning, *roughly seven hours later.*

Stockholm syndrome is the term applied when a person develops positive feelings toward their captors or abusers. It came into being in 1973, when it appeared that several people who had been held captive in a bank robbery in Stockholm had developed positive feelings for their captors, and in some cases negative feelings toward the police or authorities.

In February 1974, young heiress Patty Hearst was kidnapped from her San Francisco apartment by a group of violent radicals calling themselves the Symbionese Liberation Army (SLA). In April, she was captured on camera participating in an armed robbery of a San Francisco bank. She released a tape to the police declaring she had joined the SLA of her own free will and was later convicted of bank robbery and sentenced to seven years in prison. (President Carter commuted her sentence to twenty-one months, and President Clinton granted her a full pardon in 2001.) While the facts are far from the same—Patty admitted participating in the bank robbery—the central idea that trauma can affect someone's ability to think logically about their ability—or even their desire—to escape is corroborated by the Patty Hearst story.

44

ONE SHOULDN'T FORGET THAT DEPUTY SHERIFF ROMER testified how hysterical Caril was inside the police car when she jumped in. He described her as being in a state of shock and said she was not making sense. Once she heard on the radio that Charlie had been captured, she calmed down considerably. He was no longer a threat to her life or the lives of her family. Everyone was safe.

Lawmen, almost to a one, as well as journalists, except for two or three, believed that Caril Fugate was guilty of murder or at least that she actively and willingly participated in the murder spree. One reason for this was the belief that Charlie had passed a lie detector test in which he supposedly named Caril as a killer. It's startling how utterly lacking in credibility this evidence is.

The test was administered by Detective Henninger, and it is his notes that are quoted here. Charlie agreed to the test but told Henninger that there were some questions he would not answer. The following is a verbatim replication of Henninger's notes.

He was asked the following questions and gave the following answers.

1. Does anyone ever call you Chuck? He said YES, and this being correct,
2. Did you ever go to school? and he said Yes, this being correct
3. Do you know who stabbed the maid? And on this question he would give no answer.
4. Did you eat at all today? He answered Yes.
5. Did you stab the maid at any time? On this he would give no answer.
0. Did Caril stab the maid? On this he would give no answer.
6. Are you trying to beat the lie detector? And he said yes to this.

7. Can you drive a car? He said yes.
8. Did you shoot the Service Station Man in the head at Wichita, Kansas, with a 22 cal Rifle? And he said no, this being correct.
9. Did you ever see or handle Mr. Ward's billfold? And he said no, and this is correct.
10. Do you know where the Knife is that was used to stab the maid? But gave a indication which at this time cannot be classified.
11. Did you stab Mrs. Ward more than one time? On this he said I don't know on one chart, and no on another, and another Chart he refused to answer.
12. Did you ever wear glasses? And he said YES, this being correct.
13. Was Bartletts killed Tuesday afternoon between hours 1:30 PM and 3:00 PM on 1.21.58. On this question he said I don't know, on the first examination, I don't know on the second, and third examinations.

Henninger wrote:

He [Charlie] was then asked if he would answer the following question which had not been asked during the Polygraph, and this being, Did Caril help in any way to kill Betty Jean, and he said I can not answer this because I would be putting someone in the middle. He was then asked did Caril KILL any of the Bartletts, and again he said I cannot tell this, because of putting someone in the middle. He was then asked if the letter he wrote at the Ward home true? stating of the Murders he had done, that he had killed some, and that Caril had killed Betty Jean, and he said I cannot and will not answer this question. He was asked was Caril with you, when Colvert was shot & Robbed? He said I will answer that question and the answer was no, she was not with me. So between the refusal of the questions, *it is the opinion of the operator,* because of the fact when I asked him in question #0 (Did Caril

stab the Maid?) he did give quite an indication on the chart that
this is correct, also coupled with the fact that he refused to answer (Did you stab the Maid at any time) and (Did Caril stab the
Maid?) *that Caril stabbed the maid.* [Emphasis added.]

Apparently a little uncertain of the value of this conclusion, Henninger took a second shot with the lie detector a few days later. It was
no more successful than the first. Henninger pointed to results on the
charts indicating whether Charlie was telling the truth or lying on questions that he refused to answer. For example, when he asked Charlie if
he had cut and stabbed the maid, Charlie would not answer, but nonetheless the "charts" concluded that he had not stabbed her (meaning
Caril had). When Charlie was asked whether Caril had thrown away
the knife used on Mrs. Ward, he answered that she had not, but "the
charts" showed that in fact she had. When he was asked again whether
he had cut or stabbed the maid, Charles again refused to answer, but
"the charts" were read to indicate he had stabbed her. Finally, Henninger
voiced his frustration over the process: "Charles is not the best subject
to try and run on the polygraph, as he is seemingly enjoying all the publicity and this whole thing is more or less a joke to him, and he would lie
when the truth would be better for him."

Henninger finally wised up: Charlie was playing with him, the machine, and the truth, and he was having fun doing it. Nonetheless, word
circulated that the polygraph showed that Charlie had not killed Clara
Ward or Lilyan Fencl. If he hadn't, guess who had?

Polygraph evidence is highly controversial and has never been
widely accepted in American courts as evidence. Some courts have
described lie detectors as being no more reliable or valid a method in
determining truthfulness than flipping a coin. In *United States v. Schef-
fer*, 523 U.S. 303 (1998), the Supreme Court held that because of the lack
of any scientific consensus on the reliability of a polygraph machine, a
military rule per se excluding polygraph was constitutional. The court
said: "There is simply no consensus that polygraph evidence is reliable.

The scientific community and the state and federal courts are extremely polarized on the matter."

In our case, it is highly unlikely, for the reasons set forth earlier, if no other, that Scheele would have attempted to introduce the lie detector results into evidence were Caril put on trial for killing the maid or Mrs. Ward. Frequently, however, while the results are not used as evidence, they are often relied on by law enforcement in determining their view of the guilt or innocence of the person, as appears to have been the case here.

MERLE COLLISON

As for the tenth murder of the spree, Merle Collison, the only evidence against Caril for this crime were Charlie's March 28 and April 9 statements that she had pumped the final bullets into the unfortunate shoe salesman, directly contrary to ten previous statements in which he explicitly exonerated Caril from the killing. These statements alone are not sufficiently credible to establish Caril's guilt as Collison's killer. Caril admitted taking the second .22 to Charlie, which could have possibly supported an aiding and abetting or felony murder charge, but that would be subject to the same challenges of duress and coercion as the Bobby Jensen murder. In fact, the case of duress would seem to have been made even stronger by the most recent Lincoln murders.

So, as for the murders of Carol King, Mrs. Ward, Lilyan Fencl, and Merle Collison, the foregoing analysis shows that when you subtract Charlie Starkweather's testimony from the case, there is basically nothing to link Caril to any of these murders, much less sufficient evidence to establish her guilt beyond a reasonable doubt. Were she charged with these crimes based on the known evidence, I would find her innocent.

Which is not to say that this analysis leaves me without doubt. A skeptical voice points to the implausibility of the hostage story to begin with, the ease with which Caril could simply have walked away from Charlie so many times, the instances in which she heard mentions of her family's murder on the car radio, and the newspaper clippings in her pocket.

However, I would also consider two previously unpublished letters written by Caril, one to Charlie and one to his parents, as lending support to the finding of innocence. The first one reads:

To Charles Starkweather

I want you to know my lawyers and I did all we could to stop your execution and I felt very relieved when I found out it was stopped.

I know you didn't have the chance to make the kind of defense in your trial you wanted to make. And this is a right you should have. I didn't have a fair trial either and the police and the county attorney wear not fair with me either.

You told the truth in one of your statements at first and I know someone did something to make you change your story. Especially about my family's death. It would be best for the both of us if you would tell the truth the way it really happened especially about my family's death.

Why won't you do this. It's all I ask. And is best for the both of us. Please do this for me.

I still would like to see you and know why you did not tell the truth about my family's death.

There must be some reason why you did what you did and I want to hear it straight from you, if possible.

Please again, Caril Fugate

From York, Caril wrote to Charlie's parents:

To Mr. & Mrs. Guy Starkweather

I want you to know I did every thing I could and my lawyers did to help Charles from being executed. I know how worried you must have been.

Can you get him to tell the truth about my family death. If you could get him to do that I would every grateful and it would help him too.

Please Help him to straighten this out about my family's death.

I would be very grateful if could do this.

Thank you
Caril Fugate.

The only obvious reason Caril would write these letters if they didn't reflect the truth was if she was hoping they would be found someday and could be cited as proof of her innocence. This manner of strategic thinking was way beyond the cognitive abilities of a fourteen-year-old Caril Ann Fugate.

Finally, regardless of where she was, and who the inquisitor was, with one exception, the critical facts in Caril's story never changed. She was not a liar.

45

I FOUND IN THE PREVIOUS CHAPTERS BASED ON A CLOSE
examination of the facts that Caril was not present at 924 Belmont
when Charlie killed her parents and little sister. I found that given
current-day science on the effect of repeated trauma on the brain and
the neurological response of dissociating or freezing in the face of extreme danger, Caril did not voluntarily participate in the felony murder
of Robert Jensen or any other of the victims of the rampage.

That brings us to the second issue: Did Caril receive a fair trial?
Even if you accept a jury's verdict of guilty, the conviction could be
overturned if the methods or processes by which the conviction was
obtained violated the Constitution. The Fourteenth Amendment prohibits the states from depriving any person of "life, liberty, or property
without due process of law." The Fifth Amendment also prohibits denying someone "life, liberty, or property without due process of law," but
applies it specifically to the states. The Fourteenth Amendment was one
of three amendments passed after the Civil War and is a restriction on
state action. In lay terms, due process means that the processes of the
government in actions against citizens must be "fair." *Fair* can mean
many different things, but early on the courts held that for a confession
to be fair, it must be voluntary.

In *Brown v. Mississippi*, the Supreme Court held that involuntary
confessions violated the due process clause and could not be admitted
into evidence. In 1896, the court held in *Wilson v. United States* that to
be admitted, the confession must be given "freely, voluntarily and without compulsion or inducement of any sort."

The court has always been wary—even suspicious—of confessions
made by juveniles. In 1948 in *Haley v. Ohio*, the court laid down the
basic principle that "children cannot be judged by the more exacting

standards of maturity expected of adults." The court wrote that "special care" must be used to evaluate the circumstances surrounding custodial interrogation when a "mere child—an easy victim of the law"—is the defendant. In ruling that the boy's confession to murder was involuntary and therefore in violation of the due process clause, Justice Douglas wrote:

> Age 15 is a tender and difficult age for a boy of any race. He cannot be judged by the more exacting standards of maturity. That which would leave a man cold and unimpressed can overawe and overwhelm a lad in his early teens. This is the period of great instability which the crisis of adolescence produces. A 15-year old lad, questioned through the dead of night by relays of police, is a ready victim of the inquisition. Mature men possibly might stand the ordeal from midnight to 5 a.m. But we cannot believe that a lad of tender years is a match for the police in such a contest. *He needs counsel and support if he is not to become the victim first of fear, then of panic. He needs someone on whom to lean lest the overpowering presence of the law, as he knows it, may not crush him.* No friend stood at the side of this 15-year old boy as the police, working in relays, questioned him hour after hour, from midnight until dawn. No lawyer stood guard to make sure that the police went so far and no farther, to see to it that they stopped short of the point where he became the victim of coercion. [Emphasis added.]

In *Gallegos v. Colorado*, issued in 1962, also written by Justice Douglas, a boy charged with first-degree murder had confessed after he had been held for five days "without seeing a lawyer, parent or friendly adult" and without being taken before a juvenile court judge. Douglas noted that

> But a 14-year-old boy, no matter how sophisticated, is unlikely to have any conception of what will confront him when he is made

accessible only to the police. That is to say, we deal with a person who is not equal to the police in knowledge and understanding of the consequences of the questions and answers being recorded, and who is unable to know how to protect his own interests or how to get the benefits of his constitutional rights.

Articulating the standard that a finding of voluntariness must rely on a consideration of the "totality of the circumstances," Justice Douglas found that the circumstances in this case—the youth of the petitioner, the long detention, the failure to send for his parents, the failure to bring him before a judge, the failure to see that he had the advice of a lawyer or a friend—required finding that the confession was not voluntary, and its admission into evidence therefore violated due process.

In *Fare v. Michael*, the court reasserted the "totality of the circumstances" standard in determining whether confession was coerced or voluntary, and it noted that this approach in juvenile cases requires an inquiry into all the circumstances of the interrogation, including "an evaluation of the juvenile's age, experience, education, background and intelligence, and to whether he has the capacity to understand the warnings given him, the nature of his Fifth Amendment rights, and the consequences of waiving those rights." Other considerations are a juvenile's desire to please authorities and a desire to go home.

Applying the totality-of-the-circumstances test to Caril and her situation as the law stood in 1958, I would conclude that her confession was not freely or voluntarily given. She had been with Starkweather on a forty-six-hour murder rampage in which seven people were killed; she was fourteen years old, which essentially made her a child in the eyes of the law; she came from a deprived social and economic background; as a child she was subjected to alcoholism and emotional if not physical abuse from her father; she suffered from an educational deficit due to being transferred between six grade schools in six years; at age thirteen, she had not been protected by her parents from the emotional and sexual attentions of an adult male sociopath almost five years her senior; and she received no counseling or support from friends or family or a lawyer prior to speaking with the police or during the more than six hours of interrogation. Shortly after she was arrested, she received a sedative that put her to sleep for seventeen hours. The next day, on the advice of a doctor, she took four more sedatives. She received a telegram from her older sister, with whom she was quite close, advising her to tell the police all that she knew about the murders and advising her that she would be welcome in their home on her return. That night she was given an injection of Carbatrol, a strong sedative. She confirmed with the jail matron again that her mother, stepfather, and little sister were dead. After traveling the better part of the next day, she was confined to a hospital for the mentally ill, where she claimed to witness a patient undergoing electroshock therapy. She had no contact with family or friends that night or the next day. The following morning, February 1, the setup for the formal interrogation began.

In this isolated and traumatized state, Caril was interrogated on the first day for a minimum of two and a half hours. Facing four men and one woman, she answered questions without any advice or support. The next evening, after being advised by her father and sister to do the right thing and tell the truth, she was questioned for an additional two and a half hours under similar circumstances. The following day she was interrogated for an additional hour before going to court.

Regarding the Statement, Judge Heaney, a federal court of appeals judge, would write in a dissenting opinion on an appeal from Caril's conviction, "I am totally unimpressed with the facade of fairness that the county attorney erected to shield the interrogation process." He was particularly incensed over the failure of the government to provide Caril with an attorney prior to the taking of the Statement. The state, with all its power and resources, arrayed itself against a fourteen-year-old girl of no sophistication or worldliness for six hours and obtained a confession that could lead to her being put to death. No attorney of any competence would allow such an interrogation of a fourteen-year-old client to take place.

46

I N THE 1800S, MOST JUVENILES WERE TREATED THE SAME
as adults in the criminal justice system. If charged and convicted
of a crime, they were housed in adult jails and penitentiaries. In
the latter part of the century, reformers created what was called "houses
of refuge" for "troubled youth," which were usually large institutions
housing kids designated as abandoned, delinquent, or incorrigible. They
came to be known as "reform schools" and soon developed the same set
of problems as adult facilities, such as overcrowding and staff abuse. In
Nebraska, a juvenile facility for boys was established in Kearney in 1879,
and in 1892 a facility for girls was built in Geneva.

The first juvenile court was founded in Chicago in 1899. Within
twenty-five years, most states had set up juvenile court systems. The
courts operated on the basis of parens patriae, parent of the country,
and were aimed at the rehabilitation of youthful offenders. Under this
doctrine, the state was presumed to function in the best interests of the
child, and the purpose of intervention was rehabilitation and treatment,
not punishment. The proceedings were civil, and thus the protections
of the criminal processes were not afforded to juveniles. In many instances, the proceedings were informal and not subject to appeal. No
records were kept, and often no notices of charges were given to the
youths. Youths were seldom represented by attorneys. In 1905, Nebraska
passed its own juvenile court act. The code provided for juveniles to be
represented by attorneys in court proceedings and stated that if a juvenile was unable to afford an attorney, one would be appointed for her.

The irony in our case is that had the county attorney filed the charge
in juvenile court, there most likely would have been no issue regarding
the voluntariness of Caril's confession or her right to an attorney. While

a 1954 Nebraska case stated that a parent had certain due process rights in a dependency-and-neglect petition concerning her child, it did not address the question of the due process rights of a juvenile in a delinquency petition. Those rights were not afforded juveniles until the landmark case *In Re Gault* in 1964. In *Gault*, the Supreme Court held that a child was entitled to the protection of the "essentials of due process" in proceedings that could result in their incarceration or loss of liberty. Those essentials included the privilege against self-incrimination and the right to counsel. It also included the right to be advised of the right to counsel and to have counsel appointed by the state if the person was unable to afford one. (Justice Fortas opined that "It would indeed be surprising if the privilege against self-incrimination were available to hardened criminals, but not to children.")

In 1958, the right to counsel did not apply to juveniles in juvenile court, but by filing against Caril in an adult court where the charge could result in the imposition of the death penalty, the prosecutor had in effect attached to the proceedings the rights that an adult would have had, including the Fifth and Fourteenth Amendments protection against self-incrimination and the Sixth Amendment's right to counsel.

Although Caril was not represented by counsel at her plea hearing, she was represented by counsel at all subsequent court proceedings. However, by then, the fatal damage had already been inflicted. The record shows that on several occasions after she was taken into custody, Caril indicated that she wanted a lawyer. When Scheele asked her in Wyoming if she wanted a lawyer, she said, "Yes, but who would take it?" When Fahrnbruch asked her in February 1 if she wanted a lawyer, she first said yes, then no. Dr. Coats testified that Caril said several times at that meeting that she wanted an attorney. In her testimony, Mrs. Karnopp confirmed that Caril said she wanted an attorney. And yet Fahrnbruch proceeded as if nothing had been said.

Scheele asked Caril on cross-examination in the trial if she had ever specifically *asked* for an attorney, and she replied that she hadn't. The court would hold in *Gault* that simply because the boy's mother was aware of the fact that her son had a right to counsel, the state was not re-leased from specifically advising her of the right and inquiring whether she chose to waive it before proceeding.

Gault applied to statements made and the right to have counsel during the court proceedings. Here, we are talking about Caril's state-ment made while she was in custody but before court proceedings had begun. In *Escobedo v. Illinois*, 1964, the court held that under the Sixth Amendment a person has the right to an attorney *while being interro-gated by the police*. In *Miranda vs. Arizona*, decided two years later, the court held that a person in custody "must be warned *prior to interroga-tion* that he has the right to remain silent, that anything he says can be used against him in a court of law, that he has the right to the presence of an attorney, and that if he cannot afford an attorney one will be ap-pointed for him." In *Gault*, a key factor in the court's decision was that the juvenile was at risk of commitment to a penal institution; the same reasoning would seem to require the same warnings to a juvenile in a case where her very life was at risk.

Given the law today, Caril's statement would be excluded as a vio-lation of her Fifth and Fourteenth Amendment rights for failure of the police to give her the *Miranda* advisements before interrogating her. As for 1958, I would hold that proceeding to interrogate her on February 2 without the presence of an attorney, or at least a clear and succinct ad-visement that she had a right to an attorney, should be considered, in addition to the circumstances already mentioned, as requiring a finding that her Statement was not voluntary. Under the *Gallegos* standard, it could barely be argued with a straight face that this fourteen-year-old girl was able "to know how to protect her own interests or how to get the benefits of her constitutional rights." The written record shows that Caril didn't even know the distinction between the prosecutor and a defense attorney.

As stressed, in the absence of her Statement, the only evidence link-ing Caril to the robbery-murder of Robert Jensen was the testimony of Charles Starkweather, a notorious liar whose story about Caril's involvement changed so often as to render his testimony to be totally untrustworthy.

In my opinion, the court also violated Caril's right to a fair trial by admitting into evidence the photograph of Carol King. Caril was not charged with the murder of Carol King, but solely with the murder of Robert Jensen. Two completely separate offenses. The photo was highly inflammatory, to say the least, and bore absolutely no relevance to the case. Several jurors grimaced when it was passed to them. The admission of this photo alone should have been grounds for reversal, and the fact that the prosecution offered it and the judge allowed it suggests to the authors of *The Twelfth Victim* that the judge and prosecutor had in fact conspired to see Caril convicted.

At the conclusion of the prosecution's case, I would grant the defendant's motion to dismiss the two charges of murder in the first degree.

V

CONSEQUENCES

47

CONVICTED MURDERESS CARIL ANN FUGATE, NOW fifteen, slipped into the chilly underbelly of the Women's Reformatory in York and disappeared from public view. Caril's only visitors through the 1958 holidays were her attorneys. No one came on Christmas Eve or Christmas Day. She was in a cell all by herself in the basement and was not allowed to speak to other inmates. Her clothes didn't fit, she was allowed only one shower a week, her meals were brought to her room, and in the first few months she had no recreation or counseling.

Driving back to Lincoln after one visit, Reller declared to McArthur that they had to get Caril out of the place. They set about collecting affidavits from five former inmates, a supervisor, and a former supervisor detailing what they referred to as "brutal conditions which will undoubtedly mentally injure and disturb her ..." The current supervisor stated that the rule of complete silence "creates a condition of tension and despondency," that there was no rehabilitation, and that solitary confinement was the only form of punishment. An inmate swore that she had spent most of the first six months at York in solitary confinement, one time for smiling at another inmate. She had survived on a diet of toast and tea. Others said that the heating and cooling system didn't work and that Superintendent Bowley had refused to allow them to apply for parole, and one woman wrote that she had spent two weeks in solitary for writing a letter. There was a rule prohibiting women from lying in their beds during the day, which meant that if they were tired they had to lie on the cement floor.

On January 30, McArthur filed a motion in the Nebraska Supreme Court asking the court to suspend Caril's sentence while her appeal for a new trial was pending on the grounds that her imprisonment under those conditions constituted cruel and unusual punishment. Mrs. Bowley denied all the allegations, insisting that Caril went to chapel on Sunday and to school three day a week and that she never tried to influence the girls to get a divorce or give up their children. The doctor who served the reformatory said that the girls received excellent supervisory and medical care and that the statements in the affidavits were "typical of constitutionally psychopathic individuals." Governor Victor Anderson backed up Mrs. Bowley, claiming that she ran a good institution.

On February 6, the court denied the petition.

McArthur and Reller opened a new line of attack on their young client's conviction. In a second motion for a new trial, filed April 9, 1959, they alleged that Charles Starkweather had testified falsely against Caril Fugate and that the false testimony had been set up under the direction of the prosecuting attorney and other officials. Attached to the motion were three affidavits: one from former prison guard Carl Hefner, one from former inmate Otto Glasser, and one from current inmate Jeffrey Wheeler. The two inmates were in cells next to Charlie in the hospital ward. They both testified that three men, whom they couldn't identify, visited Charlie in his cell and they could hear what was said. Wheeler swore in his affidavit that the men told Charlie that if he testified as instructed, county attorney (Elmer Scheele) would keep him (Starkweather) from the electric chair. Glasser swore that one of the three persons "told Starkweather repeatedly that he would not get the electric chair if he said exactly what he was told to say in the Fugate case and that Elmer Scheele was a man of his word who would see to it that he did not get the chair." Glasser also claimed that Starkweather told the three men that he had done "personal violence" on Caril in the August Meyer, C. Lauer Ward and Marion Bartlett homes. Charlie told them he almost killed Caril at those homes and after Collison was shot in Wyoming because she tried to escape. The men told Starkweather not to testify to those details.

The signers of the three affidavits swore that Charlie was not allowed to watch TV, listen to the radio, or read newspapers prior to Caril's trial. Once the trial began, he was given candy and cigarettes and allowed to watch TV, read the newspapers, and listen to the radio. Glasser believed that there was a line kept open between the county attorney's office and the pen during the trial. He claimed that Charlie "laughed and shouted" when the jury found Caril guilty.

A few weeks later, Scheele answered the motion with a bevy of his own affidavits. First was one from Charlie himself, who swore that he had not been told that he would escape the electric chair if he testified against Caril, that Scheele had only urged him to tell the truth in her trial, and that Scheele had told him to keep his testimony limited to the Jensen case to avoid the possibility of a mistrial. He denied receiving any favors or promises and said he told guard Earl Clemons that he felt sorry for Caril when the jury found her guilty. Deputy warden John Greenholtz said that inmate Wheeler had been fired because he couldn't get along with his colleagues; Marjorie Marlett, a reporter for the *Journal*, said she had personally arranged to have copies of the paper and *Life* magazine delivered to Charlie in hopes of getting an interview. Scheele's affidavit said he specifically told Charlie not to expect any favors in exchange for testifying against Caril.

On June 18, after oral arguments, Judge Spencer denied the motion for a new trial. McArthur filed an appeal with the Nebraska Supreme Court, where it awaited decision along with the appeal based on juror Walenta's bet that Caril would get the chair.

The June 19 AP story on the judge's decision was on the front page of the *Hastings Daily Tribune*, beneath a photo of Louisiana governor Earl Long (Huey Long's younger brother) stepping from an automobile after being released from a psychiatric clinic in Galveston, Texas, from where he had been running the Louisiana state government.

That same day, June 19, Charlie's attorneys filed a petition for review with the United States Supreme Court.

48

BY JUNE 1959, CHARLIE HAD BEEN UNDER A SENTENCE of death for over a year. His eight-by-twelve cell in the hospital ward was comfortable; it had a window through which he could see out into the yard, and a table he could use to draw and write on, and a radio. He watched a television set in the corridor. He read daily newspapers and had special visiting privileges. He spent most of the day reading, mainly western fiction; writing his memoir; talking to visitors; or drawing. Charlie's artwork improved remarkably in his time in the cell. In the beginning, he drew in pencil; then he moved on to Crayolas and then watercolors and, finally, oils. He began one of his finest works toward the end, an elaborate Civil War battle scene, in which none of the soldiers had faces. Deputy warden John Greenholtz visited Charlie every day. Two guards sat outside his cell twenty-four hours a day.

Charlie watched TV for news of himself and was pleased whenever he showed up onscreen, no matter the story. He noticed groups of visitors touring the facility and was convinced they had come to see him, only to be crestfallen when told tours had been given at the prison long before he arrived.

Charlie presented a new face; gone was the lethal version of James Dean; in its place was a reformed, pleasant, well-spoken, and, yes, remorseful Charlie who had accepted Jesus as his savior. Perhaps he saw this version as a better fantasy: a former gunslinger/murderer trails out in a blaze of electrified glory, only to be reborn on the other side. As for the execution, he was ready whenever God wanted him.

Reinhardt was having none of it. In over forty hours of interviewing Charlie, the criminologist heard the words and saw the face but never sensed any true remorse. Charlie claimed that Jesus had forgiven him his sins but was quick to add that none of his victims would have been slain if they'd stayed out of his way. As for Caril, Charlie would say in one breath that once upon a time he had loved her, and she him, but not anymore. It was over. Then he would wonder if he would be able to see her once he passed over and if one day she would be there with him. He was feeling good about where he was, although he hoped to live a little longer so he could write a novel he had in mind.

Charlie's parents came to see him two or three times a week. They spoke through a screen in a small room. The prison chaplain stopped by to see Charlie almost daily. Charlie's favorite prayer became Psalm 23, "The Lord is my shepherd . . ." Charlie was working on his handwritten memoir, certain that it would earn him about thirty thousand dollars and be read by millions. On March 15, *Parade* magazine published a heavily edited section of it. Charlie was furious over the editing. He wondered aloud to the guards whether there would be TV shows and movies made of his life.

In February 1959, Charlie fired both attorneys Gaughan and Matschullat. He wrote Judge Spencer that he would be representing himself from now on. His first move was to file a request for clemency with the State Board of Appeals and Pardons on March 4, 1959. Prepared with the assistance of prison officials, the request sought a commutation of the sentence from death to life. The board granted his request for a hearing, issued a temporary reprieve, and set the hearing for April 21. It was the new Charlie who would appear before the board, although he must have known he had little chance of a commutation. The *Journal* wrote that, "Pale and trembling, he crossed the prison grounds to the parole board meeting room and addressed the board." Doubtful. The last thing Charlie wanted was life in prison, where he would be allowed to rot away in a cell, or even in a moldy mental hospital, to die unknown and forgotten. He had made that clear from the beginning. He knew when he fired his lawyers he would move more swiftly and surely toward his end. The time had come to honor his covenant with death, and of that he had no fear. The hearing was for show. Once again.

Charlie arrived at the hearing with hair freshly trimmed and in a tan suit, white shirt, and floral tie. He was escorted into the conference room by two guards and sat at a table in front of the board, made up of the attorney general and the secretary of state. The third member, governor Ralph Brooks, was absent "due to illness." Charlie kept his hands on the table and spoke so softly others had trouble hearing him in the crowded room. He told the board that he'd repented for his crimes. He felt sorry for his victims, and if there was any way he could bring them back, he would. Before the killings he had little concern about human life, but that had changed since he'd been in prison, "mostly by reading the Bible." He told the board that if he had been represented right at the trial, he would have gotten life. He'd never trusted his attorneys. In response to a question about his mental attitude, he insisted that he was not going nuts. He trusted that the board had an open mind. "I blame it all on myself," he said. As he left the room, he touched his mother on the shoulder.

Helen Starkweather told the board that his attorneys did not provide proper representation and had tried to get her to say that her son "acted peculiar" to support the insanity plea. Her son had changed since he was in prison, she said. He had seen a different side of life, mainly through the assistance of the chaplain and the Bible. Guy Starkweather reminded the board that there had been another participant in the crimes and asked that if she (Caril) had gotten life, why shouldn't his son?

A few days before the hearing, the citizens of Bennet held a town meeting at the local high school where 118 members signed a petition objecting to the commutation. A Lincoln attorney had been hired to represent the town at the hearing, and although twenty-one prominent members of the community were in the hearing room, he spoke for them and the signers of two additional petitions as well. He presented a six-point argument, among which were the heinous nature of Charlie's crimes, the other murders he admitted to, and the possibility of escape and commission of further murders due to his utter disregard for human life.

The hearing concluded at 10:45, forty-five minutes after it had begun. The two-member board met in executive session. At 10:50, administrative assistant Loretta Walker emerged from the room and told the gathered newsmen that the petition for "clemency" was denied. The board scheduled May 23 as Charlie's new execution date. Helen Starkweather heard the announcement in the hallway and began to cry. Secretary of state Frank Marsh explained to a reporter that the reason the board granted the hearing in the first place was because the execution had been set for March 19, Good Friday, and they didn't want any association between the death of Starkweather and that of Jesus Christ.

Ms. Walker visited Charlie in his cell and told him of the verdict. "I half expected it," he said, and turned away.

49

THE LAST TWO WEEKS OF MAY 1959 WERE EVENTFUL for both Charlie and Caril. In mid-May, Caril received her eighth-grade diploma from the school at York, of which she was quite proud. On Tuesday the twentieth, Judge Spencer denied her second request for a new trial. As usual, Reller delivered the bad news. She and her lawyers turned their attention to the fact that Charlie was scheduled to die on May 23, believing that with him would die the last real chance of a complete exoneration. Caril appealed directly to Charlie himself. She begged him "to at least confess to a minister that I am innocent so I won't be the only one who knows I am innocent. You know that you are the only who knows the truth beside God." Acting warden Greenholtz took the letter to Charlie in the cell. Charlie read it and responded that he did not want to see her. "In fact, he made it very emphatic that he didn't want to see her," and he added that he had no intention of answering the letter either.

Caril wrote Governor Brooks a letter asking him to stay the execution because "I believe there is a chance that if Charles had enough time he would tell the truth and clear me. I wish that you would stay the execution so that he would have plenty of time to tell the truth." The governor denied the request on the grounds that given the lapse of time and the trials, Starkweather had probably said all he was going to say. Caril also sent a letter to the Nebraska Board of Parole and Pardons, Judge Spencer, and other state and country officials asking that a meeting be arranged between her and Starkweather. Nothing came of her request.

On Wednesday, McArthur wrote a letter to Governor Brooks asking him to reconsider and stay the execution because in Caril's appeal, she would need the testimony of Starkweather and their contention that he lied would sound "hollow" if he was dead. Brooks denied that request the same day.

On Thursday, the day before the execution, Caril made one last try: a telegram directly to President Eisenhower. It read:

President of the United States
White House, Washington, D.C.

I am now 15 years old. Stop. About a year and half ago on a day when I was in public school 19 year old Starkweather who I had told several days before in front of my mother never to see me again went into my home and killed my 2 year old baby sister, mother and stepfather. Stop. Starkweather first confessed that I had nothing to do with his murder which is true. Stop. Later he changed his story and said I helped him do his murder which is not true. Stop. He forced me to go with him when I got home from school against my will. Starkweather will be executed tomorrow (Friday). Stop. I have been denied by Governor Brooks a request to see him and see if he will tell the truth in front of a minister of someone else who would be fair before he is executed. Stop. I know of no one else to turn to because all of my family I was living with he killed. Stop. I know you are very busy but please help me in any way you can.

Thank you
Caril Ann Fugate

David Kendall, special counsel to the president, received the telegram in the late afternoon. He made some phone calls, read the letter again, and dictated a response to his secretary:

The Starkweather case is entirely a state matter. The President has no jurisdiction or authority in any way to comply with your request.

Jim McArthur speculated that Merril Reller put Caril up to the telegram to the president.

Charlie was scheduled to die at 6:00 a.m. on Friday, the twenty-third. It appeared initially that the execution would proceed without objection or pause. But on Thursday morning, Charlie's parents filed a petition for a writ of habeas corpus ("deliver up the body") and a request for a stay of execution with Federal District Court judge Robert Van Pelt in Lincoln. The petition alleged that Charlie's rights under the due process clause had been violated. Attached to the petition was a letter from Charlie to the judge alleging he was denied effective assistance of counsel because his attorneys had failed to seek a change of venue and were inebriated on several occasions when they visited him in prison. Charlie took a final shot at Caril, claiming she had done horrible and cruel things that he was not willing to pay for. He also sought the opportunity to file an ethics complaint against John McArthur for alleging that he had lied in his testimony. His parents asked for appointment of counsel, noting that they had been unable to find an attorney willing to take the case.

Early Thursday morning, Guy brought the petition to Greenholtz at the pen, who gave it to Starkweather for his signature, which he had notarized. Judge Van Pelt denied the petition that afternoon, and the execution was on for 6:00 the next morning.

Charles wrote in a letter to his parents that he was going to the chair with a clear conscience. He claimed to have told the truth about Caril:

I have made my peace with God . . . holding on to my life is like trying to hold a handful of sand. If death is still inevitable, God will triumph. Man may take my life, but my soul belongs to him.

All my hopes now are of staying alive and repenting for the wrongs I have committed. Killing is a terrible sin against God and man. I hope that some day killing and the taking of human life, even in war, will only be a terrible memory.

At 5:00 p.m., Charlie's parents said goodbye to their son. He ate his last meal of sirloin and potatoes alone, although Greenholtz offered to bring him sandwiches and coffee throughout the night.

As the family walked to their car in the prison parking lot, Guy Starkweather figured he had seen his son for the last time. A reporter suggested he contact judge Archibald Gardner, chief judge of the Eighth Circuit Court of Appeals in Huron, South Dakota. That night, around midnight, Guy called Judge Gardner at home, and the judge told him that the matter lay with Judge Robinson, the chief district court judge. At 2:00 a.m., Guy called Judge Robinson, told him of his call with Judge Gardner, and renewed his request for a stay of execution. Judge Robinson took the matter under advisement and finally concluded that Charlie should have the opportunity to appeal Judge Van Pelt's decision denying the petition for a habeas writ. The judge noted that the habeas petition had been prepared without assistance of counsel. At 4:30 a.m., the judge signed the order granting the stay of execution until June 4.

The morning brought a predawn thunderstorm. The newsman and official witnesses had gathered at the entrance to the penitentiary, and final preparations for the execution were underway. Charlie had spent most of the night lying in his cot reading the Bible and talking with Chaplain Klein, who declared him "all set to go. We had discussed everything and he was showing no emotion whatsoever." They were only a few minutes away from shaving Charlie's head and leg for the electrodes when word of the stay reached Greenholtz by phone. Driving from Omaha, sixty miles away, a U.S. marshal delivered the warrant to him at 6:10 a.m.

The chaplain delivered news of the stay to Charlie in his cell. The condemned man broke into a big smile and shook his hand. "This is sure going to make my mother happy," he said.

Robert Jensen was at his son's gravesite in the cemetery outside Bennet at sunrise Thursday morning. Waiting, he heard on the car radio that the execution had been stayed. "I was surprised," he said. "I understood when I went to bed that it was all over." He added, "The verdict was fair and honest. I'm sure eventually it will be carried out."

Attorney Matschullat had come to the pen to witness the execution and was pleased to hear of the stay. He told a reporter that earlier he and cocounsel Gaughan had offered their services to Charlie in the appeals through the federal courts, but he had turned them down. "None of 'em I killed begged for their life," he said, "and I ain't begging for mine."

Nonetheless, Charlie typed out his notice of appeal and it was filed later that day in the federal district court by his grandmother Althea Neal.

If looked at objectively, and perhaps cynically, the ensuing appellate process resembles a judicial charade. On June 1, the court appointed three "prominent attorneys" to represent Charlie on the appeal: one was the president of the Omaha Bar Association, another the president of the Lancaster County Bar Association, and the third the president of the Omaha Barristers' Club. The Eighth Circuit covered Missouri, Nebraska, South Dakota, Arkansas, Iowa, Minnesota, and North Dakota, yet two of the three circuit court judges appointed to hear the appeal were from Omaha and one was from Sioux City, Iowa, across the river. Omaha wasn't Lincoln, and no blood had been spilled there, but it had suffered its own bout of severe anxiety and fear. The lawyers were appointed on June 1, and the hearing was held three days later, on June 4, the last day of the stay. Two days—the hearing began at ten o'clock on June 4—is a ridiculously short period of time for three attorneys to review the record, study the law, prepare briefs, and get ready for oral argument. The court could easily have extended the stay for a month or two to give the attorneys time to adequately prepare. A man's life was at stake. The attorneys could have requested that the stay be extended, but there is no record that they did.

Technically, the hearing was only to determine whether Judge Van Pelt's order denying a hearing on the petition for a writ of habeas corpus was in error. If there was probable cause to believe that Charlie's constitutional rights had been violated, then the circuit court would order the district court to conduct a hearing on the petition. If not, the appeal would be dismissed. Charlie's attorneys argued that his constitutional rights had been violated through ineffective assistance of counsel and the failure to have the case moved out of Lincoln. One of the attorneys argued that in the days of the crime, Lancaster County was an "inflamed community. I know how prejudiced I was, and still am."

The court recessed at 10:30 and reconvened at 2:00 p.m. The appeal was denied on the grounds that Charlie had not "exhausted" his state remedies; that is, he had not first sought a writ of habeas corpus in state court.

His three attorneys, their chore completed, walked away from the case. The Nebraska Supreme Court rescheduled the execution for 12:01 a.m. on June 12. Unable to find anyone in Nebraska to represent his son on a last-ditch effort, Guy Starkweather cast about for an attorney on the national stage. Two courses of action were open: filing for a writ of habeas corpus in Lincoln, or filing for a writ of certiorari with the United States Supreme Court. Guy, believing his son would never get a fair hearing in Nebraska, chose the Supreme Court.

On Tuesday, June 9, Washington D.C. attorney James Laughlin, who had gained some fame for defending Axis Sally in a sedition war crimes trial in Germany after WWII and for springing Pretty Boy Floyd's wife and mother from prison, received a collect call from Guy Starkweather asking him to intervene in his son's case. Laughlin and his partner, Albert Ahern Jr., filed a petition for a stay of execution with Supreme Court justice Charles Evans Whittaker that afternoon. On Wednesday, Justice Whittaker granted the stay for a week, until June 17, in order to give the attorneys time to seek a writ of certiorari from the full court, which if granted would stay the execution until the case was heard and disposed of, and which if denied would result in a new execution date being set. Laughlin created big headlines in Nebraska by telling reporters he might be able to delay the execution for two or more years. He said that in addition to arguing ineffective assistance of counsel and inflammatory press, he was also considering arguing that Charlie suffered from the same mental condition that had recently put governor Earl Long in a sanitarium, which was reputed to be what we now refer to as bipolar disorder. In the petition, he described his new client simply as a "mentally deficient indigent."

Greenholtz told Charlie of the new stay. He remarked that the new date didn't give them much time, then kept on talking to his brother and mother. Greenholtz phoned the executioner in Iowa—an electrician—and told him not to bother coming to Lincoln on Thursday. (Whether the executioner received a cancellation fee is unknown.)

Laughlin filed the petition for a writ of certiorari with the Supreme Court on Wednesday, June 17. On June 22, the Court denied the petition on a unanimous vote. The *Star* celebrated in broad large black letters: HIGH COURT REFUSES CHARLIE A HEARING.

On Tuesday, June 23, the Nebraska Supreme Court set the execution for Thursday, June 25, sometime between 12:01 a.m. and 11:59 p.m. Deputy Warden Greenholtz said the execution would take place shortly after midnight Wednesday. Helen, who had visited her son every day for the last month, was with Charlie when the word came. Startled, she said, "It doesn't give us much time, but we will keep right on fighting—we'll use all of our rights." They had about thirty hours. Greenholtz put in another call to the Iowa electrician.

Wednesday morning Laughlin contacted one of Caril's attorneys, Merril Reller, and asked for his assistance. He dictated motions for a new trial and a stay of execution to Reller's secretary, who typed them up. The motion for a new trial alleged, among many other things, that new evidence had been discovered, that false testimony was presented at the trial, that Harold Robinson had intimidated witnesses, that Caril had been prevented from testifying at his trial, and that the death penalty sentence was the result of great pressure. At Laughlin's request, Reller and McArthur spent the morning unsuccessfully searching for a local attorney to handle the new motions. The Starkweathers appeared in the clerk's office over the noon hour on Wednesday and filed the two motions themselves. Guy released a note from Charlie to the court: "Because of the quick date of my execution I am beginning to wonder why I am going to the chair. It doesn't seem I am going for murder, instead just to satisfy a few narrow-minded hypocrites and cover up for mistakes of judgment passed on me." Guy stated that a number of local attorneys had turned down his request to represent Charlie. "The state slipped this one over on us."

The state had appointed a new warden on June 22. The new warden said right off that he and Greenholtz, who hadn't applied for the job, had the same correctional philosophy and that he would be retained as deputy warden. The press wrongly assumed that, following protocol, the new warden would handle the execution.

At 3:51 p.m., Judge Spencer, the same judge who had presided over both Charlie's and Caril's trials, denied the two motions, ruling that the "allegations were not supported by one iota of evidence." Guy left the courtroom and reappeared in the clerk's office a few minutes later with a writ of coram nobis ("before us"), which contained the new allegation that Charlie had been promised he would be given leniency if he gave false evidence against himself. Judge Spencer denied the petition for the writ at 4:42.

Guy Starkweather did not give up. That night he filed a motion for a stay of execution with the Nebraska Supreme Court seeking a review of Judge Spencer's denial of the motion for a new trial and in order to obtain new counsel. The court met in a hurriedly convened night session, and at 8:30 the court denied the request "flat out," as the clerk noted. Starkweather had filed a new petition for a writ of habeas corpus with Judge Van Pelt, the same judge who had earlier denied a hearing on a writ, alleging newly found evidence and inadequate assistance of counsel. Judge Van Pelt denied the petition because Starkweather had not exhausted all state remedies available. In D.C., Laughlin filed a motion for a stay with justice Hugo Black, which was denied.

That was it for Charlie.

50

DEPUTY WARDEN JOHN GREENHOLTZ WAS BORN TO the job. He stood six feet four inches tall and weighed 250 pounds, which he carried easily. He had a commanding presence and, according to daughter Mary, looked a little like Broderick Crawford of the TV show *Highway Patrol*. He saw through scams and ruses and bullshit effortlessly and could put a stop to trouble with a raised eyebrow. He had no use for politics or meetings; he preferred to be out on the grounds dealing with the prisoners and sensing what was going on and listening and advising and, when necessary, imposing. The inmates called him "Big John," the staff just "Deputy."

Greenholtz began as a guard in 1949 and rose steadily through the ranks to captain of the guard, assistant deputy warden, and finally deputy warden. He knew most of the eight hundred inmates by name as well as their stories. He and his wife and two daughters, ten and twelve, lived in the deputy's second-story apartment inside the wall near the side entrance. Mary and her sister had looked out the window of their apartment to watch the arrival of Starkweather in a caravan of cars from Wyoming. They watched as he walked beneath them on the sidewalk in chains and bloody white shirt, close enough they could see the black shoe polish still in his hair. On January 29, 1958, after the Wards were found dead in their house, their classmates' parents, many of them armed, had shown up early at school in their cars to pick up their kids. Soon, Mary and her sister were the only kids left in the building. Her mother showed up at 3:15 as usual and drove her daughters to their piano lessons, and then home to their apartment inside the walls. "Don't let fear run your life," their father taught them. (Some of the girls' school friends were not allowed to visit because their living quarters were inside the walls.)

Greenholtz visited Charlie in his cell every day. He paid for some of his oils and brushes out of his own pocket. He gave him visiting privileges and accommodated reasonable requests from his family. He did his best to treat each man as an individual and to remember that whatever the man had done, he was still a human being.

This wasn't Greenholtz's first execution. In 1952, Ronald Sundahl was executed for hatcheting a sixteen-year-old carhop to death in Columbus. Timothy Iron Bear was electrocuted in 1949 for stabbing a rancher and his wife to death in the Sandhills. Nonetheless, Greenholtz didn't relish the task of running another execution.

Nebraska had executed thirty-four people before Starkweather went to the chair. The state hanged twenty-one condemned men in the first twenty years of its existence, then in 1913 switched by law from the rope to the electric chair. The chair itself was built in 1913 by a local furniture maker, but it wasn't used until 1920. It is a large, crude piece of furniture, cut from oak and stained a medium brown. It has a high, straight back with a piece of padding over a slat in the middle. The seat has a black cushion, and the armrests are narrow. On the base of the legs is a crossbar with notches to hold the prisoner's legs in place. Two thick wires run out from the wall; one snakes up the back of the chair to the top, where the head would rest, the other across the floor to the crossbar for the legs. In a small room off to the side, out of sight of the condemned man but visible to the observers, were the electrical switches.

The word had long been out that the lights at the pen, if not in all of Lincoln, would dim the moment the executioner threw the switch. When darkness fell on the night of June 25, cars full of kids began cruising and lining up on the road running directly in front of the prison. Their doors were open, and their radios were blasting rock and roll. Some were drinking beer, others pop. The boys were in jeans; the girls in shorts and blouses. The Safety Patrol shooed them off, but they soon circled back around to continue the party.

As the day wore on, Charlie painted in oil and read and talked with the chaplain. He finished a painting of a cowboy and his horse standing around a fire in snowy woods, with a haze of purple mountains in the background. The cowboy is wearing a pistol on his hip. (The *e* is missing from *Starkweather* in the signature.) "I figure this is the night," Charlie said, and he gave Greenholtz the painting. Charlie appeared calm through the evening hours.

On a rise not far away, with a good view of the prison, Charles Horst had gathered with a few friends. Charles had lived close to the Starkweathers for a few years growing up and ran a little with his older brother, Rodney. One Saturday morning he had stopped by the Starkweather house to pick up Rodney to go to the movies downtown. Charlie wanted to go along, but the two boys didn't want him along. Charlie raised hell, and when his dad told him to shut up, he kept on insisting. His dad, who had been drinking, backhanded him hard across the face, and Charlie shut up.

After the Ward slayings, when Charlie was thought to be on the loose in town, Horst and two friends drove the streets of Lincoln in a 1938 Chevy sedan with rifles poking out the windows, looking for Charlie, although they weren't sure what they would do if they spotted him. Tonight, they opened a six-pack of beer and stood on the rise and listened to rock and roll on station KFOR and waited and watched. At the cemetery outside the Community Church in Bennet, Robert Jensen again stood by his son's grave.

A representative of the local Lions Club had earlier asked Greenholtz to see if Charlie would donate his eyes to their eye bank. Greenholtz approached Charlie with the appeal. Charlie turned him down cold: "Nobody ever did a thing for me. Why should I do anything for them?"

Charlie's family gathered at the Lincoln home of his grandmother, Althea Neal. Relatives were milling about inside, making phone calls, and cars were coming and going in front. Once the Nebraska Supreme Court denied the stay at 8:30, Helen and other members of the family drove to the prison for their final visit with Charlie. Guy stayed at the house working the phone until a few minutes before midnight.

Helen; brothers Rodney and Robert; sister Laveta; Richard, a half-brother of Guy Starkweather; and Richard's wife visited Charlie that night. As they left, Charlie was allowed to hug his mother and Laveta goodbye. The family left through a side door in the prison to escape the press, but an enterprising photographer spotted the six on the walk and shot a photo of them strung out in a line behind Helen, heads down, lit up by the flash against the black night, on their way to their cars.

Greenholtz supervised final preparations for the execution, including several run-throughs with the guards, the chaplain, and the executioner from Iowa (who would earn two hundred dollars for the night's work), who had to test the electrical setup to make sure 2,200 volts would be delivered to the electrodes on the head and leg with a sharp pull of the switch. For his last meal, Charlie passed on the steak and ate cold cuts instead. The barber came and shaved the thick red hair from his head and cleared a patch on his lower left leg. Charlie dressed in denims—a slit cut in the left leg—a new blue chambray shirt with the cuffs rolled up, and loafers. He asked a guard how much time he had left and was told fifteen minutes. "Well, I guess this is it," Charlie replied. He took a plastic cross the chaplain had given him from a shirt pocket and clutched it in his fist, and the two repeated Psalm 23.

Greenholtz received a sudden shock himself. The prison physician, Dr. Bert Finkle, whose task it was to declare the man in the chair dead and who had attended all ten executions since his appointment in 1921, came to Greenholtz's office around 11:00 p.m. The two men had been close friends for years. Half an hour before midnight, the doctor suffered a fatal heart attack. Greenholtz pulled it together sufficiently to find a new doctor in time for the execution.

The execution chamber was a small whitewashed room in the basement of a stone building on the prison grounds. It was sealed by a steel door, and the room was lit only by a bare lightbulb hanging over the chair, which was a little off to the side. In front of it, rows of metal chairs were lined up on rubber mats. Of the sixty applications from the press, only twenty were granted. None of the victims' relatives were present, and Charlie, who was allowed three seats, had no one there on his behalf. In attendance, however, were his fired attorney Matschullat and criminologist Reinhardt, who was busily writing his book on Charlie.

The two attending guards, the chaplain, Greenholtz, the executioner, and several officials brought the crowd to around forty.

Del Harding was present for the *Star*. He and a few other reporters had listened to Chief Carrol tell stories about how gruesome executions were, things like moaning and smoke coming out of the bodies after the switch was thrown. His attendance at the execution made Del a little nervous, and that evening he went to the Varsity Theater in downtown Lincoln and watched Gregory Peck in *Pork Chop Hill* for distraction. He and the other reporters bunched up at the main prison door well before midnight, and he considered for a moment trying to sneak a camera through security but figured he might get caught and thrown out. When the chamber door opened, he elbowed his way into the room and grabbed a chair in the front row. Seeing he was sitting on a metal chair on a rubber mat, he moved one row back. The electric chair stood fifteen feet directly in front of him. In the small open room stood the executioner, a skinny guy, about five foot six, wearing slacks and a long-sleeve dress shirt.

Two guards entered Charlie's cell a few minutes before midnight. The last words to come from Charlie's mouth, at least words loud enough to be heard, as he sat on his cot, were, "What's the rush?" They walked Charlie and the chaplain down the hall of the ward and through a door and roughly two hundred steps down a sidewalk to the stone building. It was a clear, warm Nebraska summer night with a bright moon. Bald and without his rimless glasses, Charlie descended the stairs with his attendants and entered the chamber at 12:01 a.m. Awaiting him were Deputy Warden Greenholtz and two officers. As he walked to the chair, Charlie gave the onlookers one last half smile. One writer described him jumping onto the chair as if he were a boy in a barber shop. A green curtain was pulled to separate Charlie from view. The guards strapped Charlie's arms and legs to the chair. A strap was tightened across his chest. His pant leg was opened and a lotion to conduct the electricity was rubbed on the shaved spot. The electrode was attached. The lotion was rubbed on his scalp, and a partial leather mask was placed over his face, covering his eyes. An electrode was attached to the top of the mask, which was secured to the top slat on the chair. The green curtain was pulled back to reveal Charlie to view.

Greenholtz asked Charlie if he had any last words. Charlie seemed to reflect for a moment, then shook his head. Greenholtz signaled the executioner, stepped back, and turned to look at the faces in the audience. Tears were running down his face.

A loud hum filled the room. Charlie's fists clenched. A jolt shot through him, and he did not move. A second jolt shot through him, and he jerked like a puppet, then fell limp. A third jolt, and he jerked again, and fell limp. An officer walked over and opened Charlie's shirt, and the doctor approached and placed the stethoscope on his chest. "Is he dead?" the executioner asked. "Yes," replied the doctor. A fourth bolt shot through Charlie and he jerked against the leather straps. The stethoscope was again pressed against the chest. "Is he dead?" the executioner asked again. "Yes," the doctor answered. The executioner dropped his hand from the switch. The green curtain was pulled closed. At 12:05, four minutes after entering the execution chamber, Charles Raymond Starkweather, age twenty, was dead. The body was loaded onto a gurney, covered with a sheet, and rolled out the door of the stone building to a waiting ambulance, which drove from the grounds to the Umberger Mortuary. Reverend Klein would preside at a small family service later that day at the mortuary. Charlie was interred in public view in an unmarked grave in Wyuka.

Greenholtz explained to reporters after the execution that the tears were for the death of his close friend Dr. Finkle. Del Harding was not moved by the execution. It was kind of like the song "Is That All There Is?" It seemed quick and clean and relatively painless. His mind went to the two dead teenagers stuffed in the cellar. A lot less pain and terror than they had suffered. He drove to his office, wrote the story, and went home to bed.

Much to the disappointment of the rock and roll kids, the prison lights did not dim when the switch was thrown. (Although *the Omaha World Herald* couldn't resist claiming in a 1967 story that "The lights dimmed briefly several times.") The boys on the hill heard the guy on

KFOR announce that Charlie was dead; they tossed their empties in the back of the car and headed home.

Charlie's family learned of the moment of his death on the radio in his grandmother's home. The elder Jensen also heard it on the car radio. "It was something that had to be done," he said of the execution. "It doesn't help a bit to bring back our boy or Carol."

Caril Fugate did not learn of the execution until Reller told her on a visit he made to York on July 3. She said she was sorry. She "wasn't moved, or anything like that," he noted. But she did ask: "Did he tell the truth before he died?"

51

STARKWEATHER EXECUTED: THE HEADLINE BLAZED across the entire front page of the morning *Star*, with "Mass Killer of 11 Dies in Chair" in smaller letters above it. No photo of Charlie, only the sad picture of the family walking like ducks in a line behind the mother from the prison doors to their cars. As if to say, We've seen enough of Starkweather's face, with his thick hood-like hair, the mocking cigarette dangling from his mouth. Let's just celebrate: No more stays. He's gone. Let us absorb that. Take a deep breath and exhale and try to feel the buzz in your fingertips. The witch is dead, for God's sake. STARKWEATHER "BURNS," proclaimed an out-of-state paper joyously.

Commentators spoke solemnly of the state's loss of innocence; from now on the citizens would not leave the keys in their cars' ignitions, and their children would not walk the few blocks to school holding hands. True, but the rhythm of life in Nebraska would continue; in a few weeks, the haying season in the Sandhills would begin and green and red tractors would be crisscrossing the fields of grass, cutting, raking, and stacking, and a few yearlings would be brought to town from the ranch and sold at auction to cattlemen standing at the iron fence, straw cowboy hats pushed back on their heads, and the Niobrara River would run full out of Valentine with rafters in its waters and rattlers nestled in the grasses along its banks, all as usual, and in not too long the boys of autumn would be slipping into pads and red-and-white jerseys for another head-pounding season on the hard turf.

The citizens would mourn the victims and praise the system that brought the killers to justice and would tell each other not to sink into hate for the young man put to death. As for the girl, she got what she deserved, maybe a little less. In the years ahead they would cope with the injury to their sanity, to their pride, to their propensity for compassion.

People of America would one day forget about Charlie Starkweather, and their hearts would get right.

A letter to the editor in the *Star* just before Charlie's execution shows how difficult getting clear of the topsy-turvy emotional twists in this story would be.

> I have read many articles in Public Mind about Charles Stark-weather, and getting down to brass tacks, its people of Lincoln and classmates of school days who made the boy what he is today.
>
> He is to be pitied, now. He grew up being made fun of; no friends in school due to his bow legs, unkempt clothes and someone always whispering or gossiping about him.
>
> I have two children who attended school when he did and they told me of a boy alone in a school of many children. He started out with a complex, and why—because of people like Lincoln citizens.
>
> If "angel" Caril can get life, God only knows Charles should get the same. Being a female should not change penalties—one way or another.
>
>   Mrs. Twila Forum

52

ARIL WAS STILL VERY MUCH ALIVE AND WOULD spend the rest of her days at the reformatory, unless her indefatigable lawyers won a new trial on appeal or she obtained parole. Merril Reller, John McArthur, and eventually John's son Jim continued the fight in the courts, as they promised her they would. But the two post-conviction appeals to the Nebraska Supreme Court challenging Judge Spencer's denials of the motions for a new trial based on a biased juror (Walenta) and new evidence (perjured testimony) were denied by the Nebraska Supreme Court in December 1959.

In the Walenta case, the bias of the court is surprisingly obvious when it states, flat out: "The evidence also show that Starkweather killed ten other persons, in the killing of nine of which defendant was a participant during a series of events continuing through a period of several days." Beyond the fact that it is not clear which murder the court was excusing Caril from, the disturbing fact is that the court, on its own, tried and convicted Caril of "participating" in the murders of nine people, which would include those at 924 Belmont. It found evidence of her guilt in crimes for which she had never been charged or tried to be sufficient for conviction nonetheless. In 1969, the U.S. Supreme Court issued an order denying a review of the case.

In 1964, the U.S. Supreme Court issued *Escobedo*, holding that a suspect had the right to an attorney as soon as the investigation turned accusatory. It was an exciting moment. Clearly Caril had not been advised of her right to counsel prior to the taking of the Statement. McArthur filed a habeas corpus action in federal district court alleging that *Escobedo* should be applied retroactively. If it was, Caril's conviction would almost certainly be overturned. The Ninth Circuit Court of Appeals had already held that *Escobedo* was retroactive (which, if not overruled, would have released a great flood of inmates from prisons around the country). After oral arguments in this case, Federal District Court judge Robert Van Pelt agreed: the holding in *Escobedo* would be applied to Caril's conviction. He sent the case immediately to the Eighth Circuit Court of Appeals for review. Always cautious, McArthur nonetheless couldn't help but express his optimism to Caril. She and her lawyers felt like she stood on the doorstep of freedom.

The Nebraska State Legislature punched its way into the fight. If you want to understand how deep the animosity ran toward Caril not only among the inhabitants of Nebraska but in the state institutions, consider the fact that the legislature adopted a law just to stop Caril from getting free on a habeas corpus writ in federal court.

If the Eighth Circuit upheld Judge Van Pelt's ruling, Caril would be entitled to a hearing on the *Escobedo* issue of right to counsel, and there was little doubt that her interrogation had violated the holding in that case. It was an error that couldn't be fixed; the state could still retry her, but the only other evidence against her was Charlie's transcribed testimony. Her testimony at the first trial should be excluded as "fruit of the poisonous tree"; if the Statement had not been admitted into evidence, she would never have taken the stand. She would have to be convicted on nothing more than Scheele or Fahrnbruch's reading Charlie's testimony into the record. Still possible if not likely, given how Lincoln felt about her, but not a given.

The legislature turned to the legal maxim "exhaustion of state remedies." It means that a defendant has to go through the post-conviction remedies such as habeas corpus in state courts before she can avail herself of any federal post-conviction remedy. The problem was that at the time of the federal writ, the state didn't have any post-conviction remedies. So, while the case was pending before the Eighth Circuit in 1965, the legislature took it upon itself to adopt a law mirroring the federal statute on post-conviction remedies, so that now prisoner Fugate would have some procedures to exhaust before turning to the federal courts.

The Eighth Circuit went along with the gambit and ordered the district court to dismiss the petition, pointing out that Caril could now seek a writ of habeas corpus in the state courts, and if unsuccessful in her appeals there she would be welcome to return to federal court.

It was one step forward and two back. McArthur filed a petition for a writ of habeas corpus in state court, and the court dismissed it as insufficient on its face, which could well have been McArthur's intention so he could quickly get back to federal court. He appealed the dismissal to the state supreme court, hoping it would also uphold the dismissal, but in July 1966, the court reversed the dismissal and ordered the district court to hold a hearing. Since by now the U.S. Supreme Court had found *Escobedo* not to be retroactive, the court directed that the hearing be limited to the voluntariness of the Statement.

IN THE EARLY years at York, Caril learned how to survive: trust no one, keep to yourself, and play by the rules. If she had developed a shell to survive her childhood, she seemed to have fairly well resurrected it in prison. She stayed out of trouble by walking away from it; if something started in the TV room, she would excuse herself and return to her room. She was a great curiosity in the beginning, and other girls baited her. She learned how not to be provoked.

Life changed for the better for Caril in 1965 when a young woman by the name of Jackie Crawford began working as a correction officer at York. On her arrival, Jackie found the place to be brutal and unforgiving, with the rules of silence still enforced and solitary frequently used for punishment. Within a few years, she was promoted to assistant superintendent. One day not long after her promotion, Caril came in the administrative offices where she worked and appeared unkempt and disconsolate over her belief that she was never going to get out of York. Jackie, a small woman herself, sat her down and told her she looked terrible and had a bad attitude and to go back to her room and get cleaned up and wash her hair and put on makeup and clean clothes and come back. Returning all fixed up, Caril admitted she was feeling better, and

Jackie said good and now we're going shopping, and she took her into York for new clothes. It was the first time Caril had been in the town of York. As assistant superintendent, Jackie began implementing programs at the facility that would have a huge impact on Caril's life. In 1972, at age thirty-six, Jackie was appointed superintendent of the York reformatory.

Jim McArthur, age fifteen, met Caril soon after his father was appointed her counsel. He visited her with his father at the state mental hospital a few days after his dad was appointed. His dad encouraged him to ask her anything he wanted, and he did, and he was impressed at how easily she talked about any subject he brought up. She seemed like an ordinary person.

Jim McArthur went to court every day after school during her trial to watch his father, whom he greatly admired, and soon became as convinced of Caril's innocence as he was. He drove to Wyoming with his father and interviewed Deputy Romer and swears to this day that Romer never said that Caril told them she had witnessed the murders of her family. One evening during Caril's trial, Jim saw Charlie Starkweather being transported in a sheriff's car in the direction of the pen, and he figured he was being taken back from the county attorney's office where they had been prepping him to testify against Caril. He was convinced that the incident of the juror betting on the chair for Caril would result in a new trial and was surprised when it didn't. This earned him a mild lecture from his father about the difference between what the Constitution says and what it means when applied.

Jim attended the University of Nebraska undergraduate and law schools. During his law-student days, he became even more immersed in the case; he did the research and helped prepare the briefs for the numerous hearings in the state and federal courts. Reinhardt gave a lecture to one of his classes and stated without qualification that Caril was guilty of murder. On graduation, Jim joined his father's practice and they handled the hearings and appellate arguments in Caril's case.

Family visits at York eventually dropped off for Caril. But lawyer Reller visited her faithfully every Saturday for years. In 1968, he died of a heart attack while on a hunting trip in Perth, Australia. Caril learned of his death on the radio and was devastated. She had recently received her high school diploma and was excited about showing it to him on his return from his round-the-world trip.

In February 1967, Judge Hastings held a hearing on the voluntariness of the confession, as ordered by the Nebraska Supreme Court. Caril appeared in court in a hand-sewn jumper, high heels, and cat-eye glasses. Under Reller's questioning, she testified that many of her answers in the Statement were repetitions of what Fahrnbruch had told her, that she cooperated with officials because she was scared and because she thought she would be released after Starkweather's trial. She testified that initially she thought she was a patient at the mental hospital and that if she didn't cooperate, she would be subject to electric-shock treatments, which she had witnessed applied to a patient across the hall. To no one's surprise, the judge found the Statement to have been voluntarily given. And also to no one's surprise, the Nebraska Supreme Court affirmed the finding on appeal.

The McArthurs hustled back to federal district court on a new habeas petition. Both Nebraska federal district court judges recused themselves from hearing the petition. It took well over two years for a judge from another district to be appointed. Judge Elmo Hunter from Missouri was appointed in January 1970 and heard the petition in February 1970, three years after the first hearing.

Caril appeared for the hearing. She was now twenty-seven years old. She wore her cat-eye glasses; short, styled hair; and a white summer dress. After her testimony, she spoke freely with reporters about her life in prison. She had read over one thousand books since her incarceration, averaging two or three a week, as well as many magazines, and she wrote a column called Dear Gabby for the reformatory weekly paper, *The Hilltop*. She had learned typing and shorthand, and she worked in the office. She planned on taking extension courses at the university. Most of all, she wanted to be a nurse, so she could help people. When asked about her chances on the success on the writ, she replied, "If not this time, then the next time."

On May 6, 1970, Judge Hunter issued a decision. Basing his decision on the thirty-five-pound record of earlier hearings, he denied the petition. The legislature, in its targeted passage of the post-conviction relief statute, had successfully delayed a review by the Eighth Circuit Court of Appeals for five years.

Throughout the 1960s, the press covered every motion, every hearing, and every decision on Caril's case, usually on the front page and often as the lead story on the evening news. The photos showed her maturing from a fourteen-year-old girl to a young lady. In the early 1960s, when she had turned seventeen, the press stopped referring to her as Caril or Caril Ann. Now she was usually Miss Fugate. But not always: she was often still referred to as "the girl" in the body of the article.

After Judge Hunter's decision, Jim McArthur took over the laboring oar on the appeals, and he prepared the second appeal to a three-judge panel of the Eighth Circuit. He felt good about their chances. But on December 30, 1971, the court issued an order upholding the district court by two to one. Specifically, it found that under the "totality of the circumstances" test, Caril's statement was voluntary. In making this statement, the court said that on February 1, Fahrnbruch advised her she had the right to a lawyer, that anything she said could be used against her, and that she didn't have to talk to him if she didn't want to. What the court failed to mention in its opinion, however, was that on several occasions that day and the next day, Caril clearly indicated her desire to have legal representation and that the questioning proceeded nonetheless.

Judge Heaney wrote a highly critical dissent, but the court denied a rehearing on February 7, 1972. Petitions for a hearing en banc failed by an even vote of the entire circuit. Jim McArthur filed a petition for a writ of certiorari with the U.S. Supreme Court, although everyone understood that the chances of the court accepting it were slim or next to none. On October 10, 1972, the Court denied the petition, with only Justice Douglas voting to hear it. After almost twelve years, the long journey to have Caril's conviction overturned was finally over. There were no more appeals.

Over the years, some good fortune had come Caril's way. The superintendent had loosened up the rules; smiling, even talking was now allowed, visiting hours were extended, and the inmates were allowed to have TVs and radios in their rooms, to buy treats at a small canteen, and to wear jewelry. On learning this, Jim McArthur showed up for a visit one day with a gift for Caril: her mother's wedding ring.

By now, Caril was the longest-serving inmate in the facility, and she had long since learned to survive by keeping to herself. Her own peace did not come from getting close to a woman who might be leaving in a few months. She was good with the younger girls. One-on-one, she had a calming effect on them. She would tell them that they needed to control their minds to survive there. Hating was a waste, and you would feel better about yourself if you made use of your time doing things like sewing or working in the gardens. While she taught classes in sewing, knitting, crocheting, or "any type of fancy work," she gave away everything she made. She was baptized in the Catholic church and took on as a patron Saint Therese of Lisieux, who went into a French convent at fourteen to become a Carmelite nun and is known in America as the Little Flower of Jesus.

As superintendent, Jackie Crawford hired the first psychologist at the facility, and Caril talked to him about everything on her mind, past, present, or future. Jackie saw Caril not only as a model inmate but as a role model for the other inmates.

Jackie began a series of programs to integrate the facility into the York community and to prepare the women for reentry into society. She instituted tours of the facility, and Caril was one of the first guides. Caril introduced herself to the visitors as Therese, and when a visitor would ask her to point out Caril Fugate, she would say she didn't see her right then and added that prisoners seldom talked about what they had done to get there. Caril soon became one of three women giving talks to service organizations like Kiwanis, Rotary, and Sertoma in small towns around Nebraska.

Jackie began an incentive program that allowed prisoners on good behavior to go into York, where they shopped, bowled, and went to movies. She established a work-release program, which allowed the prisoners to work at jobs, including positions as motel maids and seamstresses. The inmates swam at the indoor community pool two days a week.

Jackie approached the minister at the Church of the Nazarene about Caril doing volunteer work at his church. Surprisingly, the minister suggested she might run the nursery while the parents were in the service. After some hesitation, the congregation agreed to give her a try. Caril insisted on using her real name with the church. "If they're giving me their kids, they deserve to know who I am." Business was a little slow at first, but soon Caril had a nursery full of babies on Sunday morning.

While Caril couldn't participate in the work-release program because of her sentence, she undertook a work-study program where she volunteered at a nursing home one day a week. After ninety hours of study and classes, she earned a certificate as a geriatric nurse's aide.

Jackie also instituted a new program called MOMS. Mothers on good behavior could have their children stay with them at the facility for up to seven days. The kids slept in the mothers' rooms and ate with them in the dining room.

Judy Glather shot her husband to death on September 17, 1971. He was a violent drunk who had beaten her badly months before. This night, he returned home drunk, slapped her and kicked her in the stomach, threw kitchen items and lamps against the wall, and threatened to strangle her with a lamp cord. After he had passed out, she crawled from bed and walked to the closet, took out a 12-gauge shotgun and two shells, and went downstairs and loaded the gun. Returning upstairs, she stepped into the darkened bedroom and shot her husband as he lay in bed. When he bolted upright, she shot him again. She was charged with second-degree murder and convicted of manslaughter. The judge gave her ten years. In 1972, the Supreme Court of Nebraska, in a four-to-three decision, found the sentence excessive and reduced it to five years. Judy was out in two.

Judy roomed across the hall from Caril in the trustees' dorm. Caril had been at York for fourteen years at that point, and Judy found her somewhat brusque and remote (although Caril would later refer to her as a friend). Caril seldom spoke or joined in group activities, such as sing-alongs or games. But sometimes it seemed as if the place revolved around Caril, with her lawyers and film crews coming and going.

Judy worked as the head cutter in the factory sewing uniforms for male prisoners in the state pen. She had a daughter, Teri, age eight, and a son, age two. She was quick to enroll in the MOMS program. In the beginning, Caril cared for the kids in the program, along with the kids of staff members, in a cottage on the grounds while their parents worked. When the cottage was closed, Caril took Teri under her wing. During her week's stay, Terri spent most of the day with Caril in her room, which was filled with cards and gifts from strangers, like candles, angels, and animals. Caril also had a guitar on the wall, and each day she would take it down and teach Teri how to play. Once a day, Caril would gather some scraps from the kitchen and the two would venture out to the cottage, beneath which lived a cat with a litter of kittens. They would feed the scraps to the mother, and then Caril would reach under the cottage and lift out a kitten or two and they would take turns holding and petting them.

Teri didn't know why Caril was in there; she only knew she had a new friend who was very good to her. Her sadness on leaving was lessened some when Caril gave her the guitar for keeps. Over the years, her affection for her prison nanny has not diminished.

Jim McArthur and his wife and kids frequently brought picnic lunches to the York facility, which they laid out on picnic tables on the grounds. They also took Caril home with them for weekends. Jackie had instituted a weekend-release program, in which prisoners could leave the facility on Saturday morning to stay with an approved person. One weekend, John McArthur held a birthday party for Caril, now in her mid-twenties, on the spacious grounds of his Lincoln home. Three generations of McArthurs attended the celebration. Tables and lawn chairs were set up, and there were cakes and gifts and games and songs. Caril spent much of the time playing with the kids and pushing the babies around in their strollers. She was touched by a birthday party being held just for her.

On Sundays, Jim and his wife would drive Caril around downtown Lincoln, past the Runza, where she and Charlie used to hang out, and out to Pioneers Park. The visits came to an abrupt end. During one weekend visit, Jim's wife had taken Caril shopping at the grocery store, and afterward the family had gone to a swimming pool at an apartment building that Jim and several other men owned. Someone spotted Caril in the pool and complained to authorities. Word came down to Jackie early the next week: Caril was not allowed in Lincoln.

In 1972, CBS aired a prime-time show entitled *Growing Up in Prison*, the brainchild of Ninette Beaver, the Omaha TV reporter who interviewed Caril in the 1958 press conference and would write, along with two others, a book on Caril. It showed clips of Caril at the 1958 press conference and clips of her at the time. A detached, shut-down child then, a composed, articulate woman now. She expressed with emotion several times how sorry she was about "what had happened" but said with force, "I swear to God, I never killed anyone." She had come to accept that she was Caril Fugate and was not embarrassed by her last name, and she believed that she was a child of God. Film showed her bowling at lanes in town and swimming at the local pool. Sheriff Heflin said on film that he believed Caril was an innocent victim, while Robert Jensen Sr. thought she might well have been the instigator of the whole thing. Nonetheless, he would not object to her parole. He would leave it to the experts on the board. "You can be destroyed by hatred and bitterness," he said, "just as love and faith can bring you salvation."

Parishioners of the Church of the Nazarene told with passion how much they trusted and cared for Caril, and several shots showed mothers handing babies into the arms of a smiling Caril. The common sentiment in town was that she deserved a chance to prove herself.

All in all, the film was quite sympathetic to Caril. It showed a side of her never imagined, much less seen, by the public. It highlighted the progressive policies of Superintendent Crawford, who would many years later end her career as director of corrections for the state of Nevada.

The film gave considerable momentum to Caril's effort to obtain parole. It also generated a truckload of mail inquiries about Caril's future. One of those came from a couple in Michigan offering to take Caril into their home and provide her with a job.

53

THE SUPREME COURT'S DENIAL OF THE PETITION FOR a writ of certiorari cleared the decks for parole. A few days after the denial, Jim McArthur filed an application for a commutation with the Nebraska Board of Parole. Again, good fortune came Caril's way. The chairman of the board was sixty-one-year-old John Greenholtz, the former deputy warden of the men's penitentiary and the presiding official at Charlie's execution. After twenty-one years as deputy warden, he'd decided to move on. Although there were two other board members—Harold Smith, the former superintendent of the boys' reformatory in Kearney, and Edward Rowley, an educational administrator for the state—Greenholtz was generally seen as "the board." His reputation for fairness and an unerring ability to see through bullshit followed him from the prison yards to the board room. He saw Caril not as monster but as a badly damaged girl. He, along with Jackie Crawford, carefully negotiated the treacherous shoals of Caril's journey through the parole process. They knew full well that there would be opposition and that if they let her out and she screwed up, it would come down on their heads.

The Nebraska law on parole was complicated. An inmate was not eligible for parole until she'd served ten years of her sentence. Since there was no minimum for someone who'd received a life sentence, it was necessary first to commute the sentence to a set number of years. No longer a lifer, the prisoner could then seek parole. The Board of Parole issued a recommended decision on the petition for commutation to the Board of Pardons, who had the final say.

The board's practice was to conduct interviews with applicants to determine if a full hearing would be granted. Caril's interview was held on June 6, 1973. The board members commented on her fifteen-year spotless record and the fact that she had obtained her high school degree and participated in almost all the programs at York. Greenholtz noted that she sang in the prison choir and took art and piano lessons. Soon after the conclusion of the hearing, Greenholtz announced that the board had voted to grant a public hearing. The hearing would be held on August 22. On July 30, Caril turned thirty.

The hearing was held in a large room in the penitentiary administration building. Shortly before 8:00 a.m., Caril arrived from York in a car driven by Jackie Crawford. She was dressed and accessorized: a white fitted dress with bell sleeves, a white summer hat, white sandals, a small white handbag, and dark sunglasses. A long way from the image of the sullen kid at her 1958 trial. Jim McArthur arrived a few minutes later. The place was swarming with press. No cameras were allowed in the hearing room. (Some enterprising photographers tried shooting the scene through a window.) Caril was the first witness. She sat across a conference table from the three board members. Greenholtz knew Caril from his visits to York. He had said more than once, "To know Caril is to like Caril."

"I know this is an important day in your life," he said to her. "Just tell us how you feel about the whole situation up to this point."

"It's hard," Caril said, "to express how you feel in the situation I am in, because I know my whole future depends on this day and the outcome of this day. Actually, I feel—if the purpose of institutions is rehabilitation—I myself feel the institution has done everything possible that they can to this point. I've participated in all the programs."

After more discussion, Greenholtz turned to McArthur for any further remarks. Jim stressed not only that Caril had a clean disciplinary record but that she had developed a positive, affirmative attitude. She had improved herself and helped many other inmates along the way.

Asked for final words, Caril said, "I want to thank you for hearing my case. I deeply appreciate it. I leave it totally up to you, whatever you decide." Caril and McArthur left the room before the other witnesses entered and waited in the warden's office.

The next witness was Victor Walker, the director of the Department of Institutions. He testified that at no time in his fifteen years had he seen a woman with Caril's record; she took every opportunity to improve herself; there was nothing else the state could do for her. He pointed out that had the crime been committed today, Caril would have been tried and committed as a juvenile. If a person has no hope for the future, he might as well be dead, because that's what he is.

Reverend Shipman and twenty members of the Church of the Nazarene spoke on Caril's behalf. They testified that they trusted her around their children, that she was a genuine, caring person that had accepted Jesus Christ as her savior. She was a good worker who deserved another chance. One parent said that Caril could handle a room full of kids better than anyone she'd ever seen. "I think she has paid her debt to society," one parishioner said. "God has forgiven her, why can't man?"

A former inmate testified that Caril had helped her and other girls at York who had bad attitudes and got in trouble. Other girls were jealous of her, but most of them respected her. All in all, thirty-one people testified in favor of Caril's release.

Four testified against it. A woman married to Carol King's brother, Warren, said Caril knew what she was doing and should spend the rest of her natural life in prison. Bobby Jensen's mother said fifteen years for ten victims wasn't much time, and she read a long, emotional statement. She had seen the NBC documentary *Growing Up in Prison*, and she didn't like it, particularly the part where Caril said she didn't have a family to come visit. Had she forgotten why she didn't have a family? A baby sister? Greenholtz patiently tried to explain the theory of rehabilitation versus punishment to her, without success. "She could not pay for her crimes if she paid a lifetime for each of the killings," she said. Carol's brother Warren delivered a petition bearing two hundred signatures from citizens of Bennet declaring that a parole would not be in the interests of justice.

Greenholtz called Caril and Jim McArthur into the warden's office and said the board would issue a decision in two days. On Friday morning, Greenholtz issued a statement saying that by a two-to-one vote, the board was recommending parole. "It is our judgment, by a majority vote, that society's purpose has been served and Miss Fugate cannot benefit by further imprisonment."

Jackie Crawford, who had herself sent a letter in support of parole for Caril, told the press that Caril was "thrilled and appreciative of the Board's decision." Caril wrote a statement:

> I deeply appreciate all the efforts that have brought this decision around. I realize that because of the magnitude of the case that people closely involved have done much soul searching to arrive at their decision to recommend commutation.
>
> I believe it was the hand of God that directed and guided their decision.

A letter to the editor regretted once again that Caril had not been sitting on Charlie's lap when the switch was thrown. Surprisingly, the *Journal* published an editorial praising the decision, as well as the courage of the members of the board for sticking their necks out for Caril.

But the decision was not truly a recommendation for parole, but rather a recommendation to the Board of Pardons that Caril's sentence be commuted. Without the commutation of the sentence to a set number of years, there could be no parole. The Board of Pardons, made up of the governor, secretary of state, and attorney general, had to accept the recommendation for commutation and then set the number of years for the revised sentence. Under Nebraska's system, if the sentence was reduced to twenty-five years, she would be immediately eligible for parole. If it was revised to thirty years, she wouldn't be eligible for three years. A commutation to fifty years wouldn't make her eligible until 1987.

On October 31, the Board of Pardons issued a two-to-one decision to reduce Caril's sentence to thirty to fifty years. She would be eligible for parole in May 1976. Jackie Crawford said that Caril was grateful for the commutation of her sentence but disappointed that she was not eligible for three years. She cried in Jackie's office.

So, after handing Caril a steady stream of defeats for fifteen years— dating back to the state supreme court deciding in 1958 that she would be tried as an adult—the system had at last held out a hand for her to leave the prison where she'd been for more than half her life, and then jerked it away.

There would seem to be little doubt that were it Greenholtz's decision, he would have reduced the sentence to twenty-five years and Caril would have been free in a number of weeks. But the elected politicians, undoubtedly aware that while God might have forgiven Caril, Nebraska never had, decided on a two-step process, so that the state would have time to get used to the idea of her freedom before it actually came to be.

On June 6, 1976, Caril appeared before the now-five-member Board of Parole in a simple white dress and shoes. Seated across the table from the members, just like three years earlier, she said she thought she'd earned parole and felt ready to join society. "I'd just like to settle down, get married, have a couple kids—you know dust the house, clean the toilet, just an ordinary little dumpy housewife. That's all I want to be— you know wash the socks, burn the toast." She also told the board, "I feel sorry for those people who hated me for eighteen years. It's destroyed their lives. It's locked them in a prison of hate."

The owner of the hospital and nursing home where Caril worked and earned her certificate stated that Caril had worked very well with the patients, although several of them rejected her because of her past, which hurt her.

Jackie Crawford again detailed Caril's unblemished eighteen-year record and told the board that Caril had prepared herself very well for a transition back into society.

No one spoke in opposition to her release. Greenholtz had the votes. The board voted to grant Caril parole, beginning June 20. The twenty-five people in the audience applauded. Caril broke into sobs.

"I just want to say thank you," she said, as she was led from the room in tears.

After the vote, Jackie told a reporter, much to her later regret, that "Caril has earned her parole. Society has gotten its pound of flesh." She shook her head over the relentless focus of the press on Caril. Reporters and cameras descended on the facility every time there was a tick in the parole process. The cameramen hung on the fence like katydids, hoping for a shot of Caril as she moved between buildings or left the facility by car.

On the evening of June 20, the couple from Lansing, Michigan, who had offered Caril a home and job, arrived at the facility. As they said goodbye, Jackie wished Caril the best and stressed that her life was now in her hands. Everything now was up to her. Caril thanked her for everything and promised she would never let her down. The two women hugged and said goodbye. In the dark of night, and after eighteen years, Caril drove off the prison grounds to begin a new life.

Caril justified Jackie Crawford's and John Greenholtz's faith in her. She disappeared from view and stayed on the straight and narrow, and in 1981 the Board of Parole released her from parole five years early.

VI

IMPACT

54

I saw her standing on her front lawn, just twirling her baton
Me and her went for a ride, sir, and ten innocent people died
From the town of Lincoln, Nebraska

—Bruce Springsteen, "Nebraska"

NOT TOO MANY SONGS HAVE BEEN WRITTEN ABOUT Nebraska, much less by the likes of Bruce Springsteen. In 1982, Springsteen, accompanying himself on a guitar and harmonica, laid down the tracks for what would become the *Nebraska* album on a tape recorder in his home. The title song, "Nebraska," is a narrative of the crimes and execution as told by Starkweather. He tells of the killings and says he's not sorry for any of them. "At least for a while, sir, me and her, we had us some fun."

Springsteen was inspired by the movie *Badlands,* produced, written, and directed by Terry Malick, which opens with a boy approaching a young girl as she is twiring her baton on her front lawn. He also read *Caril* by Ninette Beaver, B. K. Ripley, and Patrick Trese. He spoke with Beaver and offered her tickets to a show in Kansas City. Beaver declined the tickets, confessing that she didn't know who he was.

The singer painted the most powerful image of two killers going down hard since Bonnie and Clyde were spun around like tops a couple of times and ventilated in a hail of bullets: the remorseless killer in the electric chair with his "pretty baby" sitting "right there on his lap."

The image of Caril sitting on Charlie's lap is engraved in the cultural mind like a brilliant still life. Caril in a short dress, hair styled, wearing pale lipstick, sitting on Charlie's lap, a hand on his shoulder, a slightly teasing smile on her face; a handsome Charlie sitting straight in a wooden chair, limbs and chest strapped down, wearing a white shirt and denim pants, his thick red hair oiled up and over into a thick curl falling on his forehead, smiling mischievously up at her. Waiting for his "poor head" to snap back when the switch is thrown. A cruel mixture of violence and sex. Lolita in the thrall of the movie star–handsome killer outlaw. The "me and her we had us some fun" line comes from Charlie's letter to his parents in the Douglas jail.

There's been a lot of debate over who came up with the "pretty baby" line, although no one other than Springsteen says Charlie referred to Caril as "pretty baby." Some folks say that Charlie himself said he wouldn't mind going to the chair if Caril was there sitting on his lap. Others say his dad said it, others point to lawyer Gaughan.

Charlie deserves attribution. Gaughan wrote in the notes from his first meeting with Charlie that his client told him he "wouldn't mind going to the chair if Caril is sitting on my lap." Gaughan did not write his notes for public consumption—they were in fact protected by attorney-client privilege at the time—and one can't imagine why he would write them in his notes and later repeat them to the press several times if they were false.

Reporter Del Harding recalls that Guy Starkweather called him drunk one night and said his son had told him he wanted to go to the chair with Caril sitting on his lap. Professor Reinhart wrote that Charlie had said the same line to him during their sessions. It certainly seems to be something Charlie would have said. His fantasy was at risk of going off the tracks. If Caril wasn't convicted, or if he were found insane and not electrocuted, his dream of going out as the hotheaded, reckless outlaw blazing across the high plains with his sweetheart at his side would never go beyond the interior of his head.

But he could leave behind a searing, beautiful image of the bad guy taking the jolts in the chair with his young, sexy girlfriend perched on his lap, an ode to a fatally criminal love. Not that Charlie thought like this—he would simply have created the image as the rightful and natural end to the story of his life.

Charlie was dead for twenty-four years and Caril was thirty-nine when the song "Nebraska" came out in 1982. "Haunting," some reviewers called it. Mournful. And they were right. You might even end up with a disturbing twinge of sadness for Charlie when he talks about "the meanness in the world." In a piece for *Rolling Stone*, Steve Pond wrote, "This is the bravest of Springsteen's six records, also his most startling, direct, chilling." He notes the "casual cold-bloodedness" of the song itself.

Springsteen himself considers the album *Nebraska* to be his masterpiece. When he happened on the opening scene in *Badlands*, he was struggling through a deep depression after his highly successful *River* album tour. He had found himself "nowhere," to quote the phrase used by author Warren Zanes in his fascinating book *Deliver Me From Nowhere: The Making of Bruce Springsteen's Nebraska*. On January 3, 1982, by himself in the bedroom of his converted farmhouse in Coles Neck, New Jersey, Springsteen hooked up the mic to a four-track recorder and recorded the songs onto a simple cassette tape, which he carried around in his back pocket for days. (Two of the songs—"Born in the USA" and "Pink Cadillac"—didn't make the cut.) There is no studio version; the raw tracks ended up becoming the album itself. Springsteen has said that that if in fifty years he were to pick an album that most represented him, it would be *Nebraska*.

The version of *Nebraska* by singer-songwriter Aoife O'Donovan is quite powerful; it leaves a listener with an unsettling sense of melancholy.

Charlie's fantasy became larger than real life. His eight-day rampage—with Caril at his side—kicked off a blaze of storytelling far beyond what he, or anyone else for that matter, could ever have imagined. The rampage inspired at least twelve books, one major motion picture, three documentaries, one TV miniseries, and numerous short pieces in detective magazines and on YouTube. Stephen King kept a scrapbook of the headlines as a kid. The story left him so scared it inspired his career as a horror writer. Billy Joel references the "Starkweather homicide," as well as James Dean, in his song "We Didn't Start the Fire."

Why this story? There was an appeal to the alienated James Dean look-alike and his cute fourteen-year-old girlfriend who go on an eight-day murder spree shooting and stabbing ten people to death for no apparent reason, a spree that terrorized the entire state and seemingly paralyzed law enforcement. Because as boring as Nebraska might be in the national eye, at least the place was *safe*. Now, the bucolic land of farms and ranches and God-fearing people was riven with evil just as much as the mean streets of New York or Chicago.

Jim McArthur, who with his father handled the years of appeals and parole hearings for Caril without compensation, became by default the contact person for producers and writers and directors seeking to get in touch with Caril. One day in 1972, he received a phone call from Terry Malick, who said he was interested in making a film about Charlie and Caril. Malick, who had graduated summa cum laude from Harvard, taught philosophy at MIT. He had earned a master's of fine arts from the American Film Institute Conservatory and had written several screenplays but was looking for his first full-length feature. Jim was interested. He arranged for Malick and a Hollywood lawyer to meet Caril. He told the reformatory that he was bringing two lawyers with him to see Caril, and the three of them met in the visiting room at York. Malick told Caril he had a story he wanted to tell, but he would not do it without her permission. He made no promises. Caril gave her permission because, as she later told Jim, she "looked in his [Malick's] eyes and saw an honest person." She was eventually rewarded with a check for five thousand dollars and an autographed photo of Paul Newman and a few tapes of *Abbott and Costello*.

Malick selected Martin Sheen to play Charlie and Sissy Spacek to play Caril. Jim arranged for Caril to attend a showing of the film in York. He rented a movie theater in town for seventy-five dollars, after assuring the suspicious owner that the movie was not in fact a porno film. In April 1973, a month or so before the official release of the film, Caril, Jim, Terry Malick, Martin Sheen, and several others met at the Last Chance restaurant in York and had lunch. The film people were eager to meet Caril. Afterward, they watched the movie at the York movie theater. Jim sat on one side of Caril and Martin Sheen on the other. Everyone was nervous about how Caril would respond, and on the way up the aisle afterward she popped Sheen on the shoulder and said, "Charlie, you've come back to haunt me." She later told Jim that Martin did a great job as Charlie in the way he kicked the sand and booted cans down the road. She didn't care that much for the movie, though, perhaps because it suggested she might have participated in the crimes.

After the movie, the moviegoers gathered at a motel to discuss the film. Caril was not visibly upset over her portrayal. A source of some amusement was Sissy's last line in the film: she stares into the camera and says that she married her lawyer's son, which would mean that Caril married Jim McArthur. Jim was worried that Caril might be offended by the laughter at the idea, but she didn't appear to be. After an hour or so, Caril returned to the prison.

The film did not purport to tell the story of Charlie and Caril and the rampage. Malick and distributor Warner Bros. went to considerable length to prohibit any reference or linkage to the rampage or the real Charlie and Caril during the promotion of the movie. And in fact, the viciousness and brutality of the killings are softened by the score and the captivating visuals. Yet the hooks are unmistakable: When Kit first meets Holly, she is standing in her front yard wearing majorette boots and twirling her baton, and Kit manages to fit in the line "Holly and I have had fun, even if it's been rushed," in one place and "We [Holly and I] had fun though," in another. In one scene Kit is shooting into the storm cellar similar to the cellar the two Bennet teenagers were found in. One of the victims has a deaf maid, and in the police car after his arrest a smiling Kit gives the cops Charlie's famous line: "I always wanted to be a criminal, but just not this big a one."

The movie was set in South Dakota and filmed in Colorado. It opened to great reviews, was described as everything from an existential thriller to a moody and poetic meditation on violence. While a few critics called it boring, Malick himself described it as a fairy tale. Both Sheen and Malick believed strongly in Caril's innocence. In 1985, Sheen would say, "It's the one film I've done in my whole life that I'm most proud of."

Whatever the director's intent, the film had the effect of romanticizing the Starkweather-Fugate story and freezing it deep in the American psyche. It was the original visual telling of a boy and a girl turned

unfeeling murderers, of alienated youth paying back an uncaring society in blood. It would inspire Oliver Stone's *Natural Born Killers* (1994),
Brad Pitt and Juliette Lewis's *Kalifornia* (1993), and far lesser movies
such as *Starkweather* (2004).

The next serious cinematic effort was a 1993 ABC miniseries entitled
Murder in the Heartland, starring Tim Roth as Charlie, Fairuza Balk as
Caril, Randy Quaid as Scheele, and Brian Dennehy as John McArthur.
The series does not purport to be a work of art but does make a reasonable effort to stay as true to the facts as possible, given the conflicting
versions of events and cinematic limitations. (In order to give Charlie a motive to kill August Meyer, the film unfairly showed Meyer as a
mean-spirited man who saw fit to insult Charlie.) Jim McArthur was
hired as a consultant to ensure accuracy in regard to depictions of his
father and the trial scenes, but he couldn't stop the producers from con-
structing twenty-foot-high guard towers inside the courtroom. The film
also gratuitously shows Charlie sexually assaulting Mrs. Ward. Roth
does a good job depicting a sociopathic murderer and pulls off a decent
bow-legged walk but talks a little forced with a cigarette drooping from
his mouth. Balk is good but a little too weak-minded in her attempt to
show Caril as under Charlie's control. Balk, like Spacek and Malik and
Sheen, believed in Caril's innocence. Roth said, "I don't think Caril is
a murderer. She was an abused child, and the abuse continued when
she got a life sentence." Caril had nothing to do with the series and in
fact would later say that she almost lost her job at a hospital in Lansing,
Michigan, when reporters tracked her down there. Dennehy was nomi-
nated for an Emmy for best supporting actor.

In February 2023, Showtime released a four-part a series entitled
The Twelfth Victim, inspired by the book of the same name.

In 1958, with the growing prominence of television, the world was
turning more visual. People became accustomed to and insisted on
more and better images, moving or still, in Technicolor, along with the
words of the story. A simple image like white majorette boots, or a 1949
Ford with its grill torn out poking up on the top of a snowy hill, or
a powerful image like Charlie with a cigarette drooping from his lips,

or a tiny Caril busting a hard, defiant look leaving the courtroom after being convicted, imprint for lasting effect, particularly when they're shown over and over on the screen. The most powerful and lasting of all images is the photo of the happy teen couple perched on the love seat in the landlady's apartment. Almost every story written or documentary produced shows this image up front. Caril, young, cute, and innocent, shoulder to shoulder with Charlie, a little older, smiling at the camera, the cocky rebel. No matter how many times you've seen it, you look again, and again, and again, and you stare, captivated by the sense of horror waiting in the wings.

55

EFORE CHARLES MANSON; BEFORE JOHN GACY; BEFORE
Ted Bundy, the Son of Sam, the Hillside Strangler, the Zodiac
Killer; before Charles Whitman, Jeffrey Dahmer, and all the
rest—there was Charlie Starkweather. The FBI defines a mass murderer
as someone who kills four or more people in close succession in a single locale or closely related locales. Other definitions require only three
murders. A spree killer is a person who commits three or more murders
without a cooling-off period, usually in different places. A serial killer
is a person who kills three or more people in more than thirty days and
with a cooling-off period in between the killings.

Using these definitions—and there are many others—Charlie is a
hybrid mass murderer/spree killer. He killed one person (Colvert), then
seven weeks later killed three people (the Bartletts), then six days later,
and within forty-eight hours, he killed seven more people (Meyer, Jensen, King, Clara Ward, Lauer Ward, Lilyan Fencl, and Merle Collison)
at four different locations. Another way of looking at it is that Charlie
evolved from a mass murderer into a spree killer. Katherine Ramsland
writes in *Inside the Minds of Mass Murderers* that the classic mass murderer "often blames others for their failures and their motive is generally
to strike back, to punish, to annihilate, and to exact as much damage
as they can manage. Some want to make a statement, others do it for
self-glorification." In our case, Charlie was, in clinical terms, clearly sociopathic. He felt nothing for the pain and suffering of his victims. He
had a plan for the rest of his life, and he executed it rationally and in
fairly good fashion. He got what he wanted—immortality—in exchange
for a life that wasn't worth much of anything anyway.

These types of killings took place in America prior to 1958. Besides Howard Unruh, there was the notorious "Lipstick Killer," William

Heirens, who was convicted in 1946 of murdering three women and who had written in lipstick on the wall of one victim's apartment, "For heavens sake, catch me before I kill more I cannot control myself." There was the gangster and his gun moll, as played out in the Depression-era exploits of Tiger Girl and the Candy Kid, often referred to as the original gangsters, who pulled off a string of daring jewel heists around the country in the 1920s, and of course bank robbers Bonnie and Clyde who left a trail of busted banks and dead cops across the center of the country in the 1920s and 1930s. And Billy Cook, who proclaimed on his release from prison that he intended to "live by the gun and roam" and who killed six people in a twenty-two-day spree from California to Missouri in 1950 and 1951. The press played their stories, and the country was both fascinated and horrified by them. People died in the course of their criminal exploits—nine cops and four civilians in the case of Bonnie and Clyde and three cops by Tiger Girl and the Candy Kid—but, other than the victims of Cook, who was a drifter working his way across the country, they were killed in pursuit of money or jewels. The culture understood greed. In 1924, the country was mesmerized by the trials of Nathan Leopold and Richard Loeb, two wealthy students at the University of Chicago, who, believing themselves to be superior intellects, kidnapped and murdered fourteen-year-old Bobby Franks in an attempt to commit "the perfect crime."

Andrew Kehoe blew up the Bath Consolidated School in 1927, killing twenty-four kids, and Melvin Collins shot eight people to death from the window of his boarding house in 1948. There was Ed Gein, who in the mid-1950s murdered one woman and dug up bodies in the Plainfield, Wisconsin, cemetery and fashioned trophies and keepsakes from their bones and body parts, such as lampshades from skin. The Clutter murders in Holcomb, Kansas, captured in Truman Capote's *In Cold Blood*, occurred roughly five months after Charlie was executed. Familicides have always been part of the American crime scene.

In all these crimes, there was usually some sort of reason for the murders, sick or depraved as they might appear. Killing for the sheer psychopathic thrill of it had not yet arrived on the American stage.

The modern-day version of mass murderers or spree killers arrived in the mid-1960s, beginning with Charles Whitman, who in 1964, after stabbing his wife and mother to death, shot thirteen people to death from the 300-foot clock tower on the University of Texas campus in Austin. (An autopsy revealed a brain tumor pressing into Whitman's amygdala.) This was followed by Richard Speck, who was convicted in 1966 of stabbing and strangling to death eight student nurses in their Chicago residence.

These killings and the great wave that would break over the country in the 1970s and '80s were preceded by Charlie Starkweather. While you can't draw a clear line between Charlie and those who came after him, it is clear that he was the first modern-day mass killer. One reason for this was the presence of television, a much more powerful medium than newspapers and radio for dramatizing horrible events. The film of the state troopers surrounding August Meyer's farmhouse with gun stocks pressed against their cheeks in anticipation of shooting Charlie when he came out with guns blazing made it stunningly real to the viewer. There is a weird clip of a cop reaching down and grabbing poor Meyer's arm and shaking it like a rag doll as he lay dead on the floor.

To illustrate the growth in mass murders, Starkweather's killing of ten people in 1958 was the only mass murder that year. Cook was the only other spree killer of the 1950s. The Associated Press/USA Today/ Northeastern University database of mass killings shows that from 2006 through 2020, there was a total of 448 mass killings, involving 567 offenders, 2,357 victims killed, and 1,693 injured. In 2022, there were 25 mass murders, resulting in 156 dead.

There is evidence that mass murderers of recent vintage have studied previous mass murderers. In a 2019 article, Benedict Carey of *The New York Times* noted that this was true of mass murderers of all types—those that mowed down unarmed people in theaters or shooters who killed innocents in the name of ideology—and that they studied previous killings for tactics and mimicked the killers' gestures. For example, the person who killed the schoolchildren and teachers in the Sandy Hook Elementary School had studied many massacres, including

Columbine. The man who shot fifty people in the Pulse nightclub in Orlando had studied a previous attack in San Bernadino. The *Times* article concluded: "Forensic psychologists say that many would-be mass killers see themselves as part of a brotherhood of like-minded, isolated and resentful boys and men. To them, previous mass murderers may be perceived as idols and pioneers." Charles Starkweather can rightly be viewed as a founding member of the brotherhood.

Whether or not any of the subsequent mass or spree killers actually studied Starkweather, it is likely that there was a contagion effect and that Charlie Starkweather and television were the origin of it. (In an October 2015 *New Yorker* article entitled "How School Shootings Spread," Malcom Gladwell posits a theory of social contagion for school shootings, arguing there is kind of a cascading effect in mass shootings; each one makes the next one more likely. In the 2023 Nashville Covenant School shooting, *The New York Times* reported that the alleged shooter had planned the attack for months and studied in detail the actions of other mass murderers.) Although Charlie and Caril may have never achieved the celebrity status of Bonnie and Clyde, they are clearly part of the crime fabric of the country, with movies, documentaries, books, and songs telling their story.

Charlie wanted to become famous, he wanted to go down in history as a very, very bad outlaw, and he proved to whoever was watching or listening or reading that you could do that with a knife and a gun. By the time of his execution, the "bandy-legged runt" was known far and wide, even in lands across the sea. On leaving the courthouse, he would inevitably pause at the top step for a few moments and pose with an amused smirk and the ever-present cigarette pressed between his lips. *The Huntley-Brinkley Report* featured him and Caril night after night. The AP story on his conviction was carried with photos in hundreds of papers around the country. Charlie's execution was a national event. Anybody of a similar mind watching would get the idea: Here's how a nobody can become a somebody. Here's how motherfucking payback works. Here's a way to make yourself feel better. To have some fun.

In a way, Charlie is the beginning of the end of innocence, when violence had a purpose, where the killer wanted something from the victim, such as money or satisfaction, or in the case of Leopold and Loeb, the feeling of superiority that would be theirs after killing him in the perfect crime. Charlie is the precursor of what is to become almost commonplace: the violence of the common man against not one or two but many. The randomness of the selection brings an existential feel with it. You died for no reason. Therefore, you lived for no reason.

In our case, also, there were *two killers* on the run, and one was a young female. Mass murder at the time was mainly a solo male enterprise. Our killers looked like kids. There were riveting images. This cute girl in white majorette boots toting a .410 shotgun almost as big as she was; Charlie, the rebel turned killer, the gunman, with his thick red hair brushed into a ducktail, resembling a young movie star. All deserving constant coverage from the night of January 27, 1958, when the first bodies were discovered, until Charlie was put to death on June 25, 1959. The camera watched the couple on the run in a bloody cat-and-mouse game, and the mouse—or mice—outwitted the cat time and again, slipping back into Lincoln for another killing or two, or three, ramping up the fear each time, and then slipping out. And always leading the show was the happy couple on the love seat. And the famous photo of a sullen Charlie staring into the camera in Douglas after his arrest, with the dangling cigarette, hands hooked together in front, legs chained. It was the beginning of the love affair between television and violent crime. The story went from the murder rampage to the electric chair in a little less than eighteen months. The world had never seen anything like it.

56

THOSE WHO SEEK TO BRING THE HAMMER OF JUSTICE down on the head of Caril Fugate must deal with one dilemma: How does a young girl with no history of violence or aggression turn into a knife-wielding, trigger-pulling monster for eight days and subsequently transform into the perfect prisoner for eighteen years, become a trusted and caring nanny for a nursery full of kids at a local church, and basically hold a job and lead a normal, spotless life for forty-five years after her release without any hint of her previous incarnation as a coldhearted murderess?

Many people who suffer severe traumas as children or adults live with the destructive impact of the traumas for the rest of their lives. Caril was not one of them. She settled in Lansing, Michigan, living with the couple who had picked her up in York. After a year or so, she moved into her own place in Lansing. She worked twenty years as a surgical orderly at the Ingram Medical Center. She had an active social life. She went to Mexico on vacation with several of her girlfriends. She was reserved, but with friends she was funny and a good storyteller. She raised five hundred dollars in an auction for the local public radio station, and she walked as a clown in a July Fourth parade. After working a full shift at the hospital, she took care of two children for four hours a day for over seven years. She spoke at high schools about the need to make smart choices growing up and the importance of not getting mixed up with the wrong people. She didn't drink or do drugs. Her favorite pastime was reading. She was frequently off to the library to pick up a biography, a mystery, a novel, or a book on clowns.

According to a good friend, Caril has not suffered flashbacks or nightmares or extreme levels of anxiety. Other than her discussions with a psychologist in prison, she has not been involved in ongoing therapy and has not used prescription medication for her mental health. Which is not to say that the murders have slipped her mind. She told the same friend that she suffers from PTSD, and she thinks every day of the people who died—not only her family, but the other victims and the suffering of their families. She thinks about how her little sister died. She still takes a teddy bear to bed with her at night. She also fell in love and was in a ten-year relationship with a man who did not love her and exploited her for money.

Yet, for the most part, Caril lived a relatively stable, productive life as an adult. There is no indication that she continued to dissociate after her release from prison, or apparently even while she was in prison. She did not engage in any self-destructive or violent behavior.

How was Caril exempt from the long-term destructive consequences of a traumatic childhood? There is one possible explanation: sublimation. Freud saw sublimation as an unconscious mechanism that shifts the route of potentially destructive urges to neutral or even positive impulses. In his book *Dry Ice*, author and psychologist Stephen White compares sublimation to the chemical process of dry ice: it transforms from a solid into a vapor or gas without melting into a liquid. Similarly, the more snowpack is subjected to sunlight, the more likely the snowpack doesn't melt, but turns directly into uncollectable vapors. Some people melt; some don't; they skip the liquid stage and proceed to the gas stage, which would be a relatively normal, fruitful life. For those who sublimate, the destructive urges are transformed into a positive, socially acceptable behavior. In our case, Caril suffered greatly as a child. She endured poverty and the repetitive traumas of abandonment, abuse, and violence. Perhaps destructive urges of fear and anger were transformed into a strong desire, almost a need, to care for children, as she did as a twelve-year-old babysitting five kids, as she did with babies in church on Sunday for years, as she did as a nanny for the children of staff and other prisoners in prison, as she did for two children as a grown woman for many years. (The girls' grandmother wrote a glowing letter of support for Caril's pardon, as did the older girl, who wrote that she would describe Caril in three words: *kindhearted, patient,* and *generous.*) Perhaps the defense mechanism, operating unconsciously, transformed the negative emotions into remarkably positive behavior. Her traumatic childhood created the unconscious force to provide love and care for children.

Long after her release from York, Caril told Jim McArthur she realized that something positive had come out of the terrible experience of her youth. She said that she was from three generations of welfare families and, were it not for what happened, she might well have ended up on the same track: get married, have a couple of kids, get divorced, go on welfare, and live on the edge. As a girl, she had seen it as her lot in life. She turned that around into becoming a stable, caring, self-sufficient woman.

Over the years, Caril has struggled to get the truth out. The showing of *Murder in the Heartland* seemed to stimulate her efforts to reclaim innocence. She underwent a lie detector test twice on F. Lee Bailey's TV show *Lie Detector* and passed both times. (Her frozen face when she is answering questions is eerily similar to the descriptions of the fourteen-year-old girl being grilled on the stand. Caril would say that the reason she looked so cold and uncaring during the trial was that she made herself not feel anything because she was afraid if she did, she would fly apart into pieces and never come back.) She underwent hypnosis and received a report from the psychologist declaring that she had told the truth. She held a press conference and handed out packets containing Charlie's February 1 statement, in which he says on three different occasions that she was not at 924 Belmont when he killed her family, and a tape and a transcript of her hypnosis. She refused an interview with an Omaha TV station because she was convinced no one in Nebraska would ever believe she was innocent. She mailed copies of Charlie's February 1, 1958, statement to two hundred people randomly selected from the Lincoln phone book, much to the chagrin of a Lincoln police detective, who called her to complain that some of the recipients had been disturbed by the document. She called in to a Lincoln talk show in 1996 hosted by attorney Steve Berry when he was visited in studio by her former attorney, Jim McArthur. She talked for several hours with the callers, one of whom was her sister Barbara, and several of whom had been girls in school with her. Most callers said they believed her innocent; one claimed to have even seen her hiding from Starkweather in the girl's bathroom. Another said that she had witnessed Charlie pull Caril off the school bus. Caril would say later that it was the first time she had heard anyone in Nebraska admit that she might be innocent. She insisted she never had sex with Charlie and that in fact he was impotent.

CARIL MET FRED Clair in a casino in Michigan in 2004, when she was sixty. Fred, seventy-one, was a retired machinist who had lost his wife a year earlier. When she eventually sat him down and told him who she really was, he said he still wanted to marry her. Fred had four grown sons, and one of them, Tommie, recognized the Fugate name when Caril was introduced to him. He researched the case and decided that she was most likely innocent. His dad made his sons promise they would take care of her if he died first. The couple was married in 2007. They lived in Stryker, Ohio, and went to garage sales and traveled the country in a camper, stopping at casinos along the way.

In 2009, Caril suffered a heart attack and a stroke. The stroke left her with a serious speech impairment. On August 5, 2013, the couple headed out in Fred's Ford Explorer to a casino in Battle Creek. The SUV drifted to the left on Interstate 69, smacked into a median, and overturned. Fred was killed instantly. Caril's right leg and arm were broken, and her body was crushed. She remained in the hospital for over five months. After the accident, investigators pulled Tommie aside and asked if he could think of any reason why Caril would want to kill her husband.

Over the years, Caril lost touch with her attorney, Jim McArthur, who along with his father, John, had battled so relentlessly and so long on her behalf. The two ran into each other one day in the Lincoln airport. Caril was alone, except for a small dog, and she explained that a student at a local college had asked her to take the dog to her relatives in Lansing. As she talked about her life, she said that as much as she loved children, she thought it wouldn't be fair to bring a child into this world with her as the mother. In her 1996 pardon application, she wrote, "I love children too much to have them suffer because I'm their mother. Children can be cruel."

Caril never fully recovered from either the stroke or the accident. She is unable to read or write. Nonetheless, under the legal guidance of Steve Berry, Caril filed an application for a full pardon in August 2017. Her initial request for a pardon in 1996 had been denied. This application was heard by the Board of Pardons on February 18, 2020.

In the center chair behind a semicircular wooden table at the far end of the hearing room sat Republican governor Pete Ricketts, loathed by the Democratic minority in the state as a rich guy who bought his way into the governorship (his father founded TD Ameritrade). He was a bad draw for Caril; in 2015, the unicameral legislature of Nebraska (a single house, the only one in the country) voted to repeal the death penalty, and Ricketts vetoed the bill. When the legislature overrode Rickett's veto, the governor led the charge to have the repeal reversed by a referendum and contributed two hundred thousand dollars to the effort. In 2016, the voters reinstated the death penalty with 61 percent of the vote. Not the sort of man likely to respond favorably to a heartfelt appeal of a famous convicted murderer. On his left sat secretary of state Bob Evnen, on his right, attorney general Doug Peterson. The Board of Pardons considered thousands of pardon requests a year.

Caril did not attend the hearing. In her application, she maintained that she had not been present during the killings at her home and that she had been a hostage of Charles Starkweather during the murder spree. She wrote that the fact that posterity believes that she was present for her family's killing was too much for her to bear anymore. Receiving a pardon would "somehow alleviate this tremendous burden."

Caril's guilt or innocence was not on the table. The board did not have the authority to determine the guilt or innocence of the applicant on the felony charge(s). (The board erroneously claimed that she had been convicted of the first-degree murder charge in the death of Robert Jensen in addition to the felony murder charge.) The pardon only has the effect of restoring civil rights, such as the right to vote, bear arms, serve as a juror, and hold public office. But in Caril's mind, and in the minds of many of her defenders, that was a distinction without a difference. A pardon would provide her some relief from the burden she has borne since her conviction for murder in 1958.

Caril had her supporters, and there was one in particular who caught the reporters' attention. In the front row, Liza Ward, Mike Ward's daughter, sat with Steve Berry, a well-known criminal-defense attorney and coauthor of the book *The Twelfth Victim*, who represented Caril in the application. In researching and writing *Outside Valentine*, a fictionalized version of the killings, Liza became convinced of Caril's innocence. She submitted a letter to the board supporting Caril's innocence, and in the letter she stated that her father was also in favor of a pardon for Caril.

Others in the room would disagree. David Ellis's mother was a cousin of Carol King. In Ellis's mind, the mutilation of his relative's private parts was evidence of a female rage. Caril's rage.

Reporter Del Harding believed strongly—to put it mildly—in Caril's guilt. Her "hostage" rap was not believable; there were witnesses who saw her sitting in Charlie's car with a .410 on her lap while he was in the gas station. She and Charlie were *bad together*. Charlie was mean. She was worse: evil. He believed she should never receive a pardon.

The governor brought the hearing to order. Bald-headed and with a forbidding countenance, Ricketts stumbled through an explanation of the board's process. It became quickly clear that the board had already made its decision on Caril. The governor read out a list of seven names and declared that each had been denied a pardon. Fifth on the first list was "Caril Ann Clair." No hearing. Just a flat denial. Attorney Steve Berry was outraged. From his seat on the aisle in the first row he shouted out a request to be heard. The governor shouted "No!" back even louder and advised the lawyer to wait for a public-comment period if he had something to say.

Liza Ward was visibly upset; angry and seemingly on the verge of tears, she told a television reporter after the hearing that Caril had been in pain her whole life, and she demanded to know why the jury accepted the word of a man (Starkweather) rather than a girl (Caril) about the truth of her role in the murders. Paulette Newman, whose mother was a sister of Carol King, held a photo of her aunt and told a reporter she was "thrilled" by the denial of Caril's request for a pardon. The governor's spokesman, Taylor Gage, noted that Caril's crimes were horrific and depraved and had created great public fear and that her story continued to change.

Caril's quest had failed. It was her final shot at a pardon, her last shot at even the slightest official recognition that she might not have been the fourteen-year-old killer portrayed in 1958.

57

OF A GENTLE NATURE, WITH A SLY SENSE OF HUMOR, Mike Ward was in his first term at the prestigious Choate School in Wallingford, Connecticut, during the winter of 1958. He was not happy and he was not doing well. On a campus of students mainly from the northeast, Mike was somewhat of an anomaly.

On the afternoon of January 29, Mike received a message that he should go immediately to the headmaster's house. He was expecting some family friends to be visiting Choate, and he thought perhaps they had arrived. Instead, he was surprised to see the headmaster in the company of the reverend David Gracey, a former a minister at Holy Trinity Episcopal Church in Lincoln, where Mike's father had served on the vestry. Reverend Gracey was now minister of a parish in a nearby town in Connecticut. His purpose in coming to Choate that afternoon was to tell Mike that his parents had been murdered. Which he did.

Mike, feeling that the world had fallen out from under him, quickly packed up some clothes, and the two left to spend the night at Reverend Gracey's house. The following morning, they flew on a DC-4 to Lincoln, where they were met by a group of Mike's immediate family and numerous reporters and photographers. The funeral, officiated by Reverend Gracey, was held at Westminster Presbyterian Church and the interment at Wyuka Cemetery. Later, Mike would tell a friend that the photographers, always disrespectful, had stood on nearby headstones in an effort to get a good picture of him and his family. Mike was taken in by his uncle and aunt, Phil and Jeannette Sidles, who, in Mike's words, "made room" for him in their family and to whom he would be eternally grateful.

A few months after the funeral, Mike returned to Choate. Not surprisingly, his academic efforts did not improve. After graduating from

Choate, he attended Lawrence University, a small liberal arts college in Appleton, Wisconsin. It was there that Mike found that a hobby might well become a vocation. He immersed himself in the study of art and art history. He found a confidant in an English professor, and the two remained close for many years until her death. Even though, at times, Mike still felt lost and alone, he was determined to move forward with his life.

By the age of ten, Mike had become a collector. He had an almost instinctual—if not mystical—connection with unusual objects and artifacts. He set up a small museum in the basement of his house. Linda Hallam, a friend of Mike who lived across the street and whose mother, Cordy, had called Clara Ward the day she was killed, remembers that admission to the museum was a dime. There he arranged on tables, bookcases, and other available flat surfaces his collection of rare minerals, colorful agates, fossils, arrowheads, Native American pottery shards, and other objects of interest he found on trips with his parents to the Badlands of Wyoming, the Black Hills of South Dakota, and Santa Fe, New Mexico. Most items were mounted individually on wood blocks held down by wire, with typed labels for identification. On the adventures, Mike and his father would roam the hills tapping away at rocks with their hammers, turning over small boulders in search of Native American artifacts while dodging rattlers. His mother usually remained behind in the car, sitting in the front seat. On hot days she would open the car door wide and pull her skirt above her knees, always with a snake-bite kit in hand. She was her family's guardian angel—always taking care and worrying about her boys.

Mike's early interest in objects and artifacts, in things of history, as he would put it, led to a more sophisticated and lifelong interest in fine arts. He was accepted as a PhD candidate at the Institute of Fine Arts, NYU's graduate department of art history, where his main interest became the study of European twelfth-century sculpture. On his very first day at the institute, he met Stark, the woman who he would eventually marry and who would provide emotional stability in the years ahead.

Over an eight-year period, Mike, with the assistance of his wife, completed work on his PhD thesis. The subject included a large number of sculptures from the late twelfth century that still survive on the entry porch to the Cathedral of Saint James at Santiago de Compostela, a remote town in the northwest corner of Spain. Here the remains of the apostle James the Greater were venerated by the tens of thousands of pilgrims who, having walked the pilgrimage road from Paris to Santiago, sought assurance of their salvation after death.

On returning to New York, Mike received an Andrew Mellon Fellowship in the Department of Medieval Art at the Metropolitan Museum. He and Stark had a baby girl, and a few years later they began their careers as art dealers by selling works to museums, collectors, and other galleries.

The Wards' daughter, Liza, would say that her father's passion for art is best seen through his uncanny ability to envision the artist in the work, whether it is a painting or a clay pot; to see the object outside of its historical origin. He might fall in love with an illumination in a German tenth-century manuscript and ponder whether the powerful abstraction of its figures and its intense contrasting colors might have had an influence on the art of Pablo Picasso. When he looked at an interesting object, whether a piece of jewelry from ancient Greece or a Japanese painting, he wondered, "Where is the life in this piece?" Mike was also an expert at spotting fakes. If times got rough, he immersed himself even deeper in art. Had he lived a "peaches and cream" life, Liza muses, he might never have become so completely absorbed in the world of ancient artifacts.

Mike soon gained considerable international recognition as an expert and scholar in ancient Greek, Roman, and medieval art. One finds him frequently quoted in articles on topics such as the nature of the many art buyers' determined pursuit of antiquities. He was appointed by President George Bush to the U.S. Cultural Property Advisory Committee, which was formed to investigate the cultural-property laws of art-rich countries such as Greece and Italy and to consider whether the United States should recognize and enforce these countries' export laws.

Recently, he moved his gallery just down the block from the entrance to the Metropolitan Museum of Art.

With two exceptions, Mike has never given interviews or talked publicly about the tragedy that befell his family. Many of his closest friends from college were unaware of the murders. Liza grew up not knowing about her grandparents. When at age four or five she asked about them, she was told they died in their sleep. Later, around age eight, she was told they were killed by a bad man. Mike would say in the one interview he gave to *The New York Times* on the publication of *Outside Valentine* that he was determined not to let the deaths of his parents define him. He would get on with life. Mike, along with his wife Stark and daughter Liza, was also interviewed for the Showtime series.

In the *Times* article, Mike commented: "You want to go ahead and pretend that something like this never happened, though it's completely altered your life and probably altered the way you deal with people in your own family, your children. You want to get away from the pull of the thing, but you can't. And you can say, 'Oh, well, I'm an art dealer now in New York City.'"

In Mike's words, the loss of his parents left him with an "emptiness stamped forever on my soul. It's not really understandable and it never goes away." It would always define him in some manner; the loss was so overwhelming that the feeling he had when Reverend Gracey told him his parents were dead has never faded. And yet, somehow, he managed, and manages, a life of considerable accomplishment. He was not overwhelmed by bitterness or anger or depression, although he has seen how the contagion of the tragedy has deeply affected the lives of his wife and daughter. In his mind now, Mike looks back to those interests he shared with his parents as the source of his strength, and he has come to believe that this continuity of interests—of building a self, really—is what has allowed him to endure and thrive.

Mike considers himself one of the lucky ones. A psychologist might see the success of his life through the lens of sublimation. The artistic interests he developed with his parents as a child maintained and developed into his vocation, if not obsession, as he grew to adulthood. His parents were always a part of this evolution, so in a way they were always part of his life.

Sometimes the pain of loss descends into a profound, crushing silence. Dewey Jensen was fourteen when his older brother Bobby was murdered by Charlie Starkweather. Dewey became the last standing of four children of Robert and Pauline Jensen. Daniel, his twin brother, died at age three. Terry, a sister, died at a young age. And, of course, Bobby. Dewey's aloneness in face of the tragedy of his older brother's murder cast a deep shadow over his life. He decided early on to leave Bennet and live his life elsewhere.

Dewey married Peggy, his high school sweetheart, and obtained a doctorate in philosophy and religion from the University of Texas. In 1971, he began teaching at Northern Arizona University in Flagstaff. He and his wife agreed that they were going to shelter their two boys, Ethan and Thane, from the circumstances of their uncle's death and from the whole Starkweather phenomenon. How or why Bobby died was never discussed in the family, at least not in front of them. The family would vacation in Bennet in the summer, and the two boys would go to the cemetery with their parents and place flowers on Bobby's grave without ever learning the reasons for his early death. Afterward, they would walk across the cemetery and place flowers on the grave of Carol King, whom they didn't know.

It was pure chance that the two boys learned the circumstances of their uncle's death. One day, Thane's ninth-grade yearbook teacher in Flagstaff, also from Nebraska, gave him a book entitled *Caril*. Thane read of his family's tragic story in the classroom while the other students were studying math or geography or working on yearbook projects. His older brother had found out the same way, with the same teacher.

Dewey Jensen was a large-brain intellectual, deeply immersed in the philosophies and religions of humankind. He was a supportive but harsh parent. You did not argue back. He was also a high-functioning alcoholic. He drank several scotch and waters every night. He slept very little; he would stay up until 2:00 or 3:00 a.m. and then go to an eight o'clock class. He took lots of medication for depression, high blood pressure, and pain. His intellect and the alcohol and the medication seemed to wall him off from the tragedy of his brother's death. He never talked about the murder or the pain that accompanied it. By all accounts, Dewey Jensen was a tortured soul.

One morning in 1987, Dewey didn't show up for his morning class. The university contacted his wife, who told the boys, and Ethan and Thane went looking for their father. Police eventually came to the door and reported that he was dead. Katherine Ramsland, a student of his at the time and now an author and professor of forensic psychology, would later write:

> The police report read that he'd parked his car and walked half a mile into the woods with a bag of papers he'd penned and a .22 pistol. He'd built a campfire at a remote campsite and burned everything—all of his papers. I imagined him watching the flames, pondering his psycheache as they devoured the life of his mind.
>
> After the flames translated his claims about ethics, religion, and Kierkegaard into white and gray ash, Dewey had picked up his Ruger revolver and walked a few feet, and shot himself. The ranger who'd found his body near the smoldering campfire said it looked as if he were walking away.

Ramsland hadn't been surprised when she learned of Dewey's suicide. His health had seriously declined. She could feel the imminence of his death.

After their father's death, Thane and his brother began talking with their mother for the first time about Bobby's death. Thane eventually found a suitcase full of clippings at his grandparents' house after they had passed away, and he read them one by one. He was surprised to see that his grandparents gave interviews to the press, unlike their son, his father, who carried the pain of his brother's death alone and deep inside until it broke him.

—

IT'S NOT EASY to wear the name Starkweather in Nebraska. Debra Rhoades is Rodney Starkweather's daughter, born ten years after Charlie's killing spree. She has light orange hair.

"A killer's family," she told a reporter for the *Journal Star* in 2008 (the *Star* and the *Journal* merged in 1996), "are forgotten victims." Her uncle's crimes have been a part of her life for as far back as she can remember. "It keeps being brought up. It's in my face, and there's nothing I can do."

In December 2007, a nineteen-year-old man killed nine people and wounded four at the Von Maur shopping center in Omaha. A person behind her in the line at grocery store said it was some guy just like Starkweather. Debra felt for the killer's family, knowing what life would be like for them now.

She's been turned down for jobs and apartments because of the Starkweather name. When someone sees her name on a driver's license or a check, they ask her something like, "Wow . . . are you related? How does it feel?" She remembers a stranger coming up to her in a Kmart deli when Guy Starkweather was giving her a hug and saying, "Don't you know you're hugging a Starkweather?"

Bill Kelly, at the time a reporter for WOWT-TV, the NBC affiliate in Omaha, reported and produced a documentary in 1988 entitled *Charlie and Caril—Starkweather Thirty Years Later* to mark the thirty-year anniversary of the killings. In it, he interviews Barbara, who was married to Rodney Starkweather, two of her children, and other nephews and nieces of Charlie. Barbara recalls how her kids were bullied in school. She had to call the police to escort one of her sons to class to protect him. One person asked her why she would even have and raise kids with that last name.

Her son, also with orange hair, said that the abuse never let up. It was constant. Kids would call out to him, "Hey, who you going to kill next?" or simply "Killer!" All he could think of to say was "Shut up, or it'll be you next!" There were lots of fights. His sister, Debra, says it got so bad in school she finally dropped out at age sixteen. She worries that her children will have to suffer the same thing. "I just wish they would leave us the hell alone," she says bitterly. Both she and her brother had the opportunity to change their last name when their mother remarried, but they didn't. Another nephew tells of his trouble in school and getting jobs. "People hate the name [Starkweather]," he says. "They just hate it."

With Charlie in the grave, Barbara thinks people should just let the dead sleep. All it does is bring up bad memories for everyone.

Starkweather's first victim—the one that convinced him that killing was the answer—Robert Colvert, was buried where he was raised, in Beaver Crossing, a small town forty miles west of Lincoln. His daughter, Barbara, was born five months later. Her mother later remarried, and Barbara had a brother and sister from that union. She kept pictures of her father on her bedroom wall. She had lots of questions, but answers were painful for her mother and hard to come by. She did learn that he was a caring man and a good carpenter and of a sunny disposition. Barbara has a daughter of her own, and she told *Journal Star* reporter Cindy Lange-Kubick in 2008 that "she's had a good life, a different one than she would have had, but a life she wouldn't trade." Tears came to her eyes. "It's still hard though."

Charlie's last victim, Merle Collison, the shoe salesman and former WWII paratrooper whom Charlie shot to death in his car on the side of the road not far from Douglas, was buried in the Mount Olivet Cemetery in Great Falls, Montana "with little fanfare" the local paper noted. His wife remarried and moved away. His son, four months at the time of his father's death, died as a young man. Collison was an only child.

Charles (not his real name) lives in a small town outside Lincoln. His grandmother was a sister to Carol King's mother. He was twenty-two at the time of the Bennet killings. He kept a loaded shotgun at his bedside until the killers were caught. He remembers Carol as a happy, talented young girl and Bobby as a fine young man. He served as a pallbearer at Carol's funeral. Now in his nineties, the pain from the deaths has lessened little, if at all, in sixty-five years. In his nightmares, he is holding a gun on Charlie and wakes up just before he pulls the trigger.

Two employees of the Safety Patrol told him Caril stuck a rifle up Carol King, and her fingerprints were found on the gun. His voice tightens in pain as he describes his hatred of Caril Fugate. He swears he would have shot her back then if he'd had a chance and a gun. Caril Fugate killed Carol King and got off and lived happily ever after while Carol King is dead. That's justice for you.

August Meyer's farm was sold at public auction on September 11, 1958. The remains of the schoolhouse were scraped off, and the cellar filled in. The field is now pastureland with a covering of tall grass. Ditches still line either side of the narrow lane heading up the road to the site of the Meyer farmhouse. The tall, rusty pump in the tall grass tells where the schoolhouse once stood.

The current owners of the land have many stories to tell about the strangers who have over the years walked across their land searching for a connection with the dead. A few years back, two ladies from Omaha showed up in search of "orbs," which, they explained, are points of light that float in the air and represent the spirits of the dead. You can only see the orbs through special devices, which looked to the owner like modified cameras or binoculars. The ladies asked to camp out that night in hope of seeing some orbs. There were no reports of any sightings. Eventually, the house was abandoned and became a "haunted house" that drew teens and college students who stole, ransacked, and broke windows. The elements got in and the floors rotted out. In later years, druggies moved in and the owners called the sheriff. Finally, about ten years ago they got tired of running people off the property and burned the house down.

In 1964 the houses on the 900 block of Belmont Avenue were torn down. The plan was for a strip mall to be built in their place. A few spectators watched as a huge bulldozer plowed into the Bartlett house and scraped it off. The spot where 924 once stood is now an open, grassy field.

58

SIXTY-FIVE YEARS HAVE NOW PASSED SINCE THE MUR-
ders. Most of the people directly involved in the killings are dead.
Lincoln has evolved into a thriving modern-day Midwestern city.
It has close to three hundred thousand residents, and more than twenty-
six thousand students attend the university. It has become known as
the "silicon prairie" because of the number of start-ups moving there
in search of "The Good Life"—Nebraska's old slogan—which includes
a substantially cheaper cost of living and good schools. Occasionally,
a story on the killings hits the media, such as the three-part fiftieth-
anniversary series in the *Journal Star* in January 2008, or Caril's application for a pardon in 2017 and its denial in 2020, but for the students at
the University of Nebraska (it now has four campuses in the state)—anyone under thirty, really—and the newly arrived, the killings are history,
if they are aware of them at all. For those who lived through the time
as children, or even young adults, the memories might be faded around
the edges, but they haven't gone away. They recall the terror on the faces
of their parents, the fear in the school and the neighborhoods, the guns
coming out of closets, getting stuck in the basement with the pets, the
bitter relief when Charlie and Caril were finally captured.

Person after person I talked to in Lincoln said without hesitation
that Caril was at 924 Belmont when her parents were killed and that
she most likely participated in one of the killings herself, most often
the murder of Carol King, if not Lilyan Fencl as well. This holds true
for former reporters, lawmen, and average citizens. It is most always a
hard belief; that is, the person believes it so firmly that it's rarely open
for discussion. And usually without a hint of empathy for Caril's age or
circumstances. Women seem as committed if not more committed to
a belief that she participated in the murders than men. "She's a killer,"

one woman, a retired health care executive, said one evening on the phone. "Don't ever forget that." Or the swift pronouncement of a former high school teacher: "She's every bit as guilty as Starkweather." The person might give a reason, such as Caril had a lot of opportunities to escape but didn't, but often it feels like the truth lies in their gut, as it has from the beginning. Women almost never think she should have been executed, but some victims' families do. A cousin of the stoic August Meyers still has dreams of waking up holding his rifle in his hand and shooting Caril to death. There are some Lincolnites who believe she's innocent; usually they see her as a captive of Charlie, or they simply can't imagine how a fourteen-year-old girl could be a vicious murderer.

One can only speculate as to why this damnation is so prevalent. Lincoln was and still is a city of decent and fair-minded people. They are not inclined to make quick judgments about anything, much less people. One former professor at the university suggested that classism and misogyny might play a role—that Caril was seen as poor white trash, cheap and slutty in the mores of the time, and therefore less grounded in moral behavior. Charlie, as a male, was exempt from such judgment. (In fact, under Nebraska law at the time, Charlie could have been prosecuted for statutory rape because of Caril's age *unless* she was proven to be "previously unchaste.") But how does being "loose" make a girl into a killer?

It doesn't really; it may simply be a thread in the weave of the answer to the question of why the town was and is still convinced that Caril is a murderer. The major institutions in the city would seem to have done their best to make her appear so. The press portrayed Caril as a participant from almost the very beginning. Neither the headlines nor the reporting gave her a true presumption of innocence. She looked guilty, she acted guilty, she showed no remorse, her hostage theory didn't hold up, she had many chances to run, etc. County Attorney Scheele poured fuel on the fire early by releasing details of the case against Caril months before her case came to trial.

Dick Trembath, the cameraman who worked with Ninette Beaver for the Omaha NBC affiliate in 1958, developed doubts about Caril's guilt after watching *Growing Up in Prison.* As told in the book *Caril,* he lamented to his wife that they (reporters) never really tried to figure out who Caril was. They never questioned their assumptions; they photographed her and wrote copy and drew conclusions, which were quite shallow: the literal appearance of a fourteen-year-old girl who looked and acted like she could be guilty. Suppose the figure they portrayed as a nasty little girl with a dirty smile and very good posture was really just in shock? What if she was one of those people who do exactly as they are told to do?

"Even by Charlie Starkweather?" his wife asked.

"Especially Charlie."

"Oh, my God," she responded.

Trembath also articulated a not-unusual take on the question of Caril's guilt. She might be guilty of something, but what? You might not be able to convict her of murder, but you simply couldn't proclaim her innocent either. She was involved in the crimes, somehow, but how responsible could you hold her? For many people, that was about as far as they could go in not condemning her.

Tommie Clair, one of the four brothers tasked by their father with looking out for Caril after his death, is a strong advocate for Caril. He phrases his position carefully: "I think she's innocent, for the most part."

In her letter to the Board of Pardons supporting Caril's application, Liza Ward would create another option for those who might not be able to bring themselves to find Caril innocent:

Even if one were to remain unconvinced of Caril Fugate's outright innocence in the murder of Robert Jensen, perhaps one might find her not culpable, and by doing so thereby travel to a place in which she is found deserving of this pardon.

The word *culpable* means "deserving of blame" or "blameworthy." It would seem to invite a judgment of compassion in place of a legal one. As a matter of human decency, is it not the right time to let this poor woman up from the ground?

Tom Allen, who covered the story for the *Omaha World Herald*, was absolutely convinced of Caril's guilt. He was not upset that she obtained parole in 1976. He was a born-again Christian, as she claimed to be, and he felt that she had served her time. Justice had been done. Although it would have been easier to accept if she had admitted her guilt.

As for the judicial system, Judge Spencer, who would be elected to the Nebraska Supreme Court in 1960 and lived until he was a 103, had refused to allow Reller to participate in the trial other than as an adviser to McArthur. So it was three lawyers for the prosecution and one and a half for the defense in a capital case.

State and local law enforcement at every level were convinced of Caril's guilt from the beginning. Police chief Joe Carrol, Elmer Scheele, Matron Karnopp, Sheriff Karnopp, and Detective Henninger all made statements to this effect. A state patrolman high in the ranks told a close friend that there were two knives used in the killing and mutilation of Carol King. One cut into her cervix and rectum and the other cut a line of slashes across her stomach and chest. Two knives equals two killers. The friend claims to have seen a photo of the slashes. But, in fact, neither the photo introduced into evidence nor the autopsy indicate any slashes across the chest. Some lawmen also claimed that sticks and trash had been shoved up inside Carol King. The autopsy does not mention any foreign objects found inside her.

Detective Sawdon, one of the detectives who accompanied Pansy Street on the search of 924 Belmont, was absolutely convinced that Caril killed both Mrs. Ward and Lilyan Fencl. He witnessed Charlie's execution and said on *Entertainment Tonight* that his only regret in the matter was that Caril wasn't sitting on Charlie's lap in the electric chair.

One of the most firmly believed theories in law enforcement and by many citizens is that Caril mutilated King in a murderous fit of jealousy. When Charlie didn't return from the cellar after ten or fifteen minutes, Caril went there and saw Charlie having sex with the body. In a rage, she stuck a knife into King's inside.

One person close to the case recounted being told by a lawman involved in the investigation and a member of the prosecutor's office that they believed Caril was as excited by the murder spree as Charlie and that she actively participated in the crimes. They saw her as extremely jealous of Charlie, and it was their belief that when Charlie took the maid up the stairs to a bedroom, Caril became incensed and later went up the stairs and stabbed her to death.

Dr. Prudence Gourguechon, a Chicago psychiatrist and psychoanalyst who has evaluated and treated people who have been abused and traumatized for over thirty-five years, and who has served as an expert witness in civil trials, believes that whoever mutilated Carol King would have to have been in a violent, sadistic, psychotic rage, and that this does not resemble the type of jealousy a fourteen-year-old girl would have.

In no behavior before or after the spree did Caril exhibit any symptoms indicating psychosis. A more likely course of events would seem to be that in a rage over his inability to get an erection—because it was so cold, Charlie would explain to Henninger—Charlie turned his rage on Carol King with a knife.

There is an array of myths surrounding the killings. One is that prior to meeting Starkweather, Caril sold sex to boys in a place called Robbers Cave in Lincoln (a supposed hideout of real outlaws Jesse James and Texan Sam Bass); that she gave birth to Charlie's baby while in the mental hospital and that it had been adopted by her sister Barbara; that Charlie's family rescued the locks of his red hair from the floor of his cell and had a local beautician glue them on his head for the funeral viewing. A popular myth, repeated in the *Journal Star*, was that Martin Sheen had bought the marker for Charlie's grave at Wyuka. In fact, the headstone had been bought for $119 by Jerry Petty, a performer with Disney on Parade, which had been in town for the musical *Peter Pan* at the Pershing Auditorium. (He played Captain Hook. Charlie reminded him of his brother.) The cemetery only required that Petty obtain the consent of Guy Starkweather for the headstone. One rumor had it that Merril Reller had adopted Caril; another rumor had it that the charge in the electric chair was so high that it fused Charlie to the wood and that his bones had to be broken to get him off it. The wildest one might be that many years after the murder, an offspring of the Fugates married an offspring of the Starkweathers.

Yes, Lincoln has moved on. Nebraska has moved on. It's the twenty-first century. The migration of the sandhill cranes has become a widely celebrated event, with people from around the world joining tours in Kearney to watch the flapping of the great birds and hear their eerie sound as they settle in by the thousands on the Platte for the night. In 1983, Governor Bob Kerry met Debra Winger at the Zoo Bar—a popular downtown blues and folk bar since 1973—when she was in Lincoln filming *Terms of Endearment*. In October he hosted her for an overnight stay at the Governor's Mansion. She rode in a parade with him in Grand Island the next day, without a peep from the populace. In fact, a survey showed that 77 percent of Nebraskans approved of Winger's overnight at the mansion. (The story is that after a six-month romance Winger decided the life of a politician's wife was not for her and moved on.)

In 2016, Nebraska settled more refugees per capita than any state in the nation, in keeping with its long history as refugee resettlement state. In 2005, fifty languages were spoken in Lancaster County. Black people now account for 4.8 percent of the population, while Hispanic people are 11.2 percent. The University of Nebraska's women's volleyball team won national championships in 1995, 2000, 2006, 2015, and 2017. Omaha has built a multimillion-dollar stadium to host the College World Series of baseball every year. Lincoln has the new Pinnacle Bank Arena, seating 15,500 people, in the Haymarket District, the old railroad, industrial, and warehouse section of town that has been rehabilitated into an entertainment and condo venue. Omaha Steaks are sold around the world. The Lied Center, built in 1990, is a first-class performing arts facility in Lincoln. Boys Town, established in a boarding house on the edge of Omaha in 1917 by Father Flanagan and memorialized in a 1938 movie starring Spencer Tracy as Father Flannigan (for which he won an Academy Award), is now coed and has treatment facilities in twelve sites across America, as well as a major research hospital in Omaha. Omaha is also the home of the United States Strategic Command (formerly the Strategic Air Command [SAC]), which has control of two of the three nuclear delivery systems (ICBMs and land-based strategic bombers) in the country. Omaha film director Alexander Payne made a widely acclaimed black-and-white film titled *Nebraska* starring Bruce Dern, who won an Academy Award for his performance. Warren Buffett, the fourth richest man in the world, has lived in the same house in a quiet neighborhood in Omaha since 1958. In 2020, 67 percent of high school graduates in Nebraska went on to college. The state is now cool enough to market itself as "Nebraska. Honestly, it's not for everyone."

Yet in many ways, Nebraska is still Nebraska. It is the third largest producer of agricultural product—after California and Iowa—in the country. Eighty-five thousand loyal fans gather in Memorial Stadium to proudly watch the famous Big Red go to war on brisk autumn afternoons. (Nebraska won national championships in 1970, 1971, 1994, 1995, and 1997. Nebraska backs won Heisman trophies in 1972 (Johnny Rogers), 1983 (Mike Rozier), and 2001 (Eric Crouch). On weekends and in the summer months high school boys in the Sandhills hitch up their trailers, load their horses, jump in their pickups, and head out to chase a little glory and a few bucks riding bulls and roping steers in rodeo rings across the state. Small-town girls rope steers and ride their horses in barrel races in the same rodeos, but many also belong to Future Homemakers of America and bake cakes and pies for church fundraisers.

But to think that Starkweather and Fugate will fade into the shadows of the forgotten would be a serious mistake. Lincoln will always be the home of Charlie Starkweather and Caril Fugate. It is the soil in which they grew, the soil on which so much blood was spilled. Where Charlie and five of his victims are buried. The blow to the heart that dropped Lincoln to its knees and left it ashamed and embarrassed and yet seemingly proud in a strange way will be reinforced every time a book like this one or a documentary or a song about it comes out. When the boomers are long gone, the power of the searing images of love and death will keep the story of the killings and the killer(s) alive light-years beyond even Charlie's craziest fantasy. And the question of Caril's participation in the killings—ultimately, her guilt or innocence—will likely never be settled once and for all.

EPILOGUE

ONE DAY EARLY IN MY RESEARCH I CAME ACROSS A PHOTO-
graph in the *Lincoln Star* of a cluster of cops standing on the front porch
of the Ward house in their topcoats and fedoras, watching a sheet-
covered body being wheeled out of the front door on a gurney. One face
looked familiar. I scanned the names under the picture. Detective Gail
Gade (pronounced "God-e"). The fedora was pushed back on his head.
I zoomed in on his face. Olive skin, dark eyes. He was a nice guy, I remembered. He would usher my brother Mike and me into his office and
point to the wooden chairs in front of his desk in a genial manner, as if
we were his guests, not recently apprehended shoplifters. He joked with
our stepdad that we were in his office so often he would have our names
engraved on the backs of the chairs.

He wore a burgundy tie and a gold ring on his right hand, and he
was pleasant even on the day he told us that the next time we came into
his office, he would have to refer us to Hulda Roper. Mrs. Roper was your
last stop before being sent to the boys' training school in Kearney. She
signed a paper, and snap, you were gone. For two years. I'm not sure we
believed him—we were from an old and prominent Lincoln family, not
unlike the Wards—but it was a scary idea. He walked us to the door and
patted us on our shoulders like he was pulling for us, and looking back,
I think he was.

I wondered if he was one of the detectives who overlooked the scene
of violence in the Bartlett home on the morning of January 27, setting
up the next seven murders. I doubted it. I searched through the archives
and finally found an article naming the cops; he wasn't one of them.

I was thirteen when I first met Detective Gade. My grandmother, a
Lincoln grande dame, had a maid named Pearl, a student at the Seventh-
Day Adventist Union College in Lincoln. Sometimes, Pearl would come

to our house to clean or cook, and on those days she would drive over in my grandmother's 1952 black Chevy. One day, my brother Mike spotted the Chevy parked in front of our house and suggested we take it for a ride. The Chevys in those days had steel frames and steering wheels as big as flying saucers, and no power steering. And it was a standard shift. Mike drove us to the drugstore a couple of blocks away for his shift as a soda jerk. He got out, and I slipped behind the wheel and managed to get the car moving jerkily in first gear. I had three corners to navigate. I made it around the first two, and halfway around the third before spotting a girl in my junior high class that I had a crush on. I leaned out a little so she could see me driving. In the midst of this move, I failed to remember to unwind the steering wheel and the car turned into the curb, jumped it, and smashed into a tall elm in the narrow parkway. I cracked my knee on the metal dash and knocked my head against the wheel. There was a huge gash in the tree where the grill had torn into it. The car was totaled.

The incident ran on the front page of the *Star* the next day. And down to Detective Gade's office we went: Mike, our stepfather, and me. Gade was amazed that I had managed to get the car around as many corners as I did. He gave us a lecture, and that was it, we were on our way home for a faux belt strapping from our stepfather, a kind and patient man.

I came across Detective Gade in the photo of the crime scene at 924 Belmont, where ten or fifteen cops were standing around the outhouse and chicken shed. In all the official police reports and articles, his name never showed up again. I'd heard that after running the juvenile bureau in the Lincoln Police Department, he had gone on to head the security department at the University of Nebraska.

I had always felt uneasy in Lincoln. Even when I returned as an adult, it seemed as if I were crossing some threshold into the vagaries of a dark past. Now and then I would drive around the old neighborhoods. Nothing had changed; the tar strips snaked across the pavement just as they had when I rode my green-and-white Schwinn over them on the way to school. Stop signs were nonexistent at many residential intersections. And the tree. For years, I would drive by it and note the deep gash on the trunk with a strange sense of satisfaction. You were really fucked up back then, I would think. Fucked up and angry.

On my first visit to Lincoln to research this book, I drove to the old neighborhood and stopped by the tree. Or tried to. It was gone. Missing in action. I was stunned. I parked, got out, and walked over to where the tree should have been. Not even a depression in the ground to prove it had once existed. I stomped my foot on the flat ground. Why would you cut down a tree that old? It wasn't ugly; it told a story. Anyone could see that. Maybe it got infected; maybe a disease had crept into the innards through the gash and hollowed it out. I wanted to run my hand over the gash. Feel the pain in my knee. I saw a lady's face in the window of the house. I opened my hands in a "What happened?" gesture, then pointed to the ground. The face disappeared, and a curtain slid across the window. I got an inkling then of how this journey was going to go, and it made the uneasy feeling even more intense—the town, the story, the crimes, the past, even more irresistible.

Every thread sooner or later crosses another one.

Digging deep into police files, I came across a memorandum with "Hulda Roper" typed across the top and "Caril Ann Fugate" handwritten across the bottom. It recounted the incident in which Caril, age fourteen, had an accident while driving Charlie's 1941 ford. Charlie got a ticket for letting her drive it. Mrs. Roper told her to write five hundred words on what she had done. There, in the original ink, were the words of a young girl saying how sorry she was for crashing the car and promising she would never drive it again. So normal. So sweet. That was her only punishment. Then I saw an image of Hulda Roper, a pleasant-looking woman with glasses on a chain around her neck. Sitting on the bare wooden chairs in front of her desk, Mike and I were sweating as she rifled through the papers of our most recent offense, which was, if I remembered correctly, fooling around with matches in the attic of a neighbor's garage and catching the thing on fire. We were gone by the time the fire engines arrived, but the cops were at our house in minutes. Detective Gade had told us there was nothing he could do, we were on our way to see Hulda Roper, and there I sat with images of the training school in my mind.

"Your father passed away?" she asked in a kind voice.

Both Mike and I nodded.

"And your sister?"

Mike and I nodded again.

"Do you like your stepfather?'

We nodded a third time.

"Well," she said, "boys, I should put you on probation today, but I'm going to give you a warning instead. Probation, you know, is a step away from the training school."

We nodded again.

"Can't you boys talk?" she asked with a little smile.

"Thanks," Mike said. "For not sending us to Kearney."

I looked at the date on the memorandum. July 14, 1957. Our meeting with Hulda Roper would have been the same summer as Caril's, I think. Who knows? Maybe the same day. Maybe Caril was waiting in a chair in the hall when we left. Or vice versa. I closed my eyes. Caril got off easy, I thought, but then so did we.

The odd part was, while I was building my juvenile record, Charlie wasn't busted for anything serious, with one exception. I found a police report showing that in March 1957, a police officer pulled over a car with Charlie and three other boys for speeding on Highway 77. The officer found four cases of beer in their car. Charlie was sixteen. They had run south sixty miles across the Nebraska border to Marysville, Kansas, where you could buy 3.2 beer at eighteen. Nebraska boys had been crossing the border on beer runs for years, if not generations. All you needed was one guy with a car and a few bucks in your pocket. We drank beer and shot pool for a couple of hours until we were wasted, and then bought a couple of six-packs to go and drove home over the back roads. I remember the car careening through crossings and swerving up out of the ditches more than once. "Minor in possession," Charlie's rap sheet said. A lawyer got them all off without a court appearance and a fine of twenty-five bucks plus costs apiece. I was pissed. At eighteen my attempt to buy beer in Lincoln with a fake ID had resulted in charges of minor in possession *and* buying beer for minors (friends in the car). I ran my name through the newspaper database and sure enough there it was: a fine of two hundred dollars. (At eighteen, I must have been beyond Hulda Roper's reach.)

A friend of mine who knew Hulda asked her one day many years later if she remembered Mike and Harry MacLean. "Oh, yes," she said, "I remember them quite well. How did they turn out?" Mrs. Roper went on to say that she had been the only woman on the police department in those days, and even then she wasn't allowed to carry a gun (memorialized in the book *No Gun for This Lady!: The Story of Hulda Roper, First Policewoman of Lincoln, Nebraska* by Lilya Wagner). She was always the cop brought in to deal with problem kids, particularly girls. She was off work on January 24; otherwise, she would have been sent to the house at 924 Belmont to deal with Caril rather than the two uniforms. She would have ignored Caril's story of a sickness inside the house and pushed right past her. Charlie would have been waiting behind the door with the sawed-off shotgun. "I was lucky," she said. If Hulda had been killed that day, it might have stopped the killings, or maybe just the opposite.

I turned the corner I hadn't managed to navigate in the Chevy and looked at our old house. A big two-story stucco with a side yard big enough for a scrimmage. The shrubs by the porch had been replaced by shrubs on the porch. The wood trim was the same yellow. Hard times, I thought. Rough times. Two people in my life were missing. We lived in a country-club world, which wanted nothing to do with Mike and me because we were such troublemakers. Who shoplifted and set garages on fire and sat in the hall outside the principal's office and smoked and got our names in the newspapers. We didn't care about anything, I guess. I made my attitude clear: I got kicked out of Sunday school, summer camp, Boy Scouts, and prep school (and almost college). Mike wasn't persona non grata in as many places as I was (although he also got kicked out of prep school). He kind of rolled with the punches. Me, I told the world to go to hell.

I found myself driving to Irving Junior High, a half-a-block-long two-story redbrick building with white-framed windows. I parked and pressed my face against the front window. It was eerily empty, quiet. I spotted the iron railing where I'd parked my Schwinn. The stairwell where Charlie's bike had been ripped from his hands and tossed down the steps. By the time Charlie was here, he had turned from a crybaby into a vicious fighter with a big rep. Still, the world mocked him. Charlie and my brother were in a shop class together. Mike told how once during recess a bunch of boys had taken Charlie's project, a birdhouse or a boat, and glued it to the bench, all to their great amusement when he came back and tried to pick it up. I walked around the building to the yard where the fights took place. They were usually set up, and sometimes it was Irving boys against each other and other times it was a boy and his buddies from another school who showed up, a school on the north side of town, like Whittier, where Caril went. Some of the girls from Whittier had "reputations," and country-club boys, including me, used to try to pick them up. Mike had a few fights in those days, but early on he dropped an opponent to the ground with a single blow, and that pretty much put an end to it. Me? I held his coat. In his 1956 Ford Fairlane he dragged the same streets in town as Charlie, likely even ran against him once or twice. He straightened up in college and became a happy family man and successful corporate executive. Mike is gone now.

Every thread sooner or later crosses another one.

I was fifteen and away at prep school in western Massachusetts at the time of the killings. I received a phone call from my mother during the dinner hour. Her voice was shaking. "Do you remember Mike Ward?" she asked. "Yeah," I responded. "His mother and father were murdered. The killers are still on the loose." She had put the keys in the car outside and left the garage door open. The doors were locked. "Do you remember their house?" she asked. "A big white colonial just before you got to the club on the west side of the street." I didn't, but I calculated it was a little over a mile south of our house on Twenty-Fourth. She called back a few hours later and said they had captured the killers in Wyoming and everyone was safe. I remember thinking, Poor Mike, to lose your parents like that. Someone else pointed out that Mike was fortunate he was away at prep school or he would most likely have been killed himself.

Sitting in the car in front of the large colonial, I rifled through the black-and-white crime scene photos of the Ward house. The kitchen with linoleum floors and a Formica-topped table where Charlie would have eaten the pancakes prepared by Lilyan Fencl; the large dining room table with heavy silver candlesticks in the center beneath a large crystal chandelier, a matching buffet with a large silver soup tureen on top, and heavy cloth curtains reaching the floor. The bottle of 7UP Caril was drinking when she stood by the dining room window looking for Lauer Ward's car to turn in the drive was sitting close to the edge of the table. An empty package of Winstons on top of the first-floor toilet; a box of Marlboros on the coffee table. Bobby Jensen's letter jacket hanging on a chair. The large living room with the TV, where Caril took a long nap on the couch, while, so I believed, Charlie went upstairs and stabbed Mrs. Ward to death. Over-furnished with antiques and elegant pieces in the fashion of the wealthy of the time. A small library off of the hallway from the kitchen to the front of the house, looking out through French doors on a patio, an expansive back yard, and a rose garden tended by Clara Ward. The front hallway where Lauer Ward was shot and stabbed and fell on the floor to die as he tried to escape. The dark wood, inlaid with gold fleur-de-lis, stained in blood. The three bedrooms upstairs where the two women had been slain, with sheets on the floor, blood on the bed where poor Lilyan had been tied up and knifed and on the floor between the two single beds where Mrs. Ward had been found facedown, eyeglasses lying a foot away from her head. The picture of her son on her dressing table. I shuddered at the sensation. I needed to see the inside of the house. It was the only crime scene left.

The door was answered by an attractive middle-aged woman, cheery and welcoming. She and her husband, a successful Lincoln corporate lawyer, had lived in the house for twenty years and raised two kids there. Did it bother them, what happened there? (I'd heard that other kids in the neighborhood referred to it as the "murder house.") No, she said. The house had been remodeled and painted. A wall had been knocked out between the kitchen and the sitting room; the garage had been sectioned off. Previous owners had expanded the west side of the house. The linoleum floor was now white tile, and the double porcelain sink was gone. As we toured the house, we didn't talk about what happened in each room, but I could feel it. Fragments of the scenes played in my head. I took photos of everything from all angles. After an hour, my time was up, and I thanked the mistress of the house for her graciousness and left. I sat in my car for a few minutes. I looked up the drive where Charlie had parked Jensen's Ford and gone inside, leaving Caril alone in the car with the shotgun. I pictured the classy black Packard as it inched down the drive, itself now surely reeking of death, and swung north on its flight from Lincoln. It was freezing cold that day, and today was suffused in a wet heat. From the outside, the Ward house didn't look that much different from then, just like my house hadn't. Sweat rolled down my cheeks. I was beginning to feel that if I didn't get moving, something was going to catch up with me.

I drove from the Ward house east to another upscale neighborhood not far from where Charlie and Caril slept in the teenagers' car the night before hitting the Ward house and parked in front of my grandmother's old house, a lovely white two-story stucco with tall windows. I could see my room, to the right on the second floor. She kept us—Mike and I— while we awaited news of our father's death.

Something was off. The driveway descended steeply to the street and missing now I saw was a tall hedge that screened off the neighbor's house as well as cars coming from the north. On my bike I used to peel down the drive and into the street, where I hit the brakes and swung the rear around in a screeching hook in the middle of the street. I could hear my mother scream my name from the porch as a car swerved and missed me by a foot. The near miss didn't bother me; I remember that.

I remember the girl in the house next door; she was adopted, which was more unusual than not having a father and living with your grandmother. Her father, I suddenly recalled, was a psychiatrist who had examined Charlie and testified at his trial that he was sane and actually a fairly pleasant guy. He was a friendly man himself, I remember, mostly

bald, soft-spoken. Our parents were friends, until he left his wife and
daughter for a Japanese woman. I'd heard that the country club was
scandalized when he brought his new wife to play at the golf course. It
was only twenty-four years after Pearl Harbor, and a lot of the men had
fought in the Pacific. My father, Harry Norman Galleher, who went by
Norm, was officer of the day at the Schofield army base at Pearl on the
morning of the attack. My mother, in officers' housing on a hill rising
behind the base, heard the planes and, figuring they were from one of
our carriers, picked up Mike and took sister Sharon by the hand and
walked outside to watch. Overhead waves of Zeroes dropped down from
the sky so close that she could make out the pilot's faces. One of them
fired his guns as he swooped over on his way to Battleship Row. I experienced the attack in utero.

Yesterday, I recognized in a news report the name of the resident
FBI agent in charge in Lincoln; he was running the federal aspect of the
spree, which was minimal. He lived around the corner from us, and I
used to play with his son John after classes in elementary school. I also
learned yesterday that Lauer Ward was on the board of directors of the
insurance company where my stepfather was senior vice president, and
that the general counsel of the company, a friend of the family, had been
appointed by a federal court to represent Charlie on appeal. Reverend
David Gracey married my mother and stepfather in the living room
of my grandmother's home. A *Lincoln Star* clipping noted my grandmother and several other Lincoln ladies had driven to North Platte the
previous week to deliver home-baked pies and cakes to soldiers on the
troop trains traveling to the East Coast for transport to Europe. During
the summer between college and law school, I drove a Capital Cab,
the same cab company that Bob and Barbara Von Busch took to the
Belmont house on the Saturday before the spree began, the same cab
company that Rodney drove for. My mother and Clara Ward were both
in the Delta Gamma sorority at the University of Nebraska. I attended
Shattuck School in Minnesota with the son of Governor Anderson, who
called out the National Guard after the bodies were found in the Ward
house. I was born in Lincoln General Hospital, where a few floors below

the autopsies of the three Bartletts were performed on the night of January 27.

I had driven only a few blocks from my grandmother's house when I passed the grade school Mike and I attended while living with her. Sheridan School. I pulled to the curb. The front door swung open, and grade-schoolers piled out in an excited chatter. I kept an eye out for a scrawny kid with a buzz cut and wearing glasses and braces. I remembered the day the teacher called me up to the front of the room for show-and-tell. I told the class that my mother and father had gotten married over the weekend. The kids tittered. (All middle-class families, save those who lost the father in the war, were intact in those days.) I blushed and sat down. *Stepfather*, I meant to say. At least I didn't stutter and stumble, like the red-headed kid. I rolled up the window.

On it goes, I thought, as I pulled away. One thread touching another.

Our paths must have crossed on more than one occasion. The summer of 1957 was when Charlie was running stock cars at the Capitol Beach track on Sunday night. I was fourteen and Mike was fifteen, and we talked our parents into taking us to the races at least three or four times that summer. Maybe we sat behind Caril in the stands; maybe we watched Charlie accept a trophy for winning the demolition derby. And the state fair. When the electrician told me about the fit Caril threw when her dad wouldn't give her money to go to the fair for the second night in a row, I could see the brightly lit grounds stuffed with kids and cotton candy stands amid a sea of cowboy hats. That summer, Mike and I worked in booths on the Midway. Our mom dropped us off at noon and picked us up at 11:00 at night. I was in a ring-toss booth, where cowboys and farmers tried to toss a wooden ring over the top of a coke bottle. Twenty-five cents an hour. I could feel the steamy night air, hear the barkers calling out a challenge to the walkers-by. Charlie, with his thick red hair slicked back and up, a cigarette hanging from his lips, would have been wearing jeans, a snap-button western shirt, and cowboy boots. Caril in black jeans, one of Charlie's shirts untucked, her white majorette boots, a touch of lipstick, and a silver cross around her neck. He would have stopped at the booth where you shot pellet guns at Kewpie dolls perched on a shelf. He would have won a teddy bear on the first try, and Caril would have clutched it proudly as they walked on under the lights.

The thing was, the cowboys at the state fair were real cowboys. Charlie was a fake cowboy. He got it all from movies. It was a fantasy. Whereas I grew up after the war in cowboy country—the small ranch town of Bassett, in the Sandhills. My father owned a lumber yard in Stuart, a town close by, and my uncle owned a huge cattle ranch of over eight thousand acres. My father wore cowboy boots and a cowboy hat to work. I wore cowboy boots and a cowboy hat to kindergarten (I was a junior). His grandmother and her four daughters had come out on a train from Pennsylvania to Omaha in the 1880s. Her husband, an oil well inspector, had been killed by a boiler explosion in Pennsylvania a few weeks before they were to depart. From Omaha, the mother and daughters traveled a couple hundred miles west by covered wagon and homesteaded 160 acres sixteen miles south of Newport, a small town near Bassett. After three years, they moved into town so the girls could get a better education. I grew up hearing tales of Indian raids, but never got a lot of specifics. One wall of the sod hut they built by hand has been maintained. Great Grandma Barr, the homesteader, was a little girl when Abe Lincoln was alive. She lived to almost one hundred, and I remember her smiling and listening through a long, curved ear trumpet when we spoke to her.

Guns were everything to Charlie, more important than cars or girls, and I wanted to see the guns he used to kill. I wanted to hold them in my hands. Feel, pull the triggers. The weapons are maintained in a storage room by the Nebraska State Historical Society. I made an appointment to see them the day after my visit to the Ward house. The manager and I rode down an elevator to the basement, where three weapons were laid out side by side on white paper on a large table: the Winchester pump .22 Model G2A belonging to farmer Meyer that Charlie used to shoot Bobby Jensen and Carol King; the Winchester pump .22 Model 1906 belonging to the Wards that Charlie used to kill Lauer Ward and Merle Collison; and the .410 belonging to Marion Bartlett that Charlie used on his friend August Meyer. Missing was the single-shot .22 belonging to Rodney Starkweather that Charlie used to kill Marion, Velda, and Betty Jean Bartlett and the shotgun he used to kill the gas station attendant. The guns shone under a bright overhead light. At my host's request, I put on blue rubber gloves. I ran my fingers slowly over the metal. I picked up Meyer's .22 and examined the numbers on the barrel, felt it for weight and balance, and pointed it across the room at a ceiling light. I set it down, and I picked up the Wards' .22. The .410 was stocky, a crude gun, and not much longer than the Wards' .22. When I picked it up, I figured why: the last nine inches were missing. Sawed off. Meant only to shred flesh and bone at close range. The cut was rough and slightly slanted. Sixty pellets had been taken from the head of August Meyer.

I set the .410 down on the table and picked up Meyer's .22 again. Now, it felt lighter, almost weightless in my hands. I held it up to my cheek and could feel Charlie firing it like a madman: pump, shoot, pump, shoot, pump, shoot, pump, shoot, pump, shoot, pump, shoot. Six shots into the boy's head, centimeters apart, one into the side of the girl's. I slipped my finger off the trigger, released the pump, and lay the rifle carefully back down on the table. I let my breath go. My host asked if I would like to climb up on a pair of movable stairs and take photos from above. I felt a bit unstable as I climbed the stairs and bent over and aimed my phone down at the three weapons, now glittering in the overhead light.

I sat in my car in the heat. My hands were shaking. That wasn't necessary, I thought. No one needs to see a photo of the killing guns. I went to my cheesy motel, changed into shorts and a T-shirt, and lay down and tried to rest, finally rising and grabbing my camera and map and hustling out the door. The killing of the teenagers had a singular impact on me, and I had avoided a visit to the cellar for months.

My directions were bad, but finally I wandered out of Bennet and eventually came across an almost-quaint narrow lane off the gravel road. With ditches on either side, it rose out of sight over a long hill ending at the remains of the Meyer farm. This was the road that Charlie and Caril walked up and back on that frozen evening (and which I would walk this day in the drenching heat). The land was now pasture.

The grass was bent in the wind, and occasional wildflowers dotted the fields. No sign of anything now, except the long-handled pump in front of the schoolhouse. I stopped at the spot where the 1950 Ford would have stopped and then walked up the lane fifteen yards or so and off to the side in the field, toward the cellar. The photos of the crime scene were grotesque. Charlie had thrown Carol down the steps like a rag doll. I wiped the images from my mind and sat down on the grass where I figured the entrance to the cellar was. I wondered if the pump still brought up water and if any ghosts lingered down there and whether they could hear the cattle stumbling overhead. I pressed my hands flat on the earth, bending the grass flat, raised my face to the sun, and felt a vague trembling rising in my arms. You could call Charlie whatever you wanted, but in truth he was a monster. Pure and simple.

I almost missed the cemetery outside Bennet. I had to turn around a quarter mile past. I dreaded seeing their names engraved in stone. Bobby was off to the right from the entrance, under a flat stone with flowers carved in the corners, reading:

ROBERT W. JENSEN
July 31, 1940 – Jan. 27, 1958.
BELOVED SON.

Carol was on the other side of the cemetery, laying under an upright carved granite stone.

CAROL J. KING
June 28, 1941 – January 27, 1958

I looked at the green fields stretching over the horizon. Carol was the saddest, to me, of all the innocents. I shut my eyes at the thought of those few seconds after Bobby had gone down from the bullets and before Charlie turned the .22 on her and she knew her life, barely begun, was over. In the school photo you could see the kindness in her eyes.

It was early evening by the time I made it back to Lincoln. I was exhausted. I thought of going back to the motel, but I well knew the shape I was in. I would lie awake until dawn. Coming back into town I had swung a little out of the way to pass the penitentiary where Charlie had been held and put to death some sixty-four years ago. There was a new section, but the tall gray walls with guard towers built in 1876 still stood. Across the street used to be a miniature golf course. My grandmother would take Mike and me there to play, and we used to stare at the guards, rifles in hand, walking back and forth on top of the wall.

I hung a right on O Street and headed east to Wyuka Cemetery, a historic landmark and a piece of Lincoln history. Dedicated in 1869, it is a classic rural cemetery, laid out along curving brick roads with lots of shade trees, shrubs, and flowers. Many prominent Lincoln families lie in the old section. The two Wards were here, the three Bartletts, and Charlie as well. I found the Bartletts first, a flat headstone showing Marion, Betty Jean, and Velda, all with death dates of January 21, 1958. I thought of the baby's body snuggled in her mother's arms. I remembered the story Jim McArthur told about bringing Caril here after her release from prison. At her request, they went to the monument company nearby to order a headstone for her grandmother, Pansy Street. She didn't ask about her father, William, who was also buried here.

The hot, damp wind was still blowing, and I felt unsteady. I retreated to the car in search of a bottle of water. It was as hot as the air. Map in hand, I walked a couple of sections to the area of Charlie's grave. I scanned the lines of headstones where it was supposed to be and couldn't spot it. The map was stained in sweat. Then there he was, beneath a flat stone with flowers carved in the corners.

CHARLES R. STARKWEATHER
November 25, 1938   June 25, 1959
Rest in Peace

It's wrong that he lay only yards from his victims, in the same soil, as if he—and they—had died some natural, ordinary death. There should have been a pauper's grave for him somewhere, if he deserved one at all.

I stepped on the grave, as if to press him deeper into the earth. Felt for a moment the terrible irony of it all: Charlie won out. He got what he wanted. This whole story was his creation.

Guy Starkweather also found a resting place in Wyuka, although not near his son. His headstone has an engraving of the figure of Christ and the words, "The Lord Is My Shepard."

I followed the brick lane and turned left toward the family plot. My grandmother used to drive Mike and me here on Sunday afternoon with flowers for the family graves. She always slowed at a large dark red granite stone on the front of which was an exquisitely carved steam train engine. On the other side of the stone was etched the story of Walter Demeron (1884–1911), a young fireman killed along with eighteen crew and passengers when two steam engines collided head-on. Hulda Roper and Gordon MacRae are also buried in Wyuka.

RAYMOND, the upright marker said. Here are buried my mother and stepfather, younger brother, grandmother, great-grandmother and great-grandfather, an uncle who was in the Eighty-Second Airborne in WWII and jumped on D-Day and was killed on the next jump into Holland and brought home to rest, another uncle who ran allied railroads in India during WWII and took his life in 1970. And my sister. Sharon.

Sharon Galleher
Born   December 2 1939   Died   January 22 1949.

Nine years old. I was six, and loved her. She made sure I got a decent-sized piece of cake at her birthday party, that I got my turn on the slide at the Cottonwood pool. She was amused when I got into trouble. Every morning before school she would sit in a dining room chair and chat quietly with my mother as she braided her hair. She got sick suddenly, and I remember a tent over her bed and a machine creating a strange-smelling mist. Our family had disintegrated by then. My father's alcoholism and unrelenting pain from a war injury had split it apart. He came over a few days after she went into the hospital and gathered Mike and me together on the front lawn and told us Sharon had died. His eyes were red and tear-filled. I think he actually said that she was gone. A word like that. No one knew why. Some sort of respiratory paralysis. He wouldn't allow an autopsy, couldn't bear the thought of it. My mother blamed herself. Mike and I did not go to the funeral. Eight months later, drinking hard and taking over one hundred aspirins a day for pain, my father quit the journey. He came home to die. My mother took us into the bedroom to say goodbye. "Be good to your mother" were his final words.

He's not here, in the family plot in Lincoln. He lies where he belongs: in a grave under the endless blue skies of the Sandhills. Next to his mother and father and brother. The stone is etched in my mind.

Harry Norman Galleher

Nebraska

Lieut. Col. 27 Infantry 25 Div

WWII

June 15, 1911   August 18, 1949

Seven months after Sharon died. I had turned seven by then. It feels terribly lonely out there any time of year. The harsh wind flies unimpeded. The veteran's burial ceremony was held in late August. It was hotter than hell, even under the large tent. Mike and I in our heavy wool suits. I remember the dark, shiny coffin with the American flag draped over it. My grandmother—my father's mother—bent over and told me not to cry. A soldier screamed out. Then again. And again. Boom! I jumped. Screams. Boom! I looked over. The three soldiers were pointing their rifles in the sky. "Fire!" one of them screamed. I looked at Mike. His eyes were closed. Boom! I was shaking as we walked to the hearse. Now I can hear the screams and the sounds of the rifles splitting the heavens. And feel the itchiness of the wool pants on my legs.

I planned on swinging up north through the Sandhills on my trip home. Stopping by Bassett and the cemetery. On the way, I'd pass through Broken Bow, where Charlie and Caril stopped at a gas station on their run to Wyoming. I wouldn't be surprised if the gas station was still there.

On and on it goes. Every thread sooner or later crosses another one.

There is a quarter-mile dirt track outside Stuart, a small town a few miles down the road from Bassett, where my father, mother, and sister lived before the war. One summer a few years back, I raced a 1976 Monte Carlo on Sunday nights at the track. They didn't run a demolition derby there, but the track was in use before the war when my parents and sister lived there. The best I ever did was second. Good enough to get my name in the *Rock County Leader.*

When I was knee-deep in the story, I would wake up in the morning and wonder what shape I was going to be in when the journey was over. The images, the crimes, the smirk on Charlie's face after his arrest, the photo of the teenagers in the cellar, one piled on top of the other, Caril's stone-hard look, the blood splatters on the basement floor of the Ward house, Mike's picture on his mother's desk. The sounds of the rifles on that hot August afternoon. Awake or asleep, there was no way out.

In each of the true crime books I have written, terrible things were done to innocent people. Children. In each one, I kept a safe distance, like a journalist. I could read the autopsy report of a seven-year-old girl as if it were a crop report. Not here, though, and the thing is I think I sensed in the very beginning that it was going to be different, that there was a price to be paid, a measure of sanity to be served up, that the reliving of my grim childhood would leave me more vulnerable to the pain and suffering I was to encounter in the story. I didn't see that I would live each murder as I wrote it.

IN THE SPRING of 2022, even with a rough draft of a manuscript in hand, I understood I wasn't finished with my research. There was one last thread wandering off into nowhere, someone I still needed to find.

I'd heard that Caril was quite ill and approaching her end in a nursing home. No one knew where. She hadn't attended the Board of Pardons hearing in 2020; friends Linda Battisti and Liza Ward both said they were no longer in touch with her and did not know where she was. Tommie Clair, a stepson, said his brother Johnnie was her guardian and that he was no longer in touch with either of them. Johnnie refused to return my phone calls or letters. Steve Berry, Caril's lawyer, told me he hadn't talked to Caril in years. I searched databases for addresses, phone numbers, and emails. They were all out of date. Well, I thought, it wasn't like I was going to get any new information from a seventy-eight-year-old woman who couldn't talk and was reportedly on death's bed. At this point, I probably knew the details of her life better than she did. But I knew I had to at least see her. A glimpse, if nothing more. But where was she?

I found the name of the nursing home when I wasn't even looking for it, when I had almost despaired over never finding her. A simple phone call from an interested party.

"Can you direct me to room 357?" I asked the nurse at the desk halfway down the main hall of the nursing home. I'd been held up for five minutes at the sign-in desk, rattling through papers and checking no-COVID boxes. "Caril Clair," I wrote in the space for the name of the patient I was visiting. The attendant registered no concern or surprise when he glanced at the name. Still, I expected at any moment for a stern figure to appear and invite me into their office. I had an explanation ready as to why I wanted to see Caril—I was a lawyer in the area on business, and Caril's lawyer in Nebraska had asked me to drop by and say hello and pass along a few items to her—but I wasn't good at extemporaneous explanations if challenged. "Down the hall to B wing," the attendant said. "Stop at the second desk, on the right, and they'll help you."

I walked down the hall with a large manila envelope in my hand as nonchalantly as I could. It was a mistake to wear a sports coat and slacks, I realized; I was only drawing attention to myself. A week ago I finally learned the name and location of the nursing home, and the day before yesterday my wife, Julya, called the place to make sure Caril was there. A woman readily gave out her room and phone number, leading me to wonder if in fact the people there knew who she was. Twenty-four hours later, I was on a plane.

At the second desk on the right, I asked the attendant for room 357. She led me down the hall and pointed to a room. She opened the door, and I took half a step in and stopped abruptly. In front of me, in a wheel-chair, sat a very small old woman with wispy white hair. For a moment I was speechless.

"Caril?" I asked, finally.

She nodded with a smile.

The inside of my head blinked.

"I'm a friend of Jim McArthur," I finally managed, "your lawyer. I'm in the area on business, and he asked me to stop by and say hello."

She nodded and smiled.

"I brought this for you," I said, holding out a potted African violet I picked up at a grocery store on my way into town.

She smiled in delight and motioned for me to put the plant on top of her dresser. I did so and sat down. I noticed a figure in bed on the other side of a half-pulled curtain. I thought of asking if we could go to another room but worried it would only bring more attention to us. I decided to plow ahead and hope for the best.

Caril looked at me. Her face was finely lined, like harrows in a field, but pretty, with pale blue eyes. So small; the thousands of times I'd read how tiny she was and saw pictures showing her so, and still I was taken aback. She was barely there.

I would never have recognized her. The photos of her as the tough fourteen-year-old, or the grown woman at her parole hearing, or later after she'd been in the civilized world for ten or fifteen years, or when she went on *A Current Affair* to make her case, all share the same gene. Not this one, not the elfin lady in front of me with a touch of rouge on her cheeks. I couldn't see anything in there. Not pain. Bitterness. Fear. Anger. I glanced at the lady beyond the curtain. Caril was waiting expectantly. "Jim said to say hello," I said; "he still cares about you." She clicked the remote to shut off the TV. I shifted in my chair. Lifted the manila envelope to my lap.

"I have a few things for you," I said. Her back straightened a little. The risk was that the photos of her family would cause a terrible effect and send her spinning off into the past. If she'd managed to get beyond it all, somehow, I didn't want to be the one to tear open the wound. I decided to show her the photo of her and her sister. I pulled out the eight-by-ten-inch black-and-white photo of Caril and Barb meeting for the first time after her arrest on January 29, 1958, in an office in the mental hospital. The two are embracing, kissing each other on the cheek. Caril's face is wreathed in a smile of love and relief. It's here, Caril would later say, that she learned from her sister that her parents were dead.

Caril pointed to her mouth. "She can't talk," her roommate said, and Caril nodded. I glanced at the photo and handed it to her. Her face broke into a huge smile, and she managed a sound almost like a cooing. She twisted in her chair, pulled the curtain farther back, and excitedly showed it to her roommate, an elderly woman with glasses, who studied it for a second and said, "You and your sister?" Caril nodded, turned back, laid the photo on her lap, and looked expectantly at me. I lifted out a smaller photo, one of a woman I believed to be her mother, holding a baby in her arms, and a small girl in bangs and a dress holding her hand. I handed it to her. She managed a word: "Mother!" Her roommate was startled, pulled the curtain back all the way. Caril leaned toward me, holding the photo to her breast, and said with her mouth wide open, "Wow!" I noticed she was missing several teeth, up and down. She pointed to the small girl in the dress and motioned to herself. But if that was her, then the baby in her mother's arms couldn't be her little sister. Caril was probably twelve when Betty Jean was born. I didn't say anything. She was too happy. I showed her three photos of unknown men. I suspected one was Rodney Starkweather, the other maybe her stepfather or uncle. She didn't recognize any of them and handed the photos back to me. I never considered showing a photo of her and Charlie, or even just Charlie.

I had two photos left. One of a baby in diapers lying on a bed. The second, a photo of Betty Jean, Caril's little sister, in blond curls sitting in a large chair looking at the camera with big, round eyes. I had hesitated to bring the photo, and I hesitated now to show it. If she was going to crack, this was where it would happen. I showed her the baby on the bed; she studied it, then nodded and set it aside. I handed her the one of the little girl in the big chair. She looked at it, and I waited. Nothing. She continued to look at it. With no reaction. Eventually, she set it down on the other photos. And looked at me. I was taken aback. She'd cemented that one over, I finally decided. She couldn't feel a thing about her little sister. It was how she managed.

I had one item left in the envelope. The letter she wrote to her sister from inside the York reformatory. Where she talks about how good she's doing and says that things are "fine" and she is doing well in school and to say hello to little Bobby for her. After reading a page and a half to her, I glanced up. Her head was hanging down, her shoulders forward. She looked at me. Her eyes were ringed in red and teary. This, not the baby, I thought. The letter from her early days in prison. When all but her sister and grandmother were dead and there was no future.

I asked her if she would like to keep the photos, and she indicated yes and pointed to the envelope. I dropped the three of them inside. "The letter?" I asked. No, she mouthed. I stuck it in my coat pocket.

I asked Caril generally how she was doing. She pulled up her red flowery dress to mid-thigh and rubbed her leg and knee.

"She's in terrible pain," her roommate said. "She cries out when they lift her from the chair and put her in bed. And afterward she lays there and cries herself to sleep." I remembered the stories about her condition after the car accident: the car had crushed her legs.

"It happens every night," the roommate continued. "I don't understand why they can't put a sign up telling the night nurses about her leg and to be careful when they lift her." She looked at Caril with great affection. "She refuses pain medication."

Caril listened carefully to her roommate, then nodded. "They keep her clean," she said, "give her a bath every day and check on her. She played bingo today and won a box of cookies."

Caril smiled and nudged a box of cookies on her table toward me.

"How's the food?" I asked. Caril made a face. The roommate laughed.

"She always orders sloppy joes and tomato soup." Caril watched her closely. "Sometimes for two meals a day." Caril opened her mouth as if to laugh, exposing the dark spaces between her teeth.

"Does she have many visitors?" I asked.

"Nobody's been here to see her," she said.

"No one?" I asked.

"Not a one."

Caril motioned something to her roommate. "Oh," she said, "my daughter makes a special visit to see her every day." Caril nodded and leaned over and touched her roommate's wrist in gratitude.

"They tried to move her to another room and she wouldn't have it." Caril shook her head. "She can be ornery," she added. "She watches TV all day but always turns it way down when I'm ready for sleep."

The shawl around Caril's shoulders covered her right side. She carefully lifted the cloth and raised her forearm for me to see. The hand and the arm were shriveled. She lowered it and draped the shawl back over her side. I remember reading that her right arm and leg had been crushed in the car accident, that she had been in the hospital for five months.

Her roommate mentioned how she's there for rehab because she broke a hip. "I'll be up walking and out of here in a few weeks," she said. She glanced at Caril. "They claim the doctors will fix her leg, but I doubt she'll ever walk again." Caril was watching her closely, but didn't seem upset by her judgment. "I don't know anything about her, where she's from, her family. I don't think she has any kids," the woman said. Caril nodded in agreement.

"But she did have a husband, Fred . . . ," I began, but Caril made a face and batted the air. That's news. I'd heard they were in love, except for a friend of hers who told me her husband was a jerk. Or maybe for some reasons she just didn't want it talked about.

The roommate wheeled herself over to the corner of Caril's bed and announced she'd be on her way now so we could get to our business. "No need," I said, but she was already rolling toward the door.

Caril motioned for me to put the envelope with the photos in the top drawer of her tiny dresser, out of sight. I don't remember what we—or I—talked about then, but a few minutes later two women marched into the room and looked at me suspiciously. I wondered if it was time for some procedure for Caril. Her bedtime perhaps, or dinner.

"Who are you?" the severe-looking woman demanded.

"A friend of Caril's lawyer, from Lincoln, Nebraska."

"Lincoln, Nebraska," the woman parroted, then turned and headed out the door. The other woman followed in her wake.

I sensed I had little time. I leaned forward. "I wanted to meet you," I said. "I'm writing a book. I'm going to tell the complete story from beginning to end."

Instead of being upset, as I feared, Caril's face took on a look of intense interest. Her eyes held still. Stop here, I thought, but I found myself unwittingly in the thrall of this tiny figure, alone at the end of her life, such as it had been. I wanted to leave Caril with a possibility of something good. I focused on what I felt was the most important thing to her.

"I want you to know something," I said. I paused, gave it another thought. She leaned forward. Brushed a wisp of hair from her cheek. "I don't believe you were at home when your parents and little sister were murdered. You were at school."

Her face crinkled into a smile, her chin lifted and her eyes opened wide. "You can know that in your heart," I said. "I don't think you were there, and that's the way I'm going to write it."

Just then the two women came back in the room. Now puffed up, hands on hips, the first one demanded: "What is your name?"

"Harry MacLean."

"Harry MacLean," she repeated. "I've been in touch with Caril's guardian," she said, "and he doesn't want you in here. You'll have to leave."

Caril turned angry. She leaned forward, her mouth opened wide, and she tried to wave the two women out of the room. They ignored her.

"Now," the woman said.

I stood to leave. I didn't want a scene. I bent over the small, white-haired figure in the wheelchair. "Goodbye, Caril. It was nice meeting you." I touched her shoulder. She smiled up at me. Heading down the hall, hands now empty, free, I heard the squeak of the attendants' shoes behind me.

I signed out at the desk, walked through the glass doors to the outside. A soft light still shone through the trees. I continued down the steps to the parking lot and glanced back at the simple one-story brick building. I had met Caril Fugate, and in a few weeks she would turn seventy-nine, and one day she'd die in there, alone. And with her would go the truth of the killings in the winter of 1958, if she even knew the truth after all this time.

I stood on the sidewalk in the gathering dusk. The sky slowly darkened, and the room lights in the building snapped on like cat's eyes. The satisfaction of seeing the final thread fall into place was fading. What I saw now were the lingering threads of pain and sorrow tracing back to that terrible week in January in 1958. I got in the car and swung out of the parking lot. I rolled the window down, eased slowly onto the highway. Damaged souls don't recover, I thought. I'm finished.

I missed my flight back that night and ended up staying in a cheap hotel close by the airport. I lay awake in the bed for hours. When the radio clock showed 2:30 a.m., I arose and flicked off the night light in the bathroom and closed the curtains. I sat on a wooden chair next to the desk in the darkness. My breathing slowed. I pulled in a deep breath. My lungs collapsed suddenly as if a heavy hand had pushed into my chest. Then, there, I saw them all. I felt them all. The living and the dead. I was still here. For a moment, I saw the flash of light in Caril's eyes when I told her I believed her. Maybe the brightest ever.

AUTHOR'S NOTE

IN RESEARCHING THIS BOOK, I MADE USE OF THE USUAL sources for a true crime story: court transcripts, police reports, medical documents, photos, newspaper articles, television documentaries, books, magazines, and interviews with a wide range of people. The Lincoln Journal Star published an article on the project early in the process that resulted in many people contacting me with compelling stories to tell. Julya and I drove Charlie and Caril's escape route from Lincoln to Douglas, Wyoming, to get a feel for the land. We drove parts of it in the dark, as they had.

The murders happened over sixty-five years ago. This means many if not most of the people directly involved in the story have passed away. Among reporters, only Del Harding is still alive. Of the lawyers, only Jim McArthur is still around. None of the lawmen involved are alive. Accordingly, in many instances secondary sources were relied upon.

Unfortunately, most of the exhibits from the two trials are missing. The district court turned over its files and exhibits to the Nebraska Historical Society in 1966. These files are missing a majority of the exhibits for both trials. Some of this evidence would be crucial in resolving certain critical factual disputes. For example, there was a great deal of confusing testimony about the newspaper articles on the killings; more specifically, which ones did Caril cut out and read, and when. The articles themselves are nowhere to be found. While the Historical Society has three of the firearms used, it does not have Charlie's hunting knife or Velda's kitchen knife. Many photographic exhibits are missing.

The most prominent theory of what happened to the exhibits is that a court official lent them to a writer for use in an article or book and the exhibits were never returned, although this cannot be confirmed. Also missing, without explanation, are the investigative files of the Lincoln Police Department.

Police work back then is not what it is today. Crime scenes were not controlled with tape or personnel. Locals can be seen leaning into the cellar and taking pictures of the teenagers' bodies, a pool of blood next to their feet. Cops and reporters trampled all over the crime scene at 924 Belmont. Local photographers were hired to take pictures of the crime scenes. A reporter snuck into 924 Belmont and stole a photo from Caril's room right under the nose of the cops, and after copying it, snuck it back in the next day.

Most of the statements attributed to Charlie come either from his memoir, his testimony, letters, or statements made to Reinhardt or the police. Most of the statements and thoughts attributed to Caril come from her testimony, the Statement, letters, and interviews with Jim McArthur and her friends and supporters. The meaning and interpretation of the facts are solely my own.

I did extensive research into what I've come to call "trauma psychology." The main sources are the people mentioned in the acknowledgments and books and studies set forth in the bibliography.

Times were different in 1958. Witnesses in the trials were allowed to sit through the trial prior to their testimony, which would not be allowed today; Charlie's mother or father sat next to him at the defense table; the judge occasionally referred to the lawyers by their first names; reporters were allowed into the jail to take photos of Charlie and Caril; deputy sheriffs drove their personal cars on duty; the newspapers published the photos, names, and addressed of the jurors; and gas stations carried bullets for sale. On at least one occasion, a law enforcement witness left the stand during his testimony to retrieve evidence from his office and bring it to the court.

There were many versions of events in this book. Of the final versions of the killings offered by Charlie, I used mainly his testimony at his own and Caril's trial. Caril's version was taken from her Statement and her testimony at her trial. Of other disputes, I used the one that was corroborated by other facts or made the most sense given the known circumstances and context.

ACKNOWLEDGMENTS

JIM MCARTHUR SPENT HOURS WITH ME GOING OVER HIS recollection of the cases, resolving factual conflicts, suggesting people I might contact, and offering valuable insights into the history and dynamics of the events and the people. He gave me unlimited access to his massive files on the case, and I spent days in his basement searching through stacks of boxes. His wife, Margie, was a gracious hostess, always making sure I was well looked after. Thanks cannot adequately express my gratitude to Jim and Margie for their invaluable assistance. I would also like to thank Jim's son, author Jeff McArthur, for helping in the beginning of my research.

Thanks to my agent Paul Bresnick, who has stuck with me over the years and found the right home for this book. The book would not resemble its present form without the perceptive eye and guiding hand of my Counterpoint editor Dan Smetanka. Dan reordered scenes and cut excess and suggested segues and connections between people and themes that almost magically transformed a very rough and incomplete draft manuscript into a book. All of this with a genuine respect for the voice and vision of the author, as well as a great sense of humor. Every author should be so fortunate.

I would like to thank Diane Gonzolas, who has worked in Lincoln media, government, and political circles for thirty-five years, for her assistance in confirming facts, spotting flaws in the manuscript, and locating people for interviews. I would also like to thank poet Kathleen Caine, who grew up in Lincoln and provided many leads and researched a range of Nebraska issues for me. Author and psychologist Stephen White provided valuable advice on the impact of trauma on the personality, introducing me to the theory of sublimation. Author and psychologist Sharon Stanley gave freely of her time and knowledge on the nature of trauma on the processes of the human brain.

Dr. Prudence Gourguechon was kind enough to review the facts of the case and provide her valuable thoughts on the effects of trauma on Caril. I am also grateful to author and professor of forensic psychology

Katherine Ramsland for sharing her insights into the Starkweather case as well as her recollections of the struggles and suicide of Bobby Jensen's brother, professor Dewey Jensen.

I am especially grateful to Nebraska historian Jim McKee who was gracious enough to review portions of the manuscript for accuracy and to History Nebraska (formerly known as the Nebraska State Historical Society) for their assistance in locating files and photographs. Bill Kelly, now a reporter and producer with Nebraska Public Media, was generous in providing access to his files and sharing his recollections and perceptions of the Starkweather saga. I am also grateful to reporter Del Harding for sharing his recollections of the crime spree and trials and giving me permission to use his remarkable photographs in the book. Thanks to Detective Ben Peech of the Converse County Sheriff's Department for spending an afternoon driving Julya and myself around the countryside to the various spots of interest in the killing of Merle Collison and the capture of Charlie Starkweather. Author and attorney Steve Berry provided valuable research material, for which I am grateful. And thanks to Linda Battistti for sharing her recollections of Caril and their friendship. I am deeply grateful to Liza Ward for her willingness to share her thoughts on Caril and her role in the killing spree, as well as her perceptions of her father.

I would also like to thank U.S. District Court Judge John Kane for his thoughtful review of the legal and substantive issues in the book. Tom Pace was not only a solid support throughout the long process of researching and writing the book, as usual, but he also furthered my understanding of the various theories on the impact of trauma on the brain and cognitive processes.

Julya, my wife, played many roles in the evolution of this book: collaborator, editor, and unflagging supporter. She listened patiently and offered suggestions on long walks in the evenings as I recounted the day's work and attempted to reconcile the various facts and themes of the story and sort out Caril's responsibility for the murders. She pointed out key gaps or flaws in scenes, particularly in the epilogue, which she convinced me to stay with when I despaired of finding the right voice. She kept the author wired together.

BIBLIOGRAPHY

Allen, William. *Starkweather, The Story of a Mass Murderer.* Boston: Houghton Miflin, 1976.

Allen, William. *Starkweather, Inside the Mind of a Teenage Killer.* Cincinatti: Emmis Books, 2004.

Battisti, Linda M. and John Stevens Berry. *The Twelfth Victim, The Innocence of Caril Fugate in the Starkweather Murder Rampage.* Omaha: Addicus Books, 2014.

Beaver, Ninette, B.K. Ripley, and Patrick Trese. *Caril.* New York: J.B. Lippincort Company, 1974.

Cather, Willa. *O Pioneers!* Boston: Houghton Miflin, 1941.

Duwe, Grant. *Mass Murders in the United States: A History.* McFarland & Company, 2007.

Dyer, Earl. *Headline: Starkweather: From Behind the News Desk.* Hasting, NE: Cornhusker Press, 1993.

Finder, Henry, ed. *The 50s: The Story of A Decade (The New Yorker).* Edited by Henry Finder. New York: Modern Library, 2015.

Frazier, Ian. *Great Plains.* New York: Picador, 2001.

Greene, Bob. *Once Upon A Town: The Miracle of the North Platte Canteen.* New York: HarperCollins, 2002.

Halberstam, David. *The Fifties.* New York: Villard Books, 1993.

Jones, Bryan L. *North of the Platte South of the Niobrara.* Texas: Stephen F. Austin State University Press, 2018.

Jones, Stephen R. *The Last Prairie: A Sandhills Journal.* Ragged Mountain Press/McGraw Hill, 2000.

Lavergne, Gary M. *Sniper in the Tower: The Charles Whitman Murders.* Texas: University of North Texas Press, 1997.

LeDoux, Joseph. *The Emotional Brain: The Mysterious Underpinnings of Emotional Life.* New York: Simon and Schuster Paperbacks, 1996.

Levine, Peter A. *Waking The Tiger: Healing Trauma.* Berkeley: North Atlanta Books, 1997.

McArthur, Jeff. *Pro Bono: The 18-Year Defense of Caril Ann Fugate.* Burbank: Bandwagon Books, 2012.

McKee, James L. *The Prairie Capital: An Illustrated History.* Lincoln: J & L Lee Publishers.

McKee, James L. Photographs by Joel Sartore. *Visions of Lincoln: Nebraska's Capital City in the Present, Past and Future.* Lincoln: Tankworks, 2007.

Moulton, Candy. *Roadside History of Nebraska.* Missoula: Mountain Press Publishing Company. Montana: 1997.

Naugle, Ronald C. *A Brief History of Nebraska.* History Nebraska, 2018.

Newton, Michael. *Wasteland: The Savage Odyssey of Charles Starkweather and Caril Ann Fugate.* New York: Pocket Books, 1998

O'Donnell, Jeff. *Starkweather: A Story of Mass Murder on the Great Plains.* Lincoln: J & L Lee Publishers, 1993.

Olson, James C. and Ronald C. Naugle. *History of Nebraska.* Lincoln and London: University of Nebraska Press, Third Edition, 1997.

Pittman, Catherine M. and Elizabeth M. Karle. *Rewire Your Anxious Brain.* Oakland: New Harbinger Publications, 2015.

Porges, Stephen. *The Polyvagal Theory: Neurophysiological Foundations of Emotions, Attachment, Communication, and Self-Regulation.* New York: Norton and Company, 2011.

Ramsland, Katherine. *Inside the Minds of Mass Murderers: Why They Kill.* Westport, CT: Praeger Publishers, 2005.

Randall, Melanie, and Lori Haskell. "The Impact of Trauma on Adult Sexual Assault Victims." Report to Justice Canada, 2019.

Ravnikar, Michelle Barret. *Reporting a mass murder: Coverage of the Charles Starkweather case by the "Lincoln Star" and the "Omaha World Herald"* (1986). Graduate Student Thesis, Dissertations, & Professional Papers.

Reinhardt, James Melvin, *The Murderous Trail of Charles Starkweather.* Lincoln: Charles C. Thomas Publisher, 1960.

Sandoz, Mari. *Crazy Horse: The Strange Man of the Oglalas.* New York: Knopf, 1942.

Smart, Elizabeth. *My Story.* New York: St. Martin's Press, 2013.

Stanley, Sharon. *Relational and Body-Centered Practices of Healing Trauma, Lifting the Burdens of the Past.* New York and London: Routledge, 2016.

Stout, Glenn. *Tiger Girl and the Candy Kid.* Boston: Mariner Books, 2021.

Van Der Kolk, Bessel. *The Body Keeps the Score, Brain, Mind, and Body in the Healing of Trauma.* New York: Penguin Books, 2015.

Walker, Lenora. *The Battered Woman Syndrome.* Springer Publishing, 4th ed., 2016.

Ward, Liza. *Outside Valentine.* New York: Henry Holt and Co., 2004.

White, Stephen. *Dry Ice.* New York: Dutton, 2007.

Zanes, Warren. *Deliver Me from Nowhere: The Making of Bruce Springsteen's Nebraska,* New York: Crown, 2023.

HARRY N. MACLEAN is the author of the true crime classic *In Broad Daylight: A Murder in Skidmore, Missouri*, which won an Edgar Award for Best Fact Crime and was a *New York Times* bestseller for twelve weeks, selling over 1 million copies. His second book, *Once Upon a Time: A True Story of Memory, Murder, and the Law*, was named a *New York Times* Notable Book and served as the basis for *Buried*, the Emmy-nominated Showtime series. His third book, *The Past Is Never Dead: The Trial of James Ford Seale and Mississippi's Search for Redemption*, was short-listed for the William Saroyan International Prize for Writing. His first novel, *The Joy of Killing*, was selected as one of the ten best novels of 2015 by *The Denver Post*. He lives in Denver, Colorado. Find out more at harrymaclean.com.